ABORTION AND DEMOCRACY

D1557168

Abortion and Democracy offers critical analyses of abortion politics in Latin America's Southern Cone, with lessons and insights of wider significance. Drawing on the region's recent history of military dictatorship and democratic transition, this edited volume explores how abortion rights demands fit with current democratic agendas.

With a focus on Argentina, Chile, and Uruguay, the book's contributors delve into the complex reality of abortion through the examination of the discourses, strategies, successes, and challenges of abortion rights movements. Assembling a multiplicity of voices and experiences, the contributions illuminate key dimensions of abortion rights struggles: health aspects, litigation efforts, legislative debates, party politics, digital strategies, grassroots mobilization, coalition-building, affective and artistic components, and movement-countermovement dynamics. The book takes an approach that is sensitive to social inequalities and to the transnational aspects of abortion rights struggles in each country. It bridges different scales of analysis, from abortion experiences at the micro level of the clinic or the home to the macro sociopolitical and cultural forces that shape individual lives.

This is an important intervention suitable for students and scholars of abortion politics, democracy in Latin America, gender and sexuality, and women's rights.

Barbara Sutton is a professor in the Department of Women's, Gender, and Sexuality Studies at the University at Albany, SUNY. She is also affiliated with the departments of Sociology and of Latin American, Caribbean, and U.S. Latino Studies at the same institution. She earned a law degree from the Universidad de Buenos Aires in Argentina, her country of origin, as well as a doctorate in sociology from the University of Oregon. Professor Sutton's scholarly interests include body politics, reproductive justice, global gender issues, collective memory, human rights, and women's and feminist activism, particularly in Latin American contexts. Her book *Bodies in Crisis: Culture, Violence, and Women's Resistance in Neoliberal Argentina* (Rutgers University Press, 2010) received the 2011 Gloria E. Anzaldúa Book Prize by the National Women's Studies Association. She is also the author of *Surviving State Terror: Women's Testimonies of Repression and Resistance in Argentina* (NYU Press, 2018). This book received Honorable Mentions for the 2019 Distinguished Book Award by the American Sociological Association Sex & Gender Section and for the 2019 Marysa Navarro Book Prize by the New England Council of Latin American Studies.

Nayla Luz Vacarezza is an assistant researcher at the National Council for Scientific and Technical Research in Argentina. She is affiliated with the Gino Germani Research Institute and teaches sociology courses at the Universidad de Buenos Aires. She holds a Sociology degree and a doctoral degree in Social Sciences from the Universidad de Buenos Aires. She was the recipient of a doctoral and a postdoctoral fellowship from the National Council for Scientific and Technical Research in Argentina. Dr. Vacarezza's current research project focuses on the visual politics and affective aspects of abortion rights movements in Latin America. She is co-author (with July Chaneton) of the book *La intemperie y lo intempestivo. Experiencias del aborto voluntario en el relato de mujeres y varones* (Marea, 2011). The book was declared of interest by the Honorable Chamber of Deputies of Argentina's Congress in 2012. She is also co-editor (with Cecilia Macón and Mariela Solana) of *Affect, Gender and Sexuality in Latin America* (Palgrave Macmillan, 2021).

ABORTION AND DEMOCRACY

Contentious Body Politics in Argentina, Chile, and Uruguay

*Edited by Barbara Sutton
and Nayla Luz Vacarezza*

Dear Loretta,

We hope that you get insights
and inspiration from this
book.
Thank you for your support.

Nayla & Barbara
♡

Routledge
Taylor & Francis Group

LONDON AND NEW YORK

10.18.21

First published 2021
by Routledge
2 Park Square, Milton Park, Abingdon, Oxon OX14 4RN

and by Routledge
605 Third Avenue, New York, NY 10158

Routledge is an imprint of the Taylor & Francis Group, an informa business

© 2021 selection and editorial matter, Barbara Sutton and Nayla Luz Vacarezza; individual chapters, the contributors

The right of Barbara Sutton and Nayla Luz Vacarezza to be identified as the authors of the editorial material, and of the authors for their individual chapters, has been asserted in accordance with sections 77 and 78 of the Copyright, Designs and Patents Act 1988.

All rights reserved. No part of this book may be reprinted or reproduced or utilised in any form or by any electronic, mechanical, or other means, now known or hereafter invented, including photocopying and recording, or in any information storage or retrieval system, without permission in writing from the publishers.

Trademark notice: Product or corporate names may be trademarks or registered trademarks, and are used only for identification and explanation without intent to infringe.

British Library Cataloguing-in-Publication Data
A catalogue record for this book is available from the British Library

Library of Congress Cataloging-in-Publication Data
A catalog record has been requested for this book

ISBN: 978-0-367-52943-7 (hbk)
ISBN: 978-0-367-52941-3 (pbk)
ISBN: 978-1-003-07990-3 (ebk)

DOI: 10.4324/9781003079903

Typeset in Bembo
by Taylor & Francis Books

CONTENTS

ILLUSTRATIONS

Figures

Tables

CONTRIBUTORS

Sonia E. Alvarez is Leonard J. Horwitz Professor of Latin American Politics and Society, Department of Political Science, University of Massachusetts, Amherst, United States.

Lucía Berro Pizzarossa is a postdoctoral researcher at the University of Groningen, Netherlands, and the coordinator of the MAMA Network (Mobilizing Activists for Medical Abortion) for Women Help Women.

Elizabeth Borland is a professor of sociology at the College of New Jersey, United States. She currently serves as book review editor for *Mobilization*.

Magdalena Caccia is a researcher at the Gender, Body, and Sexuality Program, Anthropology Institute, School of Humanities and Educational Science, Universidad de la República, Uruguay.

Lidia Casas Becerra is the director of the Center for Human Rights of the School of Law at the Universidad Diego Portales, Chile.

Martín Couto is a researcher at the Gender, Sexuality, and Reproductive Health Program, School of Psychology, Universidad de la República, Uruguay.

Cora Fernández Anderson is an assistant professor of Comparative Politics at Mount Holyoke College, United States.

María Alicia Gutiérrez is a professor and researcher at the School of Social Sciences, Universidad de Buenos Aires. She also teaches at the postgraduate level in other national universities in Argentina.

Brianna Keefe-Oates is a doctoral student in Population Health Sciences in the Social and Behavioral Sciences department at the Harvard School of Public Health, United States.

Claudia Laudano is a professor and researcher at the School of Humanities and Science of Education, Universidad Nacional de La Plata, Argentina, where she teaches courses on digital technologies, media, women's movements, and feminist studies.

Alejandra López-Gómez is a professor and researcher at the School of Psychology, Universidad de la República, Uruguay, where she coordinates the Gender, Sexuality, and Reproductive Health Program.

José Manuel Morán Faúndes is assistant researcher at the National Council for Scientific and Technical Research (CONICET), Argentina. He is also a professor of sociology of law at the Universidad Nacional de Córdoba and a researcher in the Sexual and Reproductive Rights Program, School of Law, Universidad Nacional de Córdoba, Argentina.

Susana Rostagnol is the director of the Department of Social Anthropology at the Universidad de la República, Uruguay, and the coordinator of the Gender, Body, and Sexuality Program.

Valentina Stutzin studied Social Anthropology at the Universidad de Buenos Aires and has an MA in Theory and Practice of Documentary Filmmaking from the Universitat Autònoma de Barcelona. She has worked, both in Chile and Argentina, as an independent researcher in various feminist and queer studies projects.

Barbara Sutton is a professor in the Department of Women's, Gender, and Sexuality Studies at the University at Albany, State University of New York, United States. She is also affiliated with the departments of Sociology and of Latin American, Caribbean, and U.S. Latino Studies at the same institution.

Nayla Luz Vacarezza is an assistant researcher at the National Council for Scientific and Technical Research (CONICET), Argentina. She is affiliated with the Gino Germani Research Institute and teaches sociology courses at the Universidad de Buenos Aires.

Juan Marco Vaggione is a professor of sociology at the Universidad Nacional de Córdoba and a researcher at the National Council for Scientific and Technical Research (CONICET), Argentina. He is also director of the Sexual and Reproductive Rights Program, School of Law, Universidad Nacional de Córdoba.

Lieta Vivaldi is a research associate at the School of Philosophy, Universidad de Chile, and the director of the Gender, Justice and Law Program at the School of Law, Universidad Alberto Hurtado.

PREFACE

To describe 2020 as an eventful year would be an understatement: The COVID-19 pandemic shook the world with devastating socioeconomic and public health consequences, including a terrible death toll. The spread of a novel coronavirus brought with it the exacerbation of inequalities, rampant economic crises, political upheaval, and major disruptions to education, employment, and everyday life around the globe. It was in this tumultuous and disorienting context that this book came to be. With extraordinary effort and dedication, contributors to this volume crafted their chapters in a changing and challenging environment, which manifested itself in different ways depending on the country where the authors reside.

Academic publications often lag behind certain political events, historical turning points, or unanticipated catastrophes that might be relevant to a study's subject matter. It is particularly difficult to write about processes that are continuously evolving, when what is described in print might dramatically change by the time a book reaches the shelves of interested readers. At the time of writing, Chile is entering a new political phase after a historic popular vote in October 2020 to rewrite the country's constitution; Uruguay is months into a conservative government that won elections for the first time in 15 years; and in Argentina a significant transformation regarding the status of abortion took place as this manuscript was going into production. As the latter is directly related to the topic of this book and the analysis in several chapters, it is important to make a note here regarding this change in abortion policy in Argentina.

Around mid-November 2020, the Executive branch of the Argentine government sent a bill to the National Congress to consider the legalization of abortion along with another bill that would extend economic assistance and other support to gestating persons who choose to continue their pregnancies. The abortion legalization bill was approved by the Chamber of Deputies after a 20-hour debate that began on December 10. This is a very meaningful date for Argentines because it marks the anniversary of the restoration of democracy after the last dictatorship.

It also has wider significance as international Human Rights Day. These events illustrate the deep interconnection between democracy, human rights, and the struggle for legal abortion in the country.

With considerable speed, the abortion legalization bill moved through Congress to the next level and was passed by the Argentine Senate on December 30, 2020. A significant victory for abortion rights activists, this change is also predicted to affect the course of abortion politics in other places in the region. It is not merely a coincidence that only days after the new abortion legislation was approved in Argentina a similar debate promised to be reactivated in Chilean society, as the issue is scheduled to soon be discussed by a Congress committee in Chile. Having reached this point cannot be understood without attention to the types of political processes, mass mobilization, patient organizing, and movement-countermovement dynamics analyzed in this book. In a way, this volume can be read as a chronicle of the struggles, challenges, and victories surrounding abortion politics in Latin America's Southern Cone. It provides clues essential to understanding ongoing political processes concerning gender, sexuality, and democracy, with repercussions beyond the three countries examined.

The "Green Tide" metaphor—used to describe the rise of the abortion rights movement in the region—reflects the cumulative power of the activism considered in this volume. The image of the tide also expresses the prospects of a long-awaited overhaul in the contentious field of abortion politics. All in all, this book took on the challenge of keeping pace with this shifting scenario. Indeed, in the context of lively democracies, feminist and abortion rights organizations have managed to carve out new hopes and possibilities even in the most difficult times.

Barbara Sutton and Nayla Luz Vacarezza
January 11, 2021

ACKNOWLEDGMENTS

Abortion and Democracy is the outcome of years of feminist collaboration, friendship, and political solidarity. The vision for this volume also emerged as we interacted with scholars and activists in Latin America who nourished our understanding of the social movements and political processes in the region. We have been fortunate to participate in insightful conversations unfolding in activist and academic spaces across the hemisphere.

We thank in particular the Southern Cone Studies section of the Latin American Studies Association for selecting, as a featured panel, our session "Luchas por el derecho al aborto en el Cono Sur: Reforma legal, disputas simbólicas y movilización social" (Struggles for Abortion Rights in the Southern Cone: Legal Reform, Symbolic Disputes, and Social Mobilization). The exchanges among panelists and the feedback from attendees at the session, which took place in Boston in 2019, encouraged us to continue our focus on the panel's theme. We developed and expanded these ideas in interaction with researchers who have produced excellent scholarship on abortion politics in Argentina, Chile, and Uruguay, including those in this volume.

At the conceptualization and proposal-writing stage, this project benefited from the support of the Rockefeller Foundation Academic Writing Residency at the Bellagio Center in Italy, awarded to Barbara Sutton. Fellow residents Alexandra Adams and Bahia Shehab offered particularly valuable feedback, for which we are very appreciative. We also thank Routledge Editor Alexandra McGregor for her encouragement and support with this project since its inception, and Victoria Chow for her careful copy-editing of this volume.

Additionally, we are grateful to have supportive colleagues who have influenced our thinking and with whom we have shared our work. We would especially like to acknowledge Rajani Bhatia, Janell Hobson, and Vivien Ng at the Women's, Gender, and Sexuality Studies Department, University at Albany; as well as Alejandra Oberti, Claudia Bacci, Mariela Peller, Lucas Saprosi, and Joaquin Insausti, who are members of the group teaching "Identidades, Discursos Sociales y Tecnologías de Género" (Identities, Social Discourses and Technologies of Gender) at the Universidad de Buenos Aires. Malena Costa Wegsman, Ilona Aczel, Laura Fernández Cordero, Paula Aguilar, and Kari Norgaard also encouraged our work with warmth and wisdom. We are also grateful to Ron Friedman for his thoughtful assistance with some of the translations, and to both him and Dario Callejas for the sustained and generous support that helps these kinds of projects thrive.

We thank each of this volume's contributors for their important work and for their enthusiasm and commitment to this book project. A special thanks to Alejandra López-Gómez, Lieta Vivaldi, and Liz Borland for their comments on our introductory chapter, and to Sonia Alvarez for her attentive reading of the book manuscript as the basis for her Afterword. Chapter 11, by Lidia Casas Becerra, is a translation and adaptation of her previously published text: "La academia, entre 'los seculares y los confesionales.' Las continuidades en la reforma por la despenalización del aborto en Chile y una historia personal," in *Aborto en tres causales en Chile. Lecturas del proceso de despenalización*, edited by Lidia Casas Becerra and Gloria Maira Vargas (Santiago: Centro de Derechos Humanos, Universidad Diego Portales, 2019) and is reprinted with permission. Some fragments of Chapter 4, by Nayla Luz Vacarezza, are translated and adapted from a previously published text: "La mano que vota. Visualidad y afectos en un símbolo transnacional de las luchas por el derecho al aborto en el Cono Sur." The original article was published in *Sexualidad, Salud y Sociedad* 35(2020): 35–57, and the fragments included here are reprinted with permission.

We also extend our gratitude to the photographers, organizations, and activists who gave permission to use their images: Anita Peña Saavedra from MILES (Movimiento por la Interrupción Legal del Embarazo / Movement for the Legal Interruption of Pregnancy), Constanza Riquelme from Cultiva Audiovisual, Lilián Abracinskas from Mujer y Salud en Uruguay (Women and Health in Uruguay), Laura Salomé Canteros from the Campaña Nacional por el Derecho al Aborto Legal, Seguro y Gratuito (National Campaign for the Right to Legal, Safe, and Free Abortion), Julianite Calcagno, and Patricio Murphy. We are particularly grateful to Juli Ortiz for the book cover photo, taken in Buenos Aires during the mobilization for International Women's Day, 2020. The work of activists, archivists, and photographers documenting and keeping visual testimonies of the movement is vital to expanding the reach of these struggles and to building their memory.

We hope this book conveys at least a fraction of the extraordinary intellectual, organizational, emotional, and overall political force of the movements for abortion rights in the Southern Cone of Latin America. At a time in which democracy faces tremendous challenges around the world, these movements strive to deepen and radicalize the meanings of democracy and to reinvent politics from a feminist perspective.

1

ABORTION RIGHTS AND DEMOCRACY

An Introduction

Barbara Sutton and Nayla Luz Vacarezza

What is the connection between abortion rights and democracy, not only as a system of government but as a means of promoting social justice? How do histories of political repression and human rights violations shape abortion struggles in contemporary democracies? What broader lessons might be drawn when using "democracy" as a lens to understand the status of abortion in different societies and the activist efforts for its recognition as a right? *Abortion and Democracy* grapples with these central questions through analyses of the politics of abortion in three Latin American countries: Argentina, Chile, and Uruguay. Drawing on these nations' recent history of military dictatorship and democratic transition, the book explores how demands for abortion rights engage and influence current democratic agendas. The authors additionally offer insights of wider significance, particularly since gender, sexuality, and abortion have been at the center of political dispute in various countries. Through the examination of multiple discourses and strategies as well as the challenges and successes of abortion rights movements in the region, this volume unpacks the complex reality of abortion in specific locales and in transnational perspective.

Abortion and Democracy sheds light on key dimensions and sites of struggle pertaining to abortion: party politics and grassroots mobilization, coalition building and litigation efforts, affective and visual strategies, digital activism, healthcare and abortion accompaniment, movement-countermovement dynamics, and the role of academia in the abortion debate. As a whole, the book interrogates social inequalities and attends to the transnational aspects of political contention around abortion. It bridges different scales of analysis: from abortion experiences at the micro level of the clinic or the home to the macro sociopolitical and cultural forces that shape individual lives. The book addresses abortion as a matter of "body politics" in at least three senses, all involving relations of power: (1) how state, religious, medical, and other social discourses and regulations discipline and materially impact the bodies and lives of those

DOI: 10.4324/9781003079903-1

who need an abortion; (2) how these effects of power are contested through collective bodies in protest, individual embodied resistance, abortion accompaniment, and myriad other strategies; and (3) how these disputes delineate who is deemed to belong (or not) to the body politic, with the rights associated with full citizenship.

Abortion rights activism has made strides in different parts of the world, yet opponents have also organized to restrict or completely ban the practice. In light of such conflicts, it is important to consider contexts where abortion has been significantly restricted by law and where it is legal but under fire. Argentina, Chile, and Uruguay were selected as countries that integrate a region of Latin America—the Southern Cone—not only in terms of geographical proximity, but also based on cultural, linguistic, demographic, and historical similarities and connections.[1] Furthermore, during the last decade these countries saw important political developments related to abortion. As will be further elaborated, the legal status of abortion has varied among the three sites at different points during that period: Only late in the decade did Chile shift from a total abortion ban to the decriminalization of abortion on three grounds (*causales*); in Argentina the abortion rights movement successfully pushed to move away from a system of abortion criminalization with a few exceptions to one of legalized abortion (obtaining a favorable policy change in December 2020); and Uruguay is a pioneer among the three countries with respect to abortion liberalization, with a law approved in 2012 that permits abortion on demand during the first trimester of pregnancy. The decade was also marked by extraordinary feminist mobilizations that helped shape the public agenda in the region, including instances of transnational solidarity. Thus, in addition to similarities and variations, this book shows how certain strategies have crossed borders and how abortion rights movements in the region have developed activist connections.

Broad social and political developments, even global ones, affect the status of abortion in specific locales. Changes in government administration in 2019—for example, in Argentina toward more progressive directions and in Uruguay toward conservatism—presented the possibility of new abortion scenarios. These questions emerged: Might Argentina move closer to legalization? Will Uruguay backslide? Still, as the history of abortion politics in Latin America shows, the overall ideological orientation of the government does not neatly predict the fate of abortion (Blofield and Ewig 2017; Friedman 2019; Marcus-Delgado 2020). In Chile, a series of popular uprisings emerged in October 2019, demanding deep legal, political, and economic changes, shaking the conservative government in power. Feminists actively participated in these mobilizations, also raising questions regarding gender justice and abortion rights. In 2020, the global COVID-19 pandemic further scrambled politics and life in the Southern Cone, creating new uncertainties for the implementation of feminist agendas.

In light of these changing contexts, *Abortion and Democracy* offers a platform for comparative and transnational perspectives on abortion as a salient political issue. The contributions of international scholars, drawing on a range of disciplines and methodologies, have enriched this collection. Chapters are based on qualitative interviews, ethnographic fieldwork, archival research, media analysis, statistical information, visual analysis, and historical-comparative approaches. This introduction elaborates the volume's conceptual framework and key dimensions of abortion politics in the region, while connecting to the authors' contributions. Overall, the book presents urgently needed analyses of abortion from multiple vantage points.

Legal Contexts in Dictatorship and Democracy

The three countries studied in this volume underwent military dictatorships during overlapping periods in the last quarter of the twentieth century (Argentina 1976–83; Uruguay 1973–85; Chile 1973–90). This was a time when torture, political imprisonment, assassination, and forced disappearance were part and parcel of state-sponsored mechanisms to impose political, economic, and social agendas. It was also a period of stifled politics, when it was hard to organize for and exercise rights that might be taken for granted in democracies. This authoritarian legacy, and opposition to it, has shaped aspects of abortion politics in democracy, including activist symbols, political discourse and affects, party dynamics, and movement alliances. The book's authors address contemporary abortion struggles mindful of this history, showing the linkages between abortion rights activism and broader democratic and social justice aspirations during the post-dictatorship.

In the aftermath of dictatorial governments, abortion rights demands in Latin America's Southern Cone became entwined with the struggle for democracy. Argentina, Chile, and Uruguay began their democratic transitions with punitive abortion legislation that either preceded the dictatorship or was modified during military rule. In Uruguay, a 1938 law penalized abortion but allowed judges to reduce the sentence in certain circumstances. In Argentina, the Penal Code criminalized the practice since 1921, except for cases of rape or risk to the health or life of the woman.[2] In Chile, one of dictator Augusto Pinochet's last acts in office was to repeal the Health Code of 1931 that authorized therapeutic abortion, leading to a total abortion ban.

In democratic times, abortion rights movements grew and demanded legal reform, obtaining some victories. Uruguay legalized abortion in the first 12 weeks of pregnancy in 2012. In Chile, a legal reform in 2017 allowed abortion on three grounds: rape, danger to the woman's life, and fetal anomalies incompatible with extra-uterine life. In Argentina, criminalization remained in force, but a "procedural turn" (Bergallo 2014) and a 2012 Supreme Court decision (F., A.L. case) helped promote gradual changes toward increased abortion services for legally permitted cases (i.e., those included in the exceptions to penalization). In December 2020, the National Congress of Argentina passed a bill to legalize abortion on demand until the 14th week of pregnancy. This recent development constitutes a transformation of historic proportions, likely with ripple effects that cannot yet be fully grasped.

While democracy enabled certain progress with respect to the legal status of abortion, it did not end the clandestinity of the practice, with variations in rights and access. Given this scenario, activists have persistently pushed for abortion liberalization and effective implementation. Abortion rights activism has steadily expanded, and it gained extraordinary momentum during the 2010s. Yet even in Uruguay, which achieved earlier legalization, restrictions and obstacles remain (Correa and Pecheny 2016; Wood et al. 2016). Barriers to abortion access, including in cases that fit exceptions to penalization, have also been a major concern in Argentina and Chile (ANDHES et al. 2018; Mesa Acción por el Aborto en Chile and Fondo Alquimia 2019). In Argentina, the inclusion of conscientious objection in the newly passed law of 2020 may also be used by abortion opponents to create obstacles to the practice. Thus, activists and advocates are aware of the need to continually monitor both the effects of restrictive legislation as well as the implementation of the rights codified by law. In this sense, the production of academic knowledge about various dimensions of abortion in restrictive contexts has also contributed to the abortion rights cause (see, e.g., Johnson et al. 2011; Pecheny and Herrera 2019; Casas Becerra, this volume).

Research, Activist Legacies, and Abortion Rights

Research about abortion and its politics in the Southern Cone has followed the path of democracy. After dictatorial regimes, women's, feminist, and abortion rights movements had a better context to develop their potential. Also, scholars advocated for new research agendas that considered women's rights, gender, sexuality, and abortion. A number of studies focus on *legal analysis*,[3] while others address *health issues* such as healthcare services and women's mortality related to abortion.[4] Several works analyze *reproductive rights*, placing abortion at the intersection of women's citizenship and human rights.[5] Other studies examine the *abortion rights movement*, its history, strategies, controversies, organizational models, and coalition-building efforts.[6]

Abortion rights activism in the Southern Cone is deeply entwined with broader feminist and women's movements, including the legacy of activists who mobilized for the restoration of civilian rule after military dictatorships. Maxine Molyneux and Nikki Craske (2002, 1) point out that these movements advocated especially for what Hannah Arendt called "the right to have rights." They worked for democratization and much more than the recuperation of civil and political liberties. In the aftermath of political repression and in the context of harsh economic crises, demands for human rights protection and for support of social reproduction advanced alongside claims for political representation, against gender violence, and for reproductive rights. These movements were not fighting for gender-neutral incorporation into the political realm, nor were they focusing merely on women's individual rights. Their agendas were connected to aspirations for a substantive democracy, with genuine participation from diverse sectors of society.

Women had taken center stage in the resistance to dictatorial governments and in mobilizing for democracy. In Argentina, mothers of the disappeared, known as Madres de Plaza de Mayo, exposed the brutality of systematic political repression by the military regime. They drew on traditional roles and moral authority as *mothers* to publicly make their claims, contributing to erode the dictatorship's political power (Feijoo and Gogna 1985). While seemingly paradoxical, as this volume shows, the legacy of the Mothers was later incorporated in abortion mobilization in Argentina. In Uruguay, women also drew on gender identities as they organized to counter the effects of political repression; and during the democratic transition, women were central figures leading the charge against military impunity. Women's activism expanded during the democratic transition, promoting understandings of human rights that addressed women's rights specifically (Sharnak 2017). In Chile, women from poor neighborhoods organized communal kitchens and transformed supposedly natural and private matters into political demands for economic justice (Fisher 1993). Also in Chile, the influential feminist slogan "Democracy in the country and in the home" called for the end of authoritarianism both in private and public spaces. This demand was later expanded and adopted transnationally: "Democracy in the country, the home, and in bed"—in this way incorporating sexuality among the issues that needed to be transformed in egalitarian fashion (Sosa Gonzalez 2019).

These are only a few examples of how women's and feminist movements of the transition advanced a new way of doing politics that challenged the supposed neutrality of democracy and the traditional divide between the public and the private. According to Chilean feminist Julieta Kirkwood, the experience of the dictatorship showed that "authoritarianism is more than an economic or political problem; that it has deep roots and channels in the whole social structure; that we have to question and reject many elements and contents that were previously not considered political, as they were attributed to everyday-private life" (Kirkwood 1990, 202–3).[7] Abortion is one such issue.

Democratization processes have been enmeshed with struggles for social, political, and cultural transformation in Latin America. In Argentina, abortion rights groups bloomed during the "democratic spring" of the 1980s (Bellucci 1997; Tarducci 2018). This activism also flourished at the annual Encuentros Nacionales de Mujeres (National Women's Meetings) that started in 1986,[8] where different frames for abortion rights have been advanced (Sutton and Borland 2013). After a grave political and economic crisis in 2001, women's and feminist movements gained strength and a new nationwide organization demanding legal reform emerged: the National Campaign for the Right to Legal, Safe, and Free Abortion.[9] Obstacles and disappointment within the movement, as well as perseverance and resourcefulness, led to new strategies (Borland 2014). One major innovation has been the provision of information to and accompaniment of people intending to terminate their pregnancies with abortifacient medications.[10] Yet this was certainly not the only strategy, as activists have also challenged hegemonic legal interpretations, used health risk reduction models, and promoted access to abortion within the existing normative framework (Fernández Vázquez and Szwarc 2018; Ruibal and Fernandez Anderson 2020). In 2018, the movement reached a historic milestone with the first ever parliamentary debate of an abortion legalization bill, which ultimately did not pass. While this outcome disappointed legalization supporters, it also revealed the movement's extraordinary reach and strength. In late 2020, promoted by President Alberto Fernández, a new parliamentary debate took place and had a victorious outcome. The movement showed its force again not only in the streets, but also in social media and mass media.

In Chile, in response to Pinochet's dictatorship, women's and feminist movements demanded democracy, but also reproductive rights and abortion (Maira, Hurtado, and Santana 2010). Moderation was one of the main political characteristics of the democratic transition in Chile and, in that vein, the reproductive rights movement tended to focus largely on contraception, practically excluding the more controversial demand for abortion rights (Vivaldi Macho 2018). Later on, more radical strategies were implemented by lesbian and feminist organizations—including an abortion hotline launched in 2009, when abortion was totally prohibited—and groups that developed feminist practices of abortion accompaniment (Vivaldi and Varas 2015; Vivaldi and Stutzin, this volume). In Chile, the movement for *aborto libre* (free/unrestricted abortion) expressed dissatisfaction with the prototypical moderate strategies of Chilean democracy. Still, feminists operating pragmatically pushed for legal reform and supported President Michelle Bachelet's bill, which legalized abortion on three grounds in 2017 (Casas and Vivaldi 2014; Casas Becerra, this volume). Abortion rights supporters have continued their mobilization, visibly present in protests for wider social transformation, for example, in demonstrations denouncing gender violence and in the widespread popular uprisings of late 2019 (e.g. Feministas y Organizaciones Feministas 2019).

In Uruguay, women's and feminist movements were very active in the political processes that led to new democratic agendas, and they advocated for the inclusion of abortion rights.[11] As López-Gómez, Couto, and Berro Pizzarossa (this volume) point out, feminists first had to bring abortion out of the private sphere and present this right as a public issue and a democratic concern. Public debate on abortion escalated in the 2000s, thanks to efforts to build a broad coalition that included "trade unions, neighborhood, professional, human rights, youth and sexual diversity organizations, advocacy groups for people of African descent, and even a few religious associations" (Pousadela 2015, 129). The movement developed a wide range of strategies that emphasized the importance of women's rights, human rights, and public health for democracy (Johnson, Rocha, and Schenck 2015). The use of frames that resonated within Uruguayan democratic repertoires, the construction of alliances with key social actors, and close collaboration with sympathetic legislators were essential to the process that led to legalization (Fernandez Anderson 2017). Yet obstacles around the implementation of the law, such as conscientious objection, combined with opponents' efforts to make the legal framework more restrictive, have continued to pose barriers to abortion access (López-Gómez, Couto, and Berro Pizzarossa, this volume; Rostagnol and Caccia, this volume).

The complex legacy of feminist and women's struggles for democracy helps explain why abortion rights claims in the Southern Cone can hardly be understood merely in terms of "single issue" politics, even if particular activist efforts have focused on abortion. The fight for abortion legalization and access as a democratic claim is often bound up with, or implicitly entails, broad demands such as social justice, human rights, and public health. One example of this approach is the National Campaign for the Right to Legal, Safe, and Free Abortion in Argentina, analyzed by María Alicia Gutiérrez (this volume). This coalition focuses on abortion but is composed of a wide array of social movement organizations—feminist, labor, human rights, students,

LGBTQ,[12] and many other groups. While diverse constituencies coalesce around abortion, they in turn apply their own imprint to the demand, placing it within their own organizations' agenda. Furthermore, the Campaign's call for abortion that is *gratuito* (without charge) aims to ensure equitable and universal access.

Persistent advocacy and activism in the Southern Cone have led to abortion liberalization in the three countries, to different extents. However, even when translated into law and policy, abortion rights achievements can be fragile, followed by backlash, restrictions, and implementation obstacles. The chapters on Uruguay share a concern that some of the gains in abortion access and legal status may backslide. Additionally, legal reform and protocols do not exhaust activists' aspirations for social transformation, as we can see in the practices and frameworks of feminists who engage in abortion accompaniment in Chile and Argentina. The question then arises: What are the meanings, challenges, and possibilities of democracy in relation to abortion rights?

The Meanings, Challenges, and Possibilities of Democracy

Political Dynamics, Discourses, and Strategies

In his analysis of abortion in relation to democracy, Luis Felipe Miguel (2012) points out that while abortion is often seen as belonging to the realm of morality, it is an eminently political issue that matters for the realization of democracy. This is the case not only because of its capacity to mobilize various political constituencies, but especially because it concerns the citizenship status of around half of the population. While Miguel refers to women, the argument applies to any person who might become pregnant and need an abortion, including trans men, non-binary, and gender non-conforming individuals. The denial of full citizenship rests on unjust limitations of a basic right in a liberal democracy, which is the ability to make decisions about one's own body.

Furthermore, democracy as a political system is expected to guarantee human rights, a particularly important notion for countries that have experienced authoritarian regimes. In contexts of democracy, abortion rights activists in Latin America have used human rights arguments to support the need for abortion legalization and access, among other frames (Marcus-Delgado 2020). Not only do these frames provide a link to international institutions, treaties, and organizations concerned with human rights; they also have local resonance given the memory of massive human rights violations under dictatorship (Gudiño Bessone 2012; Sutton and Borland 2013, 2019; Morgan 2015). Even so, scholars note the limitations of humanitarian frames that emphasize the victim status of women, at the expense of their political agency (Klein 2013; MacManus 2015; Vivaldi and Stutzin 2017, this volume). Additionally, conservative groups have relied on the language of human rights, for example, referring to abortion as "genocide" and using terms such as "disappeared children," which evoke the crimes of dictatorial regimes (Gudiño Bessone 2017).

As this volume shows, conservative sectors have used the levers of democracy to oppose abortion rights and a broader spectrum of sexual and gender rights associated with what conservatives call a "gender ideology" (see, in particular, the chapter by Juan Marco Vaggione and José Manuel Morán Faúndes, comparing Argentina and Chile, and the one by Lidia Casas Becerra on Chile). Many conservative political actors are religiously inspired, including Catholic and Evangelical groups, and have transnational connections. As Miguel (2012) argues, the incursion of religious institutions in politics, including pressures on politicians, challenges the separation of church and state that is needed to uphold democracy. Importantly, conservative sectors frequently use "strategic secularism" (Vaggione 2005, 240), appearing in the guise of non-religious actors and using legal and scientific discourse. They draw on the rights and freedoms of democracy—for example, to assemble and protest, litigate in courts of justice, participate politically through party structures—to advance models of society that are not democratic or egalitarian but based on hierarchical social arrangements. The influence of abortion opponents also affects healthcare contexts, where health practitioners and institutions have invoked conscientious objection to deny abortion services. Susana Rostagnol and Magdalena Caccia (this volume) show these dynamics in the case of Uruguay, documenting the effects on abortion provision in a context of legality, under legislation enacted in democracy.

The persistence of clandestine abortions in the region, as well as repressive attitudes and policies, denotes certain continuity between democracy and dictatorship.[13] The notion of "clandestinity" itself is filled with negative connotations partly due to the memory of repressive governments that resorted to clandestine detention to achieve their goals. Thus, abortion rights movements draw on strategies, discourses, and "symbols that are historically thick with meaning, situating the abortion rights cause within a wider field of social struggles and democratic political agendas" (Sutton and Vacarezza 2020, 753). Activists and advocates in the region have denounced and challenged the injustices associated with clandestine abortion: the disproportionate risks to the lives and health of the most destitute women, the way it compounds multiple and intersecting forms of marginalization, and the selective criminalization of women who end up in prison, among others. In her analysis of the Chilean case (this volume), Lidia Casas Becerra concludes with poignant examples of the depth of such injustices, based on her personal encounters with women who experienced in the flesh the brunt of punitive abortion legislation. Such cases reveal important democratic deficits, as the promise of democracy is not just about political representation, but also about the possibility of participation in a political community in conditions of equality. Abortion criminalization actually magnifies inequality, and it has shattered the lives and voices of countless women.

Abortion rights movements in the Southern Cone have developed diverse and innovative strategies and arguments to end the injustices linked to illegal, unsafe, and inaccessible abortion. These efforts can be analyzed in relation to both distinct and overlapping political repertoires in each country during the post-dictatorships. For instance, variations on the idea that abortion legalization is "a debt of democracy" (*deuda de la democracia* / *deuda democrática*) have been advanced to different degrees by movements, politicians, and/or advocates in all three countries. This notion has specific cultural and political salience given the history of political suppression under dictatorship and the expectation that democracy would lead to greater liberty and justice. Indeed, democracy holds the potential for reproductive justice, including abortion liberalization, yet this result is by no means guaranteed (as we see, for example, in countries like the United States, where abortion has been legal for decades, but still faces a host of restrictions and challenges).

In the context of democratic systems, feminist activists in Latin America had to develop expertise using institutional channels to achieve their goals. This was facilitated by state structures dedicated to women as well as mechanisms to increase women's representation in formal politics, such as gender quota laws in various countries (Marcus-Delgado 2020). As Cora Fernández Anderson shows (this volume), the participation of feminists in political parties and elected positions is key to understanding any progress in the abortion rights policy agenda. Still, given parties' resistance to address matters traditionally seen as not relevant enough and/or as politically costly, even in progressive and leftist parties, the work of feminists in those spaces can be arduous.[14] Elizabeth Borland's analysis of cause lawyering (this volume) illustrates another way of activating institutional channels to advance abortion rights, in this instance, through litigation at various levels. Cause lawyers in the Southern Cone have drawn upon both existing national legislation and international human rights law and courts.

Different types of alliances have also promoted policy reform in the Southern Cone. Political scientist Mala Htun (2003, 5) has underscored the importance of "'issue networks'—elite coalitions of lawyers, feminist activists, doctors, legislators, and state officials—in bringing about policy change." Social and political organizations have also coalesced to push for transformation. For instance, the National Coordination of Social Organizations in Defense of Reproductive Health[15] (in Uruguay), the National Campaign for the Right to Legal, Safe, and Free Abortion (in Argentina), and the Action Committee for Abortion[16] (in Chile) show how movements can use democratic channels to advance their agendas, from coordinating with political parties, to lobbying legislators, presenting bills, and organizing civil society to participate in government-sponsored hearings.

Abortion rights activists have also resorted to the mass media to amplify their message and mobilize supporters. Media includes both non-state and state managed outlets, and freedom of the press and of expression are essential to any functioning democracy. Feminists have used these channels, both as journalists shaping news reports about gender issues, including on abortion, and as guests and interviewees in TV and radio shows. In addition, abortion rights activists have relied on Internet-based communication, such as websites and blogs, and on other platforms popularized in the 21st century, especially social media. Writing about Argentina, Claudia Laudano (this volume) shows how abortion rights activists have increasingly used social media as part of the movement's toolbox. She reveals the synergy between mobilization in the streets and social media activity on Twitter; and how this platform emerged as a vibrant site of political dispute during the abortion legalization debate of 2018.

Interestingly, conservative forces have also used Twitter as part of their counter-movement strategy, often mimicking feminist strategies—something they have done offline, too.

Advocates for abortion rights are aware of the limitations of dominant institutions as avenues for social change, and they additionally or alternatively have engaged in practices that exceed what formal politics and institutions have to offer. As a site of power and resources, and given the history of authoritarian regimes, the state has been a particularly fraught institution for feminisms in the region. In fact, some of the historical tensions within Latin American feminisms, for example, between *institucionalizadas* (institutionalized) and *autónomas* (autonomous), have been about different ways of relating to governmental and non-governmental institutions (Alvarez et al. 2002; Vargas Valente 2008; Falquet 2014). Thus, activists have at times operated within, beyond, and against the state. Organizing outside bureaucratic institutions can also create space for less hierarchical structures from which to promote social change. Some abortion rights organizations, such as the Campaign in Argentina, have experimented with transversal, horizontal, and participatory forms of organizing (Gutiérrez, this volume), in that way prefiguring the democratic futures they seek. Furthermore, as Sonia Alvarez (2019, 307–8) points out: "In the past decade or so in particular, many queer and feminist innovations arguably occurred outside/beyond the state, beyond institutionalized interactions, in the streets, in the realm of media, culture, meanings, and representations." Some of these non-institutional tactics are radical in nature, happening in the margins of the law or pushing its limits. They prefigure a more substantive democracy, including egalitarian and expansive ways of imagining gender and sexuality, everyday life, and community.

The feminist organizations that engage in abortion accompaniments illustrate the prefigurative powers of this type of activism, for instance, enacting feminist notions of autonomy and care in relation to abortion—a point made by Lieta Vivaldi and Valentina Stutzin (this volume) in their discussion of organizations such as Con las Amigas y en la Casa (With Friends and at Home). Members of this lesbian feminist organization in Chile accompany those who need to undergo abortion outside the structure of health institutions, using the pharmaceutical misoprostol. This is not only because of the failure of the state to guarantee most abortions (in fact, criminalizing them), but to bring into existence alternative visions and understandings of abortion. In Argentina, Socorristas en Red (Network of Socorristas/First Responders) fulfill a similar role, implementing a feminist ethos of solidarity that "collectivizes" abortion, and that has helped ensure safe abortions for tens of thousands of women.[17] The ways these networks accompany abortions and publicize their activities can be conceptualized as a "performative exercise" (Butler 2015, 49) of the rights of those undergoing abortions—in the sense of asserting and reinforcing the right to abortion even when the law says there is no such right in most instances. In the words of members of Lesbians and Feminists for the Decriminalization of Abortion in Argentina,[18] which launched an abortion hotline in 2009: "legality is a process that is also socially constructed through struggle and practice" (Mines et al. 2013, 143).

Drawing on the expertise gained through abortion accompaniments and sharing medical information in accessible language, these feminist networks have contributed to democratize medical knowledge and technologies, putting them to the service of those who need it. Through mutual learning and peer education, they also promote egalitarian relationships between persons seeking abortion and activists offering accompaniment. These experiences and the overall popularization of self-managed abortion with misoprostol show the importance of the availability of medication and feminist networks for safer abortions in legally restricted contexts (Hyman et al. 2013; Drovetta 2015). Still, while Uruguay made abortifacient medication widely available with legalization, circulation was restricted to the medical system (CLACAI 2017), further complicating access to safe abortions outside the law's specifications. This is particularly significant if we consider how members of the medical profession have exerted their power to deny the right to abortion, even in contexts of legality, as Susana Rostagnol and Magdalena Caccia (this volume) show in the case of Uruguay, while also acknowledging that many health professionals have been committed to abortion rights. Multiple barriers for abortion access show that places with legalized abortion may also benefit from feminist accompaniment organizations. This is the case in Uruguay, where Mujeres en el Horno (Women in Trouble) launched an abortion hotline in 2014 to provide emotional support and information (*Uypress* 2014). In Argentina, as discussed by Brianna Keefe-Oates (this volume), the Socorristas have established relationships with "friendly" health professionals, and they interact with public health institutions and the state to demand equitable policies and practices. These experiences from Uruguay and Argentina show that radical abortion activism is not necessarily about always working against the state or completely outside of it. Activists establish connections with the public healthcare system, demand the actualization of rights, and call for deep and radical changes in line with social justice and an end to patriarchy. That is, toward a more meaningful democracy.

Abortion rights activists have intervened at multiple levels: from the intimate spaces of abortion decisions and practices to their more spectacular presence in street performances and mass demonstrations. Importantly, they have engaged in forms of protest where the "assembly of bodies" (Butler 2015, 59) has been a central strategy to make their abortion rights claims heard and seen, and to influence the realm of institutional politics. Activists' embodied presence and occupation of public spaces is also a claim to democracy understood as the power of ordinary people. It is a way of bringing into the public sphere voices that may not find echo when only relying on institutional channels. Furthermore, as Judith Butler points out, through embodied protest, activists convey more than what they say. For instance, "concerted bodily action—gathering, gesturing, standing still, all of the component parts of 'assembly' that are not quickly assimilated to verbal speech—can signify principles of freedom and equality" (2015, 48). These are certainly principles that feminists around the world have aspired to and that are put at play in abortion rights protests.

In recent years, we have seen powerful forms of feminist protest. Demonstrations during the 2018 abortion debate in Argentina drew global attention for their impressive scale—in fact, there were months of sustained mass mobilizations, particularly during each crucial congressional vote (*Guardian* 2018). The magnitude and resourcefulness of these protests—also known as the *Marea Verde* (Green Tide) for the movement's color—was novel and outstanding. Still, they built on women's and feminist movements' longstanding tradition of taking to the streets as a crucial space to express dissent, exert political pressure, and exercise collective deliberation in creative and performative ways. Despite the pandemic, the streets filled with activists once again during the congressional debate of the Access to Voluntary Interruption of Pregnancy law in 2020. Uprisings against neoliberalism in Chile in 2019 also showed the pervasiveness of feminist and abortion rights demands in the midst of a radical push to re-found democracy. On International Women's Day 2020, massive protests reached a climax when activists carrying an oversized green kerchief with the slogan *Aborto legal, libre, seguro y gratuito* (Legal, unrestricted, safe, and free of charge abortion) approached a large mural painted on the ground of Plaza Dignidad consisting of the word *históricas* (historical ones).[19] These expressions have multilayered and even transnational meanings. Affirming to be "historical" (instead of *histéricas*/hysterical) points to the legacy of women's and feminist struggles to dismantle patriarchal conceptions about women's bodies and sexualities. *Históricas* is also the affectional label for the senior activists in Argentina who became like "rock stars" during the Green Tide, a space and time of protests in which "activists from different generations recognized each other, worked together, and made a significant political impact" (Sutton 2020, 10). The green kerchief symbol adopted in the Chilean protest originated in Argentina; it found resonance across borders, passing on argumentative frames and powerful political affects (Vacarezza, this volume).

Indeed, abortion politics and struggles are not only about rational deliberation and argumentation. Affect and emotions also play a crucial role and structure how abortion is perceived, imagined, and conceptualized. In this sense, clandestinity shapes stigma, secrecy, and debilitating ways of feeling that are profoundly embedded in social and political milieus.[20] In addition, emotions are more than individual experiences; they can be part of collective action repertoires. Movements express emotions like grief, rage, and even joy or pride to mobilize people around their cause, sustain their activism, and advance their goals (Goodwin, Jasper, and Polletta 2001). Abortion rights struggles in democratic times worked to transform stigma into public conversations based on women's experiences and feminist political perspectives. As early as 1989, the Uruguayan organization Cotidiano Mujer (Women Daily) published the book *Yo aborto, tu abortas, todas callamos* (*I Abort, You Abort, We all Remain Silent*) as an attempt to speak up honestly about pregnancy termination, motherhood, clandestinity, violence, sexuality, and desire. Nayla Luz Vacarezza (this volume), explores important affective dimensions of abortion rights activism in the three countries under study, through the examination of key transnational symbols of the movement—the orange "voting" hand (from Uruguay) and the green kerchief (from Argentina). These symbols have carried deep feelings of hope associated with democracy in the region, expanding political horizons and showing activist willfulness. Networks of accompaniment as well as LGBTQ activists helped bring humor, pride, and joy into abortion politics (Vacarezza 2015, 2018; Sutton and Vacarezza 2020), and younger activist generations have also imprinted protest with a festive tone (Sutton 2020). Throughout its trajectory, the abortion rights movement mobilized diverse political affects: "Pain, suffering and grief are entwined with joy, relief, sorority, mutual care, anger, pride and hope. These political affects come from the abortion experience itself and our political capacity to translate it into political action" (Vacarezza 2019, 53).

Overall, abortion rights activism in Argentina, Chile, and Uruguay have deepened the meanings of democracy, tackled its challenges, and tested its possibilities. The promise of democracy also means that the formulation of the demand for abortion rights and the strategies to advance the cause need to recognize intersecting injustices and the contributions of different groups of activists, particularly those from socially marginalized communities.

Democracy and Intersecting Injustices

Abortion can be understood as a political issue that intersects matters related to gender, sexuality, class, race-ethnicity, citizenship, and disability status, among others. Social justice arguments in the region often emphasize that poor and low-income women are the most harmed by abortion restrictions—more likely to be criminalized, undergo risky abortion procedures, or not have access at all—while women with greater economic resources have been able to access abortion in better conditions. Thus, movement participation of women from the most affected sectors is vital. Strides have been made in that regard through feminist alliances and organizing within poor people's movements, labor, and working-class organizations (e.g., Di Marco 2011). Importantly, economic deprivation often intersects with other vectors of inequality. In the United States, women of color have advanced the notion of "reproductive justice" to account for intersecting inequalities; placing abortion within broader social struggles, with deep historical roots (Ross 2006). In Latin America, varied experiences of oppression have also shaped abortion understandings; and different collectives have questioned, troubled, and pushed to transform abortion politics.

The legacies of freedom struggles against slavery and racism were felt in the early transnational organizing for abortion rights in the region. The Fifth Feminist *Encuentro* [Meeting] of Latin America and the Caribbean, held in Argentina in 1990, established September 28 as the Day of Abortion Rights for Women of Latin America and the Caribbean. On that day in the year 1871, Brazil passed the Lei do Ventre Livre (Free Womb Law) that declared the freedom of enslaved women's children who were born after the promulgation of the law (No. 2.040). By choosing that day, feminists were denouncing that almost two centuries after the start of slavery abolition in Brazil, motherhood was still not always free ("Declaración de San Bernardo" 1991 [1990]). Thus, on September 28 the feminist calendar mobilizes—more or less explicitly—abolitionist legacies, to proclaim that "womb freedom" is still an unfulfilled emancipatory project in the region.

In the past decade, regional movements have deepened their intersectional understanding of abortion practices and politics. This has been particularly salient in Brazil, where the Black feminist movement has an important presence, and where women of

African descent have suffered multiple reproductive rights violations and injustices. Black women have experienced sterilization abuse (Roland 1995), higher maternal mortality rates (Secretaria de Políticas para as Mulheres 2015), and abortion-related mortality rates three times higher than white women (IPAS Brasil and Instituto de Medicina Social 2007). Racism and legacies of colonialism are also pervasive in the countries studied in this volume. In 2018, during the abortion debate in Argentina, women of African descent participated in mobilizations and expressed their support for legal abortion and the right to bodily autonomy. They made connections between past and present, remembering how Black women's "reproductive capacity was also used as an axis of the colonial economy, which operated under a patriarchal system, of class and racist exploitation exerted by White colonists" (*Lavaca* 2018, n.p.). In Chile, lively discussions unfolded in 2019 around the March for Free Abortion, held every 25 of July since 2013, and later moved to a different date, because the date coincided with the Afrolatin, Afrocaribbean, and Diasporic Women's Day (Vivaldi and Stutzin, this volume). This led to the conjunction of struggles against racism and for free abortion, and to the slogan "abort racism." In Uruguay, Mizangas—a collective of Afrouruguayan women who assert "without racism, better democracy" (Mizangas 2020, n.p.)—participated in the political process supporting legal abortion and said that they would not be silenced, "neither by patriarchy, nor by racism" (Mizangas 2012, n.p.). In the Southern Cone, racism combined with xenophobia also manifests through prejudice and discrimination toward migrants—translated into complex intersections of class, race-ethnicity, and citizenship status when it comes to abortion access in different locales. For example, in Uruguay, barriers to migrant women's access to abortion were enshrined in the abortion law via nationality/residency requirements (López-Gómez, Couto, and Berro Pizzarossa, this volume).

As in other parts of Latin America, and in the context of colonial histories, indigenous women in the Southern Cone also have a distinct stake in reproductive politics. In Argentina, indigenous women involved in feminist and women's movements have debated abortion, presenting different political positions on the issue (Sciortino 2014). Some of these women, animated by the 2018 parliamentary debate, expressed support for abortion legalization and conveyed their own perspectives based on indigenous cosmovisions. They invoked ancestral knowledge and retrieved historic experiences of abortion as a practice used to resist colonization and sexual violence. Similarly, in Chile, indigenous women show varied viewpoints on abortion; yet traditional abortion practices with *lawen* (medicinal herbs) have been documented in Mapuche culture. Among other reasons, women from this group also resorted to abortion as resistance in "the face of the monocultural Chilean State" (Fernández Míguez and González Gronemann 2017, 432). While the 2017 abortion law reform in Chile expanded access, Sheila Fernández Míguez and Luciano Amaro González Gronemann note that its implementation "runs the risk of also becoming a form of coloniality, as it was designed within the state sphere, urban and Western, without connection to the needs of Mapuche women and the practices performed within their culture [*pueblo*]" (2017, 432). In Argentina, Relmu Ñamku (2020), a Mapuche and member of the Confederation of Indigenous Peoples and Women of Argentina,[21] advocated for the incorporation of indigenous "voice and ancestral knowledge" in the abortion legalization bill, and maintained that by "[c]reating new legal mechanisms that accompany the free decisions of each woman, we will build a more democratic society" (n.p.).

In recent years, abortion accompaniment organizations produced specific materials to facilitate access for marginalized groups and disseminated information about traditional forms of knowledge on abortion healthcare. A bi-national publication organized by Adelitas and Mansa Ballena (2016) on pre, during, and post abortion care recommends the use of medicinal herbs and plants. In Chile, the Línea Aborto Libre (2017) created a guide to self-managed abortion with medication in creole, for migrant women from Haiti.[22] In Argentina, the Consejería Pre y Post Aborto de Villa Urquiza (2018)[23] published a video guide in national sign language, produced with members of Movimiento de Sordas Feministas de Argentina (Movement of Deaf Feminists of Argentina / MOSFA).

In 2018, during the widespread abortion rights mobilizations in Argentina, organizations of people with diverse bodies and disabilities were also active participants. MOSFA participated in this activism and presented a green kerchief with the motto of the National Campaign for the Right to Legal, Safe, and Free Abortion in graphic national sign language (MOSFA 2019). In addition, the Red por los Derechos de las Personas con Discapacidad (Network for the Rights of People with Disabilities / REDI) also advocated for legalization and expressed their concerns about specific aspects of the Campaign's bill (REDI 2018). Parts of the bill were later modified, avoiding potential eugenicist interpretations (references to "grave fetal malformations" were no longer listed in the Campaign's bill as a reason to access abortion beyond the first 14 weeks of pregnancy).

LGBTQ activists have made important contributions to abortion rights struggles. Particularly in Argentina and Chile, lesbian activists were the founders of the first abortion hotlines and shaped abortion access outside the medical system. Operating in legally restrictive contexts, these activists have had to maneuver through the interstices of the law, grounding their practice in the human right to give and receive information. At the same time, they draw upon the LGBTQ movement experience and history in their abortion rights activism. Visibility and pride, alongside LGBTQ approaches to community health, have been integral to their approach. Lesbian activists have questioned the heterosexual slant of abortion politics and the hegemonic place of cis-heterosexual woman as its subject (Mines et al. 2013; Loaiza Cárdenas 2016). They have pointed to the need to broaden the understanding of whose bodies can undergo and accompany abortions, and they encourage engaging with notions of sexual freedom and autonomy often absent in dominant discourse.

Trans activism and perspectives in particular have also influenced abortion struggles, shaking dominant assumptions regarding abortion. In Argentina, there have been heated discussions about how to name the subject of abortion, denunciation of the scarce representation of trans men in the abortion debate, and calls to redress exclusionary positions within the movement (Radi 2014; Fernández Romero, 2020; Montenegro 2020). Debates over gender-inclusive language and politics permeated the National Campaign for the Right to Legal, Safe, and Free Abortion, prompting modifications of its bill to mention not only women but also any person who may gestate, no matter their gender or sexual identity (Sutton and Borland 2018). In other words, to recognize that trans men, non-binary, queer-identified, and gender non-conforming people also have abortion rights.

Feminist, LGBTQ, and abortion rights movements in the Southern Cone are redefining the meanings of democracy and social justice to include expansive notions of bodily autonomy connected to the breadth of rights promised by democracy. The first democratically elected president after the last dictatorship in Argentina, Raúl Ricardo Alfonsín (1983) asserted: *"Con la democracia no solo se vota, sino que también se come, se educa y se cura"* (With democracy we not only vote, but also eat, educate, and heal). Yet, many of these and other promises remain unfulfilled for large sectors of the population, often causing disenchantment with the system. Activists from all walks of life have been working to make democratic dreams a reality, and expanding their scope and interpretation. Sexual and reproductive rights, including abortion, are part of the bundle of rights that feminist and LGBTQ organizations have demanded as part of a transformative democratic project.

The abortion rights movement derives its strength from the various fronts of struggle that is able to handle, from its alliances with diverse social and political sectors, and from skillful activists who have used a multiplicity of strategies to create change. The popular support of wide and diverse swaths of society is what tips the scale toward legislative debate and legal reform. And that is an achievement of social movements and activists intervening at multiple levels, exercising the power of the people. At the same time, abortion rights legislation can become empty words, or may be undermined by conservative attacks, if there is not a progressive movement and civil society that monitors and demands effective access to rights— and if broader injustices persist.

This overview shows some key elements of abortion politics in Latin America's Southern Cone. *Abortion and Democracy* presents scholarship that allows us to explore how abortion rights can be productively paired with questions about democracy, citizenship, human rights, and social justice in the 21st century. In doing so, it is important to go beyond the conceptualization of democracy as a system of government, and to examine the ways in which bodies, subjectivities, and affects are mobilized to achieve just outcomes as part of the democratic inter-play. Activists, students, scholars, lawyers, politicians, healthcare workers, and other stakeholders have operated within (imperfect) democratic systems to ensure access to abortion, change unjust laws, and monitor policy implementation. At the same time, the limits and meanings of democracy are continuously being disputed as different sectors of society become disillusioned with merely formal changes and as legal reform cannot reflect and contain the breadth of democratic dreams and aspirations of activists. Some social transformations may seem utopic, but surely mark a horizon of democratic struggle worth pursuing.

Organization of the Book

Abortion and Democracy is organized into four main parts. Part I includes chapters that take comparative and transnational approaches to addressing topical issues as well as historical insights concerning abortion rights in Argentina, Chile, and Uruguay. They analyze key dimensions of legal change efforts, such as cause lawyering and political party dynamics, including the role of conservative abortion opponents. Additionally, abortion rights mobilization is explored through the study of prominent symbols and political affects linked to such activism.

Part II concentrates on Uruguay, pioneer among the three countries with respect to the legalization of abortion on demand. This section combines information and analysis of the road to legalization with ethnographic perspectives on abortion services after legalization. These accounts also hint at the implications of a new conservative political scenario for abortion access and legal status.

Part III examines different aspects of the abortion rights movement in Argentina, with special attention to the strategies and political impact of the National Campaign for the Right to Legal, Safe, and Free Abortion. Digital activism and feminist community health strategies are also analyzed as important parts of the movement's repertoire.

Part IV focuses on Chile, with insights on the struggle for decriminalization based on three grounds, including the role of academia as an arena of political dispute regarding abortion legalization and a space where secular and religious views clash. This section also sheds light on radical activist strategies that use feminist decolonial and queer perspectives to provide abortion access outside the healthcare system.

The book concludes with an Afterword by Sonia E. Alvarez, expert in social movements and Latin American feminisms, who leaves us with food for thought as we consider the future of abortion and democracy in the region and beyond.

Notes

1 While varied perspectives exist regarding which countries are part of the Southern Cone (for example, some accounts include Paraguay and Brazil), Argentina, Chile, and Uruguay have traditionally been regarded as constitutive of this region.
2 See Bergallo and Ramón Michel (2009) for a discussion of the modifications of the abortion law during the dictatorship (still maintaining criminalization), which were repealed with the advent of democracy, restoring the wording of the 1921 Penal Code.
3 For works on Argentina, see, e.g., Bergallo and Ramón Michel (2009), Bergallo (2011), and Monte (2017); for Chile see, e.g., García-Huidobro (2007), Hermosilla and van Weezel (2009), and Zúñiga Añazco (2013); and for Uruguay see, e.g., Xavier (2005) and Banfi-Vique et al. (2011).
4 See, e.g., Briozzo (2002), Romero, Zamberlin, and Gianni (2010), Casas and Vivaldi (2014), López Gómez (2016), López Gómez et al. (2017).
5 In the context of Argentina, see Checa and Rosenberg (1996), Chiarotti, García Jurado, and Schuster (1997), and Brown (2008); with regards to Chile, see Shepard and Casas Becerra (2007), Casas (2011), and Zúñiga Fajuri (2011); and about Uruguay, see Briozzo (2016), and Labandera, Gorgoroso, and Briozzo (2016).

6 About movements in Argentina, see, Bellucci (2014), Burton (2017), Sutton and Borland (2018, 2019), Sutton and Vacarezza (2020), Sutton (2020). About Chile, see Maira Vargas (2010) and Grandón Valenzuela (2020). Regarding Uruguay, see Johnson, Rocha, and Schenck (2015), Pousadela (2015), and Fernandez Anderson (2017). Transnational analysis can be found in Borland (2004) and Fernandez Anderson (2020).
7 This and all other quotes in this chapter that were originally in Spanish are our translation.
8 Changing politics in the feminist and women's movement, and in relation to broader political developments, have prompted discussion about changing the name from Encuentro Nacional de Mujeres to Encuentro Plurinacional de Mujeres, Lesbianas, Trans, Travestis y No Binaries (Plurinational Meeting of Women, Lesbians, Trans, Travestis, and Non-Binary [People]). For a journalistic account of these developments in the 34th Encuentro in 2019, see Murillo (2019).
9 In Spanish, Campaña Nacional por el Derecho al Aborto Legal, Seguro y Gratuito. See Zurbriggen and Anzorena (2013) for a history of the Campaign; and Gutiérrez (this volume) and Laudano (this volume) for more recent developments.
10 See Mines et al. (2013), Maffeo et al. (2015), McReynolds-Pérez (2017), Zurbriggen (2019), Keefe-Oates (this volume).
11 See Celiberti (2006); Abracinskas and López Gómez (2007); López-Gómez, Couto, and Berro Pizzarossa (this volume).
12 LGBTQ refers to lesbian, gay, bisexual, transgender, and queer-identified people, but as an umbrella term, it may also encompass, sometimes in modified form, other non-normative or "dissident" sexual and gender identities.
13 See Acuña Moenne and Webb (2005), Sutton (2017, 2018), and Nichols and Cuestas (2018).
14 For in-depth analyses of center-left governments of the "Pink Tide" in relation to sexual and gender rights, see Friedman (2019). For abortion rights in particular, see Blofield and Ewig (2017).
15 In Spanish, Coordinación Nacional de Organizaciones Sociales por la Defensa de la Salud Reproductiva.
16 In Spanish, Mesa Acción por el Aborto en Chile.
17 Between 2014 and 2019, Socorristas accompanied 31,936 abortions with medications and referred 1,508 women to the healthcare system for legal abortions (Socorristas en Red 2020).
18 In Spanish, Lesbianas y Feministas por la Descriminalización del Aborto.
19 See *La Izquierda Diario* (2020).
20 See Rosenberg (1994), Chaneton and Oberti (1997), Carril Berro and López Gómez (2008), Sutton (2010), Chaneton and Vacarezza (2011), Rostagnol (2014).
21 In Spanish, Confederación de Pueblos y Mujeres Indígenas de Argentina.
22 For an analysis, see Vivaldi and Stutzin (this volume).
23 In English, Pre and Post Abortion Counseling of Villa Urquiza.

References

Abogados y Abogadas del NOA en Derechos Humanos y Estudios Sociales (ANDHES) et al. 2018. "Acceso al aborto en Argentina. Informe conjunto remitido al Comité de Derechos Económicos, Sociales y Culturales (Comité DESC) de las Naciones Unidas para la cuarta evaluación periódica del país," September 11. www.cels.org.ar/web/wp-content/uploads/2018/09/20180911_Aborto_ComiteDESC.pdf.

Abracinskas, Lilián, and Alejandra López Gómez (eds.). 2007. *El aborto en debate. Dilemas y desafíos del Uruguay democrático. Proceso político y social 2001–2004*. Montevideo: Mujer y Salud en Uruguay.

Acuña Moenne, María Elena, and Matthew Webb. 2005. "Embodying Memory: Women and the Legacy of the Military Government in Chile." *Feminist Review* 79:150–161.

Adelitas, and Mansa Ballena. 2016. *Cuaderno de cuidados pre, durante y post aborto (con pastillas)*. Chile, Argentina: Adelitas and Mansa Ballena.

Alfonsín, Raúl Ricardo. 1983. "Discurso de asunción de Raúl Alfonsín," December 10. www.alfonsin.org/discurso-de-asuncion-presidencial-ante-asamblea-legislativa/.

Alvarez, Sonia E. 2019. "Afterword: Maneuvering the 'U-Turn'. Comparative Lessons from the Pink Tide and Forward-Looking Strategies for Feminist and Queer Activisms in the Americas." In *Seeking Rights from the Left. Gender, Sexuality, and the Latin American Pink Tide*, ed. Elizabeth Jay Friedman, 305–311. Durham: Duke University Press.

Alvarez, Sonia E., Elizabeth Jay Friedman, Ericka Beckman, Maylei Blackwell, Norma Stoltz Chinchilla, Nathalie Lebon, Marysa Navarro, and Marcela Ríos Tobar. 2002. "Encountering Latin American and Caribbean Feminisms." *Signs: Journal of Women in Culture and Society* 28(2): 537–579.

Banfi-Vique, Analía, Oscar A. Cabrera, Fanny Gómez-Lugo, and Martín Hevia. 2011. "The Politics of Reproductive Health Rights in Uruguay: Why the Presidential Veto to the Right to Abortion is Illegitimate." *Revista de Direito Sanitário* 12(2): 192–205.

Bellucci, Mabel. 1997. "Women's Struggle to Decide About Their Own Bodies: Abortion and Sexual Rights in Argentina." *Reproductive Health Matters: An International Journal on Sexual and Reproductive Health and Rights* 5(10): 99–106.

Bellucci, Mabel. 2014. *Historia de una desobediencia. Aborto y feminismo*. Buenos Aires: Capital Intelectual.

Bergallo, Paola (ed.). 2011. *Aborto y justicia reproductiva*. Buenos Aires: Del Puerto.

Bergallo, Paola. 2014. "The Struggle Against Informal Rules on Abortion in Argentina." In *Abortion Law in Transnational Perspective: Cases and Controversies*, eds. Rebecca J. Cook, Joanna N. Erdman, and Bernard M. Dickens, 143–165. Philadelphia: University of Pennsylvania Press.

Bergallo, Paola, and Agustina Ramón Michel. 2009. "El aborto no punible en el derecho argentino." *Despenalización.org.ar* 9:1–8.

Blofield, Merike, and Christina Ewig. 2017. "The Left Turn and Abortion Politics in Latin America." *Social Politics: International Studies in Gender, State & Society* 24(4): 481–510.

Borland, Elizabeth. 2004. "Cultural Opportunities and Tactical Choice in the Argentine and Chilean Reproductive Rights Movements." *Mobilization: An International Quarterly* 9(3): 327–339.

Borland, Elizabeth. 2014. "Storytelling, Identity, and Strategy: Perceiving Shifting Obstacles in the Fight for Abortion Rights in Argentina." *Sociological Perspectives* 57(4): 488–505.

Briozzo, Leonel (ed.). 2002. *Iniciativas sanitarias contra el aborto provocado en condiciones de riesgo. Aspectos clínicos, epidemiológicos, médico-legales, bioéticos y jurídicos*. Montevideo: Sindicato Médico del Uruguay.

Briozzo, Leonel. 2016. "From Risk and Harm Reduction to Decriminalizing Abortion: The Uruguayan Model for Women's Rights." *International Journal of Gynecology & Obstetrics* 134(S1): S3–6.

Brown, Josefina Leonor. 2008. "Los derechos (no)reproductivos en Argentina: Encrucijadas teóricas y políticas." *Cadernos Pagu* 30: 269–300.

Burton, Julia. 2017. "De la Comisión al Socorro: Trazos de militancia feminista por el derecho al aborto en Argentina." *Descentrada* 1(2): 1–17.

Butler, Judith. 2015. *Notes Toward a Performative Theory of Assembly*. Cambridge, MA: Harvard University Press.

Carril Berro, Elina, and Alejandra López Gómez. 2008. *Entre el alivio y el dolor. Mujeres, aborto voluntario y subjetividad*. Montevideo: Trilce.

Casas, Lidia B. 2011. "Women and Reproduction: From Control to Autonomy? The Case of Chile." *Journal of Gender, Social Policy & the Law* 12(3): 427–451.

Casas, Lidia, and Lieta Vivaldi. 2014. "Abortion in Chile: The Practice Under a Restrictive Regime." *Reproductive Health Matters* 22(44): 70–81.

Celiberti, Lilian. 2006. "El aborto en la agenda democrática." *Cotidiano Mujer* 42. www.cotidianomujer.org.uy/sitio/revistas/28-cotidiano-mujer-no42/367-el-aborto-en-la-agenda-democratica-lilian-celiberti.

Chaneton, July, and Alejandra Oberti. 1997. "Historia de Ana." In *Aborto no punible. Concurso de ensayo: "Peligro para la vida y la salud de la madre,"* ed. Foro por los Derechos Reproductivos, 81–95. Buenos Aires: Foro por los Derechos Reproductivos.

Chaneton, July, and Nayla Vacarezza. 2011. *La intemperie y lo intempestivo: Experiencias del aborto voluntario en el relato de mujeres y varones.* Buenos Aires: Marea.

Checa, Susana, and Martha Rosenberg. 1996. *Aborto hospitalizado: Una cuestión de derechos reproductivos, un problema de salud pública.* Buenos Aires: El cielo por asalto.

Chiarotti, Susana, Mariana García Jurado, and Gloria Schuster. 1997. "El embarazo forzado y el aborto terapéutico en el marco de los derechos humanos." In *Aborto no punible. Concurso de ensayo: "Peligro para la vida y la salud de la madre,"* ed. Foro por los Derechos Reproductivos, 19–45. Buenos Aires: Foro por los Derechos Reproductivos.

Consejería Pre y Post Aborto de Villa Urquiza. 2018. "Aborto con misoprostol en Lengua de Señas Argentina." *Facebook*, March 12. www.facebook.com/watch/?v=648242948854550.

Consorcio Latinoamericano Contra el Aborto Inseguro (CLACAI). 2017. *Mifepristona y misoprostol en seis países de América Latina: Procesos de registro y disponibilidad.* Lima: Consorcio Latinoamericano Contra el Aborto Inseguro.

Correa, Sonia, and Mario Pecheny. 2016. *Abortus interruptus. Política y reforma legal del aborto en Uruguay.* Montevideo: Mujer y Salud en Uruguay.

Cotidiano Mujer. 1989. *Yo aborto, tu abortas, todas callamos.* Montevideo: Cotidiano Mujer.

"Declaración de San Bernardo." 1991. In *Nuevos aportes sobre aborto: Publicación de la Comisión por el Derecho al Aborto* 3(5): 2.

Di Marco, Graciela. 2011. *El pueblo feminista. Movimientos sociales y lucha de las mujeres en torno a la ciudadanía.* Buenos Aires: Biblos.

Drovetta, Raquel Irene. 2015. "Safe Abortion Information Hotlines: An Effective Strategy for Increasing Women's Access to Safe Abortions in Latin America." *Reproductive Health Matters* 23(45): 47–57.

Falquet, Jules. 2014. "Las 'Feministas autónomas' latinoamericanas y caribeñas: Veinte años de disidencias." *Universitas Humanística* 78: 39–63.

Feijoo, María del Carmen, and Mónica Gogna. 1985. "Las mujeres en la transición a la democracia." In *Los nuevos movimientos sociales / 1: Mujeres, rock nacional*, ed. Elizabeth Jelin, 41–78. Buenos Aires: Centro Editor de América Latina.

Feministas y Organizaciones Feministas. 2019. "Feministas en estado de rebeldía: 'Nos sumamos al paro del 21 de octubre." *El Desconcierto.cl*, October 19. www.eldesconcierto.cl/2019/10/19/feministas-en-estado-de-rebeldia-nos-sumamos-al-paro-del-21-de-octubre/.

Fernandez Anderson, Cora. 2017. "Decriminalizing Abortion in Uruguay: Women's Movements, Secularism, and Political Allies." *Journal of Women, Politics & Policy* 38(2): 221–246.

Fernandez Anderson, Cora. 2020. *Fighting for Abortion Rights in Latin America: Social Movements, State Allies and Institutions.* New York: Routledge.

Fernández Míguez, Sheila, and Luciano Amaro González Gronemann. 2017. "Análisis crítico de la nueva ley 21.030 de despenalización del aborto en tres causales en Chile, desde la cosmovisión mapuche y la teoría decolonial de género." *Revista InSURgência* 3(2): 414–454.

Fernández Romero, Francisco. 2020. "'We Can Conceive Another History': Trans Activism Around Abortion Rights in Argentina." *International Journal of Transgender Health*, doi:10.1080/26895269.2020.1838391.

Fernández Vázquez, Sandra Salomé, and Lucila Szwarc. 2018. "Aborto medicamentoso: Transferencias militantes y transnacionalización de saberes en Argentina y América Latina." *RevIISE: Revista de Ciencias Sociales y Humanas* 12(12): 163–177.

Fisher, Jo. 1993. "Chile: 'The Kitchen Never Stopped.'" In *Out of the Shadows. Women, Resistance and Politics in South America*, 17–43. London: Latin America Bureau.

Friedman, Elisabeth Jay (ed.). 2019. *Seeking Rights from the Left: Gender, Sexuality, and the Latin American Pink Tide*. Durham: Duke University Press.

García-Huidobro, Rodolfo Figueroa. 2007. "Concepto de persona, titularidad del derecho a la vida y aborto." *Revista de Derecho* 20(2): 95–130.

Goodwin, Jeff, James M. Jasper, and Francesca Polletta. 2001. *Passionate Politics: Emotions and Social Movements*. Chicago: The University of Chicago Press.

Grandón Valenzuela, Débora. 2020. "Biopolítica y necropolítica anudadas en cuerpo de mujer: Análisis de las resistencias políticas feministas por la despenalización del aborto en Chile." In *Transversalidad y biopolíticas: Cuerpos, géneros y saberes*, eds. Rocio Moreno Badajoz and Flavio Meléndez Zermeño, 45–64. Guadalajara: Universidad de Guadalajara.

Guardian. 2018. "Argentina Holds Historic Abortion Vote as 1m Women Rally to Demand Change," August 8. www.theguardian.com/global-development/2018/aug/07/argentina-abortion-vote-legalisation-senate-mass-rally.

Gudiño Bessone, Pablo. 2012. "La disputa por la legalización del aborto en Argentina. Los usos políticos del Nunca Más." *Sociedad y Equidad: Revista de Humanidades, Ciencias Sociales, Artes y Comunicaciones* 4: 165–181.

Gudiño Bessone, Pablo. 2017. "El aborto en el campo de la memoria y los derechos humanos. Feminismo, Iglesia católica y activismo pro-vida en Argentina." *Aposta. Revista de Ciencias Sociales* 73: 86–119.

Hermosilla, Juan Pablo, and Alex van Weezel. 2009. "Contrapunto: El aborto terapéutico." *Revista Chilena de Derecho* 36(1): 205–208.

Htun, Mala. 2003. *Sex and the State: Abortion, Divorce, and the Family Under Latin American Dictatorships and Democracies*. Cambridge: Cambridge University Press.

Hyman, Alyson, Kelly Blanchard, Francine Coeytaux, Daniel Grossman, and Alexandra Teixeira. 2013. "Misoprostol in Women's Hands: A Harm Reduction Strategy for Unsafe Abortion." *Contraception* 87(2): 128–130.

Ipas Brasil and Instituto de Medicina Social. 2007. "Magnitude do aborto no Brasil: Aspectos epi-demiológicos e sócio-culturais." https://pdfs.semanticscholar.org/098e/d631db2f3f4f225d909 d99d82f8e3c4934df.pdf?_ga=2.84270105.1250562372.1599509726-89798183.1595859912.

Johnson, Niki, Alejandra López Gómez, Graciela Sapriza, Alicia Castro, and Gualberto Arribeltz. 2011. *(Des)penalización del aborto en Uruguay: Prácticas, actores y discursos. Abordaje interdisciplinario sobre una realidad compleja*. Montevideo: Universidad de la República, Comisión Sectorial de Investigación Científica.

Johnson, Niki, Cecilia Rocha, and Marcela Schenck. 2015. *La inserción del Aborto en la Agenda político-pública uruguaya 1985–2013. Un análisis desde el Movimiento Feminista*. Montevideo: Cotidiano Mujer.

Kirkwood, Julieta. 1990. *Ser política en Chile. Los nudos de la sabiduría feminista*. Santiago: Cuarto Propio.

Klein, Laura. 2013. *Entre el crimen y el derecho. El problema del aborto*. Buenos Aires: Booklet.

Labandera, Ana, Monica Gorgoroso, and Leonel Briozzo. 2016. "Implementation of the Risk and Harm Reduction Strategy Against Unsafe Abortion in Uruguay: From a University Hospital to the Entire Country." *International Journal of Gynecology & Obstetrics* 134(S1): S7–11.

La Izquierda Diario. 2020. "Chile: Más de un millón de mujeres llenaron la Plaza Dignidad y todo el país este 8M," March 9. www.laizquierdadiario.com/Chile-mas-de-un-millon-de-mujeres-llenaron-la-Plaza-Dignidad-y-todo-el-pais-este-8M.

Lavaca. 2018. "Las mujeres afro sumaron su grito #AbortoLegalYa," May 23. www.lavaca.org/notas/las-mujeres-afro-sumaron-su-grito-abortolegalya/.

Línea Aborto Libre. 2017. "Protocolo en Creole: ¡A la calle!", April 14. http://infoaborto chile.org/?p=810.

Loaiza Cárdenas, Cecilia del Carmen. 2016. *Estrategias de amor e información entre mujeres: La línea aborto libre. Una propuesta de investigación feminista.* Undergraduate thesis, Universidad de Chile.

López Gómez, Alejandra. 2016. "Tensiones entre lo (i)legal y lo (i)legítimo en las prácticas de profesionales de la salud frente a mujeres en situación de aborto." *Salud Colectiva* 12(1): 23–39.

López Gómez, Alejandra, Martín Couto, Gabriela Píriz, Ana Monza, Lilián Abracinskas, and María Luisa Ituarte. 2017. "Servicios legales de interrupción voluntaria del embarazo en Uruguay. Estrategias de los servicios públicos del primer nivel de atención." *Salud Pública Mex* 59(5): 577–582.

MacManus, Viviana Beatriz. 2015. "We are Not Victims, We are Protagonists of this History." *International Feminist Journal of Politics* (17)1: 40–57.

Maffeo, Florencia, Natalia Santarelli, Paula Satta, and Ruth Zurbriggen. 2015. "Parteras de nuevos feminismos. Socorristas en red - Feministas que abortamos. Una forma de activismo corporizado y sororo." *Revista Venezolana de Estudios de la Mujer* 20(44): 217–227.

Maira Vargas, Gloria Andrea. 2010. *Aborto y feminismo en Chile (1990–2009): Reflexiones desde el cuerpo y la sujeto.* Master's thesis, Facultad Latinoamericana de Ciencias Sociales, Ecuador.

Maira, Gloria, Josefina Hurtado, and Paula Santana. 2010. "Posicionamientos feministas en torno al aborto en Chile." https://archive.org/stream/PosicionamientosFeministasSo breElAbortoEnChile/posicionamientos_feministas_sobre_el_aborto_en_chile_djvu.txt.

Marcus-Delgado, Jane. 2020. *The Politics of Abortion in Latin America: Public Debates, Private Lives.* Boulder: Lynne Rienner.

McReynolds-Pérez, Julia. 2017. "No Doctors Required: Lay Activist Expertise and Pharmaceutical Abortion in Argentina." *Signs* 42(2): 349–375.

Mesa Acción por el Aborto en Chile and Fondo Alquimia. 2019. "Informe de Monitoreo Social. Implementación de la ley de interrupción del embarazo en tres causales." www.fondoalquimia.org/website/images/2019/06/Informe_-Monitoreo_-Social_ley_IVE.pdf.

Miguel, Luis Felipe. 2012. "Aborto e Democracia." *Estudos Feministas* 20(3): 657–672.

Mines, Ana, Gabi Díaz Villa, Roxana Rueda, and Verónica Marzano. 2013. "'El aborto lesbiano que se hace con la mano.' Continuidades y rupturas en la militancia por el derecho al aborto en Argentina (2009–2012)." *Bagoas – Estudos gays: géneros e sexualidades* 7(9): 134–160.

Mizangas. 2012. "Aborto legal ya," August 28. www.mizangas.com/post/aborto-legal-real-ya.

Mizangas. 2020. "Lineas de Acción." www.mizangas.com/.

Molyneux, Maxine, and Nikki Craske. 2002. "The Local, the Regional and the Global: Transforming the Politics of Rights." In *Gender and the Politics of Rights and Democracy in Latin America,* eds. Nikki Craske and Maxine Molyneux, 1–31. London: Palgrave Macmillan.

Monte, María Eugenia. 2017. "Abortion, Sexual Abuse and Medical Control: The Argentinian Supreme Court Decision on F., A.L." *Revista Latinoamericana de Sexualidad, Salud y Sociedad* 26: 68–84.

Montenegro, Ese. 2020. *Desandar el cisexismo en el camino a la legalización del aborto.* Buenos Aires: Puntos Suspensivos.

Morgan, Lynn M. 2015. "Reproductive Rights or Reproductive Justice? Lessons from Argentina." *Health and Human Rights Journal* 17(1): 136–147.

Movimiento de Sordas Feministas Argentina (MOSFA). 2019. "Pañuelos accesibles 'porque nosotras también abortamos,'" April 9. www.abortolegal.com.ar/panuelos-accesibles-p orque-nosotras-tambien-abortamos/.

Murillo, Eugenia. 2019. "El 34° Encuentro Plurinacional de Mujeres, Lesbianas, Trans, Travestis y No Binaries." *Página 12*, October 11. www.pagina12.com.ar/224436-el-34-encuentro-plurinacional-de-mujeres-lesbianas-trans-tra.

Nichols, Leslie, and Fedra Cuestas. 2018. "Penalización del aborto: Violencia política y abusos de la memoria en Chile." *Saúde e Sociedade* 27(2): 367–380.

Ñamku, Relmu. 2020. "La legalización del aborto en la agenda de las mujeres indígenas." *Debates Indígenas*, March 6. https://debatesindigenas.org/notas/32-legalizacion-del-aborto.html.

Pecheny, Mario, and Marisa Herrera (eds.). 2019. *Legalización del aborto en la Argentina: Científicas y científicos aportan al debate*. Los Polvorines: Universidad Nacional de General Sarmiento.

Pousadela, Inés M. 2015. "Social Mobilization and Political Representation: The Women's Movement's Struggle for Legal Abortion in Uruguay." *Voluntas: International Journal of Voluntary and Nonprofit Organizations* 27(1): 125–145.

Radi, Blas. 2014. "Aborto y varones trans." Presentation at the roundtable "Varones que Discuten Sobre Aborto Voluntario," Centro Cultural de la Cooperación, Buenos Aires, July 3. www.youtube.com/watch?v=wXSz_BmTiq8&feature=youtu.be.

Red por los Derechos de las Personas con Discapacidad (REDI). 2018. "Postura de REDI ante el proyecto de ley de interrupción voluntaria del embarazo," March 20. www.redi.org.ar/index.php?file=Prensa/Comunicados/2018/18-03-20_Postura-de-REDI-ante-el-proyecto-de-ley.html.

Roland, Edna. 1995. "Direitos reprodutivos e racismo no Brasil." *Estudos Feministas* 3(2): 506–514.

Romero, Mariana, Nina Zamberlin, and María Cecilia Gianni. 2010. "La calidad de la atención posaborto: Un desafío para la salud pública y los derechos humanos." *Salud Colectiva* 6(1): 21–34.

Rosenberg, Martha. 1994. "La reproducción de un síntoma." *El Rodaballo* 1: 22–24.

Ross, Loretta. 2006. "Understanding Reproductive Justice: Transforming the Pro-choice Movement." *Off Our Backs* 36(4): 14–19.

Rostagnol, Susana. 2014. *Aborto voluntario y relaciones de género. Políticas del cuerpo y de la reproducción*. Montevideo: Universidad de la República.

Ruibal, Alba, and Cora Fernandez Anderson. 2020. "Legal Obstacles and Social Change: Strategies of the Abortion Rights Movement in Argentina." *Politics, Groups, and Identities* 8(4): 698–713.

Sciortino, Silvana. 2014. "Violencias relatadas, derechos debatidos y mujeres movilizadas: El aborto en la agenda política de las mujeres indígenas en Argentina." *Caravelle* 102: 87–106.

Secretaria de Políticas para as Mulheres. 2015. "Relatório Anual Socioeconômico da Mulher." www.observatoriodegenero.gov.br/menu/publicacoes/relatorio-anual-socioeconomico-da-mulher-2014-1/at_download/file.

Sharnak, Debbie. 2017. "Uruguay's Long Transitional Decade and a New Era of Gendered Activism." *Journal of Iberian and Latin American Studies* 23(3): 383–398.

Shepard, Bonnie L., and Lidia Casas Becerra. 2007. "Abortion Policies and Practices in Chile: Ambiguities and Dilemmas." *Reproductive Health Matters* 15(30): 202–210.

Socorristas en Red. 2020. "Sistematización de acompañamientos a abortar realizados en 2019 por Socorristas en Red (feministas que abortamos)," https://socorristasenred.org/sistema tizacion-2019/.

Sosa Gonzalez, Maria Noel. 2019. "Una ventana para respirar. Apuntes para una genealogía feminista de las luchas por democracia en el país y en la casa en el Cono Sur en los años 80." *EntreDiversidades. Revista de Ciencias Sociales y Humanidades* 6(2): 73–97.

Sutton, Barbara. 2010. *Bodies in Crisis: Culture, Violence, and Women's Resistance in Neoliberal Argentina.* New Brunswick: Rutgers University Press.

Sutton, Barbara. 2017. "Zonas de clandestinidad y 'nuda vida': Mujeres, cuerpo y aborto." *Estudos Feministas* 25(2): 889–902.

Sutton, Barbara. 2018. *Surviving State Terror. Women's Testimonies of Repression and Resistance in Argentina.* New York: New York University Press.

Sutton, Barbara. 2020. "Intergenerational Encounters in the Struggle for Abortion Rights in Argentina." *Women's Studies International Forum* 82: 102392.

Sutton, Barbara, and Elizabeth Borland. 2013. "Framing Abortion Rights in Argentina's Encuentros Nacionales de Mujeres." *Feminist Studies* 39(1): 194–234.

Sutton, Barbara, and Elizabeth Borland. 2018. "Queering Abortion Rights: Notes from Argentina." *Culture, Health & Sexuality* 20(12): 1378–1393.

Sutton, Barbara, and Elizabeth Borland. 2019. "Abortion and Human Rights for Women in Argentina." *Frontiers: Journal of Women Studies* 40(2): 27–61.

Sutton, Barbara, and Nayla Luz Vacarezza. 2020. "Abortion Rights in Images: Visual Interventions by Activist Organizations in Argentina." *Signs* 45(3): 731–757.

Tarducci, Mónica. 2018. "Escenas claves de la lucha por el derecho al aborto en Argentina." *Salud Colectiva* 14(3): 425–432.

Uypress. 2014. "Lanzan línea telefónica para aborto seguro," March 14. www.uypress.net/a uc.aspx?49619,131.

Vacarezza, Nayla Luz. 2015. "Aborto, experiencia, afectos." In *Código Rosa. Relatos sobre abortos*, Dahiana Belfiori, 137–141. Buenos Aires: La Parte Maldita.

Vacarezza, Nayla Luz. 2018. "Perejil, agujas y pastillas. Objetos y afectos en la producción visual a favor de la legalización del aborto en Argentina." In *Aborto: Aspectos normativos, jurídicos y discursivos*, ed. Daniel Busdygan, 195–212. Buenos Aires: Biblos.

Vacarezza, Nayla Luz. 2019. "Afectos y emociones en las luchas por la legalización del aborto." In *Legalización del aborto en Argentina. Científicas y científicos aportan al debate*, eds. Mario Pecheny and Marisa Herrera, 45–55. Los Polvorines: Universidad Nacional de General Sarmiento.

Vaggione, Juan Marco. 2005. "Reactive Politicization and Religious Dissidence: The Political Mutations of the Religious." *Social Theory and Practice* 31(2): 233–255.

Vargas Valente, Virginia. 2008. *Feminismos en América Latina. Su aporte a la política y a la democracia.* Lima: Programa Democracia y Transformación Global, Centro de la Mujer Peruana Flora Tristán, and Universidad Nacional Mayor de San Marcos.

Vivaldi Macho, Lieta. 2018. *Abortion in Chile: Biopolitics and Contemporary Feminist Resistance.* PhD thesis, Goldsmiths, University of London.

Vivaldi, Lieta, and Benjamín Varas. 2015. "Agencia y resistencia feminista en la prohibición del aborto en Chile." *Derecho y Crítica Social* 1(1): 139–179.

Vivaldi, Lieta, and Valentina Stutzin. 2017. "Mujeres víctimas, fetos públicos, úteros aislados: Tecnologías de género, tensiones y desplazamientos en las representaciones visuales sobre aborto en Chile." *Zona Franca. Revista de Estudios de Género* 25: 126–160.

Wood, Susan, Lilián Abracinskas, Sonia Correa, and Mario Pecheny. 2016. "Reform of Abortion Law in Uruguay: Context, Process and Lessons Learned." *Reproductive Health Matters* 24(48): 102–110.

Xavier, Mónica. 2005. "La experiencia de Uruguay: El Proyecto de Ley de Defensa de la Salud Reproductiva." *Cadernos de Saúde Pública* 21(2): 629–633.

Zúñiga Añazco, Yanira. 2013. "Una propuesta de análisis y regulación del aborto en Chile desde el pensamiento feminista." *Revista Ius et Praxis* 19(1): 255–300.

Zúñiga Fajuri, Alejandra. 2011. "Aborto y derechos humanos." *Revista de Derecho* 24(2): 163–177.

Zurbriggen, Ruth. 2019. "Abortar y acompañar a abortar: Armándonos vidas activistas afectadas." In *Salud Feminista: Soberanía de los cuerpos, poder y organización*, ed. Fundación Soberanía Sanitaria, 199–218. Buenos Aires: Tinta Limón

Zurbriggen, Ruth, and Claudia Anzorena (eds.). 2013. *El aborto como derecho de las mujeres. Otra historia es posible.* Buenos Aires: Herramienta.

PART I

Comparative and Transnational Perspectives

2

ABORTION AND POLITICAL PARTIES IN THE SOUTHERN CONE

Electoral Costs, Platforms, and Feminist Activists

Cora Fernández Anderson

Introduction

Political parties, as foundational elements of democracy, constitute a key channel for political participation. Yet in the struggle for abortion rights in the Southern Cone, feminist movements' ties to political parties have been relatively understudied compared to the role of social movements and non-institutional activism more broadly. This chapter focuses on the complex and uneven relationship between feminism and political parties in Uruguay, Chile, and Argentina in the context of the struggle for abortion rights since these countries' democratic transitions until today.

The transition to democracy in the 1980s helped restore political and civil rights after years of military dictatorship, and with it, increased attention to gender equality alongside an invigoration of women's involvement in politics. After re-democratization, women began organizing to demand the legalization of abortion and defined this issue as a "debt of democracy" owed to women: without the right to choose over their own bodies, women were second-class citizens. Over the subsequent 20 years, other gender rights were gradually advanced. Family law was modernized to give mothers and fathers equal parental rights and gender quotas were established to advance women's political representation. In terms of public health, reproductive health programs broadened access to contraception and sexual education. However, restrictive abortion laws remained in place and the issue was initially avoided by most political parties regardless of their ideological leanings.

The landscape has been shifting in the last decade, though timidly and unevenly. After two rejected bills, Uruguay legalized abortion during the first trimester in 2012. Chile put an end to its total ban and moved into a system of exceptions in 2017. Argentina did not change its 1921 criminal code banning abortions (except for health reasons and rape) until December 2020. The country has seen massive movements erupt for abortion reform with near misses in the legislative agenda, and finally

DOI: 10.4324/9781003079903-3

achieving a hard-won victory in 2020 when abortion was legalized up to the 14th week of pregnancy. Overall, the movements have grown dramatically. In the 1980s, street actions for abortion reform gathered only a few numbers of people. Over time they grew and resulted in the current "Green Tide" that has shaken the region since 2017, when hundreds of thousands mobilized to demand legal, free, and safe abortion.

The dramatic growth of the movements alongside a lagging legislative agenda invites the question of how and whether political parties have been receptive to the abortion campaign's demands. What has been the role of feminism in advancing abortion reform within political parties? Which kind of parties have been more in touch with women's issues than others and why? Does support or hostility to abortion demands follow the left–right party divide, as is the case in North America? How have the institutional characteristics of the party system and the internal organization of parties influenced their positions around abortion?

Through the analysis of the political parties' platforms and the role of feminism, especially through feminist activists within the parties, this chapter advances the following arguments. First, all political parties, even those on the left, have been slow to integrate a feminist perspective, let alone the demands for abortion rights. Abortion reform has not been a top priority for political parties in the first decades following the democratic transition. The preference for most parties had been to support or accept the status quo, whether it was a total ban, as in Chile, or a system of exceptions, as in Argentina and Uruguay. Abortion reform was perceived as politically costly and thus most politicians preferred to avoid the issue altogether. Second, the level of institutionalization of the party system, in particular the programmatic or non-programmatic character of parties, influenced the way abortion reform has been dealt with.

Among countries with programmatic party systems—meaning that parties differentiate themselves along the ideological continuum—once the issue of abortion has entered the political agenda, there has been a rejection of abortion reform on the right, and an emerging support for reform on the left. These are the cases of Uruguay since the 1980s and more recently of Chile. In Uruguay the Frente Amplio (Broad Front) echoed women's demands for reform and in 1989 included the issue in their platform. In return, the right-wing Uruguayan Party, the Partido Nacional (National Party), stated its opposition. In Chile, both parties on the right expressed their opposition to legal abortion from early on in their platforms. The increased commitment towards abortion reform on the left took longer. The characteristics of Chile's party system, with the presence of coalitions and religious parties, delayed the inclusion of abortion reform in this country in comparison to Uruguay whose parties lack these features. On the other hand, in Argentina, where the party system is not organized ideologically, the issue of abortion has divided the main political parties: Unión Cívica Radical (Radical Civic Union, UCR), Partido Justicialista (Justicialist Party, PJ), and more recently Propuesta Republicana (Republican Proposal, PRO). As a result, multiparty coalitions were created both to support and oppose abortion reform, developing a very different dynamic than those in the neighboring countries.

Finally, the growth of feminism in the Southern Cone has been the main factor behind political parties' incorporation of abortion reform in their platforms. Two main channels have been at play in this process. First, the growing strength of the feminist movement in the last decade imposed itself in societal and political agendas forcing many parties to take a stand on feminism and its demands. Second, feminist activists have done more gradual and incremental work within their political parties, promoting feminist demands among the overwhelmingly male party leadership.

This chapter begins by reviewing the literature on party platforms and that on gender politics, and abortion in particular. Included in the chapter's core section is a brief description of each country's party system, followed by the relation of the main political parties to the abortion issue from the 1980s through 2020. It also explores the relationship of each political party with feminism and the work of feminist activists inside some of these parties.

Party Platforms and Gender Politics

Party platforms are important because they provide an easy way for parties to make their comprehensive policy positions known to the public. The literature on political party platforms has mostly emanated from case studies of Northern industrialized democracies. Some scholars believe platforms are influenced mostly by public opinion (Wagner and Meyer 2014; Klüver and Sagarzazu 2016; Benefiel and Williams 2019). "Riding the wave" perspectives argue that political parties respond to issues prioritized by voters since parties are rational actors that seek to maximize their votes. Other scholars have studied the weight of party activists, party elites, and/or interest groups in the platform's writing process, pointing to a more top-down process (Wolbrecht 2002; Coffey 2007; Conger 2010; Bawn et al. 2012). Wolbrecht (2002), for example, has found that the polarization on U.S. parties around women's rights corresponds to changes in party elites' preferences. Finally, others look into the influence of contagion and competition with other parties as an explanation of why some topics emerge simultaneously in many parties' platforms (Norris 1999; Baldez 2003; Kittilson 2013).

The literature on party platforms has mostly ignored the relationship between social movements and political parties. Can the emergence of a social movement advocating policy reform have an impact on the platform of a political party? If so, what are the mechanisms through which this influence happens? Social movement mobilization might influence public opinion and societal attitudes towards an issue, displaying the movement's growing strength, and this might be one channel through which parties pick up on new issues initially raised by a social movement. This chapter will shed light on another channel: that of double militants. These are activists who are simultaneously part of a political party and a social movement, in this case feminist movements. Thus, they have a central role in introducing the movements' demands into their party's agenda.

On the other hand, while the literature on gender politics has explored when governments address women's rights, only few scholars have looked into how political parties do so (Kittilson 2011). In researching government's gender policies, scholars have looked into factors such as the number of women in the executive and legislative branches (Soule and Olzak 2004), the existence of gender quotas

(Lovenduski and Norris 1993; Franceschet, Krook, and Piscopo 2012; Piscopo 2015), the creation of women's state agencies (Stetson and Mazur 1995; Franceschet 2003; Haas 2010), and the election of left-wing parties to power (Stetson and Mazur 1995; Htun and Weldon 2012, 2018; Blofield and Ewig 2017; Friedman 2009, 2019). Despite some important caveats, the main takeaway from this field is that an increased number of women in power, gender quotas, gender ministries, and left-wing parties have helped advance women's rights, although the relationship is often contingent. Other factors such as the budget and authority allocated to women's state agencies, or the specific characteristics of the left-wing party, interfere to make this more or less likely.

Within the field of gender politics, the research conducted on left-wing governments and their advocacy or indifference towards gender policies is particularly relevant to this study since it is one of the few areas exploring the connection between left-wing political parties and gender equality. Conventional wisdom considers left-wing parties more likely to embrace women's rights given their general focus on egalitarianism. However, studies have found contradictory evidence on this. While stronger advocacy towards women's rights among left-wing parties appeared to initially be the case in the Northern industrialized countries (Stetson and Mazur 1995), a larger global database suggested that more generally the presence of left-wing parties seemed to be more relevant to gender issues that overlap with class demands, such as childcare facilities or funding for reproductive rights services, especially when compared with issues not as narrowly associated with class, such as violence against women or family law (Htun and Weldon 2012, 2018).

Studies on the Latin American left also question the assumed coupling of left-wing parties and gender policies (Jones, Alles, and Tchintian 2012; Alles 2014; Funk, Hinojosa, and Piscopo 2017; Friedman and Tabbush 2019). For Friedman and Tabbush (2019), the Pink Tide (left-leaning) governments in Latin America improved the conditions of poor women but their projects have relied on heteropatriarchal relations of power. According to Funk, Hinojosa, and Piscopo (2017), Pink Tide governments have neither strengthened quota laws, nor have they elected more women to office than right-wing governments have. While Pink Tide governments advanced gender equality policies—for example, increasing the income of women—they have frequently rejected the expansion of reproductive rights (Friedman 2009, 2019; Blofield, Ewig, and Piscopo 2017). Studies also agree that the type of left-wing party matters. Institutionalized left-wing parties are more likely to advance reproductive rights and abortion reform in particular, such as the Frente Amplio in Uruguay. Populist parties tend to ignore those issues or even side with anti-choice positions, such as the Sandinistas in Nicaragua (Blofield and Ewig 2017). The religious or secular character of left-wing parties has also played a role in their advocacy of gender politics in general, and reproductive rights in particular. Those, like the Christian Democrats in Chile, who are closer to the Catholic Church reject a feminist agenda (Haas 2010). Following this work, this chapter adopts other institutional variables to explain when parties address the issue of abortion in the Southern Cone. Political science scholars offer definitions of party system institutionalization, highlighting one particular dimension: the programmatic character of parties, meaning alignment of parties along the ideological spectrum (Mainwaring 2018). This characteristic can help explain the different relationship between parties on the right and left towards abortion reform in countries with highly institutionalized party systems, such as Chile and Uruguay, and those with low institutionalization, such as Argentina.

While traditionally the relationship between left-wing parties and the feminist movement has been tense because of the left's exclusive focus on class and its indifference towards gender (Friedman 2009), in recent decades left-wing parties have been more receptive to feminist conceptualizations and agendas. But even when some left-wing parties have embraced the legalization of abortion as part of their platform, many times male left leaders viewed the right to abortion almost exclusively as a class issue, necessary only to prevent the deaths of poor women.[1] The work of feminist activists within the party has been key to also break with these frames and understandings. Among the few scholars who examined the role of women within political parties, some have shown that the presence of feminist activists within leftist parties increases the likelihood that the party will include gender issues in their platforms and agendas (Matland and Studlar 1996; Haas 2010; Kittilson 2011). These feminist party cadres can function as a liaison with the feminist movement in the absence of institutionalized channels that connect the party to grassroots organizations, thus increasing the chance of collaboration between activists and party members. Haas (2010) states that the openness that is seen in Chilean left-wing parties to feminist ideas is due to the internal work of feminist party members. Johnson similarly assigns women within political parties a vital role in advancing abortion reform in Uruguay (Johnson, Rocha, and Schenck 2015). Relying on these studies and expanding the analysis to new cases, this chapter looks into the presence of feminist activists and their power within left-wing parties in the Southern Cone as a possible explanation for when and how each of the political parties began to advocate for abortion reform.

Uruguay: Party Platforms and Actions Do Not Always Match

For over a century, Uruguay's political system was dominated by the Blancos (Whites) and the Colorados (Reds), traditional conservative and liberal political parties, respectively. Founded in 1836, they alternated rule and dominated Uruguay's political life through the 19th and most of the 20th century (Chasquetti and Buquet 2004). In the late 1950s and 1960s increasing unrest due to economic crisis and the incapacity of the traditional political parties to find a way out of the political crisis set the stage for the 1973 civil-military coup. Two years earlier, in 1971, a left-wing coalition termed Frente Amplio (Broad Front) emerged as a challenger of the Blancos (Partido Nacional/National Party) and Colorados, slowly eroding their domination of the political system. Bringing together communists, socialists, Christian democrats, and some independents, the Frente Amplio established itself as a force with a strong 18 percent of the vote in that year's elections. After democracy was restored in 1985, the Frente Amplio increasingly gained electoral power, winning the presidency for the first time in 2004, and again in 2009 and 2014. The emergence of the Frente Amplio as a clear left-wing party moved the Blancos and Colorados towards the right, giving Uruguay an ideologically structured party system.

Since abortion reform was included in the societal and political agenda by women's movements early in the democratic transition, political parties were forced to take a position on this issue. Given also the more institutionalized character of Uruguayan's parties, all of them discussed the issues within their internal institutions and took an institutional stand on abortion legalization based on their ideology: right-wing against it, left-wing in favor. Within the left, the work of feminist politicians within their party has been central to advance the party's commitment to abortion reform. Compared with other Southern Cone countries, Uruguay's parties have mostly supported the legalization of abortion: two out of the three political parties have explicitly done so in their platforms.[2] Having said that, for the most part institutional stances were not respected by presidents, and sometimes legislators, when bills were debated in Congress. This calls into question the relevance of party platforms at least in controversial issues such as abortion reform.

Partido Colorado

As early as 1984 (one year before the democratic transition), the Partido Colorado released a *Program of Principles* in which it stated that "the party encourages the diffusion of sexual education programs that emphasize the dignity of sexual relations and the duty of responsible parenthood. [...] [C]onsensual abortions should not be classified as crimes" (Partido Colorado 1984, 85). This document was voted and agreed on by the party's National Convention. Despite this early endorsement, the party as an institution was not active in advancing reform, aside from a few individual legislators, and it became evident that the question of abortion reform divided the party membership. As a result, the issue disappeared from their platform the following decade.

That abortion was not a priority for Partido Colorado is illustrated by the ill-fated, but pioneering effort of two legislators from the party, Víctor Vaillant and Daniel Lamas, who in 1985 introduced the first bill proposing decriminalization of abortion. Although the party had won the presidential elections and had a majority in Congress, abortion reform was never discussed. Frustration with the party's lackluster effort on gender issues led to some sharp critiques and even departures and realignments. Glenda Rondán, a legislator and key member of the Female Caucus (created in 2000), went so far as to claim she would not vote for her own party in 2010: "All the parties have at least one women candidate. What is going on with the Partido Colorado? We do not have good women candidates in Montevideo?" (*Canal 180* 2010, n.p.). Frustrated by the lack of acceptance of feminist demands, Rondán led the exit of a group of Colorado politicians who later became part of the Frente Amplio. However, the cases of these Colorado legislators in favor of abortion reform have been the exception. In a 1991 survey, most Colorado legislators either opposed decriminalization or did not have a definitive position on the issue (Johnson, Rocha, and Schenck 2015, 24). This opposition translated later in votes in Congress when a bill on sexual and reproductive health was introduced in 2002. At the time, then Uruguayan President and Colorado member Jorge Batlle (2000–05), threatened to veto the bill. As a result, only eight of 33 Colorado deputies supported the bill. In the Senate, only one of 11 legislators voted in favor (Jones 2007).

Frente Amplio

In 1989 the Frente Amplio stated in its electoral platform that the party "will study a new legal framework to support women who need to interrupt their pregnancies and guarantee adequate sanitary conditions for this practice" (Frente Amplio [Uruguay] 1989, 11). Consistent with its platform, Frente Amplio legislators have been the most active in Congress in advancing the decriminalization of abortion. As early as 1993, party legislators sponsored the first abortion bill to actually be discussed in Congress (although it never reached the plenary session) as well as the 2002, 2006, and 2011 reproductive and sexual health bills. When these bills were voted on in Congress, most legislators voted in favor with only a few exceptions.

Despite this seemingly supportive posture, President Tabaré Vázquez (2005–10 and 2015–20), from the Frente Amplio, was a major obstacle to abortion legalization. In 2008, he vetoed Article 4 of the reproductive and sexual health bill that legalized abortion during the first trimester, clearly acting against his party's platform. This move implied a return to ground zero. A new bill was thus introduced in 2011, once Vázquez was out of office, and a new Frente Amplio president, José Mujica, had been sworn in. This time when the bill legalizing abortion was passed by Congress, the president respected his party's stance and approved the abortion legalization bill.

The support for legal abortion within the Frente Amplio is not surprising. This party has been the one most influenced by feminism. Born as a movement in the 1970s, it has continued to have open channels to grassroots organizations such as unions, human rights, and women's movement organizations. This meant that feminists were able to have a place in the party early on and introduce their issues in the party's agenda. Within the Southern Cone, the Uruguayan left was the first to introduce abortion reform in their platform and bills in Congress to advance such a policy. The role of feminist Frente Amplio politicians such as Margarita Percovich, Mónica Xavier, and Carmen Beramendi were in large part responsible for this achievement.

Carmen Beramendi, union activist, former Tupamara, and political prisoner during the dictatorship, was elected to the Lower Chamber in the 1990s and later to the Senate. She recalls how she began embracing feminism:

> Women have fought to bring the dictatorship down but in the country that usually claims to be the most egalitarian of the region, there was no women in Parliament until five years after the transition to democracy. It was at that moment that I became a feminist, almost without realizing it.
>
> *(in Gentili 2017, n.p.)*

Margarita Percovich is another example of double militancy. A founder of the Frente Amplio, she was also active in women's organizations such as PLEMU (Plenary of Women of Uruguay) and connected both worlds effectively. After the transition to democracy, she was elected to the Lower Chamber and the Senate and was one of the founders of the Female Caucus. She was one of the main advocates for abortion reform in Congress. Percovich explains the work feminist legislators did since the early 1980s:

> [W]e the women of the Frente (Amplio) have worked intensely with our own political male leaders to integrate a gender perspective to all our policies and we have managed to make them understand that we cannot think about real social change if we do not pay attention to gender... we did this when we were in the city government in Montevideo and now that we are in the national government.[3]

The influence of key women in the party was clear in the construction of internal entities to bring about a gender perspective in the party's policies. As early as 1983, still under the dictatorship, the party created a Committee of Women with representatives of all the political parties that integrated the Frente Amplio. In 1989, this Committee proposed the inclusion of the abortion legalization bill in the party's platform (Johnson, Rocha, and Schenck 2015). Including a feminist perspective was not, however, without obstacles. Women activists at the time used humor and irony to expose the absurdity of male leaders' attitudes and the patriarchal underpinnings of progressive spaces such as the Frente Amplio. In a pamphlet invitation to discuss women's issues, activists wrote: "Why do we come to the Meeting for Women of the Frente Amplio? Because we have nothing to do" (De Giorgi 2017).

Even a decade later, in 1997, when feminists launched the Female Citizens' Rights Committee (UTDC) within the party, the struggles for acceptance were real. The policy document drafted by this Committee, which formulated proposals on gender equality, was not included in the party's platform (Johnson, Rodríguez Gustá, and Sempol 2019). Even when in 2009 many of the original proposals were finally included in the platform, the fact that the presidential candidates (all men) mostly ignored them in their speeches and policymaking (e.g. Tabaré Vázquez's veto against abortion legalization) showed the uphill battle that feminist politicians faced.

In 2014, Constanza Moreira became the first woman to compete for the Frente Amplio's presidential nomination and proposed a platform with a feminist perspective. This was the first sign of an attempt to renew the old male guard from the 1970s leading the party. Moreira received 18 percent of the votes despite having significantly smaller financial resources (Johnson, Rodríguez Gustá, and Sempol 2019). However, she lost the primaries to former President Tabaré Vázquez, who then won the presidential election for a second non-consecutive term.

In the past five years, feminism has become a stronger presence within the Frente Amplio, particularly led by younger generations of women at the forefront of the broader feminist tide. In 2018, a group of young activists created "La

Comité," a feminist commission within the party to discuss all the issues that have historically been relevant to the left from a feminist perspective.

Partido Nacional

The Partido Nacional (National Party) has stated its opposition to abortion in its declaration of principles. In 2002, at the beginning of the abortion congressional debate, in order to unify the party's position, former deputy Javier García presented a motion at the party's National Convention to include the principle that "life starts right after conception." The motion was quickly approved in this traditionally conservative party. Since then, the party has mandated its legislators to vote against all bills that contradict this principle. Party discipline prevailed in most cases. In 2004 only one deputy out of 22 of the Partido Nacional voted in favor of the bill on sexual and reproductive rights. In the Senate, all of the party's legislators voted against it. Only a few voices, all female, expressed support for abortion reform, such as Ana Lía Piñeyrúa. In 1993, she supported the Frente Amplio bill in favor of legalization (Johnson, Rocha, and Schenck 2015) but later changed her mind and publicly opposed the following reform bills (*Canal 180* 2012).

The fact that in Uruguay the three main parties have addressed abortion in their platforms and principles shows that the topic has been part of political debates since the democratic transition, thanks to women's activism. Although this presence did not translate into congressional debates in plenary session until 2002, it is a sign that politicians were more open to discuss the issue than in the neighboring countries, where almost no major political party referenced abortion in their early platforms. Based on their programmatic character, parties in Uruguay have taken institutional stances in favor or against legal abortion based on their ideological positionality. Platforms were not always respected, as in the case of President Vazquez's veto. Despite this temporary setback, the insider work of feminist politicians, particularly within the Frente Amplio, paid off and was a significant factor in achieving the legalization of abortion in 2012.

Chile: Early Right, Late Left

Scholars usually describe Chile as having the oldest multiparty system in Latin America, closely resembling European party systems (Mainwaring and Scully 1995): communist and socialist on the left; radicals and Christian democrats in the center; and liberals and conservatives on the right. Following the 1989 democratic transition, the historically tripartite party system was recast into two coalitions created around support or opposition to the Pinochet dictatorship. The first, opposing the military regime, was a center and left coalition under the name of Concertación de Partidos por la Democracia (Concertation of Parties for Democracy)—Nueva Mayoría (New Majority) since 2014. This coalition has consistently included the Demócratas Cristianos (Christian Democrats, PDC), the Partido Socialista (Socialist Party, PS), the Partido Radical (Radical Party, PR), and the Partido por la Democracia (Party for Democracy, PPD) together with other smaller parties depending on the specific years. The second, a right-wing coalition with numerous names throughout its history, has supported Pinochet and consistently included two main parties, the Unión Demócrata Independiente (Independent Democratic Union, UDI) and Renovación Nacional (National Renewal, RN). In 2017, a new coalition emerged as a third force in the November presidential elections, the Chilean Frente Amplio (Broad Front). Situated on the left of the political spectrum, it presents itself as an alternative to the old political system.

In one of his last acts before surrendering power, Augusto Pinochet banned abortion in 1989 with no exceptions, differentiating Chile from the other two countries. Since there is no country that has jumped from a total ban to legalization on demand, an intermediate step allowing for exceptions seemed the most likely path for Chile. As a result, the debate entailed more moderate lines. Chilean parties reacted to the total ban along ideological lines. Right-wing parties took the most active stances early on, stating their anti-choice position in their party documents defending Pinochet's measure. Those on the left took longer to explicitly state their position, evidencing the challenges within a politically heterogeneous and successful coalition that included a Christian party and the initially weak movement for abortion reform.

Renovación Nacional and UDI

During or right after the democratic transition, the two right-wing parties (RN and UDI) included in their declaration of principles the right to life from the moment of conception. RN included a declaration against abortion in their 1988 declaration of principles, anticipating Pinochet's 1989 ban. In 1991, UDI's declaration of principles explicitly included the protection of the life of the unborn. The party's main ideologist was Jaime Guzmán, the drafter of the 1980s Constitution under Pinochet, which included the defense of life from conception. The consensus around this principle within UDI is large. There was however one main political figure, Evelyn Matthei, who in 2010 introduced a bill proposing therapeutic abortion for cases of risk to the woman's life and fetal malformations incompatible with life outside the womb. Party discipline proved strong and she was threatened with expulsion. A female politician from RN, Karla Rubilar, was also one of the few voices expressing support for Matthei's bill. In both cases, it was women who challenged the otherwise broad consensus around the total abortion ban. Yet, their voices were silenced. When Matthei ran for president in 2015, she had to abandon her abortion views and support the party's adherence to the total ban (*La Tercera* 2010).

Partido Demócrata Cristiano

The Christian Democrats, although part of the center-left wing coalition, have sided against abortion, consistent with the Catholic Church's position. This was one reason why abortion reform was so hard to enact in Chile: those against liberalization had a foot in both the right and left coalitions. At the 2007 Ideological

Conference, the party reaffirmed the right to life from conception to natural death as a key principle. However, when the second Bachelet administration (2014–18) introduced a bill to reinstate therapeutic abortion under three circumstances (threat to life, fetal malformations incompatible with extra-uterine life, and rape), Christian Democrats were divided. In line with party principles, some leaders threatened bill supporters with expulsion (*La Tercera* 2015). In the end, legislators were allowed to vote "based on their conscience" and there were votes on both sides of the debate within this party.

The emergence of gender politics in the political agenda created a split among the party between a traditional conservative faction and a younger, more progressive wing (Haas 2010). This was partly due to the incessant work of feminist activists within the party. Their internal struggles to advance a feminist perspective had been even harder than within secular left-wing parties. Scholar Teresa Valdés argues that Christian Democrats such as Laura Albornoz and María Luisa España, appointed to positions to the National Service for Women (SERNAM) during the first Concertación administrations, were exposed to women's realities on a daily basis, making them more sensitive towards gender issues. As Valdés observes, "this happened through praxis, not theory."[4] As a result, these women introduced nuances into the staunch opposition against abortion historically embraced by the party, preparing the terrain for the approval of legal exceptions to abortion in the 2017 legal reform.

Partido Socialista

In contrast to the proactive stance of right-wing parties, those on the left took longer to take any institutional stand on abortion. The only party that included the decriminalization of abortion in its program from early on was an alliance of leftist parties called PAIS (Partido Amplio de Izquierda Socialista/Broad Party of the Socialist Left). It came together for the 1989 elections and quickly dissolved afterwards.

It was not until 2008 that the Socialist Party included in its platform the need to reinstate therapeutic abortion. In that year's party Congress, members passed a statement supporting "the right of women to decide over their own body through the decriminalization of therapeutic abortion" (Partido Socialista de Chile 2008, 4). However, the party's position did not translate into the government agenda until the second administration of Bachelet in 2015. Both President Lagos (2000–06) and Bachelet (2006–10), from the Socialist Party, were clear that abortion was not in their administration's agendas. This was partly due to their party's alliance with a Christian party and the lack of a strong movement for abortion reform at the time.

The Chilean Socialist Party has a long history of women's involvement in politics. Already in 1937, the party launched the Socialist Women's Action and in 1959 the Federation of Socialist Women. However, the party remained led by men for most of its history and not until 2015 did a woman—Isabel Allende—head the party. Socialist women came in contact with the feminism of the 1970s and 1980s, some while in exile and others through their party militancy and due to repeated discrimination by their peers. Carolina Carrera explains that in the 1980s, "many of the young *compañeros* that were part of the Socialist Youth and worked with me had a hard time and they looked at me like 'here comes the crazy one again with these issues'" (in Jeria 2009, 25).

The 1980s and 1990s brought some victories for feminists within the party. In 1986, the party relaunched the Federation of Socialist Women. Adriana Muñoz, recently returned from exile and a significant figure within the feminist movement and the political left, became its representative. In 1992, the party created the position of Vice-President for Women's Issues, which would be part of the Board of Directors. The power of this position would be seen some decades later. In 2018, during the party's national conference, the Vice-President for Women, Karina Del No, proposed to define the party as feminist and anti-patriarchal and the motion was approved (Delfino Mussa 2019).

Partido por la Democracia

Within the Concertación, the PPD has been the most active around abortion, despite the fact that it has not explicitly included this issue in its platform. Created in 1987 by socialist leaders as an instrumental and umbrella party to oppose Pinochet's dictatorship, the party appealed to many socialist women who preferred to be part of this new party to avoid the traditionally male-dominated Socialist Party. The PPD was the first party to pass internal gender quotas and introduce bills to reinstate therapeutic abortion in Congress. In 2013, the party actively supported the MILES[5] bill for abortion reform under three exceptions. Feminists have been a stronger presence within this party. Four feminist women were part of it from the beginning: Adriana Muñoz, Teresa Valdés, María Antonieta Saa, and Adriana Delpiano. Honoring its feminist origins, in 2018 the party rebranded itself as a "feminist party" (*La Tercera* 2018b).

Frente Amplio

Launched in 2016, the Frente Amplio is a coalition of 12 small left-wing parties many of which were part of the Nueva Mayoría coalition that took Bachelet to power in 2015. With roots in the student and feminist movement, this coalition has been the largest political force to support legal abortion on demand. Their 2017 platform, *El Programa de Muchos* (The Program of Many), explicitly talks about establishing a feminist government and advancing the legalization of abortion based on the woman's decision during the first trimester (Frente Amplio [Chile] n.d.). Despite its newness, in the 2017 election their candidate Beatriz Sánchez won 20.27 percent of the vote in the first round. In 2018, Frente Amplio legislators introduced a bill for abortion on request in Congress that has been drafted together with feminist activists from the Mesa de Acción por el Aborto (Action Committee for Abortion) (*La Tercera* 2018a).

The presence of a highly institutionalized party system with programmatic parties has meant that Chilean parties' position on abortion reform generally followed ideological stances: the right against and the left in favor. The fact that the country began the democratic period with the most restrictive abortion law of South America entailed significant obstacles to reform. This might explain the general tendency of left-wing parties to exclude the issue from their political agendas. A weak democracy with fears of its violent past produced a tendency to moderation among all political issues, abortion being no exception. In this context, the work of feminist politicians was met with many obstacles, but thirty years later the success is clear. In 2017, therapeutic abortion was reinstated, and the following year three left-wing political parties defined themselves as feminist. The competition among these parties for capturing the new feminist tide is a strong indicator in this direction.

Argentina: Multiparty Coalitions for and Against Abortion

Unlike the cases of Uruguay and Chile, Argentina's party system has not emerged from the traditional cleavages present in many Western European countries. Scholars have highlighted the low programmatic character of Argentina's party system, and most agree that traditional categories of left and right do not easily apply to Argentina's political parties (Coppedge 1997; Moreira 2006; Murillo and Levitsky 2008; Kitschelt et al. 2010). The lack of programmatic parties has allowed politicians to operate based on pragmatic and electoral calculations and, as such, parties' ideologies and class identities have shifted throughout the country's political history.

However, some general trends shed light on the Argentine political landscape. From the 1940s until the end of the 20th century, Argentine politics was dominated by two catch-all political parties, meaning parties that aim to attract a large part of the electorate despite holding diverse viewpoints: The Unión Cívica Radical (Radical Civic Union, UCR) and the Partido Justicialista (Justicialist Party, PJ), also known as Peronism because of the prominence of its founding figure, former President Juan Domingo Perón (1946–55 and 1973–74). The UCR entered politics in 1890 as a multiclass party demanding universal male suffrage and fair elections, and it has traditionally identified as the party of civil liberties, democracy, and human rights. On the other hand, the PJ came into existence in 1946 during the rise of an industrial working class, union organizing, and large-scale internal migrations to urban centers. Although not a traditional labor party, the PJ has consistently received most of the votes by working and lower-income classes, and unions have remained overwhelmingly Peronist (Levitsky 2003). Within this party system dominated by the Peronism/anti-Peronism logic, left-wing parties have been electorally insignificant and characterized by fragmentation, lack of cooperation, and high electoral volatility. On the other hand, conservative forces lacked a democratic political expression for most of the 20th century and instead supported military coups when the elected government threatened their interests. This was the case until 2010, when Mauricio Macri's new party Propuesta Republicana (Republican Proposal, PRO) emerged in the political system to fill the historical gap of a right-wing party and won the 2015 presidential elections in a coalition with the UCR called Cambiemos (Let's Change).

No main political party in Argentina has included abortion on their platform, neither in support or opposition of legal reform. The fact that the main two parties include sectors with diverse ideological identifications implies that diverse positions around abortion coexist in both of them as well. In this sense, feminists' work within these parties has been even harder. They had to fight strongholds of opposition not only on strategic terms (whether it was electorally convenient to prioritize abortion), but also ideologically (staunch abortion opponents). Still, given the ideological diversity of these parties, feminists were able to advance their perspectives and demands within both large parties, since none of them identified exclusively with the right as in the case of Chile or Uruguay. This created a very different dynamic once the issue reached Congress. Multiparty coalitions emerged both in favor and against abortion allowing for an unimaginable level of cooperation across parties under different circumstances.

Unión Cívica Radical

The UCR platforms over the years have included small sections on women's issues. In 1983 and 1989 they emphasized the need to their right to decide on the size of their family (UCR 1983, 65–69; 1989, 11). In 1995 their platform included the need to have sexual education in school's curricula and free access to birth control methods (UCR 1995). The 2003 platform was the first one to mention abortion. It called for sexual education to *prevent* sexually transmitted diseases and abortion (UCR 2003). In the midst of the 2018 congressional debate of the abortion bill, the Radical Youth (Juventud Radical), and Franja Morada (the university branch of UCR) called the party to support abortion legalization. The National Convention of the party voted in favor of the abortion bill in March of 2018 but the National Committee, the entity in charge of executive decisions, refrained from doing so (*El Cronista* 2018; *Perfil* 2018). Legislators voted based on their personal convictions with the party splitting their votes in favor of and against legalization.

The UCR has a history of organizing women within the party since early on. However, it has historically restricted women's access to leadership positions (Marx 1992; Gallo 2001; Valobra 2007). As recently as 2018, in the middle of increasing feminist mobilization in Argentina, Radical women complained about being left out of the party's decision-making process. The former president of the National Radical Convention, Lilia Puig de Stubrin, stated that "It was always this way. As a popular party, the UCR reflects the conditions of society. Ricardo Balbín [historical party leader] used to tell us 'oh here come the *flowers*'" (in Piscetta 2018, n.p.). Recently, feminist activists such as Carla Carrizo and Brenda Austin—who actively participated in the 2018 debate for legal abortion—called for women to build a collective cause and space within the party (Piscetta 2018). Still, to this day, the legalization of abortion is not included in the party's platform.

Partido Justicialista

Peronism has a history of tension with feminism. It is commonplace to state that the emergence of Peronism has actually been an obstacle for building a strong feminist movement in Argentina (Besse and Trebisacce 2013). Similar to the UCR, Peronist party documents have made no reference to an institutional position on abortion. But unlike the UCR, they did not address the issue of sexual and reproductive rights either. In fact, historically many party documents highlight the traditional links of Peronism with Christian values, in particular the Catholic Church's social doctrine (Partido Justicialista 1983). However, there is no explicit alignment with the position of the Church on abortion either.

In 2015, the progressive branch of the PJ, the Frente para la Victoria (Front for Victory) led by Néstor Kirchner and Cristina Fernández de Kirchner included sexual and reproductive rights in their party's platform for the first time, but with no reference to abortion. In the midst of the 2018 abortion debate in Congress, the Peronist party was divided among those in favor and against the proposed reform. A group of Peronist leaders not aligned with the Frente para la Victoria, among them former President Carlos Menem, signed a statement rejecting abortion and qualifying it as alien to the Peronist worldview (*Infobae* 2018). In contrast, most Frente para la Victoria politicians were vocal advocates of legalization. The votes in Congress reflected this division clearly. Finally, the 2019 platform of the Frente de Todos (Front for All, the new Peronist party name supported by the Kirchnerist branch in 2019), had no reference to abortion either, despite the explicit campaign commitment to legal abortion of their presidential candidate Alberto Fernández (Santoro and Carbajal 2019).

Since the party's early times, and following the lead of Eva Perón, women have been very active within the party. In 1949, the Peronist Women's Party was born, mobilizing thousands of women into political activity for the first time in their lives (Barry 2012). In addition, the first Peronist governments were responsible for granting women suffrage, divorce, and equal parental rights. After the 1951 elections (the first in which women could vote), 15.4 percent of legislators in the Congress lower chamber were women, and 20 percent in the Senate, all of them Peronist, a level of women's participation hardly possibly to find anywhere else at the time (Marx, Borner, and Caminotti 2007). Despite this strong activism in favor of women's mobilization and rights, until very recently most Peronist women active in the party avoided identifying with feminism.

Evita famously dismissed feminism as ridiculous and led by "women who want to be men" (Perón 1951, 195). She defined women's political participation as an extension of housework and stated repeatedly that the natural place for a woman was the home (Schaller 2020). Decades later, President Cristina Fernández de Kirchner continued the tradition of opposing feminism. When asked if she was a feminist, she used to answer "I am not a feminist, I am feminine" (Fernández de Kirchner 2019, 415). Additionally, among the heterogeneous ideas that coalesced in the origins of Peronism in the 1940s was the identification between Catholicism, Hispanicism, and nationalism. While the relationship with the Catholic Church went through phases of alliance and conflict, each time Peronism was in power strong sectors within Peronism (both within the right and the left) have upheld a Catholic worldview, clashing with any attempt to reconcile the party with the feminist movement.

Despite the general tension between Peronism and feminism, a few feminists within the party brought both identities together and have pushed for feminist demands in Congress such as legal abortion.[6] Juliana Marino is one of them. A former political prisoner, in the 1980s she rejoined her activity within the PJ. Relegated by her male *compañeros* to work on "women's issues" she decided to make the best of this opportunity and organize for the advancement of feminism within the party.[7] The battle has been uphill even under the last three Kirchnerist administrations, which, despite supporting sexual and reproductive rights policies, opposed the legalization of abortion strongly. The vertical structure of the party and the power of the president prevented legislators from setting the political agenda (Di Tullio 2018).

However, the feminist mobilization that erupted in Argentina in 2015 against femicide and abuse of women—under the motto, *Ni una menos* / Not one less— has increased the reach of feminism. Larger numbers of Peronist politicians, including Cristina Fernández de Kirchner, have come to reconcile Peronism and feminism. In 2018, after voting as a senator in favor of abortion legalization Fernández de Kirchner stated: "If you want to know who made me change my mind, it was the thousands of girls that took to the streets... we are going to add 'feminist' to our national and popular project" (*Clarín* 2018, n.p.). The influence of the growing feminist movement in this case has been clear. As a consequence, there are now more female Peronist politicians that publicly identify themselves as feminists, such as Malena Galmarini, Araceli Ferreyra, and Mayra Mendoza.

PRO

In 2010, the first successful right-wing party capable of winning a presidential election emerged in Argentine politics: PRO. Unlike its counterparts in the neighboring countries, it did not explicitly address the issue of abortion. The party's 2015 platform for the presidential elections, which they won, did not refer to any gender issue or to the protection of life from the moment of conception. Although this party harbors in its ranks some traditional conservative voices aligned with the Catholic Church who claim to defend the family and its traditional values, PRO also includes politicians that are liberal in both economic and social issues, rejecting the intervention of the state in private matters such as abortion. During the 2018 abortion debate in Congress two PRO legislators, Silvia Lospennato and Daniel Lipovetzky, were particularly vocal in favor of legal abortion and were active in the multiparty coalition promoting its approval.

In Argentina, the low institutionalization of the party system has meant that parties do not align along the ideological spectrum. As a consequence, they have not taken unified positions on abortion, neither in favor nor against. The main parties completely ignore the issue in their platforms, even until today when abortion is clearly on the societal and political agenda. Low institutionalization—particularly the Peronists, with their informal internal structures (Levitsky 2003), and the newly created PRO— has meant that the president's position holds significant weight and highly influences the party's position on an issue at the time of voting in Congress. Left-wing parties in Argentina have been the most vocal around feminism and the legalization of abortion.[8] However, within a political system mostly dominated by the logic of Peronism and anti-Peronism, the electoral gains of the left at the national level have been minimal. Within this context, multiparty alliances for and against abortion legalization have emerged, shaping the 2018 congressional debate and the following discussions ever since.

Conclusion

This chapter has analyzed the complex relationships between political parties and abortion in the Southern Cone since the time of democratization until the year 2020. The level of institutionalization of the party system and parties' relationship with feminist movements, particularly the insider activity of double militants within their ranks, help explain the different scenarios in each of the countries. Uruguay and Chile, with highly institutionalized party systems, show a correlation between parties on the right supporting restrictive abortion laws, and parties on the left advancing the legalization of the practice. This configuration has led to abortion reform in both cases—more moderate in Chile and more radical in Uruguay—once left-wing parties were in power. In Argentina, with its low institutionalized party system, parties host diverse positions and thus multiparty coalitions have emerged to both support and reject the legalization of abortion. This strategy took longer to deliver results but after a first failed attempt in 2018, in December 2020 Congress legalized abortion on demand until 14 weeks.

The timing of when parties have introduced the need for reform in their platforms is related to the presence of feminist movements. Here, this chapter contributes to the literature on party platforms, pointing to the influence of social movements in party documents and agendas—an issue that has not been widely discussed in previous scholarly work. The chapter particularly addresses two channels of influence: significant feminist mobilization in the streets, which has gradually shifted public opinion in favor of abortion legalization, and the everyday work of feminist politicians within their own parties, which helped advance feminist perspectives and with them the need for abortion reform.

The analysis of the three cases shows that in Uruguay, the early inclusion of abortion reform in the Frente Amplio's agenda could be attributed mostly to the work of double militants. At the time, the late 1980s, the feminist movement and the campaigns for abortion reform were relatively weaker than later in the 21st century, when a stronger movement was able to advance the discussion of bills in Congress and later ensured the passage of reform in 2012. In Chile, the decision to introduce therapeutic abortion in the platform of the Socialist Party, for example, was the result of gradual internal work by feminist politicians as well. However, the adoption of a feminist perspective and thus a commitment to stronger support for legal abortion on demand by the Socialists, the PPD, and the Frente Amplio seems to have been propelled mostly by the eruption of the widespread feminist mobilizations of 2018 and 2019. The competition among these parties for the "feminist" label seems to be driven by their acknowledgment of a larger shift in Chilean society brought by the feminist movement. More research regarding the timing and motivations for this change is needed. Finally, in Argentina, none of the main political parties have defined themselves as feminist nor have they included the legalization of abortion on demand in their platforms. This despite the country having seen the largest feminist mobilizations in the region and being one of the originators of the Green Tide. The fact that abortion is not present in parties' platforms is partially explained by the diversity of parties and the complexities of taking a position on such an issue in this context. However, this has not meant that politicians have ignored the feminist uprising. Many of them have taken into consideration this new shift in society and are aware that the political costs that used to be associated with advancing legal abortion might have actually turned in the other direction: it might now be costly to ignore the issue (at least in some districts and within some constituencies). Thus, many of them have made public statements in favor of legalization ever since. This lack of reference to abortion in platforms in the case of Argentina also speaks of the lack of institutionalization of political parties compared to those in the neighboring countries. Parties in Argentina, and particularly Peronism, redefine themselves with each new leader, often overriding internal institutions and conventions. In this case then, the information provided by the party's platform is less relevant than following the dynamic alliances and the public statements expressed by parties' leaders.

Notes

1 Interview with activist Soledad González quoted in Pecheny and Correa (2016).
2 At least initially. The Partido Colorado included abortion reform in its platform in the 1980s and later eliminated any reference to it.
3 Interview with Margarita Percovich, Montevideo, September 7, 2007.
4 Interview with Teresa Valdés, Santiago de Chile, August 5, 2016.
5 MILES stands for Movimiento por la Interrupción Legal del Embarazo/Movement for the Legal Interruption of Pregnancy (also, "miles" means "thousands"). MILES launched the campaign for abortion under three exceptions in 2013.
6 Legislators such as Victoria Donda (part of the Frente para la Victoria in the early years), Juliana Marino, and Juliana Di Tullio were some of them.
7 Interview with Juliana Marino, *Un Cuarto Propio* (2019).
8 The Socialist Party, founded in 1896, had among its ranks the first women who identified with feminism.

References

Alles, Santiago. 2014. "Ideología partidaria, competencia electoral y elección de legisladoras en cinco democracias latinoamericanas: Argentina, Brasil, Chile, Perú y Uruguay, 1980–2013." *América Latina Hoy* 66: 69–94.

Baldez, Lisa. 2003. "Elected Bodies: The Gender Quota Law for Legislative Candidates in Mexico." *Legislative Studies Quarterly* 26(2): 231–258.

Barry, Carolina. 2012. "Los centros cívicos femeninos: Prácticas políticas, tensiones, y continuidades con el Partido Peronista Femenino (1946)." *Desarrollo Económico* 52(206): 285–309.

Bawn, Kathleen, Martin Cohen, David Karol, Seth Masket, Hans Noel, and John Zaller. 2012. "A Theory of Political Parties: Groups, Policy Demands and Nominations in American Politics." *Perspectives on Politics* 10(3): 571–597.

Benefiel, Charlana, and Christopher J. Williams. 2019. "Taking Official Positions: How Public Policy Preferences Influence the Platforms of Parties in the United States." *Electoral Studies* 57: 71–78.

Besse, Juan, and Catalina Trebisacce. 2013. "Feminismo, peronismo. Escrituras, militancias y figuras arcaicas de la pos-colonialidad en dos revistas argentinas." *Debate feminista* 47: 237–264.

Blofield, Merike, and Christina Ewig. 2017. "The Left Turn and Abortion Politics in Latin America." *Social Politics: International Studies in Gender, State & Society* 24(4): 481–510.

Blofield, Merike, Christina Ewig, and Jennifer M. Piscopo. 2017. "The Reactive Left: Gender Equality and the Latin American Pink Tide." *Social Politics: International Studies in Gender, State & Society* 24(4): 345–369.

Canal 180. 2010. "Glenda Rondan: 'No voy a militar por el Partido Colorado,'" February 5. www.180.com.uy/articulo/9640_No-voy-a-militar-por-el-Partido-Colorado.

Canal 180. 2012. "Piñeyrúa y la contradicción de un 'delito' que no se denuncia," October 2. www.180.com.uy/articulo/29488_Pineyrua-y-la-contradiccion-de-un-delito-que-no-se-denuncia.

Chasquetti, Daniel, and Daniel Buquet. 2004. "La democracia en Uruguay: Una partido-cracia de consenso." *Política* 42: 221–247.

Clarín. 2018. "Cristina Kirchner dijo que 'las miles de chicas que se volcaron a la calle' hicieron cambiar su posición sobre el aborto," August 9. http://espectaculos.clarin.com/sociedad/cristina-kirchner-hablo-gobierno-defender-aborto-legal-siempre-vote-vida_0_H10xgSYHQ.html.

Coffey, Daniel. 2007. "State Party Activists and State Party Polarization." In *The State of the Parties: The Changing Roles of Contemporary American Parties*, eds. John C. Green and Daniel J. Shea, 74–93. Lanham: Rowman & Littlefield.

Conger, Kimberly H. 2010. "Party Platforms and Party Coalitions. The Christian Rights and State-Level Republicans." *Party Politics* 16(5): 651–668.

Coppedge, Michael J. 1997. *A Classification of Latin American Political Parties.* Helen Kellogg Institute for International Studies, Working paper 244.

De Giorgi, Ana Laura. 2017. *Un amor no correspondido. Feministas de izquierda en el Uruguay y de la post-dictadura.* Paper presented at the XII Jornadas de Sociología de la Universidad de Buenos Aires, Buenos Aires, August 22–25.

Delfino Mussa, Karina. 2019. *Mujeres Socialistas. Protagonistas de una historia.* Santiago: Partido Socialista.

Di Tullio, Juliana. 2018. "Ganar o perder. Paradojas del aborto." *Revista Anfibia.* http://revistaanfibia.com/ensayo/paradojas-del-aborto.

El Cronista. 2018. "La Convención nacional de la UCR apoyo el proyecto de aborto legal," March 12. www.cronista.com/economiapolitica/La-Convencion-Nacional-de-la-UCR-apoyo-el-proyecto-de-aborto-legal-20180312-0099.html.

Fernández de Kirchner, Cristina. 2019. *Sinceramente.* Buenos Aires: Sudamericana.

Franceschet, Susan. 2003. "'State Feminism' and Women's Movements: The Impact of Chile's Servicio Nacional de la Mujer on Women's Activism" *Latin American Research Review* 38(1): 9–40.

Franceschet, Susan, Mona Lena Krook, and Jennifer Piscopo (eds.). 2012. *The Impact of Gender Quotas.* New York: Oxford University Press.

Frente Amplio [Chile]. n.d. "El programa de muchos." www.frente-amplio.cl/sites/default/files/documentos/programa-beatriz_sanchez.pdf.

Frente Amplio [Uruguay]. 1989. "Plataforma electoral del Frente Amplio," June 4.

Friedman, Elizabeth Jay. 2009. "Gender, Sexuality and the Latin American Left: Testing the Transformation." *Third World Quarterly* 30(2): 415–433.

Friedman, Elizabeth Jay (ed.). 2019. *Seeking Rights from the Left. Gender, Sexuality and the Latin American Pink Tide*. Durham: Duke University Press.

Friedman, Elizabeth, and Constanza Tabbush. 2019. "Introduction. Contesting the Pink Tide." In *Seeking Rights from the Left. Gender, Sexuality and the Latin American Pink Tide*, ed. Elizabeth Jay Friedman, 1–47. Durham: Duke University Press.

Funk, Kendall D., Madga Hinojosa, and Jennifer M. Piscopo. 2017. "Still Left Behind: Gender, Political Parties and Latin America's Pink Tide." *Social Politics: International Studies in Gender, State and Society* 24(4): 399–424.

Gallo, Edit. 2001. *Las mujeres en el radicalismo argentino, 1890–1991*. Buenos Aires: Eudeba.

Gentili, Pablo. 2017. "Si las mujeres no nos unimos, perderemos la lucha por la igualdad. Entrevista a Carmen Beramendi." *El País*, March 6. https://elpais.com/elpais/2017/03/06/contrapuntos/1488767117_213146.html.

Haas, Liesl. 2010. *Feminist Policymaking in Chile*. University Park: Penn State University Press.

Htun, Mala, and S. Laurel Weldon. 2012. "The Civic Origins of Progressive Policy Change: Combating Violence Against Women in Global Perspective, 1975–2005." *American Political Science Review* 106(3): 548–569.

Htun, Mala, and S. Laurel Weldon. 2018. *The Logics of Gender Justice. State Action on Women's Rights around the World*. Cambridge: Cambridge University Press.

Infobae. 2018. "Contundente pronunciamiento de referentes justicialistas: El aborto es la cultura del descarte," June 7. www.infobae.com/politica/2018/06/07/contundente-pronunciamiento-de-referentes-justicialistas-el-aborto-es-la-cultura-del-descarte/.

Jeria, Claudia. 2009. "Feministas socialistas en dictadura. Una aproximación a su cultura política." *Revista Izquierdas* 3(4): 1–28.

Johnson, Niki, Cecilia Rocha, and Marcela Schenck. 2015. *La inserción del aborto en la agenda político-pública uruguaya 1985–2013*. Montevideo: Cotidiano Mujer.

Johnson, Niki, Ana Laura Rodríguez Gustá, and Diego Sempol. 2019. "Explaining Advances and Drawbacks in Women's and LGBTQ Rights in Uruguay." In *Seeking Rights from the Left. Gender, Sexuality and the Latin American Pink Tide*, ed. Elizabeth Jay Friedman, 48–81. Durham: Duke University Press.

Jones, Daniel. 2007. "El debate parlamentario sobre la Ley de Defensa de la Salud Reproductiva en Uruguay." In *Aborto en Debate. Dilemas y desafíos del Uruguay democrático. Proceso político y social 2001–2004*, eds. Lilián Abracinskas and Alejandra López Gómez, 53–98. Montevideo: MYSU.

Jones, Mark P., Santiago Alles, and Carolina Tchintian. 2012. "Cuotas de género, leyes electorales y elección de legisladores en América Latina." *Revista de Ciencia Política (Santiago)* 32(2): 331–357.

Kittilson, Miki Caul. 2011. "Women, Parties and Platforms in Post Industrial Democracies." *Party Politics* 17(1): 66–92.

Kittilson, Miki Caul. 2013. "Party Politics." In *The Oxford Handbook of Gender and Politics*, eds. Georgina Waylen, Karen Celis, Johanna Kantola, and S. Laurel Weldon, 536–553. Oxford: Oxford University Press.

Kitschelt, Herbert, Kirk A. Hawkins, Juan Pablo Luna, Guillermo Rosas, and Elizabeth J. Zechmeister. 2010. *Latin American Party Systems*. New York: Cambridge University Press.

Klüver, Heike, and Iñaki Sagarzazu. 2016. "Setting the Agenda or Responding to Voters? Political Parties, Voters and Issue Attention." *Western European Politics* 39(2): 380–398.

La Tercera. 2010. "Evelyn Matthei dispuesta a ir al Tribunal Supremo de la UDI por Proyecto de aborto terapéutico," December 15. www.latercera.com/noticia/evelyn-ma tthei-dispuesta-a-ir-al-tribunal-supremo-de-la-udi-por-proyecto-de-aborto-terapeutico/.

La Tercera. 2015. "Documento DC sugiere expulsión de parlamentarios que aprueben proyecto de aborto terapéutico," February 7. www.latercera.com/etiqueta/documento-dc/.

La Tercera. 2018a. "Diputadas de oposición presentan hoy proyecto de aborto libre," August 21. www.latercera.com/politica/noticia/diputadas-oposicion-presentan-hoy-proyecto-aborto-libre/288923/.

La Tercera. 2018b. "El PPD se recicla: Estrena logo y se declara feminista," May 4. www.later cera.com/la-tercera-pm/noticia/ppd-se-recicla-cambia-logo-se-declara-feminista/153020/.

Levitsky, Steven. 2003. *Transforming Labor-based Parties in Latin America: Argentine Peronism in Comparative Perspective*. New York: Cambridge University Press.

Lovenduski, Joni, and Pippa Norris. 1993. *Gender and Party Politics*. London: Sage.

Mainwaring, Scott. 2018. *Party Systems in Latin America. Institutionalization, Decay and Collapse*. Cambridge: Cambridge University Press.

Mainwaring, Scott, and Timothy Scully (eds.). 1995. *Building Democratic Institutions. Party Systems in Latin America*. Stanford: Stanford University Press.

Marx, Jutta. 1992. *Mujeres y partidos políticos: De una masiva participación a una escasa representación, un estudio de caso*. Buenos Aires: Editorial Legasa.

Marx, Jutta, Jutta Borner, and Mariana Caminotti. 2007. *Las legisladoras. Cupos de género y política en Argentina y Brasil*. Buenos Aires: Siglo XXI.

Matland, Richard E., and Donley T. Studlar. 1996. "The Contagion of Women Candidates in Single Member District and Proportional Representation Electoral Systems: Canada and Norway." *The Journal of Politics* 58(3): 707–733.

Moreira, Constanza. 2006. "Party Systems, Political Alternation and Ideology in the South Cone (Argentina, Brazil, Chile and Uruguay)." *Revista Uruguaya de Ciencia Política* 2, Selected Edition.

Murillo, Maria Victoria, and Steven Levitsky. 2008. "Argentina: From Kirchner to Kirchner." *Journal of Democracy* 19(2): 16–30.

Norris, Pippa. 1999. "A Gender Generation Gap." In *Critical Elections: British Parties and Voters in Long-Term Perspective*, eds. Geoffrey Evans and Pippa Norris, 65–79. London: Sage.

Partido Colorado. 1984. *Programa de Principios del Partido Colorado*, Uruguay.

Partido Justicialista. 1983. *Plataforma electoral*, Buenos Aires, Argentina.

Partido Socialista de Chile. 2008. *Resoluciones del XXVIII Congreso General Ordinario "Salvador Allende Gossens" del Partido Socialista de Chile*. Panimávida, March 14–16. https://obtienearchivo. bcn.cl/obtienearchivo?id=documentos/10221.1/25796/1/resoluciones_ps_2008.PDF.

Pecheny, Mario, and Sonia Correa. 2016. *Abortus Interruptus. Política y reforma legal del aborto en Uruguay*. Montevideo: MYSU.

Perfil. 2018. "La Juventud Radical reclama a sus senadores que voten a favor del aborto legal," August 6. www.perfil.com/noticias/politica/la-juventud-radical-reclama-a-sus-senadores-que-voten-a-favor-del-aborto-legal.phtml.

Perón, Eva. 1951. *La razón de mi vida*. Buenos Aires: Peuser.

Piscetta. Juan. 2018. "La UCR y las mujeres: La ola feminista incomoda a la 'mesa chica'." *Infobae*, July 14. www.infobae.com/politica/2018/07/14/la-ucr-y-las-mujeres-la-ola-fem inista-incomoda-a-la-mesa-chica/.

Piscopo, Jennifer M. 2015. "States as Gender Equality Activists: The Evolution of Quota Laws in Latin America." *Latin American Politics and Society* 57(3): 27–49.

Santoro, Sonia, and Mariana Carbajal. 2019. "Alberto Fernández sobre el aborto legal: 'Va a salir.'" *Página 12*, November 15. www.pagina12.com.ar/231128-alberto-fernandez-so bre-el-aborto-legal-va-a-salir.

Schaller, Paula. 2020. "Peronismo y feminismo en la historia: Mitos y verdades." *La Izquierda Diario*, March 4. www.laizquierdadiario.com/Peronismo-y-feminismo-en-la-historia-mitos-y-verdades.

Soule, Sarah A., and Susan Olzak. 2004. "When Do Movements Matter? The Politics of Contingency and the Equal Rights Amendment." *American Sociological Review* 69(4): 473–497.

Stetson, Dorothy McBride, and Amy G. Mazur (eds.). 1995. *Comparative State Feminism*. Thousand Oaks: Sage.

Un Cuarto Propio. 2019. "Juliana Marino." *Radio Cut*, October 1. https://us.radiocut.fm/audiocut/un-cuarto-propio-07-10-2019-juliana-marino/.

Unión Cívica Radical (UCR). 1983. *Plataforma electoral nacional de la Unión Cívica Radical*. Buenos Aires: UCR.

Unión Cívica Radical (UCR). 1989. *Plataforma electoral nacional de la Unión Cívica Radical*. Buenos Aires: UCR.

Unión Cívica Radical (UCR). 1995. *Plataforma electoral nacional de la Unión Cívica Radical*. Buenos Aires: UCR.

Unión Cívica Radical (UCR). 2003. *Bases para una propuesta estratégica para el cambio*. Buenos Aires: UCR.

Valobra, Adriana Maria. 2007. "La tradición femenina en el radicalismo y la lucha de Clotilde Sabattini por el reconocimiento de la equidad política, 1946–1955." *Clepsydra. Revista de Estudios de Género y Teoría Feminista* 6: 25–42.

Wagner, Markus, and Thomas Meyer. 2014. "Which Issues Do Parties Emphasize? Salience Strategies and Party Organization in Multiparty Systems." *Western European Politics* 37(5): 1019–1045.

Wolbrecht, Christina. 2002. "Explaining Women's Rights Realignment: Convention Delegates, 1972–1992." *Political Behavior* 24(3): 237–282.

3

FEMINIST LAWYERS, LITIGATION, AND THE FIGHT FOR ABORTION RIGHTS IN THE SOUTHERN CONE

Elizabeth Borland

In Argentina's northwest province of Tucumán, 25-year-old "Belén" was condemned to eight years in prison for infanticide. Belén's ordeal began in 2014, when she went to the hospital with abdominal pains and began bleeding. Hospital personnel found a 32-week fetus in the toilet and called the police, who said Belén had killed her "baby," even though she said she did not even know she was pregnant. She was sentenced to eight years in prison. After Católicas por el Derecho a Decidir (Catholics for the Right to Decide) learned about the case, their coordinator of strategic litigation, lawyer Soledad Deza, came to Belén's defense. Soon, "Free Belén" became a rallying cry in the Ni una Menos (Not One Less) movement, Argentina's large wave of protests about gender violence and femicide (Halfon Laksman 2017; Alcaraz 2018). Four months after Deza took the case, Belén was released by order of the provincial Supreme Court.

Many observers of the Belén case have focused on the vibrant street and Twitter protests that put pressure on the judicial system to release Belén (Halfon Laksman 2017; Goldsman 2018), rather than the lawyers involved.[1] Alba Ruibal and Cora Fernández Anderson (2020) argue that most scholars have focused on the decriminalization of abortion through bills in the Argentine Congress, with less attention paid to legal strategies (as they note, exceptions include the work of Argentine feminist legal scholars, as discussed in González Vélez 2012 and Bergallo 2014). The justifiable emphasis has been on a unified, federal, horizontal, autonomous coalition (Campaña Nacional por el Derecho al Aborto Legal, Seguro y Gratuito / National Campaign for the Right to Legal, Safe, and Free Abortion). This Campaign emerged in 2005 and is known for leading the "Green Tide" of protests that have swept Argentina in recent years (see Gutiérrez, this volume). As activists with green *pañuelos* (kerchiefs) took to the streets (see Vacarezza, this volume), abortion legislation first made it to a 2018 vote in Congress where it was approved in the lower house and rejected in the Senate, followed by a recent effort that culminated in the December 2020 congressional vote

DOI: 10.4324/9781003079903-4

to legalize abortion. Although it is undeniable that street protest was essential for legalization, there have been many fronts to this fight, and legal strategies deserve more attention. Shifting our focus to the role of legal mobilization in cases like Belén's highlights the important work of cause lawyers in the fight for abortion rights.

In the Southern Cone countries, new policies have increased access to abortion to different degrees. Yet in each case, abortion is limited to specific conditions that require different implementation regimes. In all three countries, feminist lawyers have organized to respond to the ongoing need to take up reproductive justice cases in the courts, and for other forms of cause lawyering related to abortion rights. This chapter draws on 35 interviews with lawyers and activists in legal collectives in Argentina, Chile, and Uruguay to examine how they play a role in the ongoing struggles for abortion rights, the litigation strategies they pursue, and the transnational connections that foster their work.[2] Focusing on cause lawyering as one mechanism for expanding democracy, this chapter views cause lawyers as important resources for each movement. It argues that while litigation contexts and strategies vary based on legal opportunity structures that differ across the three national contexts, feminist legal training and networks are key for cause lawyering toward the expansion of both rights and access to abortion. The chapter concludes with insights from the Southern Cone that can help us understand the role of cause lawyering for abortion access in other parts of the world.

Cause Lawyering and Legal Opportunity Structures

To understand the connection between cause lawyering and democracy-building in the Southern Cone, this chapter draws on scholarly literature on legal mobilization. Laws and legal institutions are the "contested terrain where hegemony is both re-created and resisted" (Marshall and Hale 2014, 302), and there is a "complex interplay" between movements, their organizations, and the law (Edelman, Leachman, and McAdam 2010, 653). When it comes to abortion rights in Latin America, much of the activist focus has been on advocating new legislation, but change has also come through court cases that serve as a testing ground for the interpretation of existing laws, and a way for lawyer-activists to demand access, often for the most vulnerable. Yet, as the literature on legal mobilization notes, it can be a double-edged sword, since court cases can also be a site for conservative interpretation and even regression of rights (Sarat and Scheingold 1998).

Scholarship on legal mobilization views litigation as a way for movements to channel demands into claims for legal rights, moving law into the political system (Zemans 1983). Scott Barclay, Lynn C. Jones, and Anna-Maria Marshall (2011) direct our attention to the ways that the law's dynamism can provide openings for movements to reinterpret existing policies, both in legal challenges and in implementation. Some take the form of what is called impact litigation: when movement activists or social movements are litigants. The goal, then, is for the trial courts and/or the appellate process "to create binding precedents that will generate new public policy" (Marshall and Hale 2014, 304), or to work for compliance in order to make legal systems more responsive. While such impact litigation is both more prevalent and more binding in the common law tradition than in civil law contexts such as those throughout Latin America, it could still be important for movements in the Southern Cone, where years of demands for new legislation could not gain traction for debate in the legislature until recently. As Anna-Maria Marshall and Daniel Crocker Hale (2014, 305) argue, "the legal system is an avenue to generate change when more traditional access to power is foreclosed." In fact, reproductive rights gains via litigation have been notable in Colombia, where Mónica Roa and Barbara Klugman (2014) highlight the potential of these strategies, but also the need for facilitating conditions.

The work of cause lawyers represents a major part of the legal mobilization literature. A form of activism, cause lawyering is "the set of social, professional, political and cultural practices engaged in by lawyers and other social actors to mobilize the law to promote or resist social change" (Marshall and Hale 2014, 303). It is distinctive in how it "services and challenges legal professionalism" (Scheingold and Sarat 2004, 2). As such, cause lawyering "is everywhere a deviant strain within the profession" (Sarat and Scheingold 1998, 3). It includes a broad set of activities that lawyers and other social actors engage in to mobilize the law as they promote or resist social change (Marshall and Hale 2014) and involves both practices and interests (Scheingold and Sarat 2004). Cause lawyering includes strategic litigation as well as efforts to change legal standards and public opinion, to foster support for collective action, and to make legal change sustainable and implementable. These roles include publicity, and Austin Sarat and Stuart Scheingold (2006, 9) note that cause lawyers who politicize a trial are "seeking resonant social meaning beyond the realm of positive law," something that may be especially relevant in contexts where other forms of mobilization are stymied.

In order to compare legal mobilization contexts, scholars have proposed the notion of legal opportunity structures. Building on the political opportunity structure concept (see Meyer and Minkoff 2004 for a review), research on cause lawyering has shown how factors such as legal rules about who can access courts and the costs involved can affect how activists mobilize the law (Hilson 2002; Andersen 2006). Yet, Lisa Vanhala (2018, 383) finds "enormous variation in how groups respond to legal opportunities." Based on her comparative research on environmental cause lawyering across and within four European countries, she proposes a "sociological institutionalist approach" to legal opportunities and cause lawyering (383) that includes "how groups frame and interpret the idea of 'the law'" (380). This approach builds on what James G. March and Johan P. Olsen (1989) term a "logic of appropriateness" which envisions institutions as "collections of inter-related rules and routines that define appropriate actions" (161). In the case of judicial institutions, a logic of appropriateness can define or delimit who can and cannot mobilize the law and gain standing.

For one, civil law systems like those in Latin America tend to have a more confined and technical role for lawyers. Lawyers specialize early in their careers, with tighter boundaries between the law and other arenas (Sarat and Scheingold 1998). With less financial support and fewer lawyers, it is rarer to find organizations with stables of lawyers (Meili 1998)—entities like the American Civil Liberties Union (ACLU) in the United States. Argentine scholar Julio Maier (cited in Thome 1993) has written that Latin American countries must also contend with greater executive control over their judicial systems, derived from Spanish colonialism. Centralized, bureaucratic, and hierarchical judiciaries that influence officials, and judges as functionaries of the state who are conceived of as a component of state power make it harder for activist lawyers to gain traction.

Given the increasing recognition of the importance of regional and extra-regional influences in feminist policy, practice, and politics (for instance, see Fernández Vázquez and Szwarc 2018), we must recognize the expansion of the transnational arena for legal mobilization (McCann 2006). Marcelo Torelly (2019) argues that domestic judges in Latin America often reference international law, producing hybridized rulings that combine constitutional and international law. In addition to edicts from the United Nations (Brown 2008), the court of the Inter-American Commission on Human Rights as well as audiences at both national and regional levels present opportunities for impact litigation and other cause lawyering. There is a trend toward transnational sociolegal mobilization in the Inter-American system over the past two decades, one that has been documented for human rights and environmental issues in Argentina and Chile, with fewer cases brought forward from Uruguay (Hincapié 2018). Increasing use of international arenas—even on issues not related to abortion rights—can build capacity for local actors to form pressure networks both inside and outside their countries (Sikkink 2005).

Argentina

When we focus on lawyer Soledad Deza's efforts in the aforementioned Belén case, we notice the diverse types of cause lawyering in abortion mobilization. Deza has written that her strategy was to show that Belén's earlier lawyers were negligent and prejudiced, that the investigation was flawed—the police never did DNA analysis and evidence mysteriously disappeared—and it violated Belén's right to privacy (Deza 2018). When interviewed, Deza outlined the many tasks involved:

> A legal defense is not [just] litigation in an abortion case, because one has to work with society [too]... To unite social movements, because you need rights but also need social mobilization.... You have to translate the law in a way that achieves social consensus... It requires many different skills. [You] have to be a bit of a lawyer but also... We are activists who work on these issues, we are public reference points, so [we] must [be] restrained... so that our activism does not turn against us. There is a whole thing that the law is neutral and objective—when all feminists know it is not—so one has to do gymnastics. [With Belén] We put together a front of organizations and political parties. From multiple identities and affiliations... to achieve consensus because otherwise you cannot unite the women's movement. It was all learning.

Deza uses the metaphor of gymnastics to explain how she worked as a lawyer, an organizer, and a media spokesperson, trying to find a balance. In her writing on the case, Deza (2018) argues that she engaged in three lines of action: using procedural law to counteract Belén's imprisonment, "rewriting history through strategic alliance with alternative media," and social mobilization (1). The latter was particularly effective and led to an "Urgent Action" campaign by Amnesty International, which Deza writes had special importance (8). The campaign also prompted a visit by a special relator and United Nations work group on arbitrary detention from UN's Committee Against Torture, resulting in a declaration calling for Belén's release by the UN Human Rights Commission in mid-July. The Mesa por la Libertad de Belén (Committee for the Freedom of Belén) called for four national marches; the most significant was on 12 August, 2016 and two days later the provincial court ordered her release.

Lawyers like Deza and Paola Bergallo—who has written about the extra-institutional "informal rules" of abortion policy in Argentina (Bergallo 2014)—cut their teeth on earlier reproductive rights cases that have had lasting impact. After all, in Argentina it was the Supreme Court's 2012 ruling on the F., A.L. case that endorsed a broad interpretation of the law's exceptions that led to more access (see Monte 2017 for a discussion of the decision). Argentina's 1921 Penal Code defined abortion as a crime, with narrow exceptions (this changed very recently with the congressional vote to legalize abortion in December 2020). Despite many years of activism demanding legalization (Sutton and Borland 2013; Ariza Navarrete and Saldivia Menajovsky 2015; Morgan 2015; Alcaraz 2018), and earlier failed attempts to get support from both the Executive and Legislative branch (Fernández Anderson 2011; Borland 2014; Ariza Navarrete and Saldivia Menajovsky 2015), the Supreme Court ruling endorsed a broad interpretation of one of the exceptions to abortion (rape), indicating that it applied to all cases of rape and not just those against women with mental disabilities (as the prevailing restrictive interpretation had asserted). This opened the door for access, and abortion services both surgical and pharmaceutical began to become more available, although still restricted (Ministerio de Salud de la Nación Argentina 2019), with continued clandestine practices and all the difficulties they imply (McReynolds-Pérez 2017; Sutton 2017). Although litigation has not been the most important tactic of the movement (Ruibal and Fernández Anderson 2020), feminist lawyers have challenged restrictions in several key cases (Tabbush et al. 2016; Ruibal 2018).

Bergallo and other lawyers explained to me that the groundwork for these cases was laid by efforts in the early and mid-2000s to form connections between feminist lawyers across Argentina, in large part by a project organized by scholar-activists at the Centro de Estudios de Estado y Sociedad (Center for the Study of State and Society, CEDES). Feminist lawyers and social scientists created a federal network, launched in 2002. Working with government agencies, bureaucracies, health ministries and the public health system, as well as with the judicial branch at the national and provincial levels, they drafted health protocols and trained judicial branch personnel and even journalists. According to Bergallo, building these relationships "increased their impact, evidence of which can be seen in their participation in the drafting of government documents and the appearance of their legal arguments in judicial rulings" (see also Ruibal and Fernández Anderson 2020). This investment has paid off in the high degree of preparation for taking on cases today as well as a network of feminist lawyers and judicial personnel who are informed about abortion rights, a network that is notably federal in nature, which is significant since many cases have arisen in provinces far from the capital.

Despite this, when the project began, the lawyers involved felt they were viewed with skepticism by other activists. Agustina Ramón Michel, a law professor who started her scholarly career working on this project, remembers it as being perceived as "conservative" because it worked on the legal grounds for abortion: "I have very clear perceptions, that we were seen as having a conservative project because... it was understood that if we worked on what we had [the existing grounds], we were leaving aside the larger proposal." She explains, "what we had was an exit door for an interpretative struggle to say: 'As it is, that's it. Rape is already covered.'" Therefore, the logic of going to Congress with a new bill should be for a "more advanced proposal" and not just one modeled on voluntary abortion in the first trimester with case-based abortion later.

In addition to being viewed with skepticism, cause lawyers who took on abortion-related cases faced ethical challenges. Sabrina Cartabia, another lawyer who was a researcher on the CEDES project as a student and later went on to work as a lawyer in the Sexual and Reproductive Health Program of the Province of Buenos Aires when its protocol was developed, explained that litigation in this area is complicated because it is about "the real bodies of women"—it seems "abstract" but it must be instrumentalized; it takes a long time and can have serious individual consequences. For this reason, creating protocols was important, and involved both lawyers like her and medical personnel working in tandem, building on the CEDES group's work.

One factor that facilitated the efforts of cause lawyers in Argentina was the concurrent expansion of women's and gender studies into academic settings (Gogna, Pecheny, and Jones 2009).[3] Feminists were interested in drawing attention to gender—including reproductive rights—in legal training. As more and more law students were exposed to gender and law, it created a fertile environment for groups of activist lawyers to form.[4] Argentina's tradition of strategic litigation and international human rights in legal training (Pinto 2016) also contributed to the expansion of knowledge networks for various professional groups in support of abortion rights in Argentina (Fernández Vázquez and Brown 2019).

These developments put pressure on human rights organizations with stables of lawyers—for example, CELS (Center of Social and Legal Studies) and Amnesty International—to get involved and join groups that were also working in this area such as CLADEM (Committee for Latin America and the Caribbean for the Defense of Women's Rights).[5] We can see early cooperation of this type in the 2006 case of L.M. R., a young disabled woman who was impregnated by her rapist uncle. She was unable to get a legal abortion, despite meeting the existing exceptions (Carbajal 2007; Alcaraz 2018). Three women's movement organizations—INSGENAR (Institute of

Gender, Rights, and Development),[6] CLADEM, and Catholics for the Right to Decide—presented the case in 2007 to the UN Human Rights Committee. In 2010, it determined that delays caused by court hearings subjected L.M.R. to physical and emotional suffering and violated her right to privacy. In a case summary, Cornell's Legal Information Institute (n.d., n.p.) concluded:

> the litigation process was so prolonged that L.M.R.'s pregnancy had advanced to the stage that her physician would no longer perform the abortion. This fact, the Committee reasoned, amounted to a violation of Article 2, because L. M.R. did not, in fact, have access to an effective remedy (the abortion) and was forced to obtain one illegally.

Moreover, the case "contributed to a growing consensus in international law that restricting women's access to an abortion may be considered torture or cruel, inhuman or degrading treatment" (Cornell's Legal Information Institute n.d., n.p.).

During deliberations before the Human Rights Committee, the Argentine representative admitted that the State had violated L.M.R.'s human rights. But according to Susana Chiarotti, then of INSGENAR, just because the nation admits this, it does not mean that the regional authorities follow suit: "It can happen that a province recognizes the rights violation when the nation does not, or the other way around" (quoted in Vallejos 2008, n.p.). Thus, continued legal vigilance is necessary at the provincial level.

Even so, because the L.M.R. case focused on a rape survivor with mental disabilities—falling clearly under the provisions in the Penal Code—and was recognized as important on its own merits, like the CEDES project, it was viewed by some activists as insufficiently progressive and perhaps even detracting from the broader legislative campaign. Despite such skepticism, according to Zoe Verón, a lawyer at the Equipo Latinoamericano de Justicia y Género (Latin American Team of Justice and Gender, ELA), these cases set the stage for contemporary cause lawyering. For instance, lawyer networks learned to gather amicus briefs, as in the 2012 Supreme Court decision. In this way, Argentina's well-connected cause lawyers have built a robust toolkit with the diverse skills needed to take on abortion rights cases and strategic litigation at multiple levels, helping to place abortion access within the scope of human rights on the democratic agenda post-dictatorship and contributing to the movement's momentum. Their efforts will likely be even more important to safeguard access under the legislation that was recently passed, in particular given the likely backlash (Economist 2021).

Chile

Legal mobilization and cause lawyer networks related to abortion rights are much less developed in Chile, which can be traced back to both the slower restoration of democracy and Chile's history of abortion restrictions. The total ban of abortion—promulgated during the regime of General Augusto Pinochet in 1989—was lifted in

2017, after years of feminist campaigning. Although many restrictions remain, the law represents significant change for a country that was long regarded as having the most restrictive laws in South America (Casas Becerra 1997; Blofield 2013; Casas and Vivaldi 2014), where cultural opportunities for abortion rights mobilization had been more limited than in Argentina (Borland 2004), and where women even resorted to crossing the border into neighboring Peru to seek clandestine abortions (Freeman 2017). When the ban was lifted with the passage of Law 21030, abortions became allowed under three strict conditions (*causales*): if the woman's life is at risk, if she was raped, or if the fetus is not viable. While statistics are scarce, activists have estimated that the *causales* account for only three percent of abortions: the other 97 percent of women do so secretly and at high risk (*Agence France-Presse* 2018). Gloria Maira, Lidia Casas, and Lieta Vivaldi (2019) demonstrate that various obstacles continue to obstruct women's access even under the *causales*, including conscientious objection, insufficient training for providers, a lack of information, and various "contradictory mandates" regarding illegal abortion (125).

Camila Maturana, a lawyer for the non-governmental rights group Corporación Humanas (Humans Corporation), has represented women who have been denied terminations. She said the conservative government of President Sebastián Piñera has made it harder for women to access their right to an abortion. Piñera's administration introduced rules in 2018 making it easier for doctors to become "conscientious objectors." Public hospitals, for example, no longer have to ensure that there are medical professionals available to terminate pregnancies. Nearly 50 percent of all providers object to abortions after rape, and some public hospitals lack a single provider willing to perform an abortion in that circumstance (Human Rights Watch 2019). Doctors who are conscientious objectors say that if the first hospital a woman goes to will not provide an abortion, she will just be taken to another one that will, but many have challenged this claim. For instance, in an interview with BBC journalists, a woman named Adriana who was turned away by a private clinic and two public hospitals said the experience was traumatic: "I was in despair, I didn't know where to turn. I knew that the fetus was going to die so why did I have to go through this torture?" she asked, "I felt so alone" (Livingstone 2019, n.p.).

Between the problem of conscientious objectors, fear and confusion among health professionals (Maira, Casas, and Vivaldi 2019), and the delays involved, the number of women who have been able to access legal abortion each year are fewer than 1,000; and this in a country with an estimated 60,000–70,000 abortions per year (Mesa Acción por el Aborto and Fondo Alquimia 2019). It is in this context that feminist lawyers are working to try and expand access. There are two principal mechanisms for Chilean cause lawyering in this context: individual grassroots case-based lawyering and the launch of a network of lawyers.

First, some lawyers take on individual cases, often with a low profile, although sometimes cases become publicized, such as the case of Karen Espíndola, who filed a letter to Constitutional Tribunal justices about her experiences being denied an abortion for an unviable fetus in 2008. Cause lawyers have worked with individuals like Karen and Adriana to denounce malpractice after women have tried to access legal abortion unsuccessfully. A veteran lawyer on many of these grassroots cases told me that they arise after women have lived through harrowing experiences. She explained that women in the first two *causales*—risk to the woman's life and unviable fetuses—actually desired pregnancies. According to Maturana, such plaintiffs are women who feel betrayed by medical institutions:

> These women are usually looking for an apology, looking for someone to acknowledge that their experience is valid, to acknowledge that [public hospital personnel] were wrong, that she had the right… to be given all the information, to respect her decision, [to] be treated properly and accompanied in that suffering.

Such cases are focused on one-on-one work with individual clients, but they are complex. In fact, the recognized expert on abortion rights law in Chile, Lidia Casas Becerra (also author of a chapter in this volume) said that it was hard to move cases forward because there is "a lot involved." When I asked her to explain, she elaborated:

> Involved in [terms of] the idea of defending women who were prosecuted, and whether those women would be willing to go forward with a full case…. I did have some clients that would not be willing. Very good cases. On issues, on criminal procedures, or on evidence testimonies, and everything that you can really push, and, really also, for taking it to court, some with provisions that one would think would be unconstitutional. But your client wants a criminal defense… to take away her criminal responsibility for her illegal abortion. So here we are stuck again.

While these difficulties are common in cases around Latin America, and for cause lawyering and abortion in general, they take on a particular weight in Chile, the one Southern Cone case where abortion was not only illegal but regularly criminalized in practice for so long. In a post-dictatorship environment with a weakened civil society, where feminists have had less impact on "setting the reproductive agenda" (Casas 2004, 429), feminist organizations were also hampered because the Chilean system does not have the amicus curiae tradition (Casas 2004). Still, several interviewees there told me that the judiciary permits public hearings in cases related to the public interest, so lawyers were involved in advocating and preparing for these presentations.

A second set of activities is newer: growing collective action by groups of feminist lawyers, particularly in a network launched in 2018, the Association of Feminist Lawyers (Asociación de Abogadas Feministas, ABOFEM). While there were feminist lawyers working before in academic sites and a few Chilean movement organizations and they cooperated with movement groups and had regional connections, ABOFEM is the first large organized group of feminist lawyers in contemporary Chile. When I met with several ABOFEM lawyers in March 2018, they said they had about 150 active members, with a broader network that helped to connect people with representation and advice as gender injustice cases came up. We discussed the need for greater publicity of the *causales*. As I sat with ABOFEM leaders, they debated whether or not it would be legal to publicize certain aspects of the law in public health settings, and how this might be achieved. Maira, Casas, and Vivaldi (2019) found similar debates and contradictions in their interviews with healthcare personnel, leading to barriers for women seeking access, making it all the more important for legal action "to make the government compliant with the law" (129).

Fear and confusion among health professionals, women, and lawyers to advance abortion cases—or even to facilitate access with the *causales*—contributes to a more closed legal opportunity structure for cause lawyering in Chile. This context highlights the importance of building networks among cause lawyers to build capacity and access by moving cases in the courts, or simply by advocating for women facing very difficult decisions. ABOFEM is well placed to serve in this capacity since it extends throughout Chile and is working to draw in and train people, from law students to judges. In fact, in my interview with her, Lidia Casas Becerra, called ABOFEM "the legal battalion of the New Wave of feminists." She linked it with an effort in the Chilean Bar Association to enact a quota to increase the number of women and greater "protagonism" in the system.

Such "protagonism" will be salient because changing the law is just one part of gaining abortion rights. Conscientious objection cases, which first appeared in 2004 regarding emergency contraceptives, are on the rise (Casas 2009) and have been expanding into a concerted strategy on the part of conservative sectors (Montero and Villaroel 2019). We can see this in the new wave of conscientious objection cases that will continue to make abortion—even with the *causales*—difficult to achieve not just in Chile but elsewhere in Latin America (see, e.g., Rostagnol and Caccia, this volume). Such policies slow implementation considerably in Chile and obstruct abortion rights (Maira, Casas, and Vivaldi 2019), further reinforcing the need for continued legal mobilization and broader reform.

Uruguay

If lawyers in Chile have only recently started to create networks for legal mobilization and "protagonism," this effort is in even earlier stages in Uruguay. After 11 years of mobilization and five failed attempts to pass legislation decriminalizing abortion (Abracinskas and López Gómez 2004, 2007; Pousadela 2016; Fernández Anderson 2017), in 2012 Uruguay removed the penalty for abortion in the first trimester (even if it is still officially classified as a crime). Its "Voluntary Interruption" law, seen as a best practices model (Berro Pizzarossa 2019) relies on a health exception (González Vélez 2012). Women must wait five days; they must be approved by a doctor, social worker, and psychologist. If approved, abortion is available free of charge in public hospitals, and there is a provision that Catholic hospitals must refer women to a provider. These changes resulted from a campaign that gathered support from the public and lawmakers, including a strong leftist coalition that emphasized harm reduction (Berro Pizzarossa 2019; Briozzo 2016). Susan Wood, Lilián Abracinskas, Sonia Correa, and Mario Pecheny (2016) attribute its enactment to Uruguay's secular values, favorable public opinion, the work of the feminist movement to build a broad coalition, and a vocal public health community that was able to gain support for a reform that critics categorize as a "modified protectionist approach that circumscribes women's autonomy" rather than achieving full rights (102). Recent scholarship has documented continuing stigma for women seeking abortion and multiple barriers to care (Makleff et al. 2019). Abortion rights activists argue that the law puts too much power in the hands of medical institutions, circumscribes women's legal access to self-administered pharmaceutical abortion (Fernández Anderson 2017) and enshrines gender stereotypes and problematic attitudes about abortion into legislation (Berro Pizzarossa 2019). Moreover, if women are denied access, they may run out of time to appeal, leading to recent challenges by lawyers in the courts (Correa and Pecheny 2016; Mujer y Salud en Uruguay 2018).

For instance, in February 2017, a Uruguayan local family judge ruled that a 24-year-old woman, Noemí, could not terminate her ten-week pregnancy after her ex-boyfriend tried to stop her. When she learned of the ruling, a feminist from Noemí's town, Lucía Berro Pizzarossa—then doing fieldwork in Uruguay for her doctorate in Amsterdam—reached out to Noemí and offered help.[7] After a Facebook post, she assembled a group of feminist lawyers who offered to work on the case as advisors through Mujer y Salud en Uruguay (Women and Health in Uruguay, MYSU). The effort began very much as a defensive action, with litigation to try and secure access to abortion for Noemí. But, after she miscarried, it also became an attempt to advance a case against the judge who tried to stop Noemí from accessing her rights. For the director of MYSU, Lilián Abracinskas, this effort is a foray into strategic litigation that is "training" for the young legal team:

> Here, what we have had is a young Uruguayan lawyer who is doing her doctorate in Holland. Then, this also serves as part of her training… Everything is… well, they are learning. We are learning. Yes, I know all the legal scaffolding, but I do not know its logic, its methodologies, its procedures. The jargon is very complex, because I read [legal documents] and I do not know if what I am understanding is the right thing. It is complex, complicated but it [strategic litigation] still seems interesting as something to think about doing [more].

An activist with years of experience, Abracinskas recognizes both the potential for cause lawyering in Uruguay, but also its difficulties. When I spoke with Lucía Berro Pizzarossa as well as Ivana Mansolido, one of the other lawyers in the group, they shared many of the challenges they are up against, from difficulty finding people to agree to be expert witnesses, to trouble accessing court documents, to difficulty gathering funds to pay for filings and insufficient help from constitutional lawyers.

The latter problem—absence of high-clout support from the legal community—is notable in Uruguay. Many of the interviewed lawyers decried the lack of gender as a topic of study for law students, which poorly prepared them for taking on cases related to gender injustice. As others have noted, legal training affects both lawyer's abilities and interest in pursuing cause lawyering (Scheingold and Sarat 2004). Uruguayan feminist lawyers complained that they were not trained in strategic litigation and even less so in gender-related law; some were working to make women's rights a required subject. Despite this, Noemí's team was learning as they went, advancing the case toward the Inter-American Court. Their efforts are earnest, but their legal opportunities are relatively limited, even in the fairly open political context in Uruguay. Mansolido said it felt like an uphill climb. "We are all the time, all the time on the defensive…. Obviously, we have to have the proper technique and judicial basis for this type of advance… at least to preserve the status that Uruguay has, it must have the adequate legal basis."

Given that one of the "foundational features" of Uruguay's movement is its "dense network among feminist NGOs [non-governmental organizations], grassroots women's groups, women in trade unions and political parties, and female legislators" (Johnson, Rodríguez Gustá, and Sempol 2018, 49), it enabled demands for abortion rights to enter and stay on the policy agenda, but it has also made it harder to push for full legalization and to make waves. As many Uruguayan interviewees emphasized, the small size of the country means that people know each other and can moderate broader disagreement. The insulated nature of many communities in Uruguay also may limit the number of women willing to come forward to make case-based legal demands. As feminist Lilian Celiberti explained to me, "We are a very small country. If you… make a report, you are personally involving, reporting doctors or nurses…. In places, in some cases where you have no other [medical] options." Celiberti also said there had been several failed attempts for legal networks to bring forward cases, so the recent effort for the Noemí case was notable. As in Chile, Uruguayan interviewees often pointed to Argentina as where I should look to understand legal mobilization and "specialized groups of lawyers."

As in the CEDES case in Argentina, activists in Uruguay have also looked skeptically at strategic litigation. In Uruguay, this skepticism was less about concerns regarding conservativism than a logic of appropriateness: the conviction that social change must be a democratic process (Pousadela 2016), and that legal action was less democratic. Lilián Abracinskas said the women's movement had never used

> strategic litigation as an advocacy strategy for change…. Because it is better under the conditions of the political system than in the legal system. In reality, we always had a better chance that in an issue that would serve to build a social movement, [so] we would actually debate in terms of normative change [rather] than in a specific personal dispute… in a case as a political strategy.

Coupled with the hegemony of health expertise in issues related to abortion—something that resulted in a law that emphasizes harm reduction and empowers doctors—skepticism about legal mechanisms has contributed to a less open opportunity structure for legal mobilization in Uruguay.

These problems are even more notable because, while strategic litigation itself is a new approach for Uruguay's movement, human rights arguments and appeals to international law have been key strategies in Uruguay for many years (Pousadela 2016). Uruguayan law gives international law "the same binding force" (Berro

Pizzarossa 2019), so international human rights treaties like CEDAW[8] can be used to ground legal cases. Despite legal barriers to using such a human rights lens (Berro Pizzarossa 2018), abortion rights are widely viewed as part of a democratic agenda (Celiberti 2006; Johnson, Rocha, and Schenck 2015)—perhaps these features may make it more likely for legal mobilization to occur in the future, if lawyers are able to gain traction and build the necessary networks.

Cross-National Comparisons and Transnational Linkages

When comparing the Southern Cone cases, we notice that cause lawyers have built on links between abortion and democracy as they have advanced individual cases. Including abortion rights as part of human rights is essential for feminists' democratic agenda in post-dictatorship, and even individual cases built to challenge lack of access serve as a signal that the collective trauma of dictatorship and the silencing and disciplining of women continue. The lawyers I interviewed were savvy about the use of human rights arguments and connections to CEDAW and international law as part of their arsenal, even as each country's differing environment for legal mobilization provided constraints and opportunities.

However, there remains skepticism about legal versus grassroots mechanisms in all three countries. In Uruguay, traditions linking popular protest to secular democracy, rather than legal action, likely make it the least amenable to strategic litigation. In Chile, of greater concern was confusion and fear stemming from abortion's history of active criminalization, which may contribute to a less hospitable environment for cause lawyering, particularly since much of the work has been focused on individual cases, often where plaintiffs seek to avoid publicity due to social stigma. In Argentina, the eventual support of longstanding human rights organizations with legal teams—places like Amnesty International and CELS—has helped build momentum and legitimacy. This may also be an important strategy to reproduce in the other two countries, particularly Chile.

Framing abortion rights as part of a "debt to democracy" (Sutton and Borland 2019; Gutiérrez, this volume) also draws attention to a generational boom of Green Tide lawyers, and its connection to legal education and exposure to activism. Feminist legal training and networks are significant for cause lawyering toward the expansion of both rights and access to abortion in the Southern Cone, and elsewhere. Lawyers have specialized technical knowledge that is key for exerting certain types of pressure. For instance, Chilean activist Fernanda Marin explained that the movement needed lawyers to help draft and collect amicus briefs, "it is also very technical knowledge but at least knowing that the instance is there. Well, because if not, I had no way. To make pressure." The Argentine case shows us how the investment in sharing knowledge and institution-building has dividends that pay off over time to build such pressure. In Uruguay, lack of both strategic litigation and women's rights in legal education has hampered the development of lawyers and networks ready to address gender-related issues. Chile's ABOFEM could be a good model for Uruguayan cause lawyers, but the years of work that it took to establish networks in Argentina suggest the effort involved, and the long timeframe that may be necessary.

In general, transnational examples and connections offer models and best practices, and can foster support among feminist cause lawyers. While constrained by different legal systems and arenas, lawyer activists in the Southern Cone are learning from one another. Argentina was held up as the regional example, both because of the protest wave that has drawn international attention but also because of the more developed strategic litigation tradition. Lawyers in all three countries had connections to others around Latin America including most prominently Colombia's Mónica Roa. There has also been collaboration on the part of legal scholars (many of whom are also engaged in cause lawyering), for example in a recent edited volume (see Bergallo, Jaramillo Sierra, and Vaggione 2018). Because international courts create a shared arena to bring forward cases, activists can seek support and build knowledge throughout the hemisphere that can generate capacity for advancing abortion rights.

Conclusion

Cause lawyering points to the numerous points of entry into legal systems, and the role of lawyers to mobilize both political and legal power, especially when they are lawyers with clout and connections who can coordinate the "gymnastics" involved. Lawyers can be enmeshed in authoritarian enclaves; the law often has a conservative bent (see Scheingold and Sarat 2004). Building network capacity among feminist lawyers is therefore even more important for the Southern Cone, particularly where there is less of a tradition for strategic litigation.

Even recognizing strategic litigation as part of abortion rights is necessary. Most of the cases that have been advanced around the region are by nature defensive rather than offensive. Although both can be considered strategic litigation, offensive tactics more often involve action litigation and are perceived of as strategic—including by the cause lawyers I interviewed. There are limits to laws and rulings that emphasize a conditions-related approach, for instance, in terms of access to information and implementation that have been common around Latin America (Bergallo 2018). Nonetheless, cause lawyering is increasingly central to this policy arena. These insights can help us to recognize and understand the role of cause lawyering for abortion access in other parts of the world.

Of course, even as feminist cause lawyers engage in legal mobilization strategies, their opponents on the right are following suit. María Angélica Peñas Defago and José Manuel Morán Faúndes (2014) detail the dynamic process by which conservatives used the courts to block women from accessing abortion, something that has only been emboldened by the "renewed influence of the Catholic hierarchy" since the accession of the pope (82).[9] Lieta Valeria Vivaldi Macho (2018, 219) argues that "the use of administrative acts (protocol) in order to limit the scope of the law can be quite efficient," and conscientious objector status is a key mechanism for administrative obstruction. Most recently, efforts to assert conscientious objector status have spread throughout the region; doctors' main opposition was to women themselves making the decision to interrupt a pregnancy, and how and when to do it (Serna Botero, Cárdenas, and Zamberlin 2019). The contingent and variable discourses through which the doctors construct the logic of their conscientious objector status arose from an unquestioning attachment to control gestating bodies; and a default sociomedical understanding of women as mothers, reproductive machines, or as fetal life-support systems. It is a cautionary tale that points to the need for robust and well-informed networks for cause lawyers willing to stand up for legal abortion rights in the Southern Cone and beyond.

Notes

1 Other scholars have scrutinized media discourse about the Belén case (Irrazabal and Felitti 2018), implications for bioethics and the health system (Rossi 2018) and legal discourse (Cano 2018).
2 This research includes qualitative interviews conducted in October and November 2018 and March and April 2019 in Buenos Aires, Santiago, and Montevideo, as well as interviews conducted via Skype/WhatsApp with those not available during fieldwork or not located in capital cities. In all, 35 activists, lawyers, academics, and current or former ministry officials were interviewed, 14 in Argentina, 12 in Chile and nine in Uruguay. Informed consent was obtained from all interviewees, who could choose to remain anonymous or not. In most cases, interviewees were willing to be quoted so their words appear in the text; in a few cases, identifying information is omitted at the request of interviewees. Interviews were supplemented by observations at public movement-related activities (marches, rallies, gallery openings, conferences, workshops, panels, etc.), as well as with materials collected from online posts (social media and websites) and publications produced by or related to movement organizations. For each case, I searched national news coverage from the top circulating newspaper and the alternative left-leaning paper)—in Argentina, *Clarín* and *Página/12*, in Uruguay, *El País* and *La República*; in Chile, *El Mercurio* and *La Nación*. For this chapter, I focus on data related to the strategies pursued and the legal opportunity structures in each country to assess the role of cause lawyering and how it varies across the cases.
3 On the relationship between feminist activism and academia in Chile, see Casas Becerra, this volume.
4 There are also networks of feminist law professors (Bergallo, personal interview) and law students (for example, Sororidad en Derecho, at the University of Buenos Aires).
5 In Spanish, Centro de Estudios Legales y Sociales (CELS) and Comité de América Latina y El Caribe para la Defensa de los Derechos de la Mujer (CLADEM).
6 In Spanish, Instituto de Género, Derecho y Desarrollo.
7 See also Berro Pizzarossa's contribution to this volume, by López-Gómez, Couto, and Berro Pizzarossa.
8 Convention on the Elimination of all Forms of Discrimination Against Women.
9 On neoconservatism in the region, see also Vaggione and Morán Faúndes, this volume.

References

Abracinskas, Lilián, and Alejandra López Gómez. 2004. *Mortalidad materna, aborto y salud en Uruguay: Un escenario cambiante*. Montevideo: Mujer y Salud en Uruguay.
Abracinskas, Lilián, and Alejandra López Gómez (eds.). 2007. *Aborto en Debate: Dilemas y Desafíos del Uruguay Democrático, Proceso Político y Social 2001–2004*. Montevideo: Mujer y Salud en Uruguay.
Agence France-Presse. 2018. "Thousands March in Chile Demanding Abortion Law Overhaul," July 26. www.voanews.com/americas/thousands-march-chile-demanding-abortion-law-overhaul.

Alcaraz, María Florencia. 2018. *¡Que sea ley! La lucha de los feminismos por el aborto legal.* Buenos Aires: Marea Editorial.

Andersen, Ellen Ann. 2006. *Out of the Closets and Into the Courts: Legal Opportunity Structure and Gay Rights Litigation.* Ann Arbor: University of Michigan Press.

Ariza Navarrete, Sonia, and Laura Saldivia Menajovsky. 2015. "Matrimonio igualitario e identidad de género sí, aborto no." *Derecho y Crítica Social* 1(1): 181–209.

Barclay, Scott, Lynn C. Jones, and Anna-Maria Marshall. 2011. "Two Spinning Wheels: Studying Law and Social Movements." *Studies in Law, Politics, and Society* 54: 1–16.

Bergallo, Paola. 2014. "The Struggle Against Informal Rules on Abortion in Argentina." In *Abortion Law in Transnational Perspective: Cases and Controversies,* eds. Rebecca J. Cook, Joanna N. Erdman, and Bernard M. Dickens, 143–165. Philadelphia: University of Pennsylvania Press.

Bergallo, Paola. 2018. "Del fracaso del giro procedimental a la inviabilidad del modelo de causales." In *El aborto en América Latina: Estrategias jurídicas para luchar por su legalización y enfrentar las resistencias conservadoras,* eds. Paola Bergallo, Isabel Cristina Jaramillo Sierra, and Juan Marco Vaggione, 155–166. Buenos Aires: Siglo Veintiuno.

Bergallo, Paola, Isabel Cristina Jaramillo Sierra, and Juan Marco Vaggione (eds.). 2018. *El aborto en América Latina: Estrategias jurídicas para luchar por su legalización y enfrentar las resistencias conservadoras.* Buenos Aires: Siglo Veintiuno.

Berro Pizzarossa, Lucía. 2018. "Legal Barriers to Access Abortion Services through a Human Rights Lens: The Uruguayan Experience." *Reproductive Health Matters. An International Journal on Sexual and Reproductive Health and Rights* 26(52): 151–158.

Berro Pizzarossa, Lucía. 2019. "'Women Are Not in the Best Position to Make These Decisions by Themselves': Gender Stereotypes in the Uruguayan Abortion Law." *University of Oxford Human Rights Hub Journal* 1: 25–54.

Blofield, Merike. 2013. *The Politics of Moral Sin: Abortion and Divorce in Spain, Chile and Argentina.* New York: Routledge.

Borland, Elizabeth. 2004. "Cultural Opportunities and Tactical Choice in the Argentine and Chilean Reproductive Rights Movements." *Mobilization. An International Quarterly* 9(3): 327–339.

Borland, Elizabeth. 2014. "Storytelling, Identity, and Strategy: Perceiving Shifting Obstacles in the Fight for Abortion Rights in Argentina." *Sociological Perspectives* 57(4): 488–505.

Briozzo, Leonel. 2016. "From Risk and Harm Reduction to Decriminalizing Abortion: The Uruguayan Model for Women's Rights." *International Journal of Gynecology & Obstetrics* 134(S1): S3–6.

Brown, Josefina Leonor. 2008. "Los derechos (no) reproductivos en Argentina: Encrucijadas teóricas y políticas." *Cadernos Pagu* 30: 269–300.

Cano, Julieta Evangelina. 2018. *Discurso jurídico sobre los cuerpos de las mujeres: El caso Belén.* Paper presented at the X Jornadas de Sociología de la Universidad Nacional de La Plata, La Plata, December 5–7.

Carbajal, Mariana. 2007. "La historial del caso L.M.R. y los derechos violados." *Página/12,* November 26.

Casas, Lidia B. 2004. "Women and Reproduction: From Control to Autonomy? The Case of Chile." *Journal of Gender, Social Policy & the Law* 12(3): 427–451.

Casas, Lidia. 2009. "Invoking Conscientious Objection in Reproductive Health Care: Evolving Issues in Peru, Mexico and Chile." *Reproductive Health Matters* 17(34): 78–87.

Casas, Lidia, and Lieta Vivaldi. 2014. "Abortion in Chile: The Practice Under a Restrictive Regime." *Reproductive Health Matters* 22(44): 70–81.

Casas Becerra, Lidia. 1997. "Women Prosecuted and Imprisoned for Abortion in Chile." *Reproductive Health Matters* 5(9): 29–36.

Celiberti, Lilian. 2006. "El aborto en la agenda democrática." *Cotidiano Mujer* 42.

Cornell Legal Information Institute. n.d. "L.M.R. v Argentina," www.law.cornell.edu/women-and-justice/resource/lmr_v_argentina.

Correa, Sonia, and Mario Pecheny. 2016. *Abortus interruptus: Política y reforma legal del aborto en Uruguay.* Montevideo: Mujer y Salud en Uruguay.

Deza, Soledad. 2018. "Una defensa legal feminista para un caso de aborto." *La Ley Online.* http://mujeresxmujeres.org.ar/wordpress/wp-content/uploads/2017/03/una-defensa-legal-feminista-para-un-caso-de-aborto.pdf.

Economist. 2021. "Argentina's Legalisation of Abortion will Provoke a Backlash," January 9. www.economist.com/the-americas/2021/01/09/argentinas-legalisation-of-abortion-will-provoke-a-backlash.

Edelman, Lauren B., Gwendolyn Leachman, and Doug McAdam. 2010. "On Law, Organizations, and Social Movements." *Annual Review of Law and Social Science* 6(1): 653–685.

Fernández Anderson, Cora. 2011. *The Impact of Social Movements on State Policy: Human Rights and Women Movements in Argentina, Chile and Uruguay.* PhD dissertation, University of Notre Dame.

Fernández Anderson, Cora. 2017. "Decriminalizing Abortion in Uruguay: Women's Movements, Secularism, and Political Allies." *Journal of Women, Politics & Policy* 38(2): 221–246.

Fernández Vázquez, Sandra Salomé, and Josefina Brown. 2019. "From Stigma to Pride: Health Professionals and Abortion Policies in the Metropolitan Area of Buenos Aires." *Sexual and Reproductive Health Matters* 27(3): 65–74.

Fernández Vázquez, Sandra Salomé, and Lucila Szwarc. 2018. "Aborto medicamentoso: Transferencias militantes y transnacionalización de saberes en Argentina y América Latina." *RevIISE: Revista de Ciencias Sociales y Humanas* (12)12: 163–177.

Freeman, Cordelia. 2017. "The Crime of Choice: Abortion Border Crossings form Chile to Peru." *Gender, Place and Culture* 24(6): 851–868.

Gogna, Mónica, Mario Pecheny, and Daniel Jones. 2009. "Teaching Gender and Sexuality at Public Universities in Argentina." *International Journal of Sexual Health* 21(4): 225–238.

Goldsman, Marta Florencia. 2018. *#LibertadParaBelen: Twitter y el debate sobre aborto en la Argentina.* Master's thesis, Universidade Federal da Bahia.

González Vélez, Ana Cristina. 2012. "'The Health Exception': A Means of Expanding Access to Legal Abortion." *Reproductive Health Matters* 20(40): 22–29.

Halfon Laksman, Florencia. 2017. "Libre. El caso Belén." *Revista Anfibia.* http://revistaanfibia.com/cronica/libre/.

Hilson, Chris. 2002. "New Social Movements: The Role of Legal Opportunity." *Journal of European Public Policy* 9(2): 238–255.

Hincapié, Sandra. 2018. "Movilización sociolegal transnacional. Extractivismo y derechos humanos en América Latina." *América Latina Hoy* 80: 51–71.

Human Rights Watch. 2019. "Chile Events of 2018." *Human Rights Watch World Report.* www.hrw.org/world-report/2019/country-chapters/chile.

Irrazabal, Gabriela, and Karina Felitti. 2018. "El Caso Belén y las construcciones sobre el 'no nacido' en Argentina. Aportes para la discusión." *Revista de Bioética y Derecho* 43: 45–60.

Johnson, Niki, Cecilia Rocha, and Marcela Schenck. 2015. *La inserción del aborto en la agenda político-pública uruguaya 1985–2013. Un análisis desde el movimiento feminista.* Montevideo: Cotidiano Mujer.

Johnson, Niki, Ana Laura Rodríguez Gustá, and Diego Sempol. 2018. "Explaining Advances and Drawbacks in Women's and LGBTIQ Rights in Uruguay." In *Seeking Rights from the Left: Gender, Sexuality, and the Latin American Pink Tide,* ed. Elisabeth Jay Friedman, 48–81. Durham: Duke University Press.

Livingstone, Grace. 2019. "The Women Seeking Abortions Turned away by Doctors in Chile." *BBC News*, August 2. www.bbc.com/news/world-latin-america-49110647.

Maira, Gloria, Lidia Casas, and Lieta Vivaldi. 2019. "Abortion in Chile: The Long Road to Legalization and its Slow Implementation." *Health and Human Rights Journal* 21(2): 121–131.

Makleff, Shelly, Ana Labandera, Fernanda Chiribao, Jennifer Friedman, Roosbelinda Cardenas, Eleuthera Sa, and Sarah E. Baum. 2019. "Experience Obtaining Legal Abortion in Uruguay: Knowledge, Attitudes, and Stigma among Abortion Clients." *BMC Women's Health* 19: 155–164.

March, James G., and Johan P. Olsen. 1989. *Rediscovering Institutions: The Organizational Basis of Politics*. New York: The Free Press.

Marshall, Anna-Maria, and Daniel Crocker Hale. 2014. "Cause Lawyering." *Annual Review of Law and Social Science* 10(1): 301–320.

McCann, Michael. 2006. *Law and Social Movements*. Burlington: Ashgate.

McReynolds-Pérez, Julia. 2017. "No Doctors Required: Lay Activist Expertise and Pharmaceutical Abortion in Argentina." *Signs: Journal of Women in Culture and Society* 42(2): 349–375.

Meili, Stephen. 1998. "Cause Lawyers and Social Movements: A Comparative Perspective on Democratic Change in Argentina and Brazil." In *Cause Lawyering: Political Commitments and Professional Responsibilities*, eds. Austin Sarat and Stuart A. Scheingold, 487–522. New York: Oxford University Press.

Mesa Acción por el Aborto and Fondo Alquimia. 2019. *Informe de monitoreo social: Implementación de la ley de interrupción del embarazo en tres causales*. Santiago: Mesa Acción por el Aborto and Fondo Alquimia.

Meyer, David S., and Debra C. Minkoff. 2004. "Conceptualizing Political Opportunity." *Social Forces* 82(4): 1457–1492.

Ministerio de Salud de la Nación Argentina. 2019. "Protocolo para la atención integral de las personas con derecho a la interrupción legal del embarazo. Segunda edición, 2019." www.msal.gob.ar/images/stories/bes/graficos/0000001792cnt-protocolo-ILE-2019-2edicion.pdf.

Monte, María Eugenia. 2017. "Abortion, Sexual Abuse and Medical Control: The Argentinian Supreme Court Decision on F., A.L." *Sexualidad, Salud y Sociedad* 26: 68–84.

Montero, Adela, and Raúl Villarroel. 2018. "A Critical Review of Conscientious Objection and Decriminalisation of Abortion in Chile." *Journal of Medical Ethics* 44(4): 279–283.

Morgan, Lynn 2015. "Reproductive Rights or Reproductive Justice? Lessons from Argentina." *Health and Human Rights Journal* 17(1): 136–147.

Mujer y Salud en Uruguay (MYSU). 2018. *Sistematización de 10 años de monitoreo para la incidencia social. Conocer la realidad para cambiarla*. Montevideo: Mujer y Salud en Uruguay.

Peñas Defago, María Angélica, and José Manuel Morán Faúndes. 2014. "Conservative Litigation Against Sexual and Reproductive Health Policies in Argentina." *Reproductive Health Matters* 22(44): 82–90.

Pinto, Mónica. 2016. "Internationalisation, Globalisation and the Effect on Legal Education in Argentina." In *The Internationalisation of Legal Education*, eds. Christophe Jamin and William van Caenegem, 37–46. London: Springer.

Pousadela, Inés M. 2016. "Social Mobilization and Political Representation: The Women's Movement's Struggle for Legal Abortion in Uruguay." *VOLUNTAS: International Journal of Voluntary and Nonprofit Organizations* 27(1): 125–145.

Roa, Mónica, and Barbara Klugman. 2014. "Considering Strategic Litigation as an Advocacy Tool: A Case Study of the Defence of Reproductive Rights in Colombia." *Reproductive Health Matters* 22(44): 31–41.

Rossi, Pablo. 2018. "Del martillo de las brujas al caso Belén." *Revista de Bioética y Derecho* 43: 77–89.

Ruibal, Alba. 2018. "Federalism and Subnational Legal Mobilization: Feminist Litigation Strategies in Salta, Argentina." *Law & Society Review* 52(4): 928–959.

Ruibal, Alba, and Cora Fernández Anderson. 2020. "Legal Obstacles and Social Change: Strategies of the Abortion Rights Movement in Argentina." *Politics, Groups, and Identities* 8(4): 698–713.

Sarat, Austin, and Stuart A. Scheingold. 1998. "Cause Lawyering and the Reproduction of Professional Authority." In *Cause Lawyering: Political Commitments and Professional Responsibilities*, eds. Austin Sarat and Stuart A. Scheingold, 3–28. New York: Oxford University Press.

Sarat, Austin and Stuart A. Scheingold. 2006. "What Cause Lawyers Do For and To Social Movements: An Introduction." In *Cause Lawyers and Social Movements*, eds. Austin Sarat and Stuart A. Scheingold, 1–36. Stanford: Stanford University Press.

Scheingold, Stuart, and Austin Sarat. 2004. *Something to Believe In: Politics, Professionalism, and Cause Lawyering*. Stanford: Stanford University Press.

Serna Botero, Sonia, Roosbelinda Cárdenas, and Nina Zamberlin. 2019. "¿De qué está hecha la objeción? Relatos de objetores de conciencia a servicios de aborto legal en Argentina, Uruguay y Colombia." *Sexualidad, Salud y Sociedad* 33: 137–157.

Sikkink, Kathryn. 2005. "The Transnational Dimension of the Judicialization of Politics in Latin America." In *The Judicialization of Politics in Latin America*, eds. Rachel Sieder, Line Schjolden, and Alan Angell, 263–292. New York: Palgrave Macmillan.

Sutton, Barbara. 2017. "Zonas de clandestinidad y 'nuda vida': Mujeres, cuerpo y aborto." *Estudos Feministas* 25(2): 889–902.

Sutton, Barbara, and Elizabeth Borland. 2013. "Framing Abortion Rights in Argentina's Encuentros Nacionales de Mujeres." *Feminist Studies* 39(1): 194–234.

Sutton, Barbara, and Elizabeth Borland. 2019. "Abortion and Human Rights for Women in Argentina." *Frontiers: Journal of Women's Studies* 40(2): 27–61.

Tabbush, Constanza, María Constanza Díaz, Catalina Trebisacce, and Victoria Keller. 2016. "Matrimonio igualitario, identidad de género y disputas por el derecho al aborto en Argentina. La política sexual durante el kirchnerismo (2003–2015)." *Sexualidad, Salud y Sociedad* 22: 22–55.

Thome, Joseph R. 1993. *Administration of Justice in Latin America: A Survey of AID Funded Programs in Argentina and Uruguay*. Arlington: Development Associates, Inc.

Torelly, Marcelo. 2019. "From Compliance to Engagement: Assessing the Impact of the Inter-American Court of Human Rights on Constitutional Law in Latin America." In *The Inter-American Human Rights System: Impact Beyond Compliance*, ed. Par Engstrom, 115–141. New York: Palgrave Macmillan.

Vallejos, Soledad. 2008. "Los derechos humanos conjugados en presente." *Página/12*, September 12. www.pagina12.com.ar/diario/suplementos/las12/13-4392-2008-09-19.html.

Vanhala, Lisa. 2018. "Is Legal Mobilization for the Birds? Legal Opportunity Structures and Environmental Nongovernmental Organizations in the United Kingdom, France, Finland, and Italy." *Comparative Political Studies* 51(3): 380–412.

Vivaldi Macho, Lieta Valeria. 2018. *Abortion in Chile: Biopolitics and Contemporary Feminist Resistance*. PhD dissertation, University of London.

Wood, Susan, Lilián Abracinskas, Sonia Correa, and Mario Pecheny. 2016. "Reform of Abortion Law in Uruguay: Context, Process and Lessons Learned." *Reproductive Health Matters* 24(48): 102–110.

Zemans, Frances. 1983. "Legal Mobilization: The Neglected Role of the Law in the Political System." *American Political Science Review* 77(3): 690–703.

4

ORANGE HANDS AND GREEN KERCHIEFS

Affect and Democratic Politics in Two Transnational Symbols for Abortion Rights

Nayla Luz Vacarezza

The fight for legal abortion in the Southern Cone generated two prominent transnational symbols: the orange hand and the green kerchief. These symbols have helped capture public attention, energize activism, stir emotions, and synthesize political meanings. The history of these symbols across borders reveals the regional construction of shared interpretative frames and common affective repertoires. Both symbols associate the struggle for abortion rights with the struggle for democracy, and they have circulated in three countries—Argentina, Chile, and Uruguay—whose recent history has been branded by dictatorships. In addition to certain values and ideas, what affective repertoires do they mobilize?

As will be shown, these symbols condense collective desires to build a democracy that extends to all areas of social life, including sexuality and reproduction. In their transnational journey, the orange hand and the green kerchief have accumulated a strong meaning of hope for what democracy could offer to women, pregnant persons, and society as a whole. These symbols mobilize not only certain ideas and values, but also emotions. In contexts where abortion has been far from an accessible right, these symbols mobilize powerful forms of disappointment, resistance, and political obstinacy.

Images, Symbols, and Affect in Social Movements

Images play a crucial role in contemporary political disputes, and social movements have used them to challenge the status quo. "From the clothes activists wear to the posters they put up to mobilize for protest, from colorful performances in the street to activist videos spread through online social networks, there is a broad range of visible expressions of dissent" (Mattoni and Teune 2014, 876). These visual productions do not appear in a vacuum; on the contrary, "social movements tap into the shared visual knowledge of the society they are rooted in. They use and reinterpret a preexisting imaginary to voice critique and

DOI: 10.4324/9781003079903-5

to form a collective actor" (Doerr, Mattoni, and Teune 2013, xiii). We could even say that the visual and artistic productions of movements do much more than beautify collective action; they have vital symbolic, communication, and framing functions as well as help mobilize activists and resources (Adams 2002).

Specifically, the symbols that identify movements are their simplest visual expression. They can be interpreted as "visual tropes" that perform at least four important functions: they explain and transmit a message, create awareness about a cause, allow people to identify participants, and sanction movement actions (Goodnow 2006). Marian Sawer showed that colors have acted as symbols that "not only served the purpose of visual identification with 'the cause' and the outward display of values but also played an important role in sustaining a sense of community" (Sawer 2007, 40). That is, in addition to playing an instrumental role, symbols emotionally connect participants to the movement. And in her study on Chilean *arpilleras* (artisanal cloth scenes), Jacqueline Adams maintains that symbols "can mark membership in a movement, allowing information to circulate, and serving as a starting point for affective bonds" (2002, 49). Recent studies on protests in South Korea also highlight the role of colors and symbols in transmitting interpretations and expressing complex affective repertoires (Kim 2018; Sarfati and Chung 2018).

Clearly, images and symbols created by social movements do more than synthesizing ideas. In this chapter, I draw on the notion that "[s]ocial movement activists diffuse still and moving images to arouse emotions that raise attention and ultimately help mobilize people into action" (Doerr, Mattoni, and Teune 2015, 11). Far from being "superficial crowd pleasers" that "might be regarded as somehow irrational, appealing to primeval emotions and gross populism" (Mac Ginty 2003, 235), movement symbols convey ideas, arguments, interpretive frames, and also politically significant emotions.

Images for Abortion Rights, Affect, and Democracy in the Southern Cone

The visual production supporting the legalization of abortion in the region is original and diverse. In the sphere of contemporary art, works by Ana Gallardo (Vacarezza 2018), Vera Grión (M.L. Gutiérrez 2011), Zaida González, and Felipe Rivas San Martín (Vacarezza 2017) show the suffering caused by abortion clandestinity and question how the fetus is personified in our culture. In the hybrid territory between art and activism, interventions by two groups stand out. In Argentina, since 2003, Mujeres Públicas (Public Women) have developed emblematic posters and performances that expose the consequences of unsafe abortion but take on the subject through irony and humor (M.A. Gutiérrez 2011; Rosa 2012; M.L. Gutiérrez 2017; Vacarezza 2018). In Chile, since 2012, the Colectivo Universitario por la Disidencia Sexual (University Collective for Sexual Dissidence) has also created posters and performances in which the figure of the fetus is used in parodic ways (Antivilo Peña 2015; Vacarezza 2017; Vivaldi and Stutzin 2017; Vivaldi 2018).

The images created by organizations supporting abortion rights have received relatively little analytical attention. In Chile, Lieta Vivaldi and Valentina Stutzin criticized the "use of humanitarian rhetoric and the construction of subjects who are victims" (2017, 139) in visuals by human rights organizations. Also, they highlighted the originality of the images by organizations that communicate the safe use of misoprostol to interrupt pregnancy. In Argentina, activist images show "original ways of speaking about the suffering associated with clandestine abortion" and also "the link between abortion and forms of joy, determination, pride, and mutual care" (Vacarezza 2018, 197). In another study on abortion visuals, Barbara Sutton and Nayla Luz Vacarezza call specific attention to the role of symbols for "their capacity to stick, to evoke affects, associate meanings, and gain adherents through repetitive use and propagation" (2020, 738). The authors analyze the centrality of the green kerchief of the Campaña Nacional por el Derecho al Aborto Legal, Seguro y Gratuito (National Campaign for the Right to Legal, Safe, and Free Abortion), whose popularity grew exponentially in the context of the first parliamentary debate on abortion legalization in Argentina in 2018. Other studies on the green kerchief tend to analyze its connection to the white kerchief of the Madres de Plaza de Mayo (Mothers of Plaza de Mayo), emphasizing linkages to the fight for human rights and democracy (Macón 2019; Barros and Quintana 2020; Felitti and Ramírez Morales 2020). The study by Sutton and Vacarezza also mentions the transnational use of the Uruguayan symbol of the "voting" hand and argues that the images of the movement in Argentina show "to what extent abortion rights struggles became intertwined with the reconstruction and strengthening of democratic life in Argentina and in other Latin American countries that underwent authoritarian governments" (2020, 750).

In this chapter, I return to the hypothesis that democracy, citizenship, and human rights are central to the visual production of the abortion rights movements in the region. While other studies show the relevance of these interpretative frames, they based their analyses on texts and discourses (Gudiño Bessone 2012; Sutton and Borland 2013, 2019; Morgan 2015; Fernandez Anderson 2017). In contrast, the present study considers how these frames are expressed in visual symbols, and additionally explores the importance of the symbols' affective force.

Studying movement symbols requires a certain heterodox methodology since they include materials that acquire meaning when they are used, that tend to have a short lifespan, and that are rarely kept. Therefore, my methodological strategy combines participant observation, conversations with key informants, and documentary research in Argentina, Chile, and Uruguay. The cooperation of activists, who kept personal archives and also treasure vivid memories of the use of symbols, was crucial. The records that were kept through the effort of organizations like Cotidiano Mujer (Woman Daily) and Mujer y Salud en Uruguay (MYSU / Women and Health in Uruguay) have been another fundamental resource for my study.

The Orange "Voting" Hand

The orange "voting" hand appeared in Uruguay and was the first prominent symbol in the abortion rights movement in the region. It was also the first symbol to spread across the three countries of the Southern Cone, helping to create a recognized political identity at the regional level.   •

Uruguay

The orange "voting" hand emerged during a rising political cycle for abortion rights, which culminated in legalization in 2012. Early in the 2000s, feminist organizations proposed "developing alliances with other social actors, broadening the social base of support and involvement regarding the issue" (Abracinskas and López Gómez 2007, 195). As a result, in 2002, the Coordinación Nacional de Organizaciones Sociales por la Defensa de la Salud Reproductiva (National Coordination of Social Organizations in Defense of Reproductive Health) was formed. It brought together women's and feminist organizations, but also other organizations connected to universities, labor unions, political parties, religious communities, and human rights, Afro-descendent, youth, and LGBTQ movements (Johnson, Rocha, and Schenk 2015; Pousadela 2015).

A hand figure rapidly appeared as one of the movement's symbols. With different aesthetics, the hand was first featured on stickers, posters, and flags, as well as in videos and illustrations. A series of ads that supported the Proyecto de Ley de Defensa de la Salud Reproductiva (Bill for the Defense of Reproductive Health) were launched in 2004 and used an open hand in the gesture of voting as a central image.[1] Also in 2004, MYSU presented two posters that also featured hands as a central motif.[2] In 2005, the cover of the magazine *Cotidiano Mujer* (No. 41) showed a hand that held out a sprig of parsley (a symbol of unsafe abortion) toward the National Congress building.[3]

The first versions of the orange "voting" hand appeared in 2004 with the design that was later popularized. They bore the slogan: "Voto a favor. Salud reproductiva" ("I'm voting in favor. Reproductive health"). The slogan did not include the word "abortion" but rather a reference to the Defense of Reproductive Health Bill (including legal abortion through the 12th week as part of a comprehensive policy of sexual education and access to birth control). Although this bill was struck down in 2004 by the Senate, the orange hand began to gain public traction as a symbol.

The symbolic relevance of the orange hand intensified in 2006 when the bill that had been rejected was presented again. President Tabaré Vázquez had promised that he would veto the law and emphasized his position in public comments prior to International Women's Day. In response, organizations carried a giant orange hand to his house at dawn on March 8. The protests continued later, when the president publicly presented a plan for equality of opportunities and rights. He was received by an auditorium packed with people holding placards in the shape of orange hands (Celiberti 2006).

The orange "voting" hand was established as a recurring visual resource in publications, documents, murals, and street paintings. Placards depicting an orange hand, that could be easily held, became the main symbol during protests. The symbol effectively demonstrated the strength of the movement, exerting pressure in public spaces. The orange hand was also central in moments of deep disappointment, for example when, in November 2008, after approval of the bill in the Senate, President Vázquez's line-item veto left without effect the article that established the right to abortion (see Figure 4.1).[4]

When José Mujica became president in 2010, prospects improved for the movement. Beginning that year, the "voting" hand placards included the slogan "Legal abortion." The demand was no longer obscured through the language of sexual and reproductive health but was explicitly expressed with the word "abortion." The year was also printed on the hands as a way of transmitting urgency, in keeping with the new slogan "El tiempo es ahora" ("The time is now").

During those years, the "voting" hand and the color orange were prominent in numerous actions. Among them, the *murga* (a traditional carnival music and dance group) La Mojigata (The Prudish) brought the topic of abortion and the orange hands to *carnaval*, the most important popular culture event in Uruguay.[5] Another notable action was the "Orange Sunrise," which, just before March 8, 2012, decorated the city of Montevideo, its emblematic public spaces and statues, with orange ribbons and hands in support of abortion legalization.[6]

In September 2012, a bill was discussed in the Chamber of Deputies that, from the point of view of activists, had been "cut up" by the modifications introduced during the parliamentary negotiation. Therefore, with the slogan "Mientras ellos ponen las condiciones, nosotras ponemos el cuerpo" (roughly meaning "Their conditions, our bodies"), MYSU held a striking public action in front of the Legislative Palace in Uruguay: with their bodies painted orange women showed the hand emblem with a piece cut out, symbolizing the incompleteness of the bill that was about to be passed.[7]

FIGURE 4.1 Protest with orange "voting" hands after presidential veto to abortion legalization. MYSU Archives, 2008.

Approval of the Voluntary Interruption of Pregnancy Law (No. 18.987) the following month was a bittersweet event for those fighting for legal reform. For one thing, the law established limitations that created forms of tutelage and barriers to abortion access (Correa and Pecheny 2016). At the same time, the conservative reaction led to initiatives aimed to repeal the law. One of them was a popular consultation in 2013, inviting people to vote in order to bring about a recall referendum. A paradoxical moment arose in which, in order to defend the law, the movement launched the "Yo no voto, ¿y vos?" ("I'm not voting, what about you?") campaign with the "voting" hand as the central symbol. Therefore, legalization did not end the cycle of struggles for abortion rights, nor did it annul the political power of a symbol that, to this day, reappears in the Uruguayan political landscape.

After this review of the symbol's history in Uruguay, we may ask ourselves: What political meanings and affective forces does it mobilize? Where does its traction come from as an emblem of the fight for the right to abortion in post-dictatorship Uruguay? The orange "voting" hand for legal abortion visually expressed one of the strongest and most resonant frames of the struggles for legal reform in Uruguay. The movement presented the demand for the right to abortion as an issue centrally related to the quality of democracy, citizenship, and human rights (Fernandez Anderson 2017). Not only did the "voting" hands conveyed the need for democratic representation, but also they argued that legal abortion implied progressing toward a more pluralistic society. In this view, the state must "offer a legal framework so that every individual has the possibility of living in accordance with their own conceptions of life, without privileging one over another" (Johnson, Rocha, and Schenk 2015, 90). In this sense, the "voting" hand was established as a symbol that expressed the need to build a pluralistic democracy.

The "voting" hand also appeared in a moment of expansion of the alliances that made up the movement and therefore was not to be directly identified with a particular political leaning. It gave a visual identity and synthesized the democratic vocation of a new and wide coalition of political subjects, built in a transversal manner. The symbol also expressed the aim to build a participative democracy with broad freedom of expression, in opposition to those who preferred silence or denial of the debate.

The orange hand appeared in very diverse forms. An important innovation was the creation of small placards that allowed protesters to show the symbol in public spaces, creating a collective attunement that was at once visual, political, and affective. Its widespread use in street protests made the movement publicly visible and established abortion as a demand that could not be ignored. The symbol also demanded attention from the system of representative democracy because it served to support and exert pressure on legislators who would have to vote for or against the bills.

The symbolic choice of the hand, a non-sexualized part of the human body, situated the debate as a matter of citizenship and democratic quality. While the demand was centered on the rights of women, the hand proposed a specific way of politicizing the body that aimed to include all citizens in the struggle, placing them on an equal footing. The hand also established a measured affective tone that managed to call upon society as a whole and not just the most convinced and radicalized sectors of the public.

It is also noteworthy that the symbol chosen was the open hand and the gesture of voting rather than the closed fist that tends to identify the leftist political groups to which a sizeable portion of the progressive forces that made up the coalition belonged. This symbolic choice demonstrates the commitment these sectors had to democracy and their desire to gain support among social groups that did not identify with the closed fist.

Voting, a basic democratic right, had accumulated enormous political and affective value in post-dictatorship Uruguay. It not only condensed forms of hope associated with democratic freedoms but was also an important channel for political resistance. A series of referendums called on the population to express itself through voting on substantial questions in democratic life, including the Referendum to Annul the Impunity Law (1989) and the Referendum to Annul the Public Enterprises Law (1992). The symbol of the orange hand managed to galvanize forms of resistance, optimism, and hope associated with voting and democracy that were already present in the Uruguayan post-dictatorship political culture.

In addition to mobilizing existing affective repertoires, the orange hand created new political hopes as it opened a different future in which democratic freedoms could be extended toward the realm of sexuality and reproduction. The symbol began to take on new affective tonalities related to persistence and tenacity every time the movement suffered setbacks and reappeared strongly in the public spaces. The very gesture of the raised hand is an expression of resistance and willfulness (Ahmed 2014), which this symbol reclaims and reinvents. In fact, the orange hand is a tool that is still useful today for defending and calling attention to the problems of a legalization that is constantly threatened by conservative onslaughts.

Argentina

The "voting" hand was adopted in Argentina by the National Campaign for the Right to Legal, Safe, and Free Abortion in 2010 when it presented its bill for the legalization and decriminalization of abortion for the third time (Zurbriggen and Anzorena 2013). The symbol took on the green color that identified the Campaign and used the slogan "Yo voto por el aborto legal" ("I vote for legal abortion"). The "voting" hand first appeared in a digital format as part of an initiative to collect signatures in support of the bill.[8] Later, Campaign activists made oversize mittens with the same slogan, which were used in public actions (see Figure 4.2).

In Argentina, the use of the hand as a symbol hearkens back to an important series of actions carried out by the human rights movement after the last dictatorship (1976–83). The "Dele una mano a los desaparecidos" ("Lend a hand to the disappeared") campaign in the summer of 1984–85 was driven by the Mothers of Plaza de Mayo—mothers of people disappeared by the dictatorship—in partnership with artists. The public was called upon to draw the outline of their hand and write their name on a poster that read "No a la amnistía. Juicio y castigo a los

FIGURE 4.2 Protest with green "voting" hands organized by the National Campaign for the Right to Legal, Safe, and Free Abortion. Photograph: Patricio Murphy, 2012. Selected for the photography exhibition "Identidades en lucha" (Identities in Struggle), by the Campaign.

culpables" ("No amnesty. Justice and punishment for the guilty") (Warley and Mango 2008).[9] This iconic action brought a multitude of people to decry the crimes of the dictatorship, symbolically offering their hand in a gesture of solidarity, and endorsing their support with their names. A million hands came together and were publicly shown in the emblematic Plaza de Mayo in a kind of democratic "referendum" against impunity.

The hand, then, was already established in Argentina as a symbol of the democratic struggle for human rights. Its use shows the degree to which Argentine activism for legal abortion "draws upon multiple ideological and experiential currents, including a collective memory of state terrorism—a memory that knows very well the costs of clandestinity, silence, and political suppression of certain lives" (Sutton 2017, 898).

The value of using the hand as a symbol and of appearing publicly in support of a cause also stands out against the infamous history of forced disappearances during the dictatorship. Showing a hand in a gesture of voting, exposing one's name, and offering one's signature as symbols that condense an identity that speaks politically in democracy are powerful political gestures in the Argentine context.

In the beginning of the 2010s, the Campaign already had the green kerchief as a symbol, and perhaps that is why the "voting" hand had a relatively short cycle of use in the public sphere. However, the symbol continued to be a recurring element in the Campaign's graphics (Sutton and Vacarezza 2020).

Chile

The orange "voting" hand was the main symbol during public debate on the decriminalization of abortion on three grounds in Chile. The bill presented by President Michelle Bachelet in January 2015 aimed to legalize abortion in three scenarios: when the woman's life is at risk, when there are fetal malformations incompatible with life, or in cases of rape. After an intense public and parliamentary debate, the bill was passed in September 2017 (No. 21.030). Through the initiative of MILES (Movimiento por la Interrupción Legal del Embarazo / Movement for the Legal Interruption of Pregnancy), the orange hand was used in both digital and physical formats, flyers, documents, and banners with a design similar to those used in Uruguay and Argentina (see Figure 4.3). Hand placards held by protesters were also visible during public marches in support of the bill.[10]

The defining feature of the symbol in Chile was that the hands appeared in groups of three, each stating one of the reasons proposed by the bill: "Por riesgo de vida y salud de la mujer" ("Because of risk to the woman's life and health"), "Por inviabilidad fetal extrauterina" ("Because of fetal non-viability outside the womb"), and "Por violación" ("Because of rape"). This triple design served to give the movement visibility, to transmit information about the bill, and to raise awareness about the necessity of legalizing each of the three abortion grounds. This final point was particularly important in a context in which there was an effort to restrict the reasons, and their scope was subject to intense debate (Vivaldi 2018).

The bill proposed by Michelle Bachelet was an opportunity to end the total ban on abortion that dictator Augusto Pinochet had left for democracy, scant months before abandoning his position (Casas and Vivaldi 2014). Perhaps that is why the symbol of the hand—associated with the democratic act of voting and with freedom of expression and assembly—resonated in Chile, where the last dictatorship

FIGURE 4.3 Flyer with orange "voting" hands in support of abortion decriminalization on three grounds. MILES, 2015.

(1973–90) had suppressed each of those rights. The "voting" hand updated hopes that democracy could end the disgraceful legacy of the dictatorship, leaving that time behind. But the "voting" hand also proposed democracy as an instrument for forging a path toward a new future with more freedom and rights.

The Orange "Voting" Hand in the Southern Cone

Multiple meanings associated with democracy are woven into the symbol of the "voting" hand. First, the emblem proclaims the value of voting, of freely expressing one's political preferences, and participating in decisions about common life. The symbol also allowed people to express a democratic will to "appear" in public individually and collectively. All of these are especially relevant issues in countries where dictatorships suppressed basic rights and forcibly disappeared political dissidents. Finally, the symbol also expressed the vocation of broadening freedoms and rights regarding the body, sexuality, and reproduction. In short, the "voting" hand shows that feminist and women's organizations in the three countries have pushed for abortion legalization as a way to deepen, reinvent, and radicalize democracy.

But the "voting" hand did much more than transfer an argumentation frame to a visual symbol. With regards to affects, the "voting" hand galvanized deep hopes associated with democracy that had matured in the post-dictatorship period in the three countries. In addition, the symbol renewed these hopes by representing a new cause and proposing a new horizon of a democratic future. Certainly, "the emotion of hope keeps something open" (Ahmed 2004, 185) and, in this case, it meant maintaining democracy as the promise of a more just and equitable common life with greater freedoms. The gesture of the hand raising up also expresses a political willfulness (Ahmed 2014). The symbol of the "voting hand" made the fight for legal abortion visible as a democratic demand and, at the same time, proposed a willful challenge to the exclusions and silences of the region's democratic agreements.

The Triangular Green Kerchief

The triangular green kerchief emerged in Argentina as an abortion rights symbol around the same time as the "voting" hand in Uruguay, but its cycle of circulation at the regional level came later. Its popularity grew exponentially in 2018 during the first parliamentary debate on the issue in Argentina. The green kerchief attained global visibility at this juncture and was adopted by the movement in Chile during the same year.

Argentina

The green kerchief was used for the first time in 2003, during the XVIII Encuentro Nacional de Mujeres (National Women's Meeting) held in the city of Rosario. Those first kerchiefs were made and handed out by the organization Católicas por el Derecho a Decidir (Catholic Women for the Right to Choose) and bore different slogans like

"Legalización del aborto" ("Legalization of abortion") and "Derecho al aborto" ("Right to abortion"), among others. Their widespread use during the march at the close of the Encuentro has been characterized as a "turning point" for the movement's visibility (Bellucci 2014, 339).

Like the orange hand, the green kerchief was a key element not only for public visibility but also for the creation of political alignment and a collective identity at the beginning of a rising political cycle. In Argentina, a process was beginning that led to the formation of the National Campaign for the Right to Legal, Safe, and Free Abortion in 2005. During those two years, the kerchief established itself within the movement and eventually received its current slogan: "Educación sexual para decidir, anticonceptivos para no abortar, aborto legal para no morir" ("Sex education for choice, contraception to prevent abortion, legal abortion to prevent death").

The color green did not aim to evoke a conventional cultural meaning (hope, environmentalism) but was rather chosen because it was not identified with any particular political leaning. Thanks to this fact, "[a]s the Campaign grew, it carved out a new activist color niche: green as the color of abortion rights" (Sutton and Vacarezza 2020, 741). The activists realized the color's ability to affirm a collective identity and also to create a particular aesthetic, political, and affective atmosphere. The Campaign's actions are always "dyed green," and the 2018 marches brought that politics of color to new heights. The green that was already present on the placards, flags, graphic materials, and kerchiefs was transferred to the marchers' bodies, clothes, hair, and faces. The commitment to the cause permeated, literally, the activists' skin and was expressed in an especially festive way by the generation of *pibas* (girls and young women):

> The glitter, the body painting, and the generally joyful quality of the young participants in the green tide is more than a style of protest. It also transforms the stigma associated with abortion, as protesters not only display the green kerchief with pride and without fear, but exuberantly celebrate their right to freedom, their resistance, and their lineage as the "granddaughters of the witches that you could not burn" (as some of the protest signs and songs declared).
>
> *(Sutton 2020, 8)*

In contrast to the color green, the triangular kerchief was already a deeply rooted symbol in Argentine political culture. Since the late 1970s, the Mothers of Plaza de Mayo established the triangular white kerchief as a persistent symbol of the struggle for justice, democracy, and human rights. To demand the "return, alive" of their children kidnapped by the military dictatorship, the Mothers protested by covering their heads with a cloth diaper, resignifying and politicizing the intimate connection to their children (Sutton and Vacarezza 2020). With this gesture, they disrupted the affective and political repertoire that, in Western contexts, associates a woman's kerchief with beauty, modesty, or tears. Instead, it made into a symbol charged with tenacity, courage, and hope. That affective and political transformation was utilized by the Campaign, and with their choice of symbol, they joined a recognized tradition of struggle. The kerchief embodies forms of transmission and affective contact with a living past of social struggles led by women, and of atrocities that have not been forgotten (Macón 2019).

The triangular green kerchief, then, has a close connection with the recent Argentine past and brought to the visual plane the interpretative frame of human rights that has become a central element for the Campaign:

> In a country that experienced a dictatorial state that applied a brutal hand to repress, censor, torture, and kill its own citizens, abortion rights activists are now saying that the democratic state needs not only to refrain from illegitimate violence but should also recognize, enable, and guarantee women's human rights, broadly defined. In that sense, the Campaign has asserted that the legalization of abortion is a "debt of democracy." This motto has varied, though related, meanings that involve both women's rights and the quality of democracy.
>
> *(Sutton and Borland 2019, 37)*

Indeed, human rights and democracy are terms that are tightly linked in Argentine political culture; and the Campaign mobilized these themes in various ways to gain support and persuade the public. The kerchief shows the extent to which a movement's values and ideas are transmitted not only through speeches, documents, or slogans but also through its symbols.

But the kerchief does much more than "translate" ideas to a visual idiom. Its materiality and versatility provide forms of identification and connection with the bodies of those who protest that have a force of their own. In contrast to the orange hand that was used as a placard someone could hold, the kerchief was worn on the body and gave rise to a performative repertoire of gestures and uses that merits analysis.

Historically, the Mothers covered their heads with white kerchiefs. In deference to the Mothers, Campaign activists generally did not wear their kerchiefs this way but rather around their necks. This conventional way of wearing them changed dramatically during 2018, when the green kerchief started being worn tied to wrists, covering faces, as a top over the naked chest, around the waist, or in the hair. Both outside and within spaces of protest, the kerchief was used to publicly show adherence to the cause, tied to purses, backpacks, and bags. Precisely because it was wearable, the green kerchief could be used broadly, on a daily basis, and over time, created a "horizontal type of communication" between supporters that expanded the space of protest to daily life (Sutton and Vacarezza 2020, 742). "Their widespread use across national, body, and political territories, as well as territories of gender, class, and age materialized the assembly of a feminist solidarity at unimagined levels" (Felitti and Ramírez Morales 2020, 136). During the 2018 protests, then, the kerchief started to mobilize new affective repertoires linked with feminist solidarity but also in contentious and assertive ways, when it was worn in irreverently (e.g., covering the face or the naked chest) or in contexts that can be hostile to the demand (e.g., at religious high schools).

In the same year, the kerchief (*pañuelo*, in Spanish) was also the protagonist of a protest action that the abortion rights movement borrowed from the Mothers of Plaza de Mayo. The *pañuelazo* is a coordinated action in which protesters raise their kerchiefs into the air at the same time, generating a collective emotional climax and powerful images for spectators. It appeared in May 2017, when the Mothers called for a march to protest the reduction in sentence of a man convicted of crimes against humanity. At the march, the Mothers asked the protesters to wear a white kerchief around their necks and at the end of the march to raise it into the air in a gesture of protest.[11] The Campaign took up this action in February 2018, when a cycle of protests began with the first parliamentary debate. Symbolically, *pañuelazos* once again placed the fight for legal abortion in the genealogy of struggles for democracy and human rights in Argentina (see Figure 4.4).

The action caused a huge visual impact as well as powerful forms of affective and political attunement among participants. Its force and simplicity facilitated quick spread. During 2018, public acts in support of legalization, no matter how big or small, ended with a *pañuelazo*. This action also served to show support and solidarity internationally, with hundreds of *pañuelazos* organized around the world.[12] The kerchief became a key agent for exerting pressure, occupying public spaces, and demonstrating collective strength. In these protests, the symbol continued to take on affects connected to urgency and a challenge to institutionalized power. The protests also activated forms of joy and pleasure connected to collective gatherings and participation. The kerchief became a hopeful symbol that pointed the way to a shared future and promised that social change is possible.

Although the bill was rejected in 2018, the widespread and daily use of the kerchief became a visible indicator of an achievement: the "social decriminalization of abortion" (see Gutiérrez, this volume). The votes in the Chamber of Deputies and the Senate were accompanied by enormous marches that brought together millions of people.[13] Something similar happened in the 2020 debate, when abortion was finally legalized. That experience of collective rising during both parliamentary debates was

FIGURE 4.4 Pañuelazo organized by the National Campaign for the Right to Legal, Safe, and Free Abortion. Photographic coverage commissioned by the Campaign. Photograph: Julianite Calcagno, non-binary photojournalist, 2020.

called the "Green Tide," a beautiful metaphor that expresses the extraordinary strength of these protests. In this new poetics of collective action, the kerchief and the color green were fundamental symbols. The "Green Tide" generated a magnetic and immersive atmosphere of protest that cannot be explained merely as the sum of the individuals present; it was much more than that. Indeed,

> Assembled bodies articulate a new time and space for the popular will, not a single identical will, not a unitary will, but one that is characterized as an alliance of distinct and adjacent bodies whose action and whose inaction demand a different future.
>
> *(Butler 2015, 75)*

The plural and embodied action of protesters dyed public spaces green and reconfigured them with their presence. In these marches, protesters fought for abortion as a right that must be recognized within institutional democracies, but they also fought for a participative and substantive democracy, built in the streets through collective occupation of public spaces for debate and action.

Chile

During 2018, the green kerchief began to be used by the Chilean movement at a moment of great revitalization of feminist struggles. In June, the Coordinadora Feministas en Lucha (Coordinating Organization of Feminists in Struggle, CFL) opened a call for logo designs for the kerchief in order to use it during the Marcha por el Aborto Libre (March for Unrestricted Abortion) that, since 2013, had brought together those fighting for the decriminalization of abortion and freedom of choice (Vivaldi 2018; Hiner and Vivaldi 2019). The context was a tumultuous one because the previous months had been marked by a powerful cycle of feminist protests and occupations of universities to denounce sexist education and violence (Zerán 2018). Multitudinous marches in Argentina had also already had a strong international impact, granting visibility and new vitality to the struggles for the right to abortion in the region and elsewhere.

Chilean activists decided to take up a symbol that was already widely popular and had proven to be an effective tool for protest. But they did not merely copy the symbol; they adapted the green kerchief to the history of Chilean feminisms. The new logo, by Carolina Lería, recreated and reformulated a 1937 poster that announced the first congress of the Movimiento Pro-Emancipación de las Mujeres de Chile (Pro-emancipation Movement of the Women of Chile).[14] The design brought into the present a key image from the democratic struggles for women's suffrage, "family planning," and "voluntary maternity" in Chile.

The logo maintained the central character from the historical poster: a woman with strong arms and long hair holding a flag that waves in the wind. But the slogan on the flag was changed to read "¡Aborto ya!" ("Abortion now!"). The association between women and motherhood from the 1937 image was also removed. In the current logo, the baby held in the woman's left arm was no longer included, and a new character appeared: another woman with her chest uncovered, holding up her left fist and wearing a triangular kerchief tied around her neck. The new figure represents the young feminists, a prominent group in the 2018 uprisings.

The logo presented the feminist struggle for abortion rights as an active, dissatisfied movement in which the memory of the past and the desire for a different future coexist. In addition, the slogans on the kerchief express the critical connection between the movement, the Chilean post-dictatorship democracy, and the legal reform of 2017: "No bastan tres causales" ("Three reasons are not enough"); "Aborto libre, seguro y gratuito" ("Unrestricted, safe, and free abortion").

The slogan "Three reasons are not enough" refers to the limitations of a decriminalization that only covers a small percentage of abortions and faces serious obstacles for implementation (Corporación Humanas 2019; Mesa Acción por el Aborto en Chile and Fondo Alquimia 2019). The feminist movement also argued that decriminalization for three reasons establishes an unfair hierarchy. The only people construed as "deserving" this right are those who can certify before the authorities that they are "victims" of an extreme situation beyond their own decisions: because their life is at risk due to pregnancy, because the fetus is not viable, or because they have been raped (Hiner 2018; Castillo 2019).

Indeed, "Unrestricted abortion" is a slogan that emphasizes autonomy to decide and the need to remove the limitations of the three grounds. The slogan appeared among autonomous feminist networks that assist with abortions and gained traction in the Chilean movement in recent years (see Vivaldi and Stutzin, this volume). It differs from the "legal abortion" slogan that was generally used in Uruguay and Argentina. One could assert that "[t]he appeal to a negative right (no interference by third parties in the 'unrestricted abortion' formula) seems to contradict the appeal to a positive right (guaranteeing the right to abortion in the 'legal abortion' formula)" (Banda and Moreno 2018, n.p.). However, in a dynamic political context in which the slogan "unrestricted and legal abortion" is used more and more often, we must pay attention to the nuances. In this sense, Karen Glavic (2019) pointed out that the slogan "unrestricted abortion" is not necessarily opposed to legalization but rather alludes to total decriminalization, abortion access outside the health system through feminist networks, abortion on demand, the absence of reasons, and the end of time restrictions.

These slogans, then, must be understood as arising from a movement that brings together both those who are fighting for legalization and those who are fighting for a utopian future of freedoms without tutelage by state power. They also express the tense relationship between Chilean feminist movements and the state and, specifically, between these movements and the terms of a democratic transition that for decades maintained criminalization in all cases—even in a political system that had institutionalized attention to women's rights and gender issues. As Nelly Richard observed,

> the tone of moderation imposed by the reconciliation logic of the "democracy of agreements" forced the transition apparatus to marginalize more confrontational positions from its circuits of speaking and to soften the tone of value debates (abortion, divorce, etc.) so that the antagonisms of positions between feminism

and the official discourse about women and the family did not unbalance the (centrist) middle ground of what had been politically agreed upon.

(Richard 2001, 230)

In brief, the slogans chosen for the green kerchief in Chile show that democracy and the language of rights do not induce the same hopeful optimism as in Argentina or Uruguay. In the Chilean context, the kerchief took on new meanings related to the possibility of moving beyond the limitations of the post-dictatorship democratic agreements.

The symbol quickly gained popularity, adopted at protests and in daily life. *Pañuelazos* were also organized in solidarity with the political process in Argentina. And, as part of the preparations for the March for Unrestricted Abortion in 2018, Coordinadora Feminista 8 M (Feminist Coordinating Organization 8 M) created a huge green kerchief approximately three meters tall and six meters wide. The giant kerchief was used as a banner and became a key element for catching the eye, occupying public space, and easily identifying the demand. Whether giant or normal-sized, used as a banner or worn on the body, the green kerchief became an emblem of the struggles for abortion in Chile.

Soon afterward, in October 2019, the country was shaken by a series of protests, initiated by high school students, over the increase in metro prices. Many of the youths that jumped the metro turnstiles en masse as a form of protest wore the green kerchief. The conflict escalated until it became a social explosion that revealed widespread exhaustion with the neoliberal model imposed during the dictatorship and deepened during democracy. The reign of the "free" market, the privatization of essential goods and services, state reduction of social spending, and work flexibilization resulted in rampant inequality and an intolerable hyper-commodification of life (Orellana Calderón 2020).

President Sebastián Piñera's administration responded to the protests by decreeing a state of emergency and unleashing brutal state repression, which brought the worst times of the dictatorship into the present. In this context, grave violations of human rights were documented, including the murder of protesters, all types of injuries (especially ocular injuries), and the use of sexual violence as a method of torture (Instituto Nacional de Derechos Humanos 2019). In the face of this intense repression, the green kerchief, in addition to expressing support of the cause of unrestricted abortion, also began to be used to cover people's faces as a safety measure since it protected against tear gas and prevented repressive forces from identifing protesters.

The visibility of the green kerchief in these protests went global in November 2019 with the performance *Un violador en tu camino* (A rapist in your path) by the feminist collective Las Tesis (The Theses).[15] In this performance, participants danced a simple choreography while singing, with a catchy rhythm, lyrics about rape that called out the structural dimension of sexual and gender violence (Serafini 2020). With their eyes covered by black blindfolds and doing squats that emulated methodologies used in police searches, protesters denounced the sexual violence endured by women arrested during the protests and pointed out the connection between these practices and the systematic use of sexual violence as torture during

FIGURE 4.5 Protest for unrestricted abortion organized by With Friends and at Home. Photograph: Constanza Riquelme / Cultiva Audiovisual, 2019.

the dictatorship. Many participants wore the green kerchief during this action, as well as during the multiple reenactments that took place in Latin America and around the world. In this viral performance, the symbol showed the intimate connection between different feminist struggles against violence and in support of the autonomy to decide about one's own body and sexuality.

During the "Chilean awakening" (interrupted by the COVID-19 pandemic), the sustained presence of the green kerchief signaled the prominence gained by feminist and abortion struggles. The green kerchief appeared in public spaces along with other symbols like the Chilean flag, the flag of the Mapuches, the color red of leftist organizations, and the black of anarchist movements and mourning. That set of symbols made evident the transversal articulation of feminist demands with the multiple demands for refounding Chilean democracy, for life with dignity, and against the increasing precariousness imposed by neoliberal capitalism. Indeed, the kerchief and the color green symbolize radical and utopian aspirations. Through these symbols, protesters manifested a deep disappointment with the neoliberal social order of the democratic transition; pushing instead for the revolutionary possibility of a new era in which feminist demands are front and center. This was expressed by a flag carried by the organization Con las Amigas y en la Casa (With Friends and at Home) in full revolt: "Sin aborto libre la revolución será siempre machista" ("Without unrestricted abortion, the revolution will always be sexist") (see Figure 4.5).

The Triangular Green Kerchief in the Southern Cone

In its trajectory through Argentina and Chile, the triangular green kerchief that identifies the fights for legal and unrestricted abortion has traveled a unique political and affective arc. The symbol began its journey by drawing on the legacy of struggles for democracy and human rights led by the Mothers of Plaza de Mayo. Its meanings and affective repertoires gained complexity in Argentina and were transformed in Chile, where the kerchief came to express deep disappointment about a democratic order that for decades blocked debate on the right to abortion and legitimized all kinds of social injustices.

In addition to mobilizing these complex affective-political repertoires, the kerchief managed to condense in a visual symbol the frame that situates the right to abortion as an issue related to human rights, citizenship, and democracy in the region. Even in Chile, where the questioning of neoliberal democracy is significant, the decriminalization and legalization of abortion was defended using arguments connected to human rights, and by pointing out the need to end, in democracy, the dictatorial legacy of total criminalization. In brief, these nuances could be interpreted as the result of the different trajectories of the movements and of the post-dictatorship democracies in each country.

Since it is a wearable symbol, the kerchief mobilized powerful forms of identification and expression that expanded the space of protest to include daily life. New protest actions like the *pañuelazo* were also key in producing both intense affective atmospheres among those who participated and poignant images for observers.

In its journey from one country to the other, the kerchief helped strengthen processes that were already in progress and did not remain identical. Rather it was reworked by local movements in order to adapt it to the new context. In fact, after the events in Chile, the Campaña 28 de Septiembre por la Despenalización y Legalización del Aborto en América Latina y el Caribe (28th of September Campaign for Abortion Decriminalization and Legalization in Latin America and the Caribbean) promoted the use of green kerchiefs across the region with different designs that brought out the particularities of each country (Gutiérrez 2019).

In both countries, the green kerchief was established as the symbol of a demand that, in order to be satisfied, requires a reexamination of the very foundations of democracy. It is also a symbol that helped advance toward new political horizons beyond what was considered appropriate, particularly since the timing never seems right for demands that question the dominant politics of gender and sexuality. Unexpected for many, the green kerchiefs became a "tide" in Argentina and were the most visible emblem for the cycle of protest that led to legalization in December 2020. Also, during the Chilean revolt, the green kerchiefs proclaimed the radical possibility of opening up a new era in a present filled with locked doors.

Concluding Remarks

Both the orange hand and the green kerchief were established as symbols of the movements for the right to abortion in the Southern Cone and were crucial elements in the political processes that led to legalization in Uruguay (2012) and Argentina (2020). They caught the attention of supporters and the general public imagination, achieving something that is usually challenging for movements: gaining recognition and visibility on their own terms. On an instrumental level, they managed to create identification among activists and were a central tool for protests in the streets and in daily life. The symbols' simplicity of design and versatility were also key to their being replicated and used in different formats and in different ways.

Both symbols appeared around the same time, during the first half of the 2000s, but they had different processes of dissemination and popularization. The hand was central in a first cycle of transnational circulation, and the kerchief gained traction later. The spread of these symbols across Argentina, Chile, and Uruguay shows the strong transnational connections of a movement that borrows and benefits from elements that were successful in other countries. At the same time, it is clear that the symbols are not mimetically reproduced but rather take on nuances related to local political history and debates.

The orange "voting" hand and the triangular green kerchief brought to the visual sphere a transnational frame that situated abortion as a human rights issue and a debt of democracy. We could even argue that both symbols are evidence of a shared visual frame in the region, grounded in common struggles for democracy, justice, and human rights in countries that experienced brutal dictatorships. This regional attunement also cannot be fully understood without considering the history of political alliances of Latin American feminisms that, at international Encuentros and conferences, have forged strong bonds and shared agendas (Alvarez 2000; Alvarez et al. 2003).

Yet the symbols did not spread only because of shared histories or modes of political articulation at a regional level. They also gained traction because they managed to touch political-affective nerves deeply rooted in post-dictatorship political cultures in the three countries. Indeed, the symbols captured, mobilized, and also transformed these affective repertoires. Hope, joy, solidarity, resistance, disappointment, and willfulness give strength to the demands for the right to abortion that aim to reinvent, radicalize, and transform the region's democracies. Their effects are long-lasting and are part of a living memory of these struggles. The insistent reappearance of the orange hand and the green kerchief over the years is evidence of the astounding achievements of the movement and also of the unfulfilled promises of the democracies of the Southern Cone. Above all, these symbols carry the notion that "perhaps willfulness is an optimistic relation, a way of holding on, of not giving up" (Ahmed 2014, 174).

Notes

1 The spots are available at: www.youtube.com/watch?v=HMpl2lXT-vM
2 One of the posters is dated May 28, 2004 (www.mysu.org.uy/multimedia/folleto/vamos-vamos-y-vamos/), and the other, September 28, 2004 (www.mysu.org.uy/multimedia/folleto/aborto-en-uruguay/).
3 The journal can be accessed at: https://cotidianomujer.org.uy/2005/2005.htm
4 For a photographic record of the protests see: www.mysu.org.uy/multimedia/galeria-de-foto/acto-contra-veto-13-de-noviembre-de-2008/
5 See video: www.youtube.com/watch?v=OXslP0gv8-E
6 A record of this action is available at: www.youtube.com/watch?v=5SoaFIRfjqo&feature=emb_logo

7 A photographic record of this action can be found at: www.mysu.org.uy/multimedia/galeria-de-foto/intervencion-palacio/
8 See: www.abortolegal.com.ar/dia-internacional-de-accion-de-la-salud-de-las-mujeres/
9 See images of this campaign and the use of hands by human rights organizations in Argentina: www.archivosenuso.org/ddhh-estrategia-creativa/manos/
10 Photos published on the MILES Facebook page show different uses of this symbol in public spaces: www.facebook.com/mileschile/photos/a.314461392013809/1292498747543397/; www.facebook.com/mileschile/photos/a.315062861953662/743720665754544/
11 See iconic picture by Eitan Abramovich: https://twitter.com/AFPespanol/status/86252 6955350093828/photo/4
12 The scope of the international actions can be seen at: www.laizquierdadiario.com/Panuelazo-internacional-en-apoyo-al-aborto-legal-en-Argentina
13 See: www.theguardian.com/global-development/2018/aug/07/argentina-abortion-vote-legalisation-senate-mass-rally
14 See poster: www.memoriachilena.gob.cl/602/w3-article-75848.html
15 See an audiovisual: www.youtube.com/watch?v=aB7r6hdo3W4.

Acknowledgments

I would like to thank all of the people and organizations that have helped me with this project since its beginnings in 2017. In Uruguay, I was given access to the archives of Cotidiano Mujer and MYSU. During my fieldwork, I enjoyed the generous cooperation of Ana Laura de Giorgi, Azul Cordo, Lilián Abracinskas, Lilian Celiberti, Lucy Garrido, Susana Rostagnol, and Rafael Sanseviero. In Argentina, I had the valuable support of Celeste Mac Dougall, Claudia Laudano, Elsa Schvartzman, Fedra Torcisi, Laura Salomé Canteros, María Alicia Gutiérrez, and Martha Rosenberg, activists in the National Campaign for the Right to Legal, Safe, and Free Abortion. In Chile, contributions to this project were made by Angie Mendoza Araneda, Lieta Vivaldi, Claudia Dides, Anita Peña Saavedra, and MILES.

References

Ahmed, Sara. 2004. *The Cultural Politics of Emotion*. New York: Routledge.
Ahmed, Sara. 2014. *Willful Subjects*. Durham: Duke University Press.
Abracinskas, Lilián, and Alejandra López Gómez (eds.). 2007. *El aborto en debate. Dilemas y desafíos del Uruguay democrático. Proceso político y social 2001–2004*. Montevideo: Mujer y Salud en Uruguay.
Adams, Jacqueline. 2002. "Art in Social Movements: Shantytown Women's Protest in Pinochet's Chile." *Sociological Forum* 17(1): 21–56.
Alvarez, Sonia E. 2000. "Translating the Global Effects of Transnational Organizing on Local Feminist Discourses and Practices in Latin America." *Meridians. Feminism, Race, Transnationalism* 1(1): 29–67.
Alvarez, Sonia E., Elizabeth Jay Friedman, Ericka Beckman, Maylei Blackwell, Norma Stoltz Chinchilla, Nathalie Lebon, Marysa Navarro, and Marcela Ríos Tobar. 2003. "Encountering Latin American and Caribbean Feminisms." *Signs: Journal of Women in Culture and Society* 28(2): 537–579.
Antivilo Peña, Julia. 2015. *Entre lo sagrado y lo profano se tejen rebeldías. Arte feminista latinoamericano*. Bogotá: Ediciones desde Abajo.

Banda, María Ignacia, and Cecilia Moreno. 2018. "Desafíos de una estrategia de aborto libre en el momento feminista." *Antígona Feminista*. https://antigonafeminista.wordpress.com/desafios-de-una-estrategia-de-aborto-libre-en-el-momento-feminista/.

Barros, Mercedes, and María Marta Quintana. 2020. "El pañuelo como artefacto político: Desplazamientos y disputas por la calle." *Millcayac. Revista Digital de Ciencias Sociales* 7(12): 175–187.

Bellucci, Mabel. 2014. *Historia de una desobediencia. Aborto y Feminismo*. Buenos Aires: Capital Intelectual.

Butler, Judith. 2015. *Notes Toward a Performative Theory of Assembly*. Cambridge, MA: Harvard University Press.

Casas, Lidia, and Lieta Vivaldi. 2014. "Abortion in Chile: The Practice Under a Restrictive Regime." *Reproductive Health Matters* 22(44): 70–81.

Castillo, Alejandra. 2019. "Aborto libre, sin pedido de disculpas." In *Aborto libre. Materiales para la lucha y la discusión en Chile*, ed. Karen Glavic, 41–48. Santiago: Pólvora.

Celiberti, Lilian. 2006. "El aborto en la agenda democrática." *Cotidiano Mujer* 42: 4.

Corporación Humanas. 2019. "Ley n° 21.030 que regula la despenalización de la interrupción voluntaria del embarazo en tres causales en Chile: Revisión de la implementación a dos años de vigencia de la ley." www.humanas.cl/wp-content/uploads/2020/03/HUMANAS-INFORME-IMPLEMENTACION-LEY-IVE-DICIEMBRE-2019.pdf.

Correa, Sonia, and Mario Pecheny. 2016. *Abortus interruptus. Política y reforma legal del aborto en Urguay*. Montevideo: Mujer y Salud en Uruguay.

Doerr, Nicole, Alice Mattoni, and Simon Teune. 2013. "Toward a Visual Analysis of Social Movements, Conflict, and Political Mobilization." *Research in Social Movements, Conflicts and Change* 35: xi–xvi.

Doerr, Nicole, Alice Mattoni, and Simon Teune. 2015. "Visuals in Social Movements." In *The Oxford Handbook of Social Movements*, eds. Donatella Della Porta and Mario Diani, 1–13. Oxford: Oxford University Press.

Felitti, Karina, and Rosario Ramírez Morales. 2020. "Pañuelos verdes por el aborto legal: Historia, significados y circulaciones en Argentina y México." *Encartes* 3(5): 111–145.

Fernandez Anderson, Cora. 2017. "Decriminalizing Abortion in Uruguay: Women's Movements, Secularism and Political Allies." *Journal of Women, Politics & Policy* 38(2): 221–246.

Glavic, Karen. 2019. "El momento del aborto libre." In *Aborto libre. Materiales para la lucha y la discusión en Chile*, ed. Karen Glavic, 9–39. Santiago: Pólvora.

Goodnow, Trischa. 2006. "On Black Panthers, Blue Ribbons, & Peace Signs: The Function of Symbols in Social Campaigns." *Visual Communication Quarterly* 13(3): 166–179.

Gudiño Bessone, Pablo. 2012. "La disputa por la legalización del derecho al aborto en Argentina: Los usos políticos del Nunca Más." *Sociedad & Equidad* 4: 165–181.

Gutiérrez, María Alicia. 2011. "Todo con la misma aguja: Sexualidad, aborto y arte callejero." In *Voces polifónicas: Itinerarios de los géneros y las sexualidades*, ed. María Alicia Gutiérrez, 117–141. Buenos Aires: Godot.

Gutiérrez, María Alicia. 2019. "Marea Verde: La construcción de las luchas feministas." *Catarsis* 1(1): 33–36.

Gutiérrez, María Laura. 2011. *Rupturas de la mirada. Discusiones sobre arte, feminismo y política en la Argentina contemporánea*. Master's thesis, Universidad de Granada.

Gutiérrez, María Laura. 2017. *Imágenes de lo posible. Intervenciones y visibilidades feministas en las prácticas artísticas en Argentina (1986–2013)*. PhD dissertation, Universidad de Buenos Aires.

Hiner, Hillary. 2018. "¿Quiénes merecen abortar y no morir?" *Antígona Feminista*. https://antigonafeminista.wordpress.com/quienes-merecen-abortar-y-no-morir/.

Hiner, Hillary, and Lieta Vivaldi. 2019. "¡Aborto libre ya! Nuevas generaciones de feministas y las luchas por el aborto en Chile." In *Aborto libre. Materiales para la lucha y la discusión en Chile*, ed. Karen Glavic, 73–95. Santiago: Pólvora.

Instituto Nacional de Derechos Humanos. 2019. "Informe anual sobre la situación de los derechos humanos en Chile 2019." https://bibliotecadigital.indh.cl/bitstream/handle/123456789/1701/Informe%20Final-2019.pdf?sequence=1&isAllowed=y.

Johnson, Niki, Cecilia Rocha, and Marcela Schenck. 2015. *La inserción del aborto en la agenda político-pública uruguaya (1985–2013). Un análisis desde el movimiento feminista.* Montevideo: Cotidiano Mujer.

Kim, Nan. 2018. "The Color of Dissent and a Vital Politics of Fragility in South Korea." *The Journal of Asian Studies* 77(4): 971–990.

Mac Ginty, Roger. 2003. "The Role of Symbols in Peacemaking." In *Contemporary Peacemaking: Conflict, Violence, and Peace Processes,* eds. John Darby and Roger Mac Ginty, 235–244. London: Palgrave Macmillan.

Macón, Cecilia. 2019. *Historia como activismo en #QueSeaLey: La lucha por la legalización del aborto en la Argentina y la cuarta ola del feminismo.* Paper presented at Latin American Studies Association Conference, Boston, May 24–27.

Mattoni, Alice, and Simon Teune. 2014. "Visions of Protest. A Media-Historic Perspective on Images in Social Movements." *Sociology Compass* 8(6): 876–887.

Mesa Acción por el Aborto en Chile and Fondo Alquimia. 2019. "Informe de monitoreo social. Implementación de la ley de interrupción del embarazo en tres causales." www.fondoalquimia.org/website/images/2019/06/Informe_-Monitoreo_-Social_ley_IVE.pdf.

Morgan, Lynn. 2015. "Reproductive Rights or Reproductive Justice? Lessons from Argentina." *Health and Human Rights Journal* 17(1): 136–147.

Orellana Calderón, Victor. 2020. "In Chile, the Post-Neoliberal Future is Now." *NACLA Report on the Americas* 52(1): 100–108.

Pousadela, Inés. 2015. "Social Mobilization and Political Representation: The Women's Movement's Struggle for Legal Abortion in Uruguay." *Voluntas* 27(1): 125–145.

Richard, Nelly. 2001. "La problemática del feminismo en los años de la transición en Chile." In *Estudios latinoamericanos sobre cultura y transformaciones sociales en tiempos de globalización 2,* ed. Daniel Mato, 227–239. Buenos Aires: CLACSO.

Rosa, María Laura. 2012. "Our Bodies, Our History: Public Women's Activism in the City of Buenos Aires." *Paradoxa: International Feminist Art Journal* 30: 5–11.

Sarfati, Liora, and Bora Chung. 2018. "Affective Protest Symbols: Public Dissent in the Mass Commemoration of the Sewŏl Ferry's Victims in Seoul." *Asian Studies Review* 42(4): 565–585.

Sawer, Marian. 2007. "Wearing your Politics on your Sleeve: The Role of Political Colours in Social Movement." *Social Movement Studies: Journal of Social, Cultural and Political Protest* 6(1): 39–56.

Serafini, Paula. 2020. "'A Rapist in your Path': Transnational Feminist Protest and Why (and How) Performance Matters." *European Journal of Cultural Studies* 23(2): 290–295.

Sutton, Barbara. 2017. "Zonas de clandestinidad y 'nuda vida': Mujeres, cuerpo y aborto." *Revista Estudos Feministas* 25(2): 889–902.

Sutton, Barbara. 2020. "Intergenerational Encounters in the Struggle for Abortion Rights in Argentina." *Women's Studies International Forum* 82: 102392.

Sutton, Barbara, and Elizabeth Borland. 2013. "Framing Abortion Rights in Argentina's Encuentros Nacionales de Mujeres." *Feminist Studies* 39(1): 194–234.

Sutton, Barbara, and Elizabeth Borland. 2019. "Abortion and Human Rights for Women in Argentina." *Frontiers: A Journal of Women Studies* 40 (2):27–61.

Sutton, Barbara, and Nayla Luz Vacarezza. 2020. "Abortion Rights in Images: Visual Interventions by Activist Organizations in Argentina." *Signs: Journal of Women in Culture and Society* 45(3): 731–757.

Vacarezza, Nayla Luz. 2017. "Los fetos de otra manera: Reflexiones sobre afectos, aborto y políticas reproductivas a partir de obras de Zaida González y Felipe Rivas San Martín." In

Afectos políticos: Ensayos sobre actualidad, eds. Cecilia Macón and Daniela Losiggio, 71–91. Buenos Aires: Miño y Dávila.

Vacarezza, Nayla Luz. 2018. "Perejil, agujas y pastillas: Objetos y afectos en la producción visual a favor de la legalización del aborto en Argentina." In *Aborto: Aspectos normativos, jurídicos y discursivos*, ed. Daniel Busdygan, 195–212. Buenos Aires: Biblos.

Vivaldi, Lieta. 2018. *Abortion in Chile: Biopolitics and Contemporary Feminist Resistance*. PhD dissertation, Goldsmiths, University of London.

Vivaldi, Lieta, and Valentina Stutzin. 2017. "Mujeres víctimas, fetos públicos, úteros aislados: Tecnologías de género, tensiones y desplazamientos en las representaciones visuales sobre aborto en Chile." *Zona Franca: Revista de Estudios de Género* 25: 126–160.

Warley, Jorge, and Laura Mango. 2008. "Madres de Plaza de Mayo: Un espacio alternativo para los artistas plásticos." In *El siluetazo*, eds. Ana Longoni and Gustavo Bruzzone, 149–187. Buenos Aires: Adriana Hidalgo.

Zerán, Faride (ed.). 2018. *Mayo feminista. La rebelión contra el patriarcado*. Santiago: LOM.

Zurbriggen, Ruth, and Claudia Anzorena (eds.). 2013. *El aborto como derecho de las mujeres. Otra historia es posible*. Buenos Aires: Herramienta.

5

NEOCONSERVATIVE INCURSIONS INTO PARTY POLITICS

The Cases of Argentina and Chile

Juan Marco Vaggione and José Manuel Morán Faúndes

Neoconservatism in Latin America, with its religious matrix, has undergone changes and adaptations in the face of sexual and reproductive rights advances in the region (Vaggione 2005, 2019; Morán Faúndes et al. 2019). While the defense of a reproductive and matrimonial morality cuts through Latin American history, the impact of feminist and LGBTI[1] movements has given rise to a new stage that manifests itself in the complexity of the actors and in the diversity of arguments and strategies that such actors favor (Peñas Defago and Vaggione 2011; Sgró Ruata et al. 2011). The Catholic hierarchy remains a central actor, yet civil society organizations (self-called "pro-life" or "pro-family" organizations) as well as Evangelical leaders also play key roles. In this context, an important question that arises is how conservative political actions intersect with the consolidation of democracy in Latin American countries.

Even though moral conservatism has displayed a special affinity with military dictatorships and authoritarian governments in the region, the transition to, and establishment of, democracy also gave way to opportunities for the construction and consolidation of a conservative agenda, with authoritarian elements. Conservative sectors maximized the democratic channels in the defense of a hierarchical conception of the sexual order, mobilizing resources permitted by the very democratic system itself. In the de-democratization processes in the region, the neoconservative agenda in its most radical versions is a key component. In some countries, for example, there has been an increase in women's criminalization, a trampling of LGBTI people's rights, and an intensification of hate speech that is connected to the impact of the most radical conservative actors.

Another aspect of neoconservatism is its functioning as a transnational phenomenon. Whereas most actions in defense of "life from conception" and of a "traditional" family occur within countries, the construction of neoconservative agendas, arguments, and strategies develops across countries, too. On the one hand, much regional activism by parishioners responded to the global call from the Vatican, which asked

DOI: 10.4324/9781003079903-6

the lay community to take action against agendas that questioned the Catholic sexual morality. On the other hand, many of the first "pro-life" groups of the region were formed, in the late 1970s and early 1980s, under the wing of organizations from the Global North, which promoted Latin American conservative activism (Morán Faúndes 2017).[2]

Finally, another point that characterizes neoconservatism is the blurring of the dichotomy between *the religious* and *the secular* (Vaggione 2005, 2017). More than a dichotomy, this is a continuum, where the differentiation of actors and arguments belonging to the religious pole or the secular pole is difficult to achieve. Without overlooking how *the religious* provides a matrix for neoconservatism, a deeper understanding of neoconservatism entails transcending the secular/religious dichotomy. Among "pro-life" or "pro-family" non-governmental organizations (NGOs), for example, there are those that explicitly recognize a religious affiliation, together with others that, in contrast, are disconnected from any such affiliation (Morán Faúndes and Peñas Defago 2016). Furthermore, many of the arguments found in the neoconservative agenda have discarded religious narratives and have, instead, favored secular elements from the fields of genetics and bioethics, among other disciplines, thus making fuzzier the limits between *the religious* and *the secular*.

Given these developments and the contemporary prevalence of electoral democracies, it is important to examine the interplay between the neoconservative agenda and the political party system, including the appropriation of neoconservative initiatives by party politics, henceforth *partidization*. Precisely, this chapter will analyze such connections, with the aim to assess how neoconservatism is channeled through, and how it influences, party politics. To this end, we look into the Argentinean and Chilean cases to identify how the neoconservative agenda, especially considering abortion as a topic in dispute, is articulated through political parties (see also Fernández Anderson, this volume, on abortion and party politics more broadly).

The Neoconservative Agenda and Party Politics

The rejection of both abortion decriminalization and LGBTI rights tends to be the common ground over which alliances are forged and which, in turn, become, in a multifarious manner, electoral platforms. In various regions of the world, conservative moral agendas are articulated and set through party politics, with long-term ramifications. In the United States, the term New Religious Right helps identify the moral and political alliance promoted, among others, by the Moral Majority organization, which was key in the politicization of conservative Christians. In different European countries, although more recently than in the United States, some political parties have taken up and channeled the conservative moral agenda and the fight against what they consider a moral decline of society.[3] In Spain, for example, the political party Vox, created in 2013, serves as a vehicle for the ideas upheld by conservative Catholic sectors and by "pro-life" organizations, such as Hazteoir or Abogados Cristianos (Christian Lawyers).

Latin America is no exception: the process through which a conservative moral agenda becomes articulated at the level of a political society is also at play in this region. Of course, this articulation is not new, for every time that novel ways of regulating the family and sexuality are debated, sectors defending a conservative sexual morality appear. Their interventions have an impact on, and are also represented in, the political party system.[4] However, the legal and political clout of, in turn, feminist and LGBTI movements has taken this conservative influence to a new level. This is evidenced in the importance that the defense of "life from conception" and of a heteropatriarchal family has attained in parliamentary debates and/or electoral agendas, even growing into a cleavage that helps explain different alliances and electoral results. This phenomenon has been more readily visible in the past few years, above all through the impact in the region of the election of Jair Bolsonaro as president of Brazil. More than an anomaly, such election seems to amount to the intensification of a process that, in different ways and with varying degrees, is underway in many Latin American countries.

Analyzing the *partidization* of the neoconservative agenda is no easy task, for it entails a multi-cause process that varies in each context. Nevertheless, it is possible to single out at least two interconnected dimensions. First, in the past few decades, we have seen a radicalization of the neoconservative agenda. If, until some time ago, this agenda centered on the defense of a moral order that perceived itself as threatened by sexual and reproductive rights, today these rights are interpreted by neoconservatism as the tip of the iceberg of a series of more extreme threats. Any politics that favors lifestyles dissonant with the heterosexual and reproductive model is deemed a part of a global agenda oriented to ideologizing and controlling populations, destabilizing the family, imposing authoritarian behavioral forms, and curtailing freedoms.

Key in this respect has been the spread of the discourse denouncing the so-called "gender ideology." Although this concept was introduced in the mid-1990s as a reaction, from the Catholic domain, against the recognition of sexual and reproductive rights in international United Nations conferences (Paternotte 2015), it was only around a decade ago that it started to be a popular concept in the neoconservative arena. By means of this discourse, conservative sectors seek to establish that, under the guise of rights, feminist and LGBTI movements are attempting to set up a global ideological project, which aims at transforming not just the economy, as was done by classical Marxism, but culture, instead (Morán Faúndes 2019). Thus, they state that sexual and reproductive rights would constitute a sort of "neo-Marxist" project, against the natural order and the biological supremacy they defend (Korolczuk and Graff 2018). "Gender ideology" is defined hyperbolically as a threat, therefore instituting feminist and LGBTI collectives not just as political adversaries but as powerful enemies intent on imposing a global domination project of ideological and cultural characteristics. The discursive effect so generated is the creation of an alterity marked by meanings that relate it to a major threat against a moral and biological order they understand as natural.

Second, and connected to the previous point, the radicalization of neoconservative discourse has had, as its opposite, the consequent generation of an actualized "we." As indicated by Chantal Mouffe (2009), every adversarial construction process entails the performative production of one's own political identity. Radicalized discourses such as that of a "gender ideology," precisely by setting up a symbolic imaginary around its antagonist, are also producing a "we" grouped together against that enemy (Garbagnoli 2016; Mayer and Sauer 2017). In a play of opposites, they create a political identity, confronting it with an enemy that the same discourse is in charge of creating (Garbagnoli 2016; Graff 2016). Therefore, in the past few years, and thanks to this sort of discourse, neoconservative sectors have been producing a consequent process of identity configuration and political subjectivation.

Discourses decrying the influence of the "gender ideology" actualize older conservative identification forms. Given that they interpret feminist and LGBTI movements' agendas as part of a broader reconfiguration of a supposed cultural Marxism with a global character, the current process of construction of a "we" is not just assembling together traditional "pro-life" and "pro-family" sectors. In fact, this process summons other sectors and agendas that did not feel particularly spoken to by matters pertaining to gender and sexuality in the past, but that rejected the ideas and politics connected to left-wing parties and communism. Therefore, by reinterpreting the sexual and reproductive rights agenda as the current ideological project of the traditional Marxist left, neoconservatism has increased its alliances, enlisting multiple sectors that mobilize various agendas. In doing so, neoconservative sectors coalesce around the lowest common denominator: their rejection of progressive and left-wing parties. In this way, the neoconservative agenda includes both traditional themes associated with sexual morality, as well as other matters such as immigration control, popular punitivism, harsher drug policy measures, and market deregulation, among others.

Neoconservatism has managed to create, in the past few years, discourses that operate as empty signifiers that permit them to oppose various policies and actors, condensing different ideas and agendas under the same conceptual umbrella (Kováts and Põim 2015; Kuhar and Zobec 2017; Mayer and Sauer 2017; Korolczuk and Graff 2018). Following Ernesto Laclau (2005), "empty signifiers" entail not only a discursive strategy, but one about political mobilization. Every collective action that operates under the construction of a "we" antagonizing with an "other," oriented to transforming or defending a specific social order, requires certain signifiers (e.g., freedom, equality, family, life, patriotism) that allow for the condensation of multiple collective demands in a single joint project. The emptier that signifier is, the better its capacity to put together heterogeneous demands and sectors. The "gender ideology" discourse belongs to this sort of narrative, creating a signifier that "may represent everything and anything" (Kuhar and Zobec 2017, 33). Thus, it operates like a symbolic glue (Grzebalska and Pető 2018), capable of joining together different actors through the rhetorical construction of an enemy.

The construction of these alterity relations, based on an us/them dichotomy, is central to current neoconservative party politics projects. By radicalizing the moral agenda, neoconservatism devises new positionings and strategies. Political parties that had traditionally followed the neoconservative agendas are less capable to continue doing so today. Yet empty signifiers such as the "gender ideology," operate as new political cleavages that go beyond and/or actualize the cleavages upon which traditional parties were founded. In this way, acknowledging that moral conservatism has been a historical cleavage in the political parties of Latin American countries, a new party politics scenario emerges partly influenced by the expanding fight against the "gender ideology." The radical nature of this expansion reveals renewed neoconservative incursions into the political party system. In particular, we examine three main types of processes that, while we differentiate for analytical reasons, are interconnected with one another in complex ways.

Confessional Parties as Channels for Neoconservatism

While it is well established that religion has strong influences on politics, these influences are diverse and fluctuating. One direct and formalized way to channel religious projects is through confessional parties, that is, parties with an explicit objective to defend the moral principles of some religious tradition. These parties have been fundamental actors in the democracies of the region, with variations across countries. Despite the ideological heterogeneity of confessional parties, it is not surprising that they are, at least potentially, a relevant path for the introduction of the neoconservative agenda into legislative debates.

In Latin America, two opposing tendencies can be identified, based on the confessional party being Catholic or Evangelical. Catholicism has, for a long time, been a relevant force for the creation and functioning of political parties. In particular, throughout the 20th century, Catholic parties in various countries had the goal to "Christianize" politics. Christian Democratic parties stood out as an alternative for the defense of moral Christian values, and to a great extent, they were a reaction against liberalism (Almeyda 1986). Although Christian Democracy (henceforward CD) continues to exist, it has lost ground as a political strategy implemented by the Catholic Church. Even Pope Francis I stated that Catholic political parties "are not the way" for believers to become involved in public debates (*Excelsior* 2015).

The Evangelical realm followed an opposite path in the region with respect to Catholic confessional parties. Although various Evangelical political initiatives existed throughout the 20th century, it has been more recently that Evangelical parties have increased their visibility and political clout through the proliferation of Pentecostal churches (Villazón 2015). In general, the 1980s and 1990s tend to be linked to the moment in which the existence (and importance) of the so-called "Evangelical vote" becomes visible, together with the creation of Evangelical political parties. Such creation entails a much more intense process, logically, in those countries with greater number of Evangelical believers. While, initially, the Evangelical political mobilization sought to obtain greater recognition as a religious minority against the privileges enjoyed by the Catholic Church, currently, this mobilization tends to be characterized by the defense of a heteronormative legal system and by its opposition to the "gender ideology," which they share with conservative Catholic sectors (Machado 2018).

The process leading to the creation of political parties with a Catholic slant in Argentina dates back to the latest decades of the 20th century (Di Stefano and Zanatta 2000). In electoral terms, they were never successful (Prieto 2014); however, CD (founded in 1954) still exists today. Notwithstanding the divisions inside the party or its heterogeneity, in later years, it has been the protagonist of a series of events against abortion, becoming involved in disputes over both the interpretations and enforcement of the law, as well as the legalization processes undertaken at a parliamentary level. In 2012, for example, the party presented a precautionary measure against the province of Santa Fe, which, following the "F., A.L." decision by Argentina's Supreme Court of Justice in the same year, had decided to adhere to and adopt the Technical Guide for the Comprehensive Attention of Non-Punishable Abortions (Guía Técnica para la Atención Integral de Abortos no Punibles), from the National Program on Sexual Health and Responsible Procreation (Programa Nacional de Salud Sexual y Procreación Responsable) of the Ministry of Health of Argentina. In addition, in 2018, while the first parliamentary abortion debate was under way in Argentina, CD publicly stated its opposition to the legal reform bill. At the beginning of that year, a few weeks prior to the start of the debate, the CD National Board decided to "ratify its commitment and militancy for the protection of human life from conception" (*AICA* 2018, n.p.).

Once the 2018 parliamentary debate on abortion legalization had begun, national deputy Juan Brügge, one of the main representatives of CD and a former president of the party, led the opposition against the bill. He stated that the bill was unconstitutional, violating the protection of the "unborn child," apart from being a bill "against the value of life." In addition to devising the strategy of a referendum (Brügge 2018), Brügge submitted a bill on the comprehensive protection of the human rights of the pregnant woman and of the "unborn girls and boys" as a counterproposal against the abortion legalization bill. The rejection of abortion by members of CD was apparent, in an extreme way, with the attempt by the political candidates from the City of Buenos Aires to include, in the party ballot, a picture of a fetus with a message that read "Light Blue City. In favor of life and the family" in direct reference to the color chosen by the anti-abortion rights movement (Angulo 2019, n.p.).

In Chile, CD evidences a different reception of the neoconservative agenda. This party, one of the most important in the country until today, has historically supported different strands, some more conservative, and others more center-oriented or even progressive in certain matters, for example, regarding sexual and reproductive rights. During the debate over the bill for abortion decriminalization in connection to three grounds, which was passed in 2017, the plurality of positions even inside the CD in areas related to sexuality became evident. Some important historical figures from CD, such as Soledad Alvear, did not only maintain a public position against the bill, but also expressed it in different commissions during the discussion of the bill. Additionally, the constitutional attorney Patricio Zapata, a CD activist, spoke before the Constitutional Tribunal on behalf of the Pontifical Catholic University of Chile, rejecting the bill's constitutionality after it had been passed by Congress. At the same time, other key CD figures supported the bill in all its stages. The CD senator back then, and presidential candidate, Carolina Goic, was a central figure in the defense of the bill. Although she has stated that she does not defend abortion under a system of terms, she did support the three grounds that the bill identified (risk to the woman's life, serious fetal anomaly, and rape) (Aguayo 2017). This diversity of positions inside CD became finally manifest when its members voted, showing no unified stance. On the contrary, in the Senate, for example, historical CD activists such as Andrés Zaldívar and Patricio Walker voted against the bill with respect to certain grounds (since each ground was voted on separately), while Carolina Goic, Jorge Pizarro, and Ignacio Walker, also emblematic Christian Democrats, approved all of the grounds. Thus, the historical confessional party from Chile has operated as a catalyst of both conservative but also more moderate and progressive positions, establishing itself as an open dispute space.

The Evangelical churches, in turn, have showed their capacity for citizen mobilization, although neither in Argentina nor in Chile have they managed to institutionalize successful confessional parties as has been the case in other countries in the region (Carbonelli 2018). The limited success that Evangelical party projects have achieved in Argentina does not mean that these sectors are not interested in holding positions of authority (in the following section, we will discuss the role played by politician Cynthia Hotton). On the contrary, in the past few years, they have undertaken several initiatives aimed precisely at this objective. To a point, the debates over sexual and reproductive rights tend to intensify these courses of action. In fact, a portion of the Evangelical world, with a particularly neo-conservative slant, strongly mobilized itself to stop abortion legalization in 2018. Moreover, interpreting the opening of the legislative debate as an act of treason by former President Mauricio Macri (who had adopted a strong position against abortion on many occasions), this same segment of the Evangelical world seeks to make more concerted attempts to enter the legislative body, be it through its own political party or not. In the Second South American Congress for Life and Family (Segundo Congreso Sudamericano por la Vida y la Familia), which took place in Punta del Este (Uruguay) in 2019, a statement made by the Evangelical leader Hugo Márquez, from the Argentine province of Neuquén, synthetically states this intention: "[W]e do not support parties, but values [...]. We are with us. They used us and so are we using them. We are going to introduce our people to Parliament through any party" (Cariboni 2019, n.p.).

In the meantime, the Evangelical realm in Chile has had political ties for at least half a century, but a *partidization* process has not taken place there either. During the military dictatorship (1973–90), a considerable number of Evangelical churches gave their full support to Pinochet's regime, and once democracy was restored in the 1990s, there were many Evangelical candidacies at the regional level, most of them unsuccessful, supported by various already existing political parties, both from the right and from the left (Mansilla and Orellana 2015). In 1988, a new generation of Evangelicals, bereft of the traditional Protestant rejection of mundane matters, created the Alianza Nacional Cristiana (Christian National Alliance), a platform whose short-term objective was to promote the failed presidential candidacy of Pastor Salvador Pino Bustos (Mansilla, Orellana Urtubia, and Panotto 2019). From these hallmarks onward, the Evangelical realm has evinced a growing interest in taking part in politics and, mostly, its projects have tended to lean toward the right and neoconservatism.

One of the most recent incursions into politics by these sectors is connected to the creation, in 2015, of the political movement Evangélicos en Acción (Evangelicals in Action) in response to a series of bills put forward by the Executive, during the presidency of Michelle Bachelet, related to abortion decriminalization and gender identity recognition. A goal of the movement is "calling up Christians across the country, who feel restless and want to oppose abortion legalization and homosexual marriage" (Chilecristiano.com n.d., n.p.). In spite of this, there is no initiative to introduce an openly Evangelical party in the country yet, in contrast with what has occurred in other Latin American countries.

Right-wing Politics and Sexuality Re-moralization

A central concern of the sectors denouncing a "gender ideology" is the connection they establish between feminist and LGBTI movements and a "new left" that wants to control the state.[5] Many neoconservatives accuse these movements of encouraging the growth of the state, as sexual and reproductive rights can only be promoted by the public apparatus. Moreover, they argue that these movements reveal an authoritarian character, given that the "gender ideology" would be imposed on society through the use of the law, therefore fostering a kind of dictatorship that favors just one way of thinking. The neoliberal concern for any idea or policy that would support state intervention instead of total individual and market freedom is voiced today by the neoconservative sectors and taken to the realm of sexual politics.

Thus, inside the neoconservative rhetoric, a somewhat explicit link between feminist and LGBTI agendas and a supposed neo-Marxist attack against individual freedoms is established. By self-proclaiming itself a defender of "the family" and freedom, neoconservative activism is adopting the role of representative of the "true liberalism." Thus, comprehensive sexual education policies, for example, are, in their view, aimed at imposing on girls and boys just one way of thinking about sexuality, undermining parents' right to decide their children's education. Another example is connected to the laws against discrimination based on sexual orientation or gender identity. According to a sector within contemporary neoconservative activism, such laws aim to impede one's freedom to ascribe to ideas that pathologize gender and sexuality expressions that move away from a cis-heterosexual norm. The neoconservative agenda thus establishes a dichotomy that is the kernel of the association between neoliberalism and neoconservatism, that is, the state/family dichotomy, by which strengthening one side amounts to weakening the other.

It is thus not surprising that the neoconservative agenda finds common ground with right-wing positions that defend a neoliberal agenda, in which individual freedom and a state with minimal intervention are political priorities. The affinity displayed between the right and moral conservatism is not new in Latin America, for the defense of a traditional family has tended to be a bulwark employed by sectors identified with the right as a political option. Even when the right has channeled its influence through realms outside of party politics,[6] democratic systems entail a new scenario for the defense of their positioning. Responding to this challenge, the fight against "gender ideology" offers the possibility of renewing alliances and public discourses that resonate with different social (secular or religious) sectors, with respect to which right-wing parties did not necessarily exercise much influence before.

The question that remains, therefore, is how the neoconservative agenda impacts party politics in Argentina and Chile. That is, how reactive politization, the mobilization against the so-called "gender ideology," is channeled through right-wing party instances. It is not our objective to reconstruct the history of the right in both countries since it exceeds the goal of the present work. In fact, we expect to identify some examples that allow us to address this question, acknowledging the limitations that the left–right dichotomy imposes on our attempt to capture the depth of sexual politics.

Argentina and Chile share the experience of a military dictatorship that, in various ways, combined a neoliberal agenda with the defense of the family based on a Catholic morality. In the respective transitions to democracy in both countries, the impact achieved by the Catholic Church was, however, different. As a reaction to the affinity that existed between the ecclesiastic authorities and the representatives of the military dictatorship in Argentina, in the first years of the transition, the Church lessened its power over the democratic government. This was evident, for example, with the passing of a divorce law in 1987 despite strong resistance from the Catholic hierarchy (Htun 2003; Matamala Vivaldi 2011). In Chile, in contrast, throughout the first years after the restoration of democracy in 1990, and even well into the 21st century, center and progressive political parties adopted moderate stances regarding the regulation of the family and sexuality. On the one hand, the Chilean Catholic hierarchy made these parties pay a high moral price for the key role the religious institution played in the democracy restoration process, which, in turn, led the center-left parties to take a moderate position in the realm of sexual morality (Htun 2003). On the other hand, the tutelage functions still held by the armed forces made the main political parties, which had opposed the dictatorship but were now in office, adopt moderate positions to avoid major conflict with the civil and military right (Araujo 2010). Among other consequences, this led to divorce being approved only in 2004, making Chile the last country in the region to do so. Additionally, for almost three decades, Chile was one of the few countries in the world to ban abortion completely, due to a legal reform put in place in the last months of the dictatorship and which was reviewed only in the 2010s by Congress.

Both countries also differ on the role that right-wing parties have performed once the democratic transition had been consolidated. In Argentina, right-wing parties have not had a notable electoral success, which does not deny the impact that right-wing leaders in other parties exert. A milepost in this respect was reached in the 1990s when the Peronist president at that time, Carlos Menem, in an alliance with (among other parties) Unión de Centro Democrático (Center Democratic Union), led a conservative government regarding sexual morality and implemented an agenda of neoliberal reforms. Precisely, Menem was a precursor of the celebration of the Day of the Unborn Child, a strategy in the fight against abortion. The day is observed on March 25 to coincide with the Catholic Feast of the Annunciation.[7] Moreover, under his government, the state ratified the Convention on the Rights of the Child (United Nations, 1989), introducing reservations and statements, among which was one that declared that, in Argentina, "a child means every human being from the moment of conception up to the age of eighteen." A few years later, in 1994, an important constitutional reform was brought about, where the introduction into the charter of the protection of life from conception was attempted without success (see also Gutiérrez, this volume).

Another moment when the neoliberal and neoconservative agendas met is exemplified by the establishment of the PRO (Propuesta Republicana / Republican Proposal), which can be categorized as a center-right party. This party, which has ruled the city of Buenos Aires since 2007, won the presidential elections in 2015, thanks to an alliance forged with other parties, thus constituting Cambiemos (Let's Change). Mauricio Macri, the main representative of PRO within the alliance, became president. Some interpretations indicate that Macri's government evidenced ambiguity in matters related to gender and sexual reproductive rights. On the one hand, his government enabled the legislative debate on abortion legalization in 2018, a milestone in a historical process that permitted the voices from different sectors, both in favor and against the initiative, to be heard. On the other hand, this government took certain actions to the contrary, such as budget cuts to policies against gender violence, the signature of an agreement (which was then broken) between the Ministry of Social Development and Evangelical sectors, with the aim of creating a National Network for the Support of Women with Vulnerable Pregnancies (Red Nacional de Acompañamiento a la Mujer con Embarazo Vulnerable), and the request for the Health Secretary, Adolfo Rubinstein, to resign after he updated the protocol for non-punishable abortions (these guidelines were immediately ignored). Moreover, during his presidential campaigns in 2015 and 2019, Macri publicly declared he was "pro-life," against abortion.

The Chilean scenario, in contrast, shows different shades with respect to the Argentinean case, as Chile is considered one of the few countries in which the right managed to successfully enter into party politics. Right-wing political parties in Chile, that is, Renovación Nacional (National Renovation, RN) and especially Unión Demócrata Independiente (Independent Democratic Union, UDI), emerged as direct channels of a conservative moral agenda. Besides, the leading role that the Catholic Church played against Pinochet's regime gave way to friendly relations between this religious institution and the center-left coalition that came to power after the dictatorship. Such amicability between these two actors brought to a halt, as we stated before, a great part of the progressive initiatives in the realm of sexuality (Htun 2003). As time went by, some of the debates connected to sexual morality caused the Catholic Church and right-wing politics to converge, especially at the turn of the century. The reactions toward governmental campaigns on the use of contraceptives for HIV prevention or the legal attack by neoconservative sectors against the commercialization of emergency contraception from 2001 onward were moments that illustrated such confluence. In addition, during the 2004 parliamentary debate on the legalization of divorce, the UDI and RN adamantly opposed the reform of the civil marriage law, in line with the ecclesiastic position. Except for six votes, all votes against the bill, both in the Senate and in the lower house, sprang from these two parties. In recent years, the most deliberate rejection of civil union, gender identity, and abortion bills has once again originated in these political parties.

Right-wing parties in Chile have drawn most of the moral conservative agenda, becoming key spaces for the consolidation of the political career of preeminent neoconservative actors, especially from the religious sphere. This strengthens the connection between right-wing politics and religious institutions. Renovación Nacional, for example, the party to which President Sebastián Piñera belongs, provided political support for three neoconservative Evangelical deputies in office today. The three have adopted extreme neoconservative positions, opposing even executive-backed initiatives, such as the public recognition given by President Piñera to trans actress Daniela Vega.

Although the neoconservative agendas in both countries have been channeled with varying degrees of intensity and success through different parties, the radicalization of neoconservative sectors that has manifested itself in the past few years has impacted in different ways the configuration of their alliances with right-wing political parties. The entrance of the abortion debate into both countries and the more and more frequent appearance of the "gender ideology" discourse have intensified conservative reactions, putting the "defense of life" on political party agendas and giving way to new configurations in the right-wing party politics scenario.

In Argentina, one manifestation of the linkage between neoconservative radicalization and right-wing party politics is the creation, in 2019, of Frente NOS (Front NOS). Formed as a conservative and right-wing party coalition aimed at competing in the presidential elections held that year, the party's formula was made up of Malvinas war veteran Juan José Gómez Centurión, running for president, and Cynthia Hotton, former Evangelical parliamentarian, running for vice-president. Frente NOS constituted a reaction against the first legislative debate on abortion, which was held in 2018, and the moral panic it generated in neoconservative sectors, due to the majority of votes that the bill obtained in the lower house of Congress.

Frente NOS drew up an explicit neoconservative agenda in matters of sexual morality, besides setting a right-wing agenda with respect to social and economic issues. In addition to rejecting legal abortion, Frente NOS promoted tax and public job reduction as well as social plan and subsidy revisions, all aiming to generate "a deep cultural change in a society used to living free of charge and seeking the provision of happiness by the State" (Frente NOS n.d., n.p.). Thus, Frente NOS emerged as an alliance founded on a radicalized right-wing agenda, with, on the one hand, a neo-conservative matrix in matters pertaining to sexual morality and, on the other, a neo-liberal project in favor of minimal state intervention. In a country where parties and coalitions such as PRO and Cambiemos adopted ambiguous or bland positions regarding sexuality, the formation of a right-wing coalition entailed, from the per-spective of a neoconservative militancy, a needed response to channel that agenda straightforwardly. At the same time, it allowed for a neoliberal right-wing vision that provided access to a larger social, economic, and political project. Another example in this direction is the creation of Renacer, a right-wing political option formed in 2020 by citizens "tired of the old politics." The main platform proposals are, precisely, to protect life from conception and the "traditional" family together with the defense of free market, private property, and a "national capitalism" (Renacer n.d., n.p.).

In Chile, since the restoration of democracy, the neoconservative agenda has been generally channeled through right-wing parties, especially the RN and UDI. Although these parties have continuously taken a position against sexual and repro-ductive rights, the radicalization of neoconservatism has also generated differences on the part of extreme right-wing groups that deem the stances adopted by these parties not extreme enough. One of the clearest examples of such discrepancies is the recently formed Republican Party (Partido Republicano). Its founder, politician José Antonio Kast, is a former Catholic deputy who used to be a member of the extreme-right party UDI, in favor of Pinochet. Kast has a proven track record in neoconservative actions.

Kast participated for years in one of the most important parties inside the right-wing coalition of Chile. Yet he stepped aside from it to compete for its electorate outside of the Chilean bipartisan system, which controlled the electoral scenario since the return of democracy in 1990. Although the Republican Party's political agenda is multifarious, the fight against sexual and reproductive rights, and more generally, against the "gender ideology," occupies an important place in its plat-form. In 2019, for example, Kast took part in Transatlantic Summit III, held in Colombia, where neoconservative leaders from Europe and the Americas con-vened. In his presentation, Kast pointed out that "there is not a more perverse ideology than a gender ideology. Should there exist anything more perverse than the concept of communism it is precisely that of a gender ideology" (Kast 2019).

On Kast's agenda specifically, and on the Republican Party's agenda in general, the opposition against abortion plays a pivotal role. Both Republican Action (Acción Republicana) and the Republican Party define themselves as organizations that defend "life from conception until a natural death," while they also state that they "promote the family" and "believe in God" (Acción Republicana n.d., n.p.). However, they do not express that they embrace any specific religious creed. In addition, even before the start of the parliamentary debates on abortion decrimi-nalization on three grounds in Chile, Kast and his party submitted, in 2007, a request to declare emergency oral contraception and the intrauterine device unconstitutional. The reason they provided was that they understand these prac-tices to cause abortions. Moreover, ten years later, when Kast was still a national deputy in 2017, he voted against the bill for abortion decriminalization on three grounds, stating that the bill would permit the "murder of innocent children, Chilean children who do not have a voice to defend them" (Kast 2017, n.p.).

Similar to Frente NOS in Argentina, the Republican Party's agenda does not limit itself to topics related to sexual morality. Its postulates reveal a social and economic neoliberal agenda, espousing individual freedom and protection of private property. The party's principles express the following:

> our resolute and unyielding defense of free private initiatives in matters connected to the economy, our defense of constitutional guarantees so as to stop the State from interfering with an individual's economic and social affairs and our defense and support of the right to property for all, since we are convinced that private property, inasmuch as it results from the fruits of people's exercise of their liberty, entails one of the pillars of a truly free and responsible society.
>
> *(Partido Republicano n.d., n.p.)*

In the Republican Party's agenda, the defense of a free market and a conservative sexual morality converge harmoniously within a project seeking to renew right-wing politics outside of the traditional Chilean coalition of center and far-right parties.

Both in Argentina and in Chile, the radicalization of the neoconservative agendas has provoked fissures in the party systems, particularly in right-wing parties. What is striking is that while the role and strength of such parties have been different, the two countries show similarities regarding the emergence of new far-right parties that channel both neoconservative moral matters and neoliberal tenets concerning political, economic, and social issues. Precisely, the new political textures that Latin American neoconservatism has accorded its discourses—the association between sexual and reproductive rights and a supposed new left, neo-Marxism and state control—is triggering political projects that oppose feminist and LGBTI claims, but from heterogeneous right-wing political platforms.

The Formation of Pro-life/Pro-family Parties

One of the main actors defending the neoconservative agenda in Latin America is the group comprised of the self-called "pro-life" or "pro-family" organizations. While their development and functioning are country-specific, their emergence in the region dates back to the 1980s and was influenced by Human Life International, a Catholic "pro-life" organization from the United States. Since then, these organizations started to appear at an intensified pace and, today, they lead the fight against the "gender ideology." This growth also meant that the constituencies these NGOs appeal to have become more complex. If, initially, they were associated with *the religious* (a feature that could even be apparent in their name), in the past few years, they do not just self-identify as ecumenical (seeking to include different religious traditions) but as secular too (Morán Faúndes and Peñas Defago 2016).

The expansion of these NGOs has also implied a higher degree of institutionalization. Although many of them become visible almost exclusively as a reaction to specific public debates at a given moment, others have achieved formal recognition and take an active part in policy-related processes. For example, they have undertaken litigation (as plaintiff or through the presentation of *amicus curiae*) to prevent the implementation of rights or deny them altogether, in particular those linked to sexual education, birth control methods, or legal abortion, among others. These strategic forms of *judicialization* have become one of the major obstacles for different sectors to enjoy sexual and reproductive rights already recognized. Regarding abortion, for instance, these NGOs litigate against guidelines that are in effect and that regulate the voluntary interruption of pregnancy with the purpose of blocking altogether or hindering their legal application.[8]

Apart from strategic judicialization (Monte and Vaggione 2018; Peñas Defago 2019), "pro-life" activism has tried to influence legislative bodies (both national and regional) in the dispute over the regulation of a sexual order. Thus, there are increasing and recurrent references to a "gender ideology" in parliamentary debates. Very rapidly, this phrase appears not only in street demonstrations, but is also employed by legislators. Bills have even been proposed that explicitly mention the "threat of a gender ideology," and that have the purpose of eliminating, from the legal system and from public policies, any linguistic form pointing to this "gender ideology." In Brazil, Guatemala, or Peru, for example, there have been bills aiming to foreclose gender perspectives as they are considered ideology-ridden and totalitarian.[9]

As part of "pro-life" activism's growing institutionalization, some of its leaders have become involved in elections. In Argentina, such involvement is not an isolated event, but has a history. In 1999, for example, Cristina González Delgado, president of the "pro-life" NGO Mujeres por la Vida (Women for Life) in Córdoba, ran for provincial deputy for the party Acción por la República (Action for the Republic). Similarly, Rodrigo Agrelo, a member of "pro-life" NGO Portal de Belén, was a provincial legislator for Unión de Centro Democrático (Center Democratic Union) and ran for vice-governor in Córdoba in 2003, for the party alliance called Frente de la Lealtad (Front of Loyalty). As mentioned before, these examples also show the affinity between neoconservatism and neoliberalism, given than in both cases, "pro-life" leaders belong to parties that can be understood as right-wing.

In the past few years, "pro-life" activism took yet another step toward institutionalization and the advancement of the neoconservative agenda: the formation of political parties for the "defense of life from conception" and/or the heteronormative family. In this agenda, abortion figures most prominently, even when other topics are included too. "Pro-life" activism thus exceeds the civil society arena, and emerges into the political society realm through what we have called *partidization*. When considering the number of votes, their success level is low, but this activism manages to mobilize the electorate most reactive to feminist and LGBTI movements.

"Pro-life" parties' institutionalization points to the growing significance that gender/sexuality cleavages acquire in contemporary politics. Additionally, as these parties (and their leaders) are inscribed outside the traditional party system, they are able to display an anti-politics positioning, which they capitalize on, given the crisis of representation in the region. In Argentina, regional parties (at municipal or provincial levels) have functioned, historically, as vehicles for leadership, and even political parties, against party politics. The limited demands of formal prerequisites have permitted the subnational realms to be more prone to create parties that position themselves on the margins of politics, employing a discourse that is critical of current party leaderships.

The emergence of neoconservative provincial and municipal parties underscores the significance of *the local* as the appropriate arena for *the political*. Indeed, this is one way in which a "pro-life" and "pro-family" agenda is *partidized*. An example of this is Partido Encuentro Vecinal Córdoba (Party Neighborhood Encounter Córdoba), formed in 2011. Per the party's information, it "began as a group of Cordobese citizens disconnected from any sort of political activity who decided to become involved in politics so as to change it" (Encuentro Vecinal n.d., n.p.). The party's members and main promoters happen to also belong to the NGO Portal de Belén, one of the most active "pro-life" movement organizations in Argentina. Among the party's stated priorities are the following: "the dignity of every human being, from the beginning of their life until their natural death," "the fostering of marriage between a man and a woman," and "the tutelage of parents' right and obligation to educating their children in accordance with their convictions" (Encuentro Vecinal n.d., n.p.). In this party's legislative work, the centrality of abortion opposition is quickly evidenced, together with the aim to re-moralize politics. This conservative positioning also surfaced up, for example, on International Women's Day with a manifesto, in which the party celebrates

> fecundity, which, in some of us [women], is evidenced through our children, but which goes beyond, and its importance also transcends, biological motherhood. Instead, fecundity is expressed in our capacity to give, embrace, listen and find ourselves in our neighbor.
>
> *(Encuentro Vecinal 2018, n.p.)*

In this same text, there is a warning about the "difficult moments we are going through in our country, where, in the midst of great social and economic problems, an ideological colonization is in full swing, attacking us where it hurts us the most: the life of the weakest." This party has become stronger: in 2015, it won a new seat when competing at the provincial legislative elections and in 2019, party member Aurelio García Elorrio ran for governor.

Another, more recent, example is the creation of the party called Partido Celeste (Light Blue Party), which reportedly "strengthens and promotes the defense of the first human right, as it is the right to life" (*La Nación* 2018, n.p.). The emergence of this party is the direct consequence of the 2018 parliamentary debate about abortion legalization in Argentina. The party's very name explicitly refers to the color that identified "pro-life" sectors during the debate. It was a color chosen in reaction to the green kerchiefs that were popularized by the National Campaign for the Right to Legal, Safe, and Free Abortion, then worn by anyone supporting abortion rights. It was also another "pro-life" organization, Fundación Más Vida (More Life Foundation), the one that endorsed the creation of Partido Celeste. According to Raul Magnasco, president of the foundation, the decision to form the party was in line with what "people had been demanding for some time, above all, after the result that the voting of the bill obtained in the lower house of Congress, i.e. to have a pro-life party that represents those Argentineans who are in favor of both lives" (in De Sousa 2018, n.p.). Magnasco characterizes the party as non-confessional, given that "we have religious, atheist and Jewish voluntary workers, while there is also a Muslim woman and we used to have an Umbanda woman volunteering for 'Más Vida'" (in De Sousa 2018, n.p.).

Besides defending a neoconservative moral agenda, Partido Celeste also proposes an economic liberalization of the market and the reduction of the state apparatus, of taxes, and of subsidies for vulnerable sectors. The model aims to attain fiscal surplus and thus the country's ability to reject "loans from international organisms that demand antinatalism and abortion policies" (Partido Celeste n.d., n.p.). The argument is noteworthy due to the relationship it establishes between financial institutions and abortion policies, and because free market policies tend to be associated with external debt that permits the affordance of public works and policies in the long run. The party's rhetoric includes a national sovereignty logic for a state capable of sustainable fiscal balance, which would help avoid taking out international loans from institutions supporting abortion.

The Chilean case differs from the Argentinean one on this matter. In Chile, there are no parties that originate directly from "pro-life" activism, such as Partido Celeste. There are at least two factors that may help explain this difference. On the one hand, up until 2015, Chilean parliamentary elections were based on a binominal electoral system, which promoted the formation of only two large opposite political coalitions, discouraging, therefore, the existence of vehemently opposing views in Congress (every electoral project was forced to strike up alliances, which, in turn, promoted negotiation spaces among allied parties). Thus, an eventual pro-life party would have been obliged to compromise with traditional parties, given that competing as a third choice would have drastically reduced the possibilities for this third option to get a parliamentary seat. Parties that are set up around a non-negotiable agenda, such as the "pro-life" project, do not have any leeway to accept less than what they want on certain topics, which in practice is a disincentive to create and sustain them.

On the other hand, with the return of democracy, initiatives connected to sexual and reproductive rights tended to be checked, and on many occasions outright rejected, by the actual vetoing function performed by the Catholic Church in Chile (Htun 2003). In addition, the neoconservative agenda was fervently supported by the traditional right, together with hundreds of other sectors within Christian Democracy, which meant that there was no need to create "pro-life" parties. Neoconservative activism, more than forming a party of its own, tended to associate itself with those parties able to channel its demands successfully. Now, with the reconfiguration of the electoral system, and after a series of battles that the conservative realm has lost lately, such as the one connected to abortion decriminalization on three grounds or to the gender identity law, the question that emerges is whether or not "pro-life" activism will decide to embark itself on its own electoral adventure or, in contrast, if it will continue channeling its demands through its joint work with right-wing parties and certain Christian Democracy spaces.

Conclusions

Although the influence of the conservative moral agenda upon political leaders is not new, the radical reaction against sexual and reproductive rights has given way to new alliances and, thus, new impacts on the political system. For analytical purposes, we have laid out three neoconservative *partidization* processes in Argentina and Chile. First, we focused on confessional parties, particularly Christian Democracy and its different track records in each country. In Argentina, the Christian Democratic party is a minority party that advocates for the defense of life from conception as it searches for support of sectors of society identified with Catholicism, which consider abortion a crime and a sin. In Chile, in contrast, Christian Democracy evidences a broad array of positions on abortion, which is indispensable for a majority party that encompasses a much more important constituency.

Second, we focused on right-wing political parties that continue to be one of the main channels for the defense of a conservative sexual morality. In both countries, we see new right-wing leaders and parties, for whom the defense of life from conception is a fundamental pillar of their electoral platforms. Neoconservatism provides a new agenda, leaders, and constituencies for right-wing political initiatives. In the third place, we have identified the incipient development of leaders and parties that directly represent the pro-life movement. Thus, this movement exceeds civil society and enters into the realm of party politics seeking support from the sectors most fiercely opposed to abortion. Although uncommon, this type of initiative can be seen as a single-issue party with strong affinities with the previous two.

Finally, we would like to underscore two key aspects of this *partidization* process. On the one hand, this process permits to explicitly outline the way in which neoconservatism and neoliberalism are entwined together. The mobilization against a "gender ideology," inasmuch as this category is an empty signifier, is susceptible to being appropriated from diverse ideological positions. However, an affinity with neoliberalism seems to mark the main political party initiatives. In particular, right-wing parties and some leaderships and "pro-life" parties find in the defense of family and freedom a legal realm in which a conservative sexual morality and a neoliberal economic project converge. As has been found in other contexts, the resonances between neoliberalism and neoconservatism, between an economic rationality and a moral rationality (Brown 2006, 2019; Acar and Altunok 2013; Cooper 2017), are also apparent in Latin America.

On the other hand, another significant aspect of this process is the presence of *the religious* as an integral part of neoconservative *partidization*. *The religious* emerges, in more or less explicit ways, as a feature that characterizes the three types of parties outlined. The fight against the "gender ideology" constitutes common ground for alliances among different sectors that consider that both specific Christian values and also society's very foundations are in danger. Neoconservative incursions into party politics enhance, then, the impact that religious beliefs, morality, and institutions exert on contemporary societies. Yet they exert this influence in innovative ways, opening new analytical and normative challenges.

Notes

1 Lesbian, gay, bisexual, transgender, and intersex.
2 Organizations such as Movimento em Defesa da Vida (Movement in Defense of Life) in Brazil (1978), Ceprofarena in Peru (1981), ProFamilia (Pro-Family) in Argentina (1983), and Movimiento Anónimo por la Vida (Anonymous Movement for Life) in Chile (1985), were formed in close connection to Human Life International.
3 For a detailed analysis of this process, known as Agenda Europe, see Datta (2018).
4 The fight for divorce is an example from the 20th century.
5 One of the most influential works in this sense is Márquez and Laje (2016).
6 Such as economic or military networks (Cannon 2016).
7 This is a Catholic celebration that commemorates the annunciation to the Virgin Mary that she would become pregnant with Jesus Christ.
8 Cause lawyering is used both by the neoconservative movement and the abortion rights movement (see Borland, this volume).
9 Bill 3610/2018, Peru.

References

Acar, Faride, and Gülbanu Altunok. 2013. "The 'Politics of Intimate' at the Intersection of Neo-Liberalism and Neo-Conservatism in Contemporary Turkey." *Women's Studies International Forum* 41(1): 14–23.
Acción Republicana. n.d. "Nuestros principios e identidad," Santiago. www.accionrepublicana.cl/principios/.
Aguayo, David. 2017. "Carolina Goic por aborto: 'No es un tema para evaluar el voto con la calculadora.'" *La Tercera*, May 20. www.latercera.com/noticia/carolina-goic-aborto-no-tema-evaluar-voto-la-calculadora/.
AICA. 2018. "La Democracia Cristiana rechazó toda iniciativa que favorezca el aborto," March 2. www.aica.org/32529-la-democracia-cristiana-rechazo-toda-iniciativa-que-favorezca-el-aborto.html.
Almeyda, Clodomiro. 1986. "La democracia cristiana en América Latina." *Nueva Sociedad* 82: 139–149.
Angulo, Martín. 2019. "Debate por el aborto: Impugnaron a un partido político que lleva la imagen de un feto en su boleta." *Infobae*, July 3. www.infobae.com/politica/2019/07/03/debate-por-el-aborto-impugnaron-a-un-partido-politico-que-lleva-la-imagen-de-un-feto-en-su-boleta/.
Araujo, Kathya. 2010. "Sobre ruidos y nueces: Debates chilenos en torno a la sexualidad." In *El activismo religioso conservador en Latinoamérica*, ed. Juan Marco Vaggione, 77–108. Córdoba: Ferreyra Editor.
Brown, Wendy. 2006. "American Nightmare: Neoconservatism, Neoliberalism, and De-Democratization." *Political Theory* 34(6): 690–714.
Brown, Wendy. 2019. *In the Ruins of Neoliberalism: The Rise of Antidemocratic Politics in the West*. New York: Columbia University Press.

Brügge, Juan. 2018. "Juan Brügge: El proyecto de legalización del aborto va contra la construcción nacional." *YouTube*, June 14. www.youtube.com/watch?v=YeWU8wtpu8w.

Cannon, Barry. 2016. *The Right in Latin America: Elite Power, Hegemony and the Struggle for the State*. New York: Routledge.

Carbonelli, Marcos. 2018. "Political Parties and Churches in Argentina: Intersections in Quicksand." *Politics and Religion Journal* 12 (1): 75–97.

Cariboni, Diana. 2019. "El género es el nuevo demonio." *Perfil*, February 1. https://noticias.perfil.com/noticias/general/2019-02-01-el-genero-es-el-nuevo-demonio.phtml.

Chilecristiano.com. n.d. "Evangélicos en acción, un movimiento político." http://chilecristiano.cl/index.php/noticias/447-evangelicos-fundan-movimiento-politico.

Cooper, Melinda. 2017. *Family Values: Between Neoliberalism and the New Social Conservatism*. New York: Zone Books.

Datta, Neil. 2018. *"Restoring the Natural Order": The Religious Extremists' Vision to Mobilize European Societies Against Human Rights on Sexuality and Reproduction*. Brussels: European Parliamentary Forum on Population & Development.

De Sousa, Florencia. 2018. "Lanzaron el Partido Celeste para 'erradicar el flagelo social del aborto.'" *Perfil*, August 29. www.perfil.com/noticias/politica/lanzaron-el-partido-celeste-el-cual-se-opone-a-la-legalizacion-del-aborto.phtml.

Di Stefano, Roberto, and Loris Zanatta. 2000. *Historia de la iglesia argentina. Desde la conquista hasta fines del siglo XX*. Buenos Aires: Grijalbo Mondadori.

Encuentro Vecinal. 2018. "Jornadas de encuentro y formación política 2018." https://evcba.com.ar/2018/02/26/jornadas-de-encuentro-y-formacion-politica-2018/.

Encuentro Vecinal. n.d. "Principios." https://evcba.com.ar/principios/.

Excelsior. 2015. "Los partidos políticos católicos no son el camino, asegura el Papa," April 30. www.excelsior.com.mx/global/2015/04/30/1021658.

Frente NOS. n.d. "Política económica." www.afiliatenos.com.ar/plataforma/#Politica-economica.

Garbagnoli, Sara. 2016. "Against the Heresy of Immanence: Vatican's 'Gender' as a New Rhetorical Device Against the Denaturalization of the Sexual Order." *Religion and Gender* 6(2): 187–204.

Graff, Agnieszka. 2016. "'Gender Ideology': Weak Concepts, Powerful Politics." *Religion and Gender* 6(2): 268–272.

Grzebalska, Weronika, and Andrea Pető. 2018. "The Gendered Modus Operandi of the Illiberal Transformation in Hungary and Poland." *Women's Studies International Forum* 68: 164–172.

Htun, Mala. 2003. *Sex and the State: Abortion, Divorce, and the Family Under Latin American Dictatorships and Democracies*. Cambridge: Cambridge University Press.

Kast, José Antonio. 2017. "Intervención de José Antonio Kast en votación sobre el aborto." *YouTube*, July 20. www.youtube.com/watch?v=3wVG4Lk12Ys.

Kast, José Antonio. 2019. "José Antonio Kast—Cumbre Transatlántica Colombia 2019 (05.04.2019)." *YouTube*, April 5. www.youtube.com/watch?v=Gu7wpZ20JNk&t=479s.

Korolczuk, Elżbieta, and Agnieszka Graff. 2018 "Gender as 'Ebola from Brussels': The Anticolonial Frame and the Rise of Illiberal Populism." *Signs: Journal of Women in Culture and Society* 43(4): 797–821.

Kováts, Eszter, and Maari Põim. 2015. *Gender as Symbolic Glue. The Position and Role of Conservative and Far Right Parties in the Anti-gender Mobilizations in Europe*. Brussels: Foundation for European Progressive Studies and Friedrich-Ebert-Stiftung.

Kuhar, Roman, and Aleš Zobec. 2017. "The Anti-Gender Movement in Europe and the Educational Process in Public Schools." *Center for Educational Policy Studies Journal* 7(2): 29–46.

Laclau, Ernesto. 2005. *On Populist Reason*. London: Verso.

La Nación. 2018. "Aborto: Tras el rechazo en el Senado, los 'provida' lanzaron un partido político," August 28. www.lanacion.com.ar/politica/aborto-rechazo-senado-provida-lanzaron-partido-politico-nid2166476.

Machado, Maria das Dores Campos. 2018. "Religion and Moral Conservatism in Brazilian Politics." *Politics and Religion Journal* 12(1): 55–77.

Mansilla, Miguel Ángel, and Luis Orellana. 2015. "Participaciones activas y pasivas de los evangélicos en los espacios públicos y políticos en Chile entre 1973 y 1999." *Revista Estudios Sociales* 51: 146–159.

Mansilla, Miguel Ángel, Luis Orellana Urtubia, and Nicolás Panotto. 2019. "La participación política de los evangélicos en Chile (1999–2017)." *Revista Rupturas* 9(1): 179–208.

Márquez, Nicolás, and Agustín Laje. 2016. *El libro negro de la nueva izquierda. Ideología de género o subversión cultural*. Buenos Aires: Grupo Unión.

Matamala Vivaldi, María Isabel. 2011. "La iglesia vaticana y su poder en Chile, a pesar de los crímenes." In *Miradas y reflexiones feministas. Sebastián Piñera, año uno: Conmociones y exigencias sociales*, ed. Carmen Torres Escudero, 43–74. Santiago de Chile: Fundación Instituto de la Mujer.

Mayer, Stefanie, and Birgit Sauer. 2017. "'Gender Ideology' in Austria: Coalitions Around an Empty Signifier." In *Anti-Gender Campaigns in Europe. Mobilizing Against Equality*, eds. Roman Kuhar and David Paternotte, 23–40. New York: Rowman & Littlefield.

Monte, María Eugenia, and Juan Marco Vaggione. 2018. "Cortes irrumpidas. La judicialización conservadora del aborto en Argentina." *Revista Rupturas* 9(1): 107–125.

Morán Faúndes, José Manuel. 2017. *De vida o muerte. Patriarcado, heteronormatividad y el discurso de la vida del activismo "Pro-Vida" en la Argentina*. Córdoba: Editorial del Centro de Estudios Avanzados.

Morán Faúndes, José Manuel. 2019. "The Geopolitics of Moral Panic: The Influence of Argentinian Neo-Conservatism in the Genesis of the Discourse of 'Gender Ideology.'" *International Sociology* 34(4): 402–417.

Morán Faúndes, José Manuel, and María Angélica Peñas Defago. 2016. "The Strategies of the Self-Proclaimed Pro-Life Groups in Argentina. The Impact of New Religious Actors on Sexual Politics." *Latin American Perspectives* 43(3): 144–162.

Morán Faúndes, José Manuel, María Angélica Peñas Defago, María Candelaria Sgró Ruata, and Juan Marco Vaggione. 2019. "La resistencia a los derechos sexuales y reproductivos. Las principales dimensiones del neo-activismo conservador argentino." In *Sexualidad, religión y democracia en América Latina*, ed. Gloria Careaga, 53–94. Mexico: Fundación Arcoíris.

Mouffe, Chantal. 2009. *En torno a lo político*. Buenos Aires: Fondo de Cultura Económica.

Partido Celeste. n.d. "Propuestas del partido." www.partidoceleste.org/partido-celeste/.

Partido Republicano. n.d. "Conócenos." https://partidorepublicanodechile.cl/partido-republicano/nosotros-partido-republicano/.

Paternotte, David. 2015. "Blessing the Crowds: Catholic Mobilisations Against Gender in Europe." In *Anti-Genderismus. Sexualität und Geschlecht als Schauplätze aktueller politischer Auseinandersetzungen*, eds. Sabine Hark and Paula Irene Villa, 129–148. Bielefeld: Transcript Verlag.

Peñas Defago, María Angélica. 2019. "Jóvenes, vida y conciencias tutelados/as. Principales discursos legales de la oposición católica a las leyes de salud sexual y reproductiva y matrimonio igualitario en Argentina." *Sociedad y Religión* 29(51): 11–36.

Peñas Defago, María Angélica, and Juan Marco Vaggione. 2011. *Actores y discursos conservadores en los debates sobre sexualidad y reproducción en Argentina*. Córdoba: Ferreyra Editor.

Prieto, Sol. 2014. "El desempeño de los partidos confesionales católicos en Argentina: Una revisión crítica." *Religião & Sociedade* 34(2): 114–138.

Renacer. n.d. "Nuestras Bases." www.renacerfederal.org/nuestras-bases/.

Sgró Ruata, María Candelaria, Hugo H. Rabbia, Tomás Iosa, Mariana Manzo, Maximiliano Campana, and José Manuel Morán Faúndes. 2011. *El debate sobre matrimonio igualitario en Córdoba. Actores, estrategias y discursos.* Córdoba: Ferreyra Editor.

United Nations. 1989. *Convention on the Rights of the Child.* New York: United Nations.

Vaggione, Juan Marco. 2005. "Reactive Politicization and Religious Dissidence: The Political Mutations of the Religious." *Social Theory and Practice* 31(2): 233–255.

Vaggione, Juan Marco. 2017. "La Iglesia Católica frente a la política sexual: La configuración de una ciudadanía religiosa." *Cadernos Pagu* 50: e175002.

Vaggione, Juan Marco. 2019. "The Conservative Uses of Law: The Catholic Mobilization Against Gender Ideology." *Social Compass* 67(2): 252–266.

Villazón, Júlio Córdova. 2015. "Velhas e Novas direitas religiosas na América Latina." In *Direita Volver!*, ed. Sebastião Velasco e Cruz, 163–175. São Paulo: Fundação Perseu Abramo.

PART II
Uruguay

6

"PUSH AND PULL"

The Rocky Road to the Legalization of Abortion in Uruguay

Alejandra López-Gómez, Martín Couto, and Lucía Berro Pizzarossa

Introduction

Uruguay's development of a "human rights agenda" has been closely followed and monitored by regional and international human rights systems, non-governmental organizations working on human rights, and gender equality and academic institutions of significant stature. Indeed, our small country managed to advance and legally protect—not without contradictions and controversies—human rights related to sexuality, reproduction, and gender equality. These advances are framed within a wider agenda responding to the needs and demands of recognition, wellbeing, and social inclusion by historically marginalized communities.

From 1938 to 2012, abortion was criminalized by Law No. 9763. After many years of social and political debates, Uruguay placed itself as one of the first South American countries to legalize voluntary abortion on demand and implement services in the National Health System with the adoption of Law No. 18.987 in 2012 (Diario Oficial 2012) (hereinafter abortion law). This law comes to complement Law No. 18.426 (Diario Oficial 2008a), which recognizes sexual and reproductive rights as human rights, with the state as responsible for their protection and fulfillment.

These achievements in the human rights agenda must be understood in the context of the social and economic transformations that Uruguay underwent particularly in the post-dictatorship period (since 1985), geared toward furthering democracy and citizen participation. The recognition of women's right to voluntary termination of pregnancy is part of this broader process. As such, the Uruguayan case is of particular importance not only for the country itself, but for Latin America and other countries around the globe.

This chapter critically examines the process of social and political discussion that led to the legalization of abortion in Uruguay, the lights and shadows in the implementation of the new law, and the lessons that can be drawn from this experience. We

DOI: 10.4324/9781003079903-8

take into account the country's political culture regarding how conflicts are dealt in the Uruguayan public opinion and political party system as well as the role of the different actors who participated in the construction of the agenda, noting the arguments and administrative mechanisms that the opposition groups put in place.

To develop the chapter's arguments, we draw on the accumulated body of research about the process of abortion decriminalization in Uruguay and the implementation of the law in force. We have updated the review of scientific and popular articles published between 2012 and 2020. To this end, we consulted official government sources, refereed scientific journal databases, websites of feminist and other social organizations at the national level, academic databases of master's and doctoral theses, public opinion surveys of recognized quality, and data from empirical studies we have conducted in recent years. The chapter includes a critical description of the discursive turns, actors, and milestones in the process leading to the adoption of the abortion law, which can be understood as a "push and pull"—in the words of Uruguayan historian Carlos Real de Azúa (1964). Based on the text of the law and its implementation, we then discuss how this push and pull—characteristic of Uruguay's democratic conversations—coexist in the current system.

A central goal in this chapter is to understand how the decriminalization of abortion first appeared as a demand of the feminist movement to later turn, since the beginning of the new millennium, into a wider citizen demand driven by diverse actors and framed in connection to democracy. This shift from feminist demand to citizens' demand (Abracinskas and López Gómez 2006) is one of the keys to understanding the complex process of building a political agenda in defense of sexual and reproductive rights, with strong social support, which took place early on relative to other countries in the region.

This process can be traced back to 1985 after the culmination of the civil-military dictatorship that took place between 1973 and 1985. It intensified towards the early 2000s, with unique characteristics resulting from the alliances between social, academic, trade union, political, and religious actors as well as the development of a strategy of social involvement in the debate, led by the country's feminist organizations.

The argumentative construction of women's right to abortion as a matter of democracy, equity, and social justice, a public health issue, and a central axis of human rights, was the result of a coalition of actors who united forces to sustain the debate and promote relevant normative and social transformations in this regard. November 2020 marks the eighth anniversary of the adoption of the Voluntary Interruption of Pregnancy Act. This chapter will analyze the "push and pull" process of its adoption, the possibilities and limitations of this instrument, and the main barriers to its implementation.

After 15 years of government by the Frente Amplio (Broad Front, a coalition of left-wing and center-left parties), a new political era has begun in Uruguay. In this new national and global scenario, it is difficult to predict what will happen to the country's human rights agenda. However, some current developments allow us to try out hypothetical scenarios. In March 2020, a new coalition of right and center-right parties (Coalition for Change) took office for the period 2020–25. This happened just a few days before the global pandemic of COVID-19 landed its first case in the country. The emergency created by this new global health scenario—and its consequences at the social and economic level—has generated substantial changes in people's lives, exposing and worsening preexisting social inequalities and generating uncertainty about the future.

The authors of this chapter have been direct participants in the development and consolidation of a research agenda on abortion, and have actively contributed to the recognition and guarantee of sexual and reproductive rights in Uruguay, whether in the academic, social, and/or parliamentary spheres. We feel that we are protagonists of this collective history and that we bear responsibility for its future. The writing of these pages is part of our commitment to women's historic struggle to be recognized as full subjects of rights and fundamental actors in the democratic life of our countries.

Abortion Rights in the Public Agenda

The public demand for the right to decide can be reconstructed in Uruguay considering it intimately linked to the strengthening of democratic life, in at least two ways. First, the right to abortion was constructed as a public issue, which accounts for a specific process of broad social debate that led to this definition. Second, the right to abortion was raised as a crucial matter for the life of Uruguayan women as members of the body politic. In this section we present a sociohistorical analysis of the construction of abortion as a public concern, organized in three periods: (1) from 1985 to 2000, (2) from 2001 to 2012, and (3) from 2013 to 2020.

1985–2000: The Abortion Debate Enters the Public Sphere

The beginning of this period is marked by the transition to democracy in Uruguay after 12 years of dictatorship. During this period, political parties and social organizations (particularly the trade union center and student movements) were harshly targeted and persecuted—although they managed to maintain a continuous clandestine activity—so they were forced to reduce their expression and activities. The democratic restoration allowed for the return of social movements to action in the public sphere, now freely and without state repression. However, two more movements joined the historical and powerful movements of workers and students: the movement for cooperative housing and the feminist movement. They had an important role in the dictatorship's exit and the democratic discussion that followed.

As for the agenda for the decriminalization of abortion, the first task of the feminist organizations was to make it an element of debate in the public sphere. The law in force since 1938—which considered abortion a crime in all circumstances, except for extenuating and exempting reasons—had not been applied to either prosecute the crime of abortion or to enable legal abortions under the permitted grounds (Abracinskas and López Gómez 2008; Baltar da Rocha, Rostagnol, and Gutiérrez 2009). Thus, abortion was seen as a matter belonging to the private sphere, with little respect for public opinion, but with objective possibilities of being prosecuted: a clandestine phenomenon.

According to Roger Cobb and Charles Elder (1986, 33), in reference to the process of formulation of political demands, "demands are generated from needs, through a process of politicization." At the beginning of the period studied here, feminists managed to politicize a "personal" or private matter, gradually positioning it in the public arena and as a matter of importance to public opinion. The great challenge was to influence the social debate and develop effective communication and awareness strategies to position public opinion in favor of the decriminalization of abortion in the country.

Elisabeth Noelle-Neumann points out that there are two ways of defining public opinion: while one is to understand it as "a rationality that contributes to the process of opinion formation and decision-making in a democracy," the other way is to conceive of it as form of "social control" (Noelle-Neumann 1995, 280). In developing the second definition, she states that

> public opinion as social control seeks to ensure a sufficient level of social consensus on common values and objectives. According to this concept, the power of public opinion is so great that neither the government nor individual members of society can ignore it. This power comes from the threat of isolation that society directs against deviant individuals and governments, and from the fear of isolation due to the social nature of [hu]mankind.
>
> *(Noelle-Neumann 1995, 289)*

But how do issues enter public opinion? How do majorities, minorities, and exclusions arise? According to the author, the fear of social isolation generates successive spirals of silence by which a position, because it is a majority one, will be adopted by more and more people (and conversely a minority position will lose support). Likewise, those positions that do not find a minimum of support in public opinion will be discarded, being considered taboo. Thus, the inclusion of abortion in the public debate must be understood, first of all, as a successful operation to avoid it being considered as taboo.

It was during this period that public opinion gradually turned to a position in favor of decriminalization. Analyzing Uruguayan's public opinion, Oscar Bottinelli (2010, 17) notes that "support for the decriminalization of abortion has oscillated in a decade and a half (from 1993 to 2008) in a range of 55 to 63 percent, with a maximum in 2003 and a minimum in 1993." The author adds that the measurements show a great stability of opinions and also a very high percentage of people who have an opinion on the matter, "which has oscillated between 88% and 94%" (Bottinelli 2010, 17). On the basis of the evidence available on public opinion during this period, the majority of the population was in favor of decriminalization (55 percent) and the percentage against was significantly lower (38 percent), although not negligible. Only a very small sector of the population stated that they had no position on the subject (7 percent).

As for the legislative expression of the debate, bills to decriminalize abortion were introduced in all legislatures from 1985 to the approval of the current abortion law (Johnson 2011; López Gómez 2014).[1] However, in the period between 1985 and 2000, no bill was passed by either legislative chamber, and all drafts were tabled by the advisory committees of these bodies.[2] Thus, in these first 15 years, public support for legal reform did not have a reasonable correspondence in the behavior of political parties within the Legislative branch (Selios 2007).

It should be emphasized that during the 1990s two international policy milestones took place, which cemented the demand for the decriminalization of abortion as a central human rights issue, particularly as a matter of sexual and reproductive health and rights. We refer to the United Nations Conference on Population and Development in 1994 (Cairo) and the Fourth World Conference on Women in 1995 (Beijing). These events had a direct effect on the country's public policies, when in 1996 sexual and reproductive health programs and services began to be implemented at the departmental level in Montevideo (the country's capital) and shortly afterwards, at the national level.

2001–12: The Right to Abortion as a Social Demand for a Stronger Democracy

This period is characterized in its beginnings by two relevant dimensions. The first is linked to the occurrence of clandestine abortions. The second concerns the definition of the public issue and the consolidation of a broad social and political alliance in favor of decriminalization.

During 2001, Uruguay suffered a grave economic crisis with extremely serious social consequences. This was compounded by the increase in women's deaths from unsafe abortion as the main isolated cause of maternal mortality (Briozzo 2003; Abracinskas and López Gómez 2006). As a result of this public health problem, an initiative against unsafe abortion was created, which promoted pre- and post-abortion counseling as an obligation of the health system, without legal consequences for the women who consult it, which was adopted as a health policy in 2004 by the Ministry of Public Health (Ministerio de Salud Pública 2004). The medical sector that promoted this initiative entered the scene of political debate as a relevant actor due to its legitimacy and influence in Uruguayan society.

The reports of the increase in maternal deaths in 2001 can be regarded as an event of such force that it catapulted the matter of abortion further into the public debate agenda. As Elder and Cobb (1993, 100) put it when discussing the formation of the public agenda, "a dramatic event, or a whole combination of circumstances, can have the effect of powerfully raising attention to the problem."

In this scenario, the social mobilization gains more strength, as new voices are added: the pronouncement of the Sindicato Médico del Uruguay (Medical Union of Uruguay) and the Universidad de la República (University of the Republic, Udelar) through its highest governing body. As a result of this new social impulse, the National Coordination for the Defense of Reproductive Health was established in 2003, bringing together feminist, union, religious, human rights, health professional, sexual diversity, and youth organizations. This milestone reflects the expansion of the historical subject that sustains the demand to be installed as a social and citizen demand. This was accompanied by increasing media attention, which amplified the discussion on the matter.

The manner in which an issue is presented and defined is as important as its inclusion in the public agenda. This definition should be seen as a social process by which some features are highlighted and others are ignored, with the result that the public demand or problem is on the agenda (Elder and Cobb 1993). By way of example, abortion could be defined as a rights or public health matter but also as an economic or a legal one. The ways in which it is defined is part of the dispute in the public sphere, and conditions the possibility of success of the demand.

In the case of Uruguay, the matter of abortion was defined, with greater force at the beginning of the 21st century, as a matter linked to the quality of democracy and the exercise of citizenship. Consequently, the platform in favor of the legal change denounced that the penalty in force was a clear and concrete limitation to women's citizenship and a deficit in the quality of Uruguayan democracy. At that time, the defense of democracy was not exclusively related to the processing of the demand, but was strongly linked to its content. The symbols that accompanied the campaign of the coalition of organizations are an example of this: the orange hand with the slogan "vote in favor" began as a sticker and was transformed into posters, flyers, and other applications that were identified by the citizens and used in public events since 2004 (see Vacarezza, this volume). This symbol was later adopted by other feminist organizations in the region in their strategies to defend women's right to choose as a matter to be decided democratically. Furthermore, the main slogan used in this period to promote abortion law reform read, "It is a matter of rights. It is a matter of democracy."

During this period, legislative progress should be noted, although it was accompanied by reactions that slowed down the adoption of a new law. On the one hand, a bill legalizing abortion was passed by the House of Representatives for the first time in 2002. However, in 2004, the bill was rejected by the Senate and was therefore archived.

In 2005, the Frente Amplio party took over the national administration of the government for the first time. Tabaré Vázquez was elected president of the Republic and the new government had an absolute majority in both legislative chambers. Although in 2008 the Uruguayan parliament approved a Law in Defense of the Right to Sexual and Reproductive Health (a law that included the decriminalization of abortion), the president exercised his constitutional right to a partial veto, leaving the approved law without the articles referring to the decriminalization of abortion. The rationale used in the veto has been analyzed from different angles and perspectives, and it is interesting to observe the medical discursive record in the argumentative bases that sustained it (Banfi Vique et al. 2010). This political event generated controversy within the governing party and between the Executive and organized civil society. After decades of social mobilization and parliamentary approval, the presidential act of vetoing—based on personal convictions and ignoring the political position of the party and the social movements—prevented the state from recognizing women as full citizens. Paradoxically, from that moment on, the country had a law that recognized sexual and reproductive rights as human rights (Diario Oficial 2008a), but maintained the crime of abortion as defined since 1938 (Law No. 9.763, 1938).

In 2010, a new Executive Power and a new parliament took office, with the same characteristics of the previous period: the Frente Amplio obtained the majority in both chambers and the ownership of the Executive Power, and José Mujica was elected as president.

That year, Senator Monica Xavier presented a new bill containing the chapters vetoed by the previous president. The law was approved in the Senate, but the Frente Amplio could not secure the votes for its approval in the House of Representatives, so it had to resort to the vote of opposition members of parliament. As a result of the hard negotiations to obtain the necessary majorities, the law that was finally adopted was a watered-down version—it contained fewer guarantees for women and provided for greater state guardianship over women's decisions. The law was adopted in November 2012 (Diario Oficial 2012) and was quickly regulated by the Ministry of Public Health for implementation in January 2013 in the National Integrated Health System (Ministerio de Salud Pública 2012).

During this period, the social alliance in favor of the decriminalization of abortion was strengthened and included in a larger agenda, the so-called "new rights agenda," concerning matters of sexuality and gender identity as well as the use of cannabis. Three important laws were adopted during this period: Voluntary Interruption of Pregnancy, Marriage Equality, and Regulation of the Cannabis Market (Arocena and Aguiar 2017). These initiatives were accompanied by public policies for universal access to sexual and reproductive health services and sex education in the national education system.

The Voluntary Interruption of Pregnancy Law states that abortion can only take place in the National Integrated Health System and it is free for all users. The law sets a series of prescriptive requirements and conditions for access, and establishes a route through the health system that involves at least three consultations. In the first, the woman declares her willingness to have an abortion in front of a doctor; in the second, she must attend a consultation with a multidisciplinary team for counseling; and before the third consultation with a gynecologist—the abortion itself—there is a mandatory five-day waiting period in which the woman needs to "reflect" on the decision to be made. Other requirements, such as prior residence of one year in the country, as well as lax conscientious objection for professionals and ideological objection for institutions, are fundamental aspects that limit women's decisions and diminish the guarantees for the full exercise of sexual and reproductive rights. Waiving of criminal penalties apply to voluntary termination until 12 weeks of gestation and after that, until 14 weeks in the case of rape and without a time limit for cases of serious risk to the woman's health and life and fetal malformation incompatible with extra-uterine life. Any abortion that does not meet these requirements and takes place outside the health system or the procedure prescribed by the law is considered a crime.

2013–2020: Push and Pull in the Implementation of the Law

Since the 2012 abortion reform, women have increasingly used the services permitted by the law. According to official figures from the Ministry of Public

Health,[3] in 2019, the number of abortions performed in health services was 10,227, while in 2018 there were 10,373 abortions.[4] Table 6.1 summarizes the main official data available from 2013 to 2019.

With regards to age, between 2013 and 2019, women aged 20 and over who accessed abortion services accounted for between 82 percent and 87 percent of abortions in each year of the period. Abortions among women aged 15–19—for the same period—ranged from 13 percent to 17 percent. Finally, abortions of women under 15 years have ranged from 1.03 percent to 0.34 percent in the same period (see Table 6.2).

According to data from the Ministry of Public Health, the percentage of women who have desisted from the abortion process after consultation with the multidisciplinary team varies between 6 and 8 percent per year (Ministerio de Salud Pública 2018)[5] (see Table 6.3).

Although legal abortion services have been functioning—as the data on the use of these services show—several deficits remain, which are partly rooted in the political compromises associated with the law's political debate and approval process. Carlos Real de Azúa, an eminent Uruguayan historian, defined our society as a "buffer society" (1973). He observed that the Uruguayan political discussions tended to be of "consensus," and that the country managed to achieve a social and political system that "buffered" any strong hegemony. Analyzing the period of state reforms that commenced in the 20th century in Uruguay, he uses the metaphor of "push and pull" to explain how the more radical transformative impulses (push) were always followed by a significant backlash (pull) that resulted in middle-ground, consensus solutions (Real de Azúa 1964). Real de Azúa's conceptualization

TABLE 6.1 Absolute frequency of abortion per year and abortion rate per 1,000 women

	2013	2014	2015	2016	2017	2018	2019
Absolute frequency	7,171	8,537	9,362	9,719	9,830	10,373	10,227
Rate/1,000 m.	8.56	10.18	11.11	11.3	11.39	⋆	⋆
% growth	—	+20%	+9.6%	+3.8%	+1.1%	+5.5%	−1.5%

Source: Table prepared by the authors according to data released by the Ministry of Public Health.
⋆No official data was made available.

TABLE 6.2 Percentage of abortions according to age group

	2013	2014	2015	2016	2017	2018	2019
Under 15 years old	1.03	0.81	1	0.76	0.65	0.51	0.34
15 to 19	16.73	16.44	17.12	16.43	15.02	13.70	12.95
20 or more	82.23	82.75	81.87	82.81	84.33	85.70	86.71

Source: Table prepared by the authors according to data released by the Ministry of Public Health.

TABLE 6.3 Percentage of women who initiated but did not finish the abortion process

	2013	2014	2015	2016	2017
Abortion	94	92	94	94	94
Desist process	6	8	6	6	6

Source: Table prepared by the authors according to data released by the Ministry of Public Health.

★ No data was made available on this for 2018 and 2019

of the Uruguayan democratic debates is very useful to analyze the developments around abortion.

Indeed, throughout the long and complex process of liberalization of abortion, the pushes were rapidly faced by a pull. It is important to note that the democratic discussion of this abortion law did not end in 2012. Once the law was passed in parliament, the "pull" changed locus; the courts and ballots became the new sites of contestation of the legal advances. Since its adoption, the law has been the target of many legal and political challenges. In June 2013, anti-abortion advocates called a referendum to overturn the law. In the end, it fell significantly short of the percentage threshold needed to succeed (well below the 25 percent required for the referendum to even take place) (Coppola et al. 2016). Along similar lines, the regulatory decree of the law was challenged in July 2013 by several doctors arguing that it unduly restricted their right to freedom of thought. Doctors sought to have ten out of the 42 articles included in the decree annulled (hereinafter *Alonso et al. v. Poder Ejecutivo*). On August 21, 2015, the highest administrative court effectively annulled several (seven out of 42) of the provisions that limit the exercise of conscientious objection (Tribunal de lo Contencioso Administrativo 2015).

While the law was widely celebrated and it is a step towards the decriminalization of abortion, a closer look shows it may not be an ideal model in the eyes of women seeking an abortion. The law that was passed in 2012 itself represents a serious "pull" from the previous versions (i.e., the law that was adopted—and partially vetoed—in 2008 and the first draft bill that was submitted in 2010). The procedure set by the law requires multiple consultations with healthcare professionals and is far more restrictive than the earlier versions (López-Gómez et al. 2017; Stifani, Couto, and Lopez Gomez 2018). The complex democratic process outlined in the previous section and the tensions between the different frames and ideas continue to coexist in the implementation of the law. Thus, the "compromise" that this law represents translates into a complex model of access that liberalizes abortion (push) but poses a series of burdensome barriers to access the services (pull).

First of all, it is important to underline that abortion remains a crime under Uruguayan law; the criminal penalties are waived when the abortion is obtained according to the process/timelines/methods set in the law and after complying with an extensive list of requirements. The liberalization of access to abortion provided by the Uruguayan abortion law actually reflects not a decriminalization of abortion, but an affirmation of abortion's illegality—except in certain circumstances. During the parliamentary debates that preceded the law, feminist organizations criticized this transactional solution—product of the "push and pull" noted by Real de Azúa—highlighting the burdensome requirements and barriers set by the law. For some of the actors involved in the parliamentary discussion, this legislative amendment brought no real change, as the voluntary termination of pregnancy continues to fall within the realm of penal law (Johnson, Rocha, and Schenck 2013). Furthermore, the mainstream discourse used to promote the law relied heavily on a "public health" narrative. This has proven very powerful in the Uruguayan context as an instrument to regulate societal issues and undoubtedly was more politically palatable and convincing (Wood et al. 2016). However, this professional, medical management of social problems translates into a model of access in which reproductive autonomy is heavily regulated and medicalized (Berro Pizzarossa 2019). The over-medicalization of abortion effectively hinders access to legal abortion services, undermines women's agency, and, at its most extreme, continues to put women's lives at risk by forcing them to resort to clandestine abortions (CEDAW 2016). This legislative model, which continues to regulate abortion as both a criminal matter and an overly medicalized procedure, feeds stigma and obstructs safe, legal, and accessible abortion care (WHO 2011). In that sense, feminists have played a crucial role confronting medical power, making visible its strategies and corporate interests, and questioning an authoritarian medical habitus that restricts and/or inhibits the exercise of women's health rights (López Gómez 2018).

The Costs of the Democratic Compromise in the Implementation of the Law

Using four features of democratic systems, this section will enquire whether this law—and the model proposed by it—further contributes to full citizenship and democracy for women.

Freedom of Belief: "Conscientious Objection" or "Conscious Oppression"[6]

The scope of conscientious objection is regulated generally by Law No. 18.987, and in more detail by the adjusted version of Decree 375/2012 following *Alonso et al. v. Poder Ejecutivo* (Tribunal de lo Contencioso Administrativo 2015). However, limits to its exercise, accountability mechanisms, and measures to ensure the effective provision of the services were not included in the law.

The law recognizes an explicit right to "conscientious objection"—otherwise unregulated for other areas of medicine or else—and also a collective right of "ideological objection" enabling private health institutions to invoke an institutional objection and abstain from providing abortion services altogether (Cabal, Arango Olaya, and Montoya Robledo 2014). The second was criticized given that freedom of belief—underpinning the right to refuse to perform abortions—belongs to individuals and hardly can be considered a right for institutions (even less medical legal entities) (Adriasola 2013).

Some measures were regulated by the regulatory decree but most of them were stricken down by the court. As mentioned above, the regulatory decree was challenged before the administrative court and its ruling annulled many of the limitations to the exercise of conscientious objection. Among others, it annulled Article 12 that required physicians to avoid value judgments regarding the patient's decision to terminate her pregnancy, and mandated that no further inquiry into the reasons ought therefore to be carried out. Moreover, the decision in *Alonso et al. v. Poder Ejecutivo* enables doctors to refuse participation in any of the steps relating to the termination of pregnancy (not only the abortion procedure), hindering access to pre-abortion and post-abortion care (Tribunal de lo Contencioso Administrativo 2015). As a result of the sentence of the Administrative Court (No. 586/015 of August 11, 2015), the Ministry of Health had to make adjustments to the regulations of the law and the clinical guidelines. The resolutions No. 243 of April 22, 2016 (Ministerio de Salud Pública 2016) and No. 469 of May 23, 2017 establish the new technical guidelines for abortion services throughout the country (Ministerio de Salud Pública 2017).

Unsurprisingly, empirical evidence shows that conscientious objection is being used in an ad hoc, unregulated, and at times outright incorrect manner. It is used as a means to oppose abortion on very broad grounds—to the extent that some authors speak of a "civil disobedience" (Cabal, Arango Olaya, and Montoya Robledo 2014; International Women's Health Coalition and Mujer y Salud en Uruguay 2018)—resisting the application of the law. Objection, therefore, becomes an all-encompassing opportunity for non-participation in abortion services. In 2015, research showed that in some areas of the country up to 100 percent of medical service providers refuse to terminate pregnancies, making it virtually impossible to obtain timely access to services (MYSU 2015). In some regions with high numbers of objectors, respondents explained that women are required "to travel 200 or even 300 km just to get a prescription" for medical abortion (Fiol et al. 2016). Strictly speaking, opposing the law does not configure conscientious objection, and the Uruguayan situation merits further monitoring and accountability to ensure effective provision of the service.

Moreover, in July 2016, the Convention on the Elimination of all Forms of Discrimination Against Women (CEDAW) Committee considered the reports from Uruguay and noted its concern about the widespread use of conscientious objection among medical practitioners, "thereby limiting access to safe abortion services, which are guaranteed by law" (CEDAW 2016, 11/14). It recommended that the state takes active measures to ensure that women have access to legal abortion and post-abortion services, and "introduce[s] stricter justification requirements to prevent the blanket use by medical practitioners of their right to conscientious objection to performing an abortion" (CEDAW 2016, 12/14).

The solution proposed by the Ministry of Health follows the line of the "compromise/conciliation" nature of the parliamentary discussion in Uruguay. Access to abortion services is "ensured" by covering women's expenses when they need to travel to another location. However, its "conciliatory" model that is grounded on a strategy of referral increases the barriers to access. For example, media reported that some women travel 2,400 km to access abortion services (Barquet 2013). A provider's refusal to perform abortion services compounds the effects of the many barriers that women face in healthcare: discrimination, stigma, financial burdens, lack of information, transportation difficulties, and limited autonomy to make decisions about their own bodies.

A truly democratic debate would take into account the freedom of belief of the woman seeking services—that may include the right to select their providers of care accordingly—and would reframe the discussion as "refusal to provide services" or "denial of services based on conscience claims," which subverts the asymmetry of power that currently exists between doctors and patients.

Access to Public Information

Tied to abortion barriers is the lack of access to public information on services and providers, which seriously undermines this democratic pillar. First, the law itself stated that the Ministry of Health should set up a data collection system that allowed for the periodic evaluation of the law (Article 12). However, it is not clear to the users of the services or general population, what data is being collected and for which purpose. The Ministry of Health does not release disaggregated data and does not give citizens access to the dataset. The only information made publicly available is via a periodic PowerPoint presentation. Besides breaching the provisions of the law, this lack of transparency undermines the health of democracy. Citizens only have access to data as presented and interpreted by governmental entities, and citizens are presented with an "official" reading of the information. Thus, it is virtually impossible for civil society to monitor the implementation of the law, for academics to build knowledge on the topic, and for the state itself to monitor and evaluate its public policies on abortion.

Second, besides the lack of general data, the serious lack of transparency on particular issues hinders access to abortion services. There is no available information, for example, of the costs of the "referral system" set up for the cases of conscientious objection. Indeed, accommodating providers who refuse to perform essential aspects of their jobs could cause costly disruptions and inefficiencies in the healthcare system and divert precious resources away from service provision (Schuklenk and Smalling 2017). Moreover, there are no official registries of conscientious objectors. This mechanism would allow women to know beforehand if particular gynecologists refuse to perform abortions, therefore enabling informed decisions about their professional of choice. There were some initiatives—even within the Ministry of Health—but nothing has been implemented (Ministerio de Salud Pública 2016). Much more transparency is needed to understand the impact of the law and whose interests and needs it is actually serving.

Right to Quality Health (Care) and to Benefit from Scientific Progress

In terms of implementation, the investment in professional training and equipment for abortion has been very limited. The Ministry of Health in its "Technical Guide for the

Voluntary Termination of Pregnancy" stated a strong preference for medication abortion (Ministerio de Salud Pública 2012). Access to abortion medication (misoprostol and mifepristone) is provided exclusively within the National Integrated Health System and has no cost for women. Since the adoption of the law, around 98 percent of abortions were carried out with pills prescribed by the gynecologist and self-administered by women at home (Fiol et al. 2016). Surgical abortion is performed very rarely, and training for methods such as surgical abortion and manual or electric vacuum aspiration has not been made available (Fiol et al. 2016). This limitation reportedly appears to be a "practical, logistical, and political decision" (Stifani, Couto, and Lopez Gomez 2018) that had mostly to do with the health system and/or doctors themselves: medication abortion was easier to implement and as it requires minimal participation it could decrease the number of conscientious objectors. As reported by Stifani, Couto, and Lopez Gomez (2018, 47), a key stakeholder considered that "[t]here is a lot less conscientious objection to prescribing a termination than there is for performing a termination with instrumentation."

However, while medication abortion has undeniable advantages (WHO 2011), the limitation in range and availability of methods shows that the model was not built with women's needs and preferences at the center. Furthermore, it did not necessarily succeed in terms of the political acceptability of medication abortion, given the high numbers of objectors (Coppola et al. 2016). Additionally, research from the field shows how health professionals generally display paternalistic, disciplinary, or condemnatory attitudes towards women seeking abortion services (Labandera, Gorgoroso, and Briozzo 2016). Some even publicly declare their desire to show sonograms or speak to their patients about the "right to life" (Muñoz 2018).

It is also noteworthy that the model proposed by the law allows for a serious degree of violence that has not been addressed by the system. Recent data collected in the National Survey on Prevalence of Gender Based Violence shows that 54.4 percent of women experienced some kind of violence during the abortion process (Instituto Nacional de Estadística 2019).

Non-discrimination

Another legal barrier to abortion is the requirement set by Article 13 of the law. This provision permits access to abortion only to women of Uruguayan nationality, or who have resided permanently in the country for at least one year. In the discussions around this requirement, members of parliament considered—with virtually no opposition— that setting requirements of citizenship and/or permanent residency was appropriate. According to the transcript, this was aimed at preventing "abortion tourism."[7] The nationality/residency requirement, the parliamentarians argued, will prevent the creation of an image of Uruguay "as a country in which it is possible to obtain abortions." Abortion is singled out as an exceptional healthcare service, as no other services are subjected to these requirements (Diario Oficial 2008b). In terms of national standards, this prerequisite constitutes an exception to the guarantees provided by the Constitution and the law regulating the healthcare system, which applies to all "inhabitants" of the national territory (Diario Oficial 2008b).

Furthermore, by using the word "tourism," evoking images of ease and leisure, legis-lators obscured discriminatory dynamics preventing access to basic healthcare services, solely based on nationality or citizenship or even location within the Uruguayan territory. Singling out abortion as the only healthcare service that requires a particular nationality or period of residence contributes to the stigmatization of the procedure—hindering safe, legal, and accessible abortion care and services that are warranted to nationals. Some migrants gain access to abortion via the provisions of Article 7 of Law No. 19.580 that exempts migrant women from the requirements of citizenship/residence in cases when they are victims of domestic violence (the law does not require a criminal complaint).

While legal exceptions open up an avenue of access, we must acknowledge the symbolic power of a law that creates different categories of abortions and therefore different categories of women. Women experiencing violence are regarded by the law as morally and therefore legally deserving of protection. This regime deter-mines a "hierarchy of deservingness" (Aragón 2016), in which some reproductive decisions are valued and others are despised. While undoubtedly we must address gender-based violence, and in particular for women in vulnerable situations, must a woman be a victim of violence to be granted access to basic healthcare? This pro-vision continues to put migrant women in unequal conditions.

Final Reflections

Uruguay has made significant progress in gender equality policies and in the recogni-tion of sexual and reproductive rights. Latin America and Caribbean countries lauded the most progressive regional document 20 years after the International Conference on Population and Development (ICPD) Programme of Action, called the "Mon-tevideo Consensus" (CEPAL 2013). In recent years, however, the regional landscape, including Uruguay, has changed, with the growth of conservative movements. This situation generates a scenario of uncertainty regarding state guarantees of women's human rights, and sexual and reproductive rights specifically.

The broad coalition that developed an open and public strategy to promote and to defend the decriminalization of abortion in Uruguay faced a different opposition strategy. Conservatives opted for a silent and reticular strategy that focused parti-cularly on lobbying political elites, in building a social base in the towns and vil-lages far from the capital, and on the "evangelization" of the poorest.

During the national election campaign in November 2019, the main women lea-ders of the right and center-right coalition parties (Coalition for Change) made a public commitment to support the rights agenda. One of their spokeswomen pointed out that "women's rights and the rights agenda that has been approved will not go backwards. Our idea is to build on that" (Betancur 2019). Despite these encouraging words, the agreed consensus platform is limited and offers no guarantees.

The new president of the Republic, Dr. Luis Lacalle Pou (leader of Coalition for Change), publicly declared during a press conference on May 4, 2020—in the midst of the COVID-19 pandemic—that the government has a "pro-life" agenda. He also said that the current abortion law would not be amended, but abortions will be "discouraged" during his term (*Televisión Nacional de Uruguay* 2020). His speech expresses an empowered conservative position that undermines abortion access and adopts a regressive approach to gender and sexual and reproductive rights.

The contradictory messages fit clearly with a shift in anti-abortion activism observed in other countries. Given conservatives' lack of success in outlawing abortion completely, they now support burdensome barriers that effectively erode women's access to legally recognized rights (Cannold 2002; Finer and Fine 2013). While there is a vague reassurance that the legal gains will not be backtracked, the "discouragement" of abortion and the general "pro-life" stance set a substantially different tone for the implementation of the law.

This situation places feminists and civil society at a crossroads. On one hand, the lack of political will to push forward the rights agenda, and to implement and interpret the current abortion framework in a progressive manner, further worsens the shortcomings of the law. On the other, the imminent risk of backtracking on abortion rights—and the whole sexual and reproductive rights agenda—forces a protective response that shields the achievements, but allows little room for criticism and improvement of the existing framework. This creates a chilling effect on any proposal to improve the current law, as opening up the debate for reform could mean opening up space for regression.

Some questions arise about the current state of the rights agenda and its future implications. For one thing, influential political actors have sought to confront and discredit gender policies and feminist demands. Still, abortion and sexual and reproductive health services have functioned normally during the first semester of 2020—despite the health emergency and the change in the national government. The COVID-19 health crisis, with its economic and social repercussions, has dominated public opinion and the concerns of the population. This context does not contribute to a clearer vision of how Uruguayan society positions itself in the face of these neoconservative postures in the country.

The relationship between legal and social decriminalization of abortion is not linear, and legal change itself does not ensure social transformation in the meaning of abortion. We know that abortion stigma (Kumar, Hessini, and Mitchell 2009; Norris et al. 2011)—expressed at the political, social, and professional levels, and incorporated in women's subjective experiences—survives despite legal reform (Cárdenas et al. 2018; Makleff et al. 2019). In this sense, the effect of stigma on access to legal abortion services and consequently the perpetuation of clandestine abortion practices should be examined in the future. Some evidence indicates that abortions have been taking place outside the law. Wood et al. note that:

> As a consequence, women continue to face the threat of jail and risks to their health. In fact, in 2015, three women were prosecuted, and two of these imprisoned, for the crime of abortion. After six months in jail, these women had to move to another town because of the stigma and discrimination they faced at home.
>
> (*Wood et al. 2016, 105*)

Further research is needed to understand why women undergo abortions outside legal channels and how abortion stigma impacts those trajectories.

In addition, it will be important to analyze how conservative discourses that are pronounced from positions of political power affect the ways in which Uruguayan society perceives, understands, or rejects women who experience situations of abortion. What is the impact of the contemporary public milieu, which seems to legitimize conservative discourses of discrimination and misogyny? Will it influence a public opinion that for decades has been in favor of legal abortion in Uruguay?

The political project of conservative sectors involves a deep restoration model with economic, legal, and cultural components. Abortion is once again settled in the public arena as a field of ideological dispute and a political bargaining chip. It is premature to say what the future will look like, although there are some signs that allow us to hypothesize a scenario of tensions in trying to safeguard the rights agenda—and even go beyond it. At the same time, efforts to remove the barriers that limit access to abortion services will still be needed. Therefore, once again, organized civil society has a fundamental role to play in defense of human rights and democratic gains. This scenario demands continued vigilance regarding initiatives that undermine the achievements of the sexual and reproductive rights agenda.

Notes

1 With the exception of a project presented in the period 2015–20 that sought to modify the law approved in 2012. In Uruguay, the five-year term of elected parliamentarians is called a "legislature." It coincides with the mandate of the Executive.
2 One of the bills to decriminalize abortion, introduced in 1993, was approved by the House Bioethics Committee in 1994. This favorable report from the committee, addressed to the plenary of the House, was never dealt with, this being the end of the legislative process of that project.
3 One of the implementation problems is the quality, systematization, and lack of open access to micro-data in the figures reported, which means that secondary analysis of the information is not possible. The absence of an information system on abortion clearly hampers social monitoring of the implementation of the law.
4 For these years it is not available the official data of abortion rates.
5 There is no available data related to people not identified as women as well (e.g., trans men or non-binary individuals) who might have used the service.
6 We borrow here the term from Alegre (2009).
7 See Cámara de Senadores (2011, 117). The term refers to a fairly common phenomenon where women are forced to travel, sometimes to other countries, in order to access abortion or other reproductive healthcare services.

References

Abracinskas, Lilián, and Alejandra López Gómez. 2006. "Análisis feminista del debate social sobre el aborto en Uruguay. Un tema de la agenda democrática." In *Realidades y coyunturas del aborto. Entre el derecho y la necesidad*, ed. Susana Checa, 189–199. Buenos Aires: Paidós.
Abracinskas, Lilián, and Alejandra López Gómez. 2008. "Social Consensus, Democratic Conflict: The Debate on the Decriminalisation of Abortion in Uruguay." *IDS Bulletin* 39(3): 72–76.

Adriasola, Gabriel. 2013. "La objeción de conciencia y la interrupción voluntaria del embarazo: ¿Cómo conciliar su ejercicio con los derechos de las usuarias?" *Revista Médica del Uruguay* 29(1): 47–57.

Alegre, Marcelo. 2009. "Conscious Oppression: Conscientious Objection in the Sphere of Sexual and Reproductive Health." *SELA (Seminario en Latinoamérica de Teoría Constitucional y Política) Papers* 65: 1–34.

Aragón, Beatriz Martín. 2016. "Women's Rights or 'Unborn' Rights? Laws and Loopholes in Madrid's Public Healthcare Services Abortion Provision to Migrant Women." In *A Fragmented Landscape: Abortion Governance and Protest Logics in Europe*, eds. Silvia De Zordo, Joanna Mishtal, and Lorena Anton, 169–186. New York: Berghahn Books.

Arocena, Felipe, and Sebastián Aguiar. 2017. "Tres leyes innovadoras en Uruguay: Aborto, matrimonio homosexual y regulación de la marihuana." *Revista de Ciencias Sociales* 30(40): 43–62.

Baltar da Rocha, María Isabel, Susana Rostagnol, and María Alicia Gutiérrez. 2009. "Aborto y parlamento: Un estudio sobre Brasil, Argentina y Uruguay." *Revista Brasileira de Estudos de População* 26(2): 219–236.

Banfi Vique, Analía, Oscar A. Cabrera, Fanny Gómez Lugo, and Martín Hevia. 2010. "El veto del Ejecutivo uruguayo a la despenalización del aborto: Deconstruyendo sus fundamentos." *Cuadernos. Aportes al Debate en Salud, Ciudadanía y Derechos* 1(1): 13–68.

Barquet, Paula. 2013. "La mujer que viajó 2.400 kilómetros para hacerse un aborto legal." *El Observador*, February 16.

Berro Pizzarossa, Lucia. 2019. *Abortion, Health and Stereotypes: A Critical Analysis of the Uruguayan and South African Abortion Laws Through a Human Rights Lens*. Groningen: Ipskamp Printing.

Betancur, Lucía. 2019. "'Compromiso por las Mujeres': Documento que firmaron mujeres referentes de la coalición." *Universal* 970, November 17.

Bottinelli, Oscar. 2010. "La opinión pública en los últimos quince años, la relación entre el sistema político y opinión pública." *Cuadernos. Aportes al debate en Salud, Ciudadanía y Derechos* 1(2): 13–29.

Briozzo, Leonel. 2003. "Aborto provocado: Un problema humano. Perspectivas para su análisis - Estrategias para su reducción." *Revista Médica del Uruguay* 19(3): 188–200.

Cabal, Luisa, Mónica Arango Olaya, and Valentina Montoya Robledo. 2014. "Striking a Balance: Conscientious Objection and Reproductive Health Care from the Colombian Perspective." *Health Human Rights Journal* 16(2): 73–83.

Cámara de Senadores (República Oriental del Uruguay). 2011. *Diario de Sesiones de la Cámara de Senadores*. Segundo Período de la Legislatura, 61ª Sesión Extraordinaria, Nº 131, Tomo 491, December 27.

Cannold, Leslie. 2002. "Understanding and Responding to Anti-choice Women-centred Strategies." *Reproductive Health Matters. An International Journal on Sexual and Reproductive Health and Rights* 10(19): 171–179.

Cárdenas, Roosbelinda, Ana Labandera, Sarah E. Baum, Fernanda Chiribao, Ivana Leus, Silvia Avondet, and Jennifer Friedman. 2018. "'It's Something that Marks You': Abortion Stigma After Decriminalization in Uruguay." *Reproductive Health* 15: 150.

Comisión Económica para América Latina (CEPAL). 2013. *Consenso de Montevideo sobre población y desarrollo*. Santiago: Comisión Económica para América Latina.

Convention on the Elimination of all Forms of Discrimination Against Women (CEDAW). 2016. *Concluding Observations on the Combined Eighth and Ninth Periodic Reports of Uruguay*. UN Doc. CEDAW/C/URY/CO/8–9.

Cobb, Roger W., and Charles D. Elder. 1986. *Participación en política americana: La dinámica de la estructuración de la agenda*. México: Noema.

Coppola, Francisco, Leonel Briozzo, Fernanda Nozar, Verónica Fiol, and Diego Greif. 2016. "Conscientious Objection as a Barrier for Implementing Voluntary Termination of

Pregnancy in Uruguay: Gynecologists' Attitudes and Behavior." *International Journal of Gynecology & Obstetrics* 134(S1):S16–19.

Diario Oficial. 2008a. *Ley 18.426 sobre Salud Sexual y Reproductiva.* www.impo.com.uy/bases/leyes/18426-2008.

Diario Oficial. 2008b. *Ley 18.211 Creación del Sistema Nacional Integrado de Salud.* www.impo.com.uy/bases/leyes/18211-2007.

Diario Oficial. 2012. *Ley 18.987 Interrupción Voluntaria del Embarazo.* www.impo.com.uy/bases/leyes/18987-2012.

Elder, Charles D., and Roger W. Cobb. 1993. "Formación de la agenda. El caso de la política de los ancianos." In *Problemas públicos y agenda de gobierno,* ed. Luis Aguilar Villanueva, 77–104. México: Porrúa.

Finer, Louise, and Johanna B. Fine. 2013. "Abortion Law Around the World: Progress and Pushback." *American Journal of Public Health* 103(4): 585–589.

Fiol, Verónica, Leticia Rieppi, Rafael Aguirre, María Nozar, Mónica Gorgoroso, Francisco Coppola, and Leonel Briozzo. 2016. "The Role of Medical Abortion in the Implementation of the Law on Voluntary Termination of Pregnancy in Uruguay." *International Journal of Gynecology & Obstetrics* 134(S1): S12–15.

Instituto Nacional de Estadística. 2019. *Encuesta Nacional de Prevalencia de Violencia Basada en Género y Generaciones (EVBGG).* Montevideo: Instituto Nacional de Estadística.

International Women's Health Coalition and Mujer y Salud en Uruguay. 2018. *Unconscionable: When Providers Deny Abortion.* New York: IWHC.

Johnson, Niki. 2011. "El tratamiento de la despenalización del aborto en el ámbito político-parlamentario" In *(Des)penalización del aborto en Uruguay: Prácticas, actores y discursos. Abordaje interdisciplinario sobre una realidad compleja,* eds. Niki Johnson, Alejandra López Gómez, Graciela Sapriza, Alicia Castro, and Gualberto Arribeltz, 185–228. Montevideo: Universidad de la República.

Johnson, Niki, Cecilia Rocha, and Marcela Schenck. 2013. *La inserción del aborto en la agenda político-pública uruguaya 1985–2013: Un análisis desde el movimiento feminista.* Montevideo: Cotidiano Mujer.

Kumar, Anuradha, Leila Hessini, and Ellen M. H. Mitchell. 2009. "Conceptualising Abortion Stigma." *Culture, Health & Sexuality. An International Journal for Research, Intervention and Care* 11(6): 625–639.

Labandera, Ana, Mónica Gorgoroso, and Leonel Briozzo. 2016. "Implementation of the Risk and Harm Reduction Strategy Against Unsafe Abortion in Uruguay: From a University Hospital to the Entire Country." *International Journal of Gynecology & Obstetrics* 134 (S1): S7–11.

López Gómez, Alejandra. 2014. "Aborto legal en Uruguay: El largo proceso para garantizar el acceso a la salud y los derechos reproductivos de las mujeres." In *Comportamiento reproductivo y fecundidad en América Latina: Una agenda inconclusa. Serie e-Investigaciones No.3,* eds. Suzana Cavenaghi and Wanda Cabella, 121–145. Río de Janeiro: Asociación Latinoamericana de Población.

López Gómez, Alejandra. 2018. "La salud sexual y reproductiva en Uruguay: Posibilidades y limitaciones de su análisis desde la teoría de los campos de Bourdieu." In *Pierre Bourdieu en la sociología latinoamericana. El uso de campo y habitus en la investigación,* eds. Roberto Castro and Hugo José Suárez, 167–188. Cuernavaca: Centro Regional de Investigaciones Multidisciplinarias and Universidad Nacional Autónoma de México.

López-Gómez, Alejandra, Martín Couto, Gabriela Píriz, Ana Monza, Lilián Abracinskas, and María Luisa Ituarte. 2017. "Servicios legales de interrupción voluntaria del embarazo en Uruguay. Estrategias de los servicios públicos del primer nivel de atención." *Salud Pública de México* 59(5): 577–582.

Makleff, Shelly, Ana Labandera, Fernanda Chiribao, Jennifer Friedman, Roosbelinda Cardenas, Eleuthera Sa, and Sarah E. Baum. 2019. "Experience Obtaining Legal Abortion in Uruguay: Knowledge, Attitudes, and Stigma Among Abortion Clients." *BMC Women's Health* 19: 155.

Ministerio de Salud Pública. 2004. *Medidas sanitarias para la prevención del aborto provocado en condiciones de riesgo.* Ordenanza No. 369. Montevideo.

Ministerio de Salud Pública. 2012. *Manual de Procedimientos para el Manejo Sanitario de la Interrupción Voluntaria del Embarazo.* www.mysu.org.uy/wp-content/uploads/2014/11/Descargue-aqu%C3%AD-el-Manual-de-Procedimientos-IVE.pdf.

Ministerio de Salud Pública. 2016. *Ordenanza No. 243/016.* www.gub.uy/ministerio-salud-publica/institucional/normativa/ordenanza-2432016.

Ministerio de Salud Pública. 2017. *Manual de procedimientos para el manejo sanitario de la interrupción voluntaria del embarazo. Segunda Edición corregida.* Resolución No. 469/017. www.gub.uy/ministerio-salud- publica/institucional/normativa/resolucion-4692017.

Ministerio de Salud Pública. 2018. *Presentación sobre natalidad, fecundidad y mortalidad infantil en Uruguay 2018.* www.gub.uy/ministerio-salud-publica/comunicacion/publicaciones/presentacion-sobre-natalidad-fecundidad-y-mortalidad-infantil-en-uruguay.

Mujer y Salud en Uruguay (MYSU). 2015. *Informe sobre el estado de situación y desafíos en salud sexual y reproductiva y aborto en los departamentos de Paysandú, Río Negro y Soriano. Observatorio en Género y Salud Sexual y Reproductiva.* Montevideo: MYSU.

Muñoz, Amanda. 2018. "A cinco años de la aplicación de la Ley de Interrupción Voluntaria del Embarazo." *La Diaria*, May 7.

Noelle-Neumann, Elisabeth. 1995. *La espiral del silencio. Opinión pública: nuestra piel social.* Barcelona: Paidós.

Norris, Alison, Danielle Bessett, Julia R. Steinberg, Megan L. Kavanaugh, Silvia De Zordo, and Davida Becker. 2011. "Abortion Stigma: A Reconceptualization of Constituents, Causes, and Consequences." *Women's Health Issues* 21(S3): S49–54.

Real de Azúa, Carlos. 1964. *El impulso y su freno. Tres décadas de batllismo.* Montevideo: Ediciones de la Banda Oriental.

Real de Azúa, Carlos. 1973. *Uruguay, ¿una sociedad amortiguadora?* Montevideo: Centro de Informaciones y Estudios del Uruguay.

Schuklenk, Udo, and Ricardo Smalling. 2017. "Why Medical Professionals Have No Moral Claim to Conscientious Objection Accommodation in Liberal Democracies." *Journal of Medical Ethics* 43(4): 234–240.

Selios, Lucía. 2007. "La opinión pública, la democracia representativa y el aborto." In *El aborto en debate. Dilemas y desafíos del Uruguay democrático. Proceso político y social 2001–2004*, eds. Lilián Abracinskas and Alejandra López Gómez, 151–166. Montevideo: Mujer y Salud en Uruguay.

Stifani, Bianca, Martín Couto, and Alejandra Lopez Gomez. 2018. "From Harm Reduction to Legalization: The Uruguayan Model for Safe Abortion." *International Journal of Ginecology & Obstetrics* 143(S4): 45–51.

Tribunal de lo Contencioso Administrativo. 2015. *Alonso, Justo y otros con Poder Ejecutivo. Acción De Nulidad.* Decisión 586/2015. Montevideo: Tribunal de lo Contencioso Administrativo.

Televisión Nacional de Uruguay. 2020. "Tenemos una agenda pro-vida." *Portal Televisión Nacional Uruguay*, May 5.

Wood, Susan, Lilián Abracinskas, Sonia Correa, and Mario Pecheny. 2016. "Reform of Abortion Law in Uruguay: Context, Process and Lessons Learned." *Reproductive Health Matters* 24(48): 102–110.

World Health Organization (WHO). 2011. *Unsafe Abortion: Global and Regional Estimates of the Incidence of Unsafe Abortion and Associated Mortality in 2008*, 6th edition. Geneva: World Health Organization.

7

WOMEN'S BODIES, AN ETERNAL BATTLEFIELD?

Susana Rostagnol and Magdalena Caccia

Introduction

Abortion has an array of meanings, and it is therefore a phenomenon that encompasses political, biological, social, religious, moral, legal, and psychological aspects, among others. Abortion occurs largely in the bodies of women; that is, the *locus* where these multiple meanings crisscross, and where relations of power are settled. As such, masculine domination has concentrated considerably on controlling bodies and reproduction (Tamayo 2001).

In Uruguay, Law 18.987 for Voluntary Interruption of Pregnancy (herein VIP) passed in 2012. This legislation has not brought an end to the battles over the (reproductive) bodies of women, although it was a significant step forward. It made Uruguay the first South American country in which women can choose to have an abortion based on their own free will.

In this chapter, we will explore some of the issues that exist in the implementation of the VIP Law, which bring into play the control over bodies. We will examine aspects of guardianship contained in the Law, as well as in the practices through which voluntary interruption of pregnancy is carried out, the ways in which women traverse it, and finally what we consider to be the current greatest barrier for proper functioning of the VIP Law: conscientious objection.

As the previous chapter in this volume (López-Gómez, Couto, and Berro Pizzarossa) has addressed the process that led to passage of the VIP Law, here we will concentrate on its implementation. Different research projects recently conducted have analyzed the application of the law, shedding light on the tensions that arise in guaranteeing its effective enforcement (Correa and Pecheny 2016; Romanutti 2016; Rostagnol 2016; López-Gómez et al. 2017; Moncalvo 2017; Mujer y Salud en Uruguay 2017; Caccia 2018). In brief, all of them show that women's bodies are still a battlefield of masculine domination. That is the issue that this chapter will explore.

DOI: 10.4324/9781003079903-9

Ethnographic Process

Ethnography is one of the most comprehensive ways to address the practices and meanings of the voluntary interruption of pregnancy for the different actors involved, taking into account both what individuals do and the meanings they attribute to their practices. In preparing this chapter, we have relied on previous ethnographic research completed both by ourselves and by colleagues in our research program, as well as material from an ongoing study.[1] In order to understand implementation of the VIP Law, fieldwork was carried out in the public clinics in Municipality A in Montevideo, the most populous and poorest municipality in the city (Romanutti 2016), and we are currently working on a study on the "entryways" to the voluntary interruption of pregnancy in the private sector. In both studies, the information related to ethnographic records and informal conversations was organized in tables according to the categories of analysis central in each case.

We also conducted a study on the discourses related to conscientious objection by gynecologists (objectors and non-objectors) and graduate students of gynecology (Caccia 2018). That study was then continued through interviews with objectors in different parts of the country. The interviews from both studies were analyzed in accordance with different thematic axes, including the preparation of conceptual maps related to central concepts used in the different discourses. Finally, we have included an exploratory research about migrant women regarding sexual and reproductive rights.

A Right with Guardianship?

In the 1960s and 1970s, European feminists shouted far and wide that their bodies belonged to them. In Uruguay in those years, the body, sexuality, and abortion were not on the agenda. Only with the return of democracy did feminism take to the streets, demanding the right to abortion (Johnson, Rocha, and Schenck 2015; Rostagnol 2018a) through the assertion of women's ownership of their bodies (Cotidiano Mujer 1989). During the 1990s, women's and feminist movements were strengthened in step with United Nations conferences. The early 21st century was marked by the growing visibility of unsafe abortion. Therefore, the demand for the legalization of abortion came from the exclusive sphere of feminism, to be backed by various groups in civil society and gain a place on the political agenda (Johnson, López Gómez, and Schenck 2011; Correa and Pecheny 2016; Rostagnol 2016). Abortion became a matter of public health and social justice. This framing implied a depoliticization of abortion as a feminist demand, but it proved to be a successful political strategy. Uruguay had all the optimal conditions for passage of a law that legalized abortion: governments led by an institutionalized left, a strong feminist movement, a favorable public opinion, and general secularization (Blofield and Ewig 2017).

The law finally enacted was the product of negotiations that distanced it from the original proposal. As tends to occur when a consensus is not reached, the law became less radical. The alterations the bill underwent led to losses for women's rights and showed the success of certain conservative strategies centered on mechanisms of control over reproductive bodies. All in all, the result was a law that introduces an aspect of guardianship to the practice of abortion. VIP Law 18.987 does not *legalize* abortion per se but rather allows women to legally terminate their pregnancies based on their own will if they approach a healthcare service within the Integrated National Health System[2] during the first 12 weeks (14 in cases of rape) and follow the steps set forth by the law.

The Uruguayan state stands out for its early secularization and a definitive separation of church and state. However, the pressure of conservative activism both from the Catholic Church and Evangelical churches has been significant. It has been exercised in the way of a secular power through the political system—not through parishioners. Conservative sectors have tried to exert a "moral guardianship" of sexual issues, in line with the notion of a "single morality." This view implies believing that wide sectors of civil society lack the capacity to make their own decisions or manifest their interests; that is, that they require guardianship, some kind of protection or control (Nugent 2010). This situation is exacerbated in the case of women, who are not always recognized as moral subjects (Tamayo 2001).

In the case of the VIP Law, there is a kind of guardianship at three levels: legal abortion can only be performed in an institution that is part of the Integrated National Health System;[3] women are required to take five days to consider their decision once they have received information from an interdisciplinary team; and the only available method is medication abortion, meaning that women cannot select the method they prefer.

Why the need for guardianship? We continue to find the concept coined by Giulia Tamayo (2001) to be thought-provoking: "patrimonial control of the body" for women, with "patrimonial" referring to the patriarchal appropriation of women's bodies. Since the practices and representations of abortion are the product of the gender relations they simultaneously give rise to, the decision to terminate a pregnancy challenges the "patrimonial control of the body" (Rostagnol 2016). For conservatives, gender is central because the machinery of control and dominance over feminine bodies makes it possible to regulate reproductive behavior. During debates on the legalization of abortion, a central point revolved around who had the legitimacy to make the decision, and under what circumstances abortion would be performed. Biological life was not in question but rather the mechanisms used to regulate, control, and order life (Mujica 2007).

The instrument for maintaining control over bodies is the action of imposing guardianship. Thereby, guardianship is at odds with democracy. For Guillermo Nugent (2010), a "guardianship order" (*orden tutelar*) is incompatible with pluralism, because pluralism demands that collectives be able to express themselves and enter into dialogue. The absence of dialogue leads to incommensurability between the moralities of collectives, such that the institutionality of guardianship defines the moral value of actions, allowing or prohibiting certain practices. By contrast, in a democratic environment, it is necessary to "advocate for tolerance and individual responsibility in a context established by ideals of equality [which] require a criticism of the order of things that we typify as guardianship" (Nugent 2010, 108). Guardianship is at odds with the autonomy of individuals. As Flavia Biroli puts it:

The affirmation of women's autonomy to make a decision about the termination of their pregnancy is therefore an issue that touches on questions that go beyond the scope of abortion to the functioning of democracy, to the spaces and ways in which the state regulates, to the hierarchies and tolerable forms of domination, to individual rights, and to the relationship between all of these issues and the principle of a secular state.

(Biroli 2016, 21)

Women's freedom to access voluntary interruption of pregnancy places men and women at greater equality to exercise their citizenship in order to construct a truly inclusive democracy.

One could say that in Uruguay there is increased flexibility of guardianship, while guardianship is absolute in totally restrictive legislation. If we focus solely on the letter of Law 18.987, we see that while it establishes a margin of guardianship, it does not correspond to a "guardianship order." We must go beyond the law because it leaves holes that allow for different practices, such that the consultation with an inter-disciplinary team can be both an instance of counsel and accompaniment for the woman, and a form of "biopower" as conceptualized by Michel Foucault (1977). Given the laxity of the law, we must analyze regular and reiterative practices through which it is implemented. There is a wide array of these, including processes of women's empowerment but also the obstruction of rights.

Scope and Weaknesses of Law 18.987 for Voluntary Interruption of Pregnancy

Passage of the VIP Law is a milestone, but it is part of a broader process in which the practice of clandestine abortions gave rise to a risks and harm reduction policy, and finally to the voluntary interruption of pregnancy. Throughout this process, doctors have moved from reporting crimes to providing counselling to practicing abortions. Others have remained reticent and exercise conscientious objection.

Many women with post-abortion complications waited to seek medical advice for fear of being reported (Rostagnol 2016). This led to an increase in deaths among pregnant women due to post-abortion complications, a fact that is at the foundation of the policy of reducing risks and harm, which has been promoted by healthcare professionals and led to a protocol for pre- and post-abortion care, leaving aside the act of abortion itself (Briozzo 2002). In 2008, this was included in the Law for the Defense of the Right to Sexual and Reproductive Health. At the time, there was widespread (illegal) use of the pharmaceutical misoprostol to interrupt pregnancy. Different medical groups have fought for the legalization of abortion, and there were a significant number of healthcare professionals committed to the cause. As a consequence, the law was implemented immediately after it was passed, through Regulatory Decree 375/2012 of the Public Health Ministry. Healthcare professionals followed the technical guides for the procedure. There was also a group of gynecologists who immediately opposed the practice through conscientious objection.

Before the law was passed, training courses were carried out on sexual and reproductive rights and on pre- and post-abortion counselling (Labandera, Gorgoroso, and Briozzo 2016), which allowed for voluntary interruption of pregnancy services to be put in motion in public health centers (Fiol et al. 2016; Rostagnol 2016). While all have followed the same strategy to facilitate women's access to the services offered, possibilities vary between centers depending on the material and human resources available to them. The Ministry of Health opted for medication abortion based on scientific evidence and the experience of managing this procedure as part of the strategy for reducing risks and harm (Fiol et al. 2016). The services are provided by professionals, most of whom were already part of the sexual and reproductive health services system (Rostagnol 2016; López-Gómez et al. 2017).

In the private sector, Institutions of Collective Medical Assistance (ICMAs) are heterogeneous. Two of them have *objeción de ideario* (institutional conscientious objection), a legal concept created to exempt denominational institutions from practicing abortions, although they must guarantee provision of services to their female members. In contrast to the public sector, there was no common strategy. Indeed, modifications have been made over time.

As in other countries, when permissive legislation is achieved, the actual right to abortion comes into play in the regulations related to access to it, as do the practices of healthcare providers, ranging from conscientious objection to a commitment to women seeking voluntary interruptions of pregnancy.

A study of public health centers in a municipality of Montevideo (Romanutti 2016) shows members of interdisciplinary teams who are on the side of women and attentive to resolving their problems, many of which are the product of economic hardship. As such, they decided to coordinate appointments for sonograms along with the team interviews so that women would only need to make a single visit. But there were also objectors, as well as personnel who tried to discourage women from seeking pregnancy interruptions. Some made them listen to the embryo's heartbeat during the sonogram. In the words of one gynecologist: "They can't mistreat a person, tell them what they told them, 'to look,' 'that maybe they won't be able to go through with it,' 'that they're going to regret it,' value judgments" (Dr. B).

Access to voluntary interruption of pregnancy differs from one part of the country to another. In some places it is accessible, while in others access is impossible. As a result, many women prefer to go to Montevideo rather than to a local clinic (Moncalvo 2017). In addition, in many smaller towns, it is not always possible to maintain the anonymity of people seeking to interrupt their pregnancies. Some women prefer to travel or even undergo abortions outside of the health system in order to avoid stigma (Caccia 2018). However, access to misoprostol is more difficult since approval of the VIP Law. In fact, according to some of the women we interviewed, it is even more difficult to obtain in Uruguay than in countries with more restrictive legislation, as was the case with Argentina.

All the same, the greatest difficulty lies in the lack of available professionals due to conscientious objection, a stance which in some parts of the country is assumed by the majority, and in others, all. Likewise, there is little information about the law, which adds to fears and preconceptions among women. Between 2015 and 2019, feminist organizations held workshops and meetings in different parts of the country to help women understand their reproductive rights and take ownership of their bodies.[4] This shows how feminist movements continue to monitor and defend women's rights after the VIP Law.

There are both private and public health centers where women feel comfortable and respected, while at others they feel mistreated. This is illustrated in the testimonials of some healthcare providers: "a woman comes in for an appointment and tells you, 'the girl who gave me the appointment, when I told her it was for a voluntary pregnancy interruption, she made a face'" (Dr. N). Or as Dr. B told us, making reference to one of his patients: "One came in who was told [at the outpatient clinic]: 'I won't give you an appointment for a voluntary interruption of pregnancy.'"

This shows the importance of administrative personnel as to whether the health center is friendly or not. Some outpatient clinics in underprivileged neighborhoods are characterized by their close and personalized treatment (Romanutti 2016; Rostagnol 2016).

The majority of middle-class women receive care in ICMAs. We will present some preliminary results of our current research. The study covered the "entryways" for a voluntary interruption of pregnancy process in eight Montevideo ICMAs. Six of them had information desks, but only one actually offered information. At one of them, standing next to the unattended information desk was a security guard, with whom the following dialogue took place:

"What do you need?"
"I need information to get an abortion."
"Pahhh! I don't know, but do you know what? Go down that hallway at the end, turn right, and there's the outpatient clinic. Ask there."

(N, Quintela field diary, May 7, 2018)

With more or less ease, patients were always directed to the sexual and reproductive health outpatient clinic or to a gynecologist, without mention of whether or not that gynecologist was a conscientious objector. There is a general lack of knowledge regarding the location of voluntary interruption of pregnancy services. This is even more pronounced in small towns, where information is obtained through word of mouth. We could say that there is a structural discouragement caused by the difficulties in reaching the correct place. The women we came into contact with went to their appointments with the decision already made, so they generally overcame these obstacles. The vast majority of these women seemed already certain that they wanted a voluntary interruption of their pregnancies.

Once they reached the correct area, care was given in some ICMAs. In one case, the importance of psychological support was highlighted; in others, patients found caring attitudes. It is worth noting that the eight ICMAs—including two with institutional conscientious objection—provided information, and in no case gave a refusal or discouragement from proceeding with the voluntary interruption of pregnancy. However, the fact that the law was followed does not mean that the process is always fast and easy to access. The practices of institutions and healthcare teams define the process. Both public and private health centers have changing dynamics that often depend on the people in charge of carrying out tasks.

The greatest obstacle to tackle is always time. Sometimes the problem arises from women themselves. Healthcare professionals mention that some women experiencing poverty do not seem to be aware of their pregnancies, and when they find out, they are already well into the pregnancy. But in other cases, the postponement comes from delays in scheduling appointments. One woman had to wait four weeks from her first visit until the abortion was scheduled; another, after having completed the five days of consideration, had to wait several more to receive misoprostol (Blanchard et al. 2017, 13–14). A lack of human, material, and financial resources in some health centers does not allow them to offer these services with the appropriate frequency and hours of availability.

Among women who live in underprivileged neighborhoods with low schooling, the cultural and economic barriers become significant. The smallest health centers do not offer blood tests or sonograms, and women must go to a different center, which means money for the trip, someone to provide childcare, and possibly missing work. Despite the fact that services are free, economic hardship is a specific difficulty with regards to access to a voluntary interruption of pregnancy.

Migrant women are an especially vulnerable group: they must have been residents for a year before they can get access, unless they have undergone a situation of violence or rape. In accordance with some of the stories we heard, proving violence is very difficult for these women. They achieve it only when they find a healthcare team committed to women's rights. But even migrant women who are protected by the legal framework face various obstacles, both material and symbolic: language codes, access to information, the difficulty of understanding technical jargon used by health services, material limitations, and a lack of knowledge about voluntary interruption of pregnancy as a right. In addition, since voluntary interruption of pregnancy is an outpatient procedure, housing plays a central role since many of these women live in boarding houses with few amenities and a lack of privacy (Rostagnol et al. 2020). We can see that the obstacles are not only legal or regulatory.

In all cases reviewed in our studies and in others that we have consulted (Moncalvo 2017; Blanchard et al. 2017), we see time and again a similar pattern: healthcare teams do not address the emotional processes experienced by women undergoing an abortion. Therefore, while it existed, many women sought moral and emotional support on the Safe Abortion hotline (Blanchard et al. 2017).

Despite all this, much has been accomplished if we take into account the scarcity of resources, the existence of professionals committed to the voluntary interruption of pregnancy process and also the objectors, and the women themselves who must overcome the obstacles they encounter.

What Are Objections Based On?

Conscientious objection is a key obstacle to the proper implementation of the VIP Law. Serna Botero, Cárdenas, and Zamberlin (2019) point out that healthcare professionals justify their objections to performing abortions through discourses that show how they conceive pregnant bodies and their rights. Objectors' discourse reproduces the medicalization of reproduction while also reinforcing the role of women as mothers above all else. In what follows, we will analyze how these discourses include elements of religion and medical-scientific power in order to legitimize conservative opinions.

Science and religion—separated by the secularism widely celebrated in Uruguay for more than 100 years—seem to have met at a certain point in the discourse of gynecologist objectors: "You've got patients who don't come because they have an illness; they come because they've got a family on the way, [gynecology] is the only specialty that is involved with that [...] believe in life, not in taking life" (Dr. Q). The "right to life" and choosing the "profession of life" are presented as reasons for justifying objection. Gynecology is made out to be the only specialty within medicine that does not have to deal with the pain of death. "It isn't the same thing to provide care during a birth and to provide care to a patient with a voluntary interruption of pregnancy, it's exactly the opposite" (Gynecology student).

In response to this, we must ask what notions of life are at play. On this point, "scientific truths" and religious dogma are not easy to tell apart. Conservative groups adhere to the discourse of family as the primary mandate and defend a life guided by tradition, heterosexuality, and reproduction. In this context, activists fighting for the right to abortion have been portrayed as a sort of "promotors of death," an opposing signifier (Mujica 2007). The self-proclaimed "pro-life" discourses have widely spread this idea, so it is not unknown to healthcare professionals: childbirth is thereby configured as medical intervention in favor of life, while abortion is situated on the opposite plane.

In the conservative discourse of safeguarding life, there is an intention to impede the exercise of women's sexual and reproductive freedom. In other words, under the false pretense of scientific objection, a form of guardianship is reinforced with regards to bodies and subjectivities. Alluding to the right to life in an abstract fashion, without thinking about people specifically, or rather thinking about pre-people, is at the very least dangerous for a society that boasts of its ability to guarantee human rights. The anti-abortion lobby has aimed to separate the pregnant woman from the *zef* (zygote-embryo-fetus) as if they were two independent lives, and this is reflected in biomedical discourses.[5]

We must therefore ask what agency is recognized for women who decide to terminate their pregnancy? In the eyes of healthcare professionals who are conscientious objectors, women are not entirely conscious of the decision they are making. With regards to reproductive autonomy, women continue to exercise passive citizenship, suspended in a perpetual state of being minors (Brown 2007). Interesting in this sense is the analysis by Elixabete Imaz (2010) based on Tahon (1995): women's exercise of the right to citizenship necessarily requires that they have control of their reproductive capacity. Achieving this right is what truly breaks the woman-mother formula and makes women citizens. The body is disputed territory; as women take ownership of it, democracy is deepened.

Rostagnol and Viera (2006) warn of situations in which powerful sectors—for example, doctors—act in the name of protecting people's rights, using an array of justifications such as women's presumed inability or ignorance:

> This [women interrupting their pregnancies on more than one occasion] makes me a bit angry in a way, but more than anything, I think it's a real shame because I say to myself, "what a shame that this woman isn't aware of other possibilities."
>
> (Dr. T)

This means not recognizing women as moral subjects able to make their own decisions and know what is best for them at a given moment. It is clear that this conception is rife with biases and stigmatizing notions about women who have abortions. For instance, according to Dr. T, "We can't discuss voluntary interruption. If a woman isn't able to access birth control methods, if a woman doesn't have the ability to think about what the best birth control method is, if she is still ashamed to ask."

In the construction of women as passive subjects, doctors feel that they have some responsibility for unintended pregnancies because they do not "educate" women as they should, they do not explain what they have to do or what is best in light of their age, social, partnership, or professional situation. They mention the need to "empower" women to make reproductive decisions, but what does "empowerment" refer to? Does it mean simply providing information about birth control methods? And going deeper into this question, are doctors the ones who should be empowering women? Does that not reinforce the paternalistic medical tradition and guardianship that social sciences have been questioning for decades? In the words of a doctor:

> we have to try to find out a lot of things, so that we can make those kinds of patients see that perhaps the decision they're making isn't the right one because it will harm them, you know? I mean, there will be a toll...
>
> (Dr. P)

The act of abortion takes on a tenor of tragedy, something that "marks you for life in terms of suffering and remorse" (Dr. T), something that sooner or later women will regret. "I don't have the numbers, but my sense is that about half of the patients who have an abortion have a child the next year by their own choice" (Dr. P). The motherhood mandate is so strong that if a woman makes the decision to undergo an abortion, she will later try to find all available options to become pregnant to "make up for" that abortion. In the case of patients undergoing treatment due to difficulties conceiving, this guilt would be even greater: "the ones who had an abortion, you don't even know how hard it is for them because deep down they feel like it's a punishment life is giving them" (Dr. C). Another doctor commented:

> I've never had a patient who became pregnant by chance and just through bad luck and the famous condom that broke. Behind an unplanned and unwanted

pregnancy, there's an act of irresponsibility […] And always, or almost always, these pregnancies end up being beloved children.

(Dr. Q)

For some professionals, the product of pregnancy is always wanted, even if it is not planned. The lack of planning, in turn, is presented as an act of irresponsibility, which only reinforces the idea that women are not sufficiently capable of making decisions about their sexual and reproductive behaviors. In addition, it does not seem possible for a pregnant woman—even if that pregnancy is not wanted—to avoid developing a strong affective connection to the "unborn child." Therefore, any attempt to interrupt pregnancy seems clearly unnatural.

The romanticization of motherhood, even teenage motherhood, gives rise to a dangerous discourse in which difficulties or limitations become characterized as those of the individual, rather than being social or contextual. Caring for a child, even in totally adverse circumstances, is presented as an "act of courage," of "challenging oneself" (Dr. Q). The "mother" thereby becomes a kind of "heroine" who sets aside her fears or insecurities for the good of the "unborn child." In parallel, the figure of the father disappears, ignoring the indisputable fact that reproduction is an act carried out by two individuals.

For some gynecologists, a woman's body is a mere materiality, a mute territory upon which they can act, assuming the authority to decide in her place. On the other hand, it would seem that some abortions are valid while others are not. Petchesky uses the expression "morality of the situation" (1990, 365) to refer to these constant negotiations in which a single person oscillates between the extremes. In this sense, morality is not something static but rather adapts to different situations. All medical acts could be described as unique since they imply a personal decision by the doctor about how to apply scientific-technical knowledge. Social and historical reasons come into play in this decision; individualized medical attention means that the healthcare professionals' subjective judgments appear before each patient. "I've had patients where termination of pregnancy is more understandable, right? I could even share in it" (Dr. Q).

In this sense, we agree with López Gómez and Couto (2017) that the relationship established between the healthcare professional and the woman using the system is a key piece in the real possibilities of exercising the right to choose. Therefore, there are "expected" abortions that are somehow encouraged by healthcare professionals, while others are totally discouraged and morally condemned. As Serna Botero, Cárdenas and Zamberlin (2019) point out, doctors have the power to "exempt" some women in particular circumstances from their destiny of motherhood.

We also believe it is important to address the issue of stigma among healthcare professionals who participate in voluntary interruption of pregnancy services. Historically, the association of certain gynecologists with the practice of abortion has meant a loss of esteem within the profession (Rohden 2002; Harris 2013). Stigmatization becomes an effective tool to maintain the social order. A gynecology student related: "Where I worked before, we had to send a doctor from SHSA to perform the abortions because no one wanted to do them, and we all call her the 'abortionist'; nobody actually knows her name, I think, she's the 'abortionist.'"

There is what Alejandra Ciriza (2013) calls a "slippage of meaning," referring to the act of equating abortion with a "culture of death" such that people who are in favor of abortion rights take on this position and are pejoratively referred to as "abortionists." This creates a separation among healthcare personnel: those who perform abortions and those who do not, with the former becoming "dirty workers" (Kumar, Hessini, and Mitchell 2009) in the eyes of the rest of the medical profession and society.

> What happened here was that when the law was approved, there was a really militant "anti-law" chief who applied a lot of pressure, he exercised power brutally and people were afraid, [...] the chief even said that non-objecting doctors couldn't look our children in the face doing what we were doing—that was the level of manipulation [...] So the level of social stigma is high, I think [...] it picks up the old idea of the "abortionist" that was ethically the worst thing when we studied.
>
> *(Dr. L)*

Nowadays, gynecologists who perform abortions are stigmatized in many places, leading to negative consequences for their labor and social integration (Harris 2013). In practice, this situation creates an obstacle for women to access services. Practicing gynecologists voice the fear of stigma and being professionally discredited. In a country where voluntary interruption of pregnancy is permitted, conscientious objection becomes one of the manifestations of abortion stigmatization.

In this context, we wonder whether Uruguayan gynecologists distinguish between voluntary abortions and those performed because of a medical diagnosis that shows health risks (for the woman, for the *zef*, or for both). In Andalucía, Rostagnol (2018b) found that in the latter case, doctors had no trouble participating in the procedure, although when the abortion was the outcome of the woman's decision, they were reticent. The stigma of being labeled as doctors who perform abortions makes them hold back even if they are not explicitly objectors. Additionally, there are objections raised by medical leadership. In Uruguay, this situation became evident both among practicing gynecologists and students specializing in gynecology. Dr. M commented: "What happened with conscientious objection here was that we had bad information, we had a leader who was totally opposed to the [VIP] law, and we were a little scared because it could harm our work." As early as a few decades ago, Menéndez (1988) pointed out that medical students basically learned about biological concepts in their courses of study. Fieldwork conducted by Caccia (2018) shows that during medical training, voluntary abortion is not addressed as a social fact. According to a gynecology student: "There are sexual and reproductive health outpatient clinics, so if you want you can go there, but it's not part of the education in the course of study, it's not part of the degree. If you're a professional and you're interested in it, you'll learn."

What is left out of a given curriculum is not random (Ibáñez 2010). Students express that the contents related to sexual and reproductive health, sexual diversity, and gender violence are given in an "artisanal" way and depend almost exclusively on the professors' interest in the relevant topic. At the same time, OB/GYN clinics are run in accordance with their leadership's convictions: if the chief doctors are objectors, their clinics will be objectors. In this context, it is evident that professors' moral convictions also play a role, influencing students' decisions:

> I like to participate in the appointments, I do that when I can. There are professors who have asked me if I'll be an objector, and I've said that I don't know. They've told me that everyone's opinion is respected.
>
> *(Gynecology student)*

Gynecology students are not able to make abortion prescriptions, but once they graduate, if they do not claim conscientious objection, they will immediately become the "protagonists" of voluntary interruption of pregnancy appointments. Despite the discourse of acceptance, there is a kind of persuasion here: why ask a resident if s/he will object when s/he has not made a statement in that regard and is, in fact, choosing to participate in voluntary interruption of pregnancy appointments? University education, just like social practices, is also political. The fact that voluntary interruption of pregnancy is absent throughout educational programs despite being decriminalized years ago is not an innocent fact: academic training and its ethical-political orientation are also disputed territory.

Conscientious Objection as One of the Main Obstacles

Conscientious objection is a manifestation of the right to freedom of conscience, a fundamental guarantee for the recognition of a diversity of beliefs. In legal terms, this concept is activated to protect the private and individual conscience when there is a conflict between the public duties that must be fulfilled as professionals and individual rights. Objectors are generally not looking to change a law but rather to differentiate themselves individually. When an objector refuses to perform a certain action, they should be responding solely to "save their conscience," whether for religious, philosophical, or moral reasons (Casas and Dides 2007; Diniz 2011). Conscientious objection is individual and does not have a political goal or seek to convince others to become objectors.

In medicine, conscientious objection is traditionally raised with regards to practices associated with birth and death, which tend to have religious significance (Frader and Bosk 2009). In recent decades, debates around conscientious objection became important in the sphere of sexual and reproductive health regulations (Alegre 2009). In the health sector, the resulting problem lies between objectors' right to act in accordance with their moral convictions and the state's obligation to guarantee a population access to relevant services.

There are contrasting opinions in this regard. Julian Savulescu (2006) holds that if doctors are not prepared to provide adequate care to their patients because the patients' decisions conflict with the doctors' moral values, then they should not be doctors because care can never be partial. Any person may have their beliefs and convictions, but when they act in representation of the state in public health services, they must remain neutral. "To be a doctor is to be willing and able to offer appropriate medical interventions, that are legal, beneficial, desired by the patient and a part of a just health care system" (Savulescu 2006, 295). This stance is known as the "incompatibility thesis." If health services are based on the beliefs and values of doctors and not on health policy, it is impossible to guarantee basic care. It is understood that religious and/or philosophical freedom is subordinate to the duty to provide care, and if care is not provided, the situation could be labeled as discriminatory, immoral, or illegal, depending on the consequences for patients (Diniz 2011).

However, another position, known as the "integrity thesis" in legal vocabulary, understands the concept of conscientious objection as an absolute and individual right that may be used by all people in the event of a situation that compromises their moral integrity. This thesis presupposes that a person is a member of a moral community more than a professional (Diniz 2011), and as such holds that the rights of healthcare personnel are above the patients' right to receive care. In this context, a question raised by Frader and Bosk becomes relevant: "Why would individuals choose a specialty in which the provision of routine service involves so many procedures they find morally objectionable on personal grounds?" (2009, 67)

Although conscientious objection in medicine has been widely discussed at the international level, Francisco Cóppola (2013) maintains that its implications and limitations have not received the debate they deserve in Uruguay. In fact, he states that there are healthcare professionals engaging in a masked civil disobedience through conscientious objection, whom he calls "pseudo-objectors."

Conscientious objection to voluntary interruption of pregnancy is a complex phenomenon tangled with diverse interests and convictions that extend well beyond religious, philosophical, or moral motives, although these are included in many cases. In reality, a recourse that should be limited to the respect of individual conscience ends up being used for reasons that are far from the protection of deep and personal convictions. Moral values, as cultural products, are not external to social groups. The most conservative factions have invoked "morality" to legitimize their positions (Rostagnol 2016).

It is worth noting the medical community's support for the VIP bill when it was debated in parliament, in contrast to the increase in objectors once it passed. At the time, there was tension between gynecologists who quickly implemented the law, and others who developed a strategy to create barriers to its application. The latter looked for "adherents," which explains the high number of objectors across the country and the mass objection in some cities in the interior. Not satisfied with this, a group of gynecologists presented an appeal to the Administrative Court to contest 11 articles in the law. In broad terms, the changes following the court's ruling further weakened women's autonomy as time periods were extended, the figure of the progenitor was introduced, and professionals who were objectors were allowed to "inform" women about possible alternatives to abortion.

When it became evident that in some cities conscientious objection by gynecologists was part of a corporate decision, family practitioners offered to participate in all appointments in the voluntary interruption of pregnancy process, including administering medication, in order to make up for the lack of gynecologists willing to implement the law. This proposal was rejected, so gynecologists are still the only doctors allowed to make up the team that receives voluntary interruption of pregnancy consultations. Could this situation be understood as an "abuse of professional power"? (Frader and Bosk 2009, 67).

Additionally, some gynecologists declare themselves objectors because they refuse to participate in a greater number of tasks without an increase in salary, since abortion is not charged as a medical procedure, or simply because they are not interested in it. The fact that abortion is not a paid practice—to avoid it being performed for profit—can become a disincentive for gynecologists (Correa and Pecheny 2016). However, if public health is a right for all individuals, what actions must be taken when the commodification of public health becomes apparent?

Medical professional power appears in different ways in the implementation of the Law. Medicine continues to control women's bodies, and in the process of abortion, gynecologists hold a central role.[6] At a medical appointment, when a woman states her intention not to continue her pregnancy, the social meanings of abortion and gender relations become apparent (Rostagnol 2016). The appointment is a social process (Helman 2003) in which the *habitus* of the participating actors determine the nature of the interactions.

Now, *habitus*, as characterized by Pierre Bourdieu (1997), is embodied history; it is about people's dispositions to feel, value, and act in a certain way to the detriment of another. Individuals internalize these dispositions throughout the course of their history. The medical *habitus* could be defined as the set of predispositions incorporated throughout a long process of socialization that begins in education and is reinforced in professional practice, providing content to the doctors' daily interventions (Castro 2010).

> The *habitus* of doctors [...] can create practices that, from the point of view of the agents, are professional, disinterested, and apolitical, and that also simultaneously fulfill a pedagogical role to reproduce a particular order and sanction practices (like abortion) that defy the basic assumptions of that order.
>
> *(Castro, Ervitti, and Sosa Sánchez 2006, 641)*

Medical practice carries a double dimension, both clinical and political, but in the majority of cases, doctors are conscious only of the former since their own *habitus* makes the latter invisible (Castro 2010). Behind the conscientious objection that allows doctors not to perform certain professional duties hides a strong moral persuasion. A disciplinary structure functions in health institutions that presupposes obedience and the patients' approval of the mandates of medical power (Castro 2010). Conscientious objection is an action carried out in the framework of an asymmetrical relationship of power between doctor and patient in which the hierarchy is well defined (Alegre 2009). According to Michel Foucault (1999), medicine is imposed upon the individual as an act of authority; in the case of voluntary interruption of pregnancy, the obligation to attend more than one appointment to access abortion (whether or not the woman considers it necessary) is evidence of this authoritarian imposition.

The feminist movement has advocated for "bodily autonomy," identifying the political control of the reproductive and sexual dimensions as an emblematic expression of female subordination. According to Barbara Sutton (2017), reducing women to "reproductive wombs" means stripping them of the possibility of being part of the "body politic." Along the same lines, Rosalind Petchesky (2000) questions whether women can act as citizens when their bodies and sexuality are regulated by others (medical power, the state, religious authorities). The pregnant body (or the body that can become pregnant) "would seem to exempt the person in question from full citizenship and their human rights" (Sutton 2017, 896).

In this sense, abortion implies much more than the mere interruption of a pregnancy; it means, in fact, that women have regained autonomy over their bodies (Gutiérrez 2004). It therefore makes sense to wonder whether what is being repressed is the practice of abortion or that very autonomy. The "deconstruction of the maternalization of women" (Tahon 1995, in Imaz 2010), implies a long process of retracing a historical path that subsumes women to their possibility of pregnancy.

Conclusion

One of the most effective forms of guardianship over women is the loss of control over their own bodies. In the Uruguayan case, the VIP Law put guardianship into practice through a professional mechanism. Indeed, passage of the law did not end the tradition of guardianship by the Uruguayan state, but rather constituted a shift from repressive guardianship to healthcare guardianship (Correa and Pecheny 2016) protected by scientific, medical, and religious arguments. As discussed throughout this chapter, abortion challenges the prevailing order mainly because it recognizes women's capacity to make decisions about their sexual and reproductive lives outside of "relationships of subordination" (Bard Wigdor, Johnson, and Vaggione 2017, 38) that are constantly imposed in patriarchal societies.

Conscientious objection is a quintessential mechanism of control in the case of abortion. A state that does not guarantee the right to abortion in practice is allowing patriarchal guardianship to raise itself above sexual and reproductive rights. If institutional forms of violence (such as medical power) are not subject to deep analysis, they end up becoming legitimized as the norm, making invisible the relationships of power they produce and reproduce. In this sense, healthcare authorities cannot overlook situations in which women's autonomy is infringed upon, but must rather guarantee that services function properly and that all women have access to them.

In a political context such as the one unfolding in 2020, in which a new government in Uruguay proclaimed itself as a "defender of life," the challenges lie in ensuring that women's reproductive autonomy is not brought into question again.

Groups that defend women's rights must be more alert than ever to guarantee that women's bodies do not become *the eternal battlefield*.

Notes

1 All of the studies—some of them are theses—fall within the Gender, Body, and Sexuality Program in the Social Anthropology Department at FHCE/UdelaR. Gabriela Romanutti and Noelia Quintela are colleagues. CSIC/UdelaR have financed most of them.
2 The SNIS is made up of services provided by the State Health Services Administration (SHSA) and services by Institutions of Collective Medical Assistance (ICMA), both systems make up the National Health Fund (NHF), as well as private insurance.
3 This means that they cannot go to a doctor's private practice, even though it is an outpatient procedure.
4 See, for example, the campaign "Nuestro cuerpo, nuestro territorio. Aborto legal y seguro" ("Our Bodies, Our Territory. Legal and Safe Abortion") at https://cotidianomujer.org.uy/sitio/98-proyectos/aborto/2180-nuestro-cuerpo-nuestro-territorio-aborto-legal-y-seguro. Also see the campaign "Sin barreras al acceso al aborto legal y seguro" ("Without Barriers to Legal and Safe Abortion") at https://cotidianomujer.org.uy/sitio/sin-barreras
5 This aspect is broadly addressed in Vacarezza (2013).
6 Since its beginnings, gynecology has been a field of intervention on women's bodies that implies much more than "care" of their reproductive organs (Rohden 2002).

References

Alegre, Marcelo. 2009. "Opresión a conciencia: La objeción de conciencia en la esfera de la salud sexual y reproductiva." *SELA (Seminario en Latinoamérica de Teoría Constitucional y Política) Papers* 66: 1–37.
Bard Wigdor, Gabriela, Cecilia Johnson, and Juan Marco Vaggione. 2017. "Prácticas tuteladas. Masculinidad y adultocentrismo en la decisión del aborto." *Revista de Ciencias Sociales* 28: 20–44.
Biroli, Flavia. 2016. "Aborto, justiça e autonomia." In *Aborto e democracia*, eds. Flavia Biroli and Luis Felipe Miguel, 17–46. San Pablo: Alameda.
Blanchard, Kelly, Caitlin Gerdts, Yasmin Reyes, Laura Fix, and Chelsea Tejada. 2017. *Estudio para comprender el avance hacia el acceso seguro al aborto en América Latina. Objetivo 2: Una evaluación a profundidad de las experiencias de mujeres que usaron una línea de aborto seguro en Uruguay.* Unpublished manuscript, Ibis Reproductive Health.
Blofield, Merike, and Christina Ewig. 2017. "The Left Turn and Abortion Politics in Latin America." *Social Politics: International Studies in Gender, State & Society* 24(4): 481–510.
Bourdieu, Pierre. 1997. *Razones prácticas. Sobre la teoría de la acción.* Barcelona: Anagrama.
Briozzo, Leonel (ed.). 2002. *Iniciativas sanitarias contra el aborto provocado en condiciones de riesgo. Aspectos clínicos, epidemiológicos, médico-legales, bioéticos y jurídicos.* Montevideo: Sindicato Médico del Uruguay.
Brown, Josefina. 2007. "Mujeres y ciudadanía. De la diferencia sexual como diferencia política." *Kairos. Revista de Temas Sociales* 11(19): 1–18.
Caccia, Magdalena. 2018. *Derechos en disputa: Interrupción Voluntaria del Embarazo y Objeción de Conciencia. Una aproximación etnográfica.* Undergraduate thesis, Universidad de la República.
Casas, Lidia, and Claudia Dides. 2007. "Objeción de conciencia y salud reproductiva en Chile: Dos casos paradigmáticos." *Acta Bioethica* 13(2): 199–207.
Castro, Roberto. 2010. "Hábitus profesional y ciudadanía: Hacia un estudio sociológico sobre los conflictos entre el campo médico y los derechos a la salud reproductiva en

México." In *Poder médico y ciudadanía: El conflicto social de los profesionales de salud con los derechos reproductivos. Avances y desafíos en la investigación regional*, eds. Roberto Castro and Alejandra López Gómez, 50–72. Montevideo: Facultad de Psicología de la Universidad de la República and Centro Regional de Investigaciones Multidisciplinarias de la Universidad Nacional Autónoma de México.

Castro, Roberto, Joaquina Erviti, and Itzel Sosa Sánchez. 2006. "Las luchas clasificatorias en torno al aborto: El caso de los médicos en hospitales públicos de México." *Estudios Sociológicos de El Colegio de México* 24(72): 637–665.

Ciriza, Alejandra. 2013. "Sobre el carácter político de la disputa por el derecho al aborto. 30 años de lucha por el derecho a abortar en Argentina." In *El aborto como derecho de las mujeres. Otra historia es posible*, eds. Ruth Zurbriggen and Claudia Anzorena, 63–83. Buenos Aires: Herramienta.

Cóppola, Francisco. 2013. "Interrupción voluntaria del embarazo y objeción de conciencia en Uruguay." *Revista Médica Uruguaya* 29(1): 43–46.

Correa, Sonia, and Mario Pecheny. 2016. *Abortus interruptus. Política y reforma legal del aborto en Uruguay*. Montevideo: Mujer y Salud en Uruguay.

Cotidiano Mujer. 1989. *Yo aborto, tu abortas, todos callamos*. Montevideo: Cotidiano Mujer.

Diniz, Debora. 2011. "Objeção de consciência e aborto: Direitos e deveres dos médicos na saúde pública." *Revista Saúde Pública* 45(5): 981–985.

Fiol, Verónica, Leticia Rieppi, Rafael Aguirre, María Nozar, Mónica Gorgoroso, Francisco Coppola, and Leonel Briozzo. 2016. "The Role of Medical Abortion in the Implementation of the Law on Voluntary Termination of Pregnancy in Uruguay." *International Journal of Gynecology & Obstetrics* 134(S1): S12–15.

Foucault, Michel. 1977. *Historia de la sexualidad. 1-La voluntad de saber*. México: Siglo XXI.

Foucault, Michel. 1999. *Estrategias de poder*. Barcelona: Paidós.

Frader, Joel, and Charles L. Bosk. 2009. "The Personal is Political, the Professional Is Not: Conscientious Objection to Obtaining/Providing/Acting on Genetic Information." *American Journal of Medical Genetics. Seminars in Medical Genetics* 151C(1): 62–67.

Gutiérrez, María Alicia. 2004. "Silencios y susurros: La cuestión de la anticoncepción y el aborto." In *Ciudadanía sexual en América Latina: Abriendo el debate*, eds. Carlos F. Cáceres, Timothy Frasca, Mario Pecheny, and Veriano Terto Júnior, 129–139. Lima: Universidad Peruana Cayetano Heredia.

Harris, Lisa. 2013. "La conciencia y el aborto: Acerca de los estigmas." In *Objeción de conciencia: Un debate sobre la libertad y los derechos. Seminario Regional*, ed. Cotidiano Mujer, 23–30. Montevideo: Cotidiano Mujer.

Helman, Cecil. 2003. *Cultura, saúde e doença*. Porto Alegre: Artmed.

Ibáñez, Ana. 2010. "Algunas reflexiones en torno a la formación ética en la Universidad." In *Formación ética en la Universidad. Aportes para docentes y estudiantes*, eds. María del Huerto Nari and Ana Ibáñez, 45–58. Montevideo: Universidad de la República.

Imaz, Elixabete. 2010. *Convertirse en madre. Etnografía del tiempo de gestación*. Madrid: Cátedra.

Johnson, Niki, Alejandra López Gómez, and Marcela Schenck. 2011. "La sociedad civil ante la despenalización del aborto: Opinión pública y movimientos sociales." In *(Des)penalización del aborto en Uruguay: Prácticas, actores y discursos. Abordaje interdisciplinario sobre una realidad compleja*, eds. Niki Johnson, Alejandra López Gómez, Graciela Sapriza, Alicia Castro, and Gualberto Arribeltz, 237–263. Montevideo: Universidad de la República.

Johnson, Niki, Cecilia Rocha, and Marcela Schenck. 2015. *La inserción del aborto en la agenda político-pública uruguaya 1985–2013. Un análisis desde el movimiento feminista*. Montevideo: Cotidiano Mujer.

Kumar, Anuradha, Leila Hessini, and Ellen M. H. Mitchell. 2009. "Conceptualising Abortion Stigma." *Culture, Health & Sexuality. An International Journal for Research, Intervention and Care* 11(6): 625–639.

Labandera, Ana, Mónica Gorgoroso, and Leonel Briozzo. 2016. "Implementation of the Risk and Harm Reduction Strategy Against Unsafe Abortion in Uruguay: From a University Hospital to the Entire Country." *International Journal of Gynecology & Obstetrics* 134 (S1): S7–11.

López Gómez, Alejandra, and Martín Couto. 2017. "Profesionales de la salud, resistencia y cambio en la atención a mujeres que deciden abortar en Uruguay." *Descentrada* 1(2): 1–16.

López-Gómez, Alejandra, Martín Couto, Gabriela Píriz, Ana Monza, Lilián Abracinskas, and María Luisa Ituarte. 2017. "Servicios legales de interrupción voluntaria del embarazo en Uruguay. Estrategias de los servicios públicos del primer nivel de atención." *Salud Pública de México* 59(5): 577–582.

Menéndez, Eduardo. 1988. "Modelo médico hegemónico y atención primaria." In *Segundas jornadas de atención primaria de la salud*, 451–464. Buenos Aires: Asociación de Médicos Residentes del Hospital de Niños Ricardo Gutiérrez and Comisión Argentina de Residentes del Equipo de Salud.

Moncalvo, Lorena. 2017. *Barreras de acceso a la interrupción voluntaria del embarazo: Dificultades del aborto legal en Uruguay*. Undergraduate thesis, Universidad Federal de la Integración Latinoamericana.

Mujer y Salud en Uruguay. 2017. *Los servicios de salud sexual y reproductiva y el aborto legal*. Montevideo: Mujer y Salud en Uruguay.

Mujica, Jaris. 2007. *Economía política del cuerpo. La reestructuración de los grupos conservadores y el biopoder*. Lima: Centro de Promoción y Defensa de los Derechos Sexuales y Reproductivos.

Nugent, Guillermo. 2010. *El orden tutelar. Sobre las formas de autoridad en América Latina*. Lima: Centro de Estudios y Promoción del Desarrollo and Consejo Latinoamericano de Ciencias Sociales.

Petchesky, Rosalind Pollack. 1990. *Abortion and Woman's Choice: The State, Sexuality and Reproductive Freedom*. Boston: Northeastern University Press.

Petchesky, Rosalind Pollack. 2000. "Sexual Rights: Inventing a Concept, Mapping an International Practice." In *Framing the Sexual Subject: The Politics of Gender, Sexuality and Power*, eds. Richard Parker, Regina María Barbosa, and Peter Aggleton, 81–103. Berkeley: University of California Press.

Rohden, Fabíola. 2002. "Ginecologia, gênero e sexualidade na ciência do século XIX." *Horizontes Antropológicos* 8(17): 101–125.

Romanutti, Gabriela. 2016. *Intervenciones de profesionales de la salud del primer nivel de atención del sector público en el Zonal 17 de la ciudad de Montevideo, en el proceso de implementación de la Ley de Interrupción Voluntaria del Embarazo No. 18.987. Análisis desde la perspectiva de los Derechos Humanos de las mujeres*. Master's thesis, Universidad de la República.

Rostagnol, Susana. 2016. *Aborto voluntario y relaciones de género: Políticas del cuerpo y de la reproducción*. Montevideo: Universidad de la República.

Rostagnol, Susana. 2018a. "'Mi cuerpo es mío'. Movimientos de mujeres, derechos sexuales y reproductivos a fines del siglo XX." In *Notas para la memoria feminista. Uruguay 1983–1995*, ed. Lilian Celiberti, 195–211. Montevideo: Cotidiano Mujer.

Rostagnol, Susana. 2018b. "Abortion in Andalusia: Women's Rights after the Gallardon Bill." *Antropología* 5(2): 113–136.

Rostagnol, Susana, and Mariana Viera. 2006. "Derechos sexuales y reproductivos: Condiciones habilitantes y sujetos morales en los servicios de salud. Estudio en el Centro Hospitalario Pereira Rossell, Uruguay." In *Realidades y coyunturas del aborto. Entre el derecho y la necesidad*, ed. Susana Checa, 299–316. Buenos Aires: Paidós.

Rostagnol, Susana, Pilar Uriarte, Magdalena Caccia, Natalia Magnone, Federica Tuban, Juana Urruzola, and Mariana Viera. 2020. *Salud sexual y reproductiva de mujeres migrantes en*

Uruguay: Ideas, contextos, obstáculos y potencialidades para un ejercicio pleno de derechos. Unpublished manuscript, Comisión Sectorial de Investigación Científica/Universidad de la República.

Savulescu, Julian. 2006. "Conscientious Objection in Medicine." *BMJ Clinical Research* 332: 294–297.

Serna Botero, Sonia, Roosbelinda Cárdenas, and Nina Zamberlin. 2019. "¿De qué está hecha la objeción? Relatos de objetores de conciencia a servicios de aborto legal en Argentina, Uruguay y Colombia." *Sexualidad, Salud y Sociedad* 33: 137–157.

Sutton, Barbara. 2017. "Zonas de clandestinidad y 'nuda vida': Mujeres, cuerpo y aborto." *Estudos Feministas* 25(2): 889–902.

Tahon, Marie-Blanche. 1995. "La lente absorption de la femme dans l'individualisme abstrait: La mère est-elle un individu?" In *Individualismes et individualité*, ed. Jean-François Coté, 91–101. Québec: Editions du Septentrion.

Tamayo, Giulia. 2001. *Bajo la piel. Derechos sexuales, derechos reproductivos.* Lima: Editorial del Centro de la Mujer Peruana "Flora Tristán."

Vacarezza, Nayla. 2013. "Política de los afectos, tecnologías de visualización y usos del terror en los discursos de los grupos contrarios a la legalización del aborto." In *El aborto como derecho de las mujeres. Otra historia es posible*, eds. Ruth Zurbriggen and Claudia Anzorena, 209–226. Buenos Aires: Herramienta.

PART III
Argentina

8

RIGHTS AND SOCIAL STRUGGLE

The Experience of the National Campaign for the Right to Legal, Safe, and Free Abortion in Argentina

María Alicia Gutiérrez

The National Campaign for the Right to Legal, Safe, and Free Abortion,[1] a political coalition that emerged in Argentina in 2005, is the expression of an ongoing history of struggles for the dignity and rights of women. The decriminalization and legalization of abortion has been an important demand made by feminist and sexual diversity organizations under different political, economic, and social circumstances. The year 2018 was a turning point. The Voluntary Interruption of Pregnancy (VIP) Law (Ley de Interrupción Voluntaria del Embarazo or IVE in Spanish) was debated for the first time in the National Congress. A series of conditions converged to give rise to this debate, which had long been demanded by the Campaign.[2]

This chapter offers an account of the Campaign's history, related political debates and disputes, and the arguments and alliances that appeared after the presentation of a bill to legalize and decriminalize abortion in Argentina. It is an exploratory reflection on an object of study that is in constant formation. The Campaign is a collective political construction of which I have been and continue to be a part of. From this perspective, I have analyzed the Campaign's trajectory, the various elements that characterize it, and the interrelation between them through records of participation, observation, documentary information (declarations, newsletters, and articles), and interviews collected from different media outlets and periodicals. I also offer contextual historical background to help understand the evolution of the demand for abortion rights in Argentina.

Genealogy of the Demands for the Right to Legal Abortion

The 1980s: The Transition to Democracy

The genealogy of the fight for legal abortion is key to understanding the Campaign's influence and action, and to interpreting the way in which an individual right to

DOI: 10.4324/9781003079903-11

autonomy and freedom has been resignified as a collective right (Gutiérrez 2016). In recent years, the Campaign has established itself as a legitimate and increasingly recognized political interlocutor. It includes various and individually articulated struggles by the feminist movement, with the legalization of abortion at the center. These efforts began during the 1960s and 1970s through declarations, articles, and publications as well as concrete actions (Bellucci 2014). The transition to democracy in 1983 allowed for political participation to advance human rights, and for the enrichment of this participation through the contributions of women who returned from exile and introduced feminism from a theoretical, philosophical, and political perspective. This led to the emergence of innumerable civil society organizations and, within the structures of the state, the creation of the Undersecretariat of Women (Subsecretaría de la Mujer) to handle demands regarding work, care, violence, discrimination, and body politics, among others (Tarducci, Trebisacce, and Grammático 2019).

Reproductive rights, abortion, and diverse corporealities became commonplace topics in social and popular political organizations. In 1986, the organization of the Encuentros Nacionales de Mujeres (National Women's Meetings), which has continued to take place annually and includes women from all sectors of society, was a milestone. The Encuentros became a space for national and pedagogical debate on the growth of feminisms and the incorporation of the issue of abortion (Alma and Lorenzo 2009; Maffia et al. 2013). The demand for abortion rights has led the closing marches at the Encuentros—with the Campaign's green banner at the forefront—demonstrating the transversal nature of the fight for abortion legalization.[3]

In March 1988, a group of women, including the emblematic figure of Dora Coledesky, came together to form the Commission for the Right to Abortion (Comisión por el Derecho al Aborto) and undertook effective actions in different political and social spaces (e.g., petition signing, events in public venues, interventions in unions, and presentations in the media) with the motto "Contraceptives to prevent abortion, legal abortion to prevent death" (Anticonceptivos para no abortar, aborto legal para no morir).[4] These experiences are part of a tradition and practice of advocacy that later influenced the formation of the Campaign.

Globally, the United Nations Decade for Women between 1975 and 1985 also had an impact on the actions undertaken during the following decade in Argentina, showing the connections between local and global feminist struggles.

The 1990s: A National and Global Turning Point

The implementation of neoliberal models in the Latin American region led to economic crises and an exponential increase in unemployment and poverty (Williamson 1999; Morley 2000). However, even in such adverse socioeconomic contexts, the demands of women's organizations were still expressed at both the national and global levels. Participation in United Nations conferences—in Cairo in 1994 and in Beijing in 1995—helped place sexual and reproductive rights and the right to abortion within the international human rights framework. These events prompted broad participation by all relevant actors in the field:

governmental organizations, grassroots women's movements, ethnic and sexual minorities, and civil society as a whole. In addition, sexual and reproduction matters became increasingly understood from the perspective of women's human rights, including freedom and autonomy in decisions about sexuality and procreation without coercion, discrimination, or violence.

After these conferences, the coalition of Self-Organized Women for the Freedom to Decide (Mujeres Autoconvocadas para Decidir en Libertad, MADEL) was organized in Argentina, and had important interventions during the process of Constitutional Reform of 1994. In this reform, a conservative alliance between the ecclesiastical hierarchy and the governing Justicialist Party tried to introduce a clause to protect life from the moment of "conception." In contrast with the antiabortion stance that gave impetus to that proposal, the motto "Defending life," in MADEL's view, meant the application of social policies in accordance with women's needs and an active role of the state to improve the deteriorated conditions of healthcare— basically sexual and reproductive health (Gutiérrez 2000; Theumer 2018).

A group of legislators, social communicators, and sexual diversity groups coalesced around common concerns and, in 1995, presented a bill for a Sexual Health and Responsible Procreation Law at the national level, which was approved by the Chamber of Deputies, but rejected in the Senate. This fight led to a domino effect in some provinces, and the national debate moved to the level of different districts. Finally, a series of articles relevant to sexual and reproductive rights were introduced in the 1996 constitution of the Autonomous City of Buenos Aires, a politically important district given that it is also the site of the national government. In addition, coordinated actions on different fronts—unions, universities, public spaces, political parties, and the media[5]— led to the organization of a comprehensive strategy to give political visibility to abortion issues. The goal was to raise awareness and urge society to reflect on the right to abortion and build an active commitment to achieving it.

The 21st Century: New Ground

The new century began with another deep economic and political crisis. Public demonstrations in late 2001 allowed for the emergence of new forms of social organization and participation. Political strategies were constituted to question power and the formally democratic system of representation.

Gender issues, including sexual and reproductive rights and abortion, had an amplified space, both in neighborhood assemblies and popular organizations of unemployed workers known as *piqueteros* (picketers). In the academic sphere, new research was developed to analyze access to decriminalization of abortion. The spirit of this moment gave rise in Buenos Aires to the Assembly for the Right to Abortion (Asamblea por el Derecho al Aborto) that met once a week during 2002 with attendance by feminists, assembly members, picketers, student organizations, political parties, and independent parties. This new grouping was not free of conflict and differences, however, which eventually led to its dissolution. Some ex-members of the Asamblea formed the Strategies for the Right to Abortion Group (Grupo Estrategias por el Derecho al Aborto) that still functions today. In the words of Martha Rosenberg—one of the historical activists in the abortion rights movement and a continuously active participant—"the proposal came out of the Assembly for a workshop of strategies, which took place in the Rosario Encuentro with more than 300 attendees who agreed on legalization and not continuing the eternal debate with fundamentalists" (personal interview, 2010).

Around this time, important legislation concerning sexual and reproductive rights advanced in specific districts and the national level. In 2000, the Reproductive Health Law (Ley de Salud Reproductiva) was passed in the City of Buenos Aires. In 2002, with very little participation by the women's movement, a law creating the National Program of Sexual Health and Responsible Procreation (Programa Nacional de Salud Sexual y Procreación Responsable) was achieved, with articles agreed upon by legislators and representatives of the Catholic Church. In 2006, the Comprehensive Sex Education Law (Ley de Educación Sexual Integral) was approved nationally, although there are still great difficulties in properly enforcing it.

The 18th National Women's Encuentro in Rosario in 2003 was a key moment. Not only was the Strategies Workshop (Taller de Estrategias) on abortion legalization carried out, leading to various activities, but the issue became a transversal concern through an intensive campaign by participants in all the Encuentro's workshops on different topics. It was the first time that the march at the end of the Encuentro closed with a green banner that demanded legal, safe, and free abortion. In the 19th National Women's Encuentro in Mendoza in 2004, a meeting was held to establish the basis for the creation of an abortion rights campaign of national reach. In Córdoba in May 2005, the first national meeting was held, with more than 70 women from all over the country in attendance. They agreed on the Campaign's motto and the strategy for launching it country-wide. A federal organization was thereby created, a plural and diverse group that brought together historical struggles for legal abortion (Anzorena and Zurbriggen 2013).

The Campaign

The National Campaign for the Right to Legal, Safe, and Free Abortion was created with the goal of decriminalizing and legalizing abortion. It established the importance of these two actions: decriminalization to free women from the punitive aspect, and legalization to achieve conditions for access and avoid the risk to life and health, as well as defending personal safety. Women and gestating persons carry in their bodies the permanent marks of deprivation of the conditions that would allow them to make decisions freely.

The Campaign was formally launched on May 28, 2005, International Women's Health Day, in different places in Argentina. The first action was to gather 100,000 signatures country-wide for a petition that was given to legislators after a march in Buenos Aires with the motto: "Sex education for choice, contraception to prevent abortion, legal abortion to prevent death" (Educación sexual para decidir, anticonceptivos para no abortar, aborto legal para no morir).

Feminist activist and journalist Liliana Daunes and the actress Cristina Banegas read the document, which demanded: "Decriminalize and legalize abortion so that the women who decide to interrupt their pregnancies during the first twelve weeks have safe, free care in public hospitals and through health insurance programs throughout the country." It also called for "enforcement of the ministerial resolution on humanized post-abortion care and effective care for women and girls who decide to have an abortion in cases in which their life and health are in danger, or in cases of pregnancies caused by rape, which the Penal Code already exempts from punishment." The document proposes "creation of a tripartite commission made up of women's and other organizations, and representatives of the Legislative and Executive powers" to prepare a new bill (Campaña 2005, n. p.). The enormous level of participation, the diverse hair and skin colors, the different ages represented, and the various types of clothing all reproduced the diversity that, despite being characteristic of Argentine society, is rarely present in protest marches. This demonstrated the support already shown in public opinion surveys.

From the presentation of the first bill in 2007 until 2018—the first time abortion legalization was debated by both legislative chambers in the National Congress—seven presentations were made. Furthermore, during its 15 years of existence, and given the diversity and growth of the struggle, the Campaign engaged in various actions and strategies to socially amplify the demand, reaching multiple levels of society. This is referred to as "social decriminalization of abortion," which will be analyzed later.

Organizational Strategies

The Campaign is organized in a federal, plural, diverse, and inclusive manner, and its functioning is characterized by horizontality. Many organizations supported the coalition—today more than 500 organizations have joined—along with individuals who participate independently in the various actions and declarations.[6] The Campaign's organization includes regional groups by territory, networks, and work groups. The annual National Plenary Session (Plenaria Nacional) collectively decides on the strategies to be pursued, and a National Coordination body (Articulación Nacional), elected for one year, implements those decisions. In each territory and/or network, a representative is chosen based on members' criteria. This is a new power of organization and political functioning. Horizontality implies attending to multiple voices, situations, and geographic spaces, and counteracts concentration in decision-making. We infer that this method, which breaks with traditional forms of political and/or social organization, is one of the reasons for the enormous growth of the movement, with new generations of young people who feel engaged by horizontal forms of organization rather that hierarchical structures. It requires participation in intense discussion to arrive at a consensus. This allows for the establishment of common ground for decision alignment which, in each space, is implemented in accordance with political, social, and cultural conditions. These deliberative structures are complemented by commissions and collectives for various actions and groupings.

The Lobbying Commission (Comisión de Cabildeo) was created after presentation of the first bill by women activists who participated in actions within the

National Congress to develop a lobby for debate of the law. Although there is precedent for this type of work, it requires great ability to perceive and map the political stage in order to establish priorities: strategies are built as processes unfold. This does not mean that there are no previous experiences and lessons that can provide examples. The presentation of bills on multiple occasions contained their lessons, including the importance of the project being collectively debated.

In the 2018 debate, the role of the Lobbying Commission was key in cooperating with a group of legislators in the Chamber of Deputies called Las Sororas (The Sisterly), with whom an agreement was reached on the names of people to be called upon to speak and interact with undecided representatives. This group held informational meetings, prepared a dossier with arguments and rationales, and established a space for ongoing dialogue. It also worked on the necessary actions for the process of modifying the original bill in order to achieve ratification. The Senate debate reflected a different context. The Lobbying Commission began its work in an unknown space, and the acceleration of the debate forced them to rethink strategies. The eventual rejection of the bill opened a space for reflection and evaluation, which led to the creation of lobbies in the provinces and the city of Buenos Aires, and to the training and education of legislators.

Another key element in the Campaign's development has been the Communications Commission (Comisión de Comunicación). It is made up of a national assembly that is subdivided by regions and into groups that operate on social networks. Iconography was created to give identity to the struggle at the social level. The Commission worked with journalists, collectives of feminist communicators, and audiovisual media specialists, with whom they made collaborative productions on many occasions.[7]

A Collective of Sex/Gender/Political Dissidents for the Right to Abortion (Colectiva de Disidencias Sexogeneropolíticas por el Derecho al Aborto) has recently formed at the national level and is made up of individuals who have been active in the Campaign for many years. In their proposal, they call for understanding abortion outside the heterosexual matrix, given that the Campaign is a social group that includes diverse participants with respect to "gender, sexuality, class, age, migratory status, labor, educational, and religious context, racialized people, and people of body, functional, intellectual, and psychosocial diversity" (Colectiva de Disidencias 2019, n.p.). In that sense, they propose building intersectionality in order to "defend individual and collective life projects that are the object of persecution, discipline, and violence" (Colectiva de Disidencias 2019, n.p.).

The Campaign's Foundations

The Campaign's foundations are centered on the consideration of freedom and autonomy to make decisions about one's own body as a human right, and of reproductive and social justice as a debt of democracy. The notion of justice is central to the demand for the legalization of abortion. In particular, the Campaign takes up the idea of class-based injustice; and the intersection of gender and class as systems of inequality has a strong presence in the Campaign's analysis. This is related to the notion of reproductive justice that amplifies the concept of reproductive rights given that it incorporates the importance of social, political, and economic factors as conditions that allow individuals to make decisions regarding reproduction. This perspective questions the notion of individual rights and establishes a relationship with inequalities and the deterioration of the human and non-human world.

In the Campaign's words:

> To work for the right to abortion as a matter of social justice is to recognize that in the Latin American context, engulfed as it is by poverty and social inequality, it is poor women who suffer or die due to clandestine abortions, and who are excluded from other cultural and material goods. The illegality of abortion gives rise to different practices according to the woman's socio-economic condition and the lack of information.
>
> *(Campaña 2010a, n.p.)*

Additionally, and in accordance with the idea of justice, the Campaign proposes that the legalization of abortion is a "debt of democracy." If the body is the territory of freedom, the inexistence of a right that promotes freedom of choice violates a basic principle of democracy. This implies a limited democracy that does not include a significant sector of the population in the exercise of their freedom from discrimination (Ávila 1999; de Sousa Santos 2006).

Regarding the need to achieve democratic ideals, the Campaign states the following:

> We want to broaden democracy, guaranteeing this right to women affected by a patriarchal society that limits, infringes upon, and subordinates 52% of the population. A true democracy must serve our health, protect our lives, and empower our decisions with regards to the dilemma of an unwanted pregnancy.
>
> *(Campaña 2010a, n.p.)*

The Campaign proposes a substantive and participative democracy in relation to abortion by shifting understandings from a mere individual right to a collective right. In doing so, it resignifies the notion of autonomy in terms that are critical and transformative with regards to social relations, and establishes a link between the individual moral dimensions of autonomy and its collective political expression. Autonomy, in both its personal and collective dimensions, is conceived of as an "endless movement" in a constant process of construction and deconstruction along with the other, opening a space for questioning both at the individual and social levels (Gutiérrez 2016). Therefore, the legalization of abortion involves all of civil society; it is not the exclusive demand of those who identify as women.

The Bills

As mentioned earlier, the first bill for abortion decriminalization and legalization was presented within the framework of International Women's Health Day in

2007. With the slogan, "Not one more death because of clandestine abortion" (Ni una muerta más por abortos clandestinos), a march took place outside the National Congress, along with similar activities throughout the country (Rosenberg and Schvartzman 2014).

A drafting commission was created and carried out an intense debate, inquiries, consultations, and comparative analyses of legislation. The bill established

> the decriminalization of abortion, except when it is performed against the woman's will, and legalization of voluntary abortion, by the woman's choice until the twelfth week of pregnancy and without a time limit in cases of rape, danger to health or life, and severe fetal malformations.
>
> *(Campaña 2010b, n.p.)*

The bill demanded women's right to choose about their own bodies as well as their right to autonomy as a just cause, a matter of human rights.

After this rite of passage, the Campaign presented bills on several occasions, with necessary adjustments based on the exchanges and debates in the Campaign's different organizations. The decision was made in 2015 to entirely reformulate the bill. A new drafting commission made a proposal to the entire Campaign as a result of Forums for Debate that took place in different parts of the country throughout one year. With the suggestions from the forums, the commission reformulated the bill that was debated and agreed upon in that year's plenary session. The bill proposed on March 6, 2018 was the product of that collective and participatory process.

Thereby, with the impact and momentum of feminisms from Not One [Woman] Less (Ni Una Menos) (2015), the International Women's Strikes (2017/ 18), and the Global Cry for Legal Abortion (Grito Global por el Aborto Legal) (2017), the demand for legalization had reached streets, homes, educational centers, and underprivileged neighborhoods.

Social Decriminalization of Abortion: Building Alliances

The many years of failed bills prompted Campaign members to generate strategies from and for society. Activism, in its desire to achieve women's access to information and safe abortions, outlined methods of access taking into account the existing legal framework. The development and spread of these strategies contributed to what is referred to as "social decriminalization of abortion." The time waiting for debate of the law became a productive period that also allowed different viewpoints to join the fight. Networks and alliances were formed at the national level among diverse groups, organized under different dynamics with respect to the expansion of rights. The Campaign's slogan, "Sex education for choice, contraceptives to prevent abortion, legal abortion to prevent death," was put into practice in the multiple activities carried out by the networks and commissions operating under the Campaign's umbrella.

Some networks arose because of the Campaign's need to act on the epidemio-logical information showing that unsafe abortion was a key reason for pregnancy-related deaths (REDAAS, ELA and CEDES 2018). These networks also aimed to alleviate social inequality with regards to access. They aimed to spread information, and to produce, perhaps without realizing it, a form of implementation that bought time for passage of the law.

In 2012, one of the first groups that emerged was Socorristas en Red (Network of First Responders), formed by women who accompany those who need to have an abortion (see Keefe-Oates, this volume). They set up a network that has been expanding across the country over time. The Socorristas operate where there is demand, and make a loving and feminist practice into a mode of action. They provide accompaniment throughout the abortion process. Additionally, they establish pedagogies for accompaniment, debate strategies, compile information, carry out artistic and public interventions, work with healthcare professionals, and create knowledge that enriches the feminist tradition.[8]

Another network is Teachers for the Right to Legal, Safe, and Free Abortion (Docentes por el Derecho al Aborto Legal, Seguro y Gratuito), which was created in 2014. A large number of activists are teachers, and they attest to the difficulty of implementing the Comprehensive Sex Education Law in schools. They organized in order to put into practice the slogan "Sex education to decide" and work with knowledge in the actual classroom space. They have produced materials, spread the educational strategy nationwide, and become a cornerstone of the understanding of clandestine abortion in all its dimensions.[9]

The Network of Healthcare Professionals for the Right to Choose (Red de Profesionales de la Salud por el Derecho a Decidir), created in 2015, was launched by activists that work in the public health system who create the conditions for access to legal abortions. The appearance of misoprostol and medication abortion (mifepristone is not legally available in Argentina) were key. Healthcare professionals realized the importance of organizing to set up networks of solidarity, exchange of experiences and knowledge, and interaction with healthcare authorities to demand enforcement of laws and access to materials. The network is currently made up of more than a thousand professionals throughout the country and has become a key element in providing access.[10]

The RUDA Network of University Cátedras [teaching teams/courses] for the Right to Abortion (Red RUDA or Cátedras Universitarias por el Derecho al Aborto) was created in 2019 to expand and include in university curricula abortion as an issue that was largely silenced. It is made up of cátedras from 23 national universities—in social sciences, humanities, psychology, law, and medical sciences. The goal is to bring into the sphere of students' knowledge the arguments and scientific developments about abortion from a perspective of law, ethics, subjectivity, healthcare, and social sciences. The group has built support for abortion legalization in each university, as well as promoted declarations from the National Inter-University Council (Consejo Interuniversitario Nacional). The coalition of these cátedras requires interaction with authorities, professors, non-academic staff, and students.[11]

Additionally, during the 2018 debate, there was cooperation with collectives of actresses, poets, illustrators, photographers, and other kinds of artists who expressed their support through their own mechanisms in the streets and other spaces.[12]

All of these actions created a social climate for abortion—a word that had been cursed and clandestine—to "come out of the closet" and establish itself in streets, plazas, neighborhoods, schools, universities, hospitals, unions, the media, social networks, public institutions, and many other spaces. The Campaign's symbol, a triangular green kerchief, became the widespread symbol of a fight that transcended the Campaign in its significance (see Vacarezza, this volume).

The Voluntary Interruption of Pregnancy Bill: The 2018 Debate

The bill presented by the Campaign included time periods and reasons for abortion. Voluntary interruption, by the free will of the woman or pregnant person, would be available up to 14 weeks into the pregnancy. Then, following the 1921 Penal Code exceptions to penalization and a Supreme Court decision of 2012 (known as F., A.L. case), reasons for abortion after the 14 weeks were introduced: in cases of rape, risk to the life or health of the pregnant person, and malformations incompatible with life outside the womb. There was no inclusion of conscientious objection as a right for healthcare professionals or for institutions. Beneficiaries of the law were described as all pregnant people in accordance with existing regulations in the Gender Identity Law No. 26.743 (Ley de Identidad de Género). The bill proposed legality of access for adolescents and children in accordance with the regulations of the new National Civil and Commercial Code (Código Civil y Comercial de la Nación) (Honorable Cámara de Diputados 2018).

A combination of situations at the beginning of 2018 allowed for the abortion debate to take place. One factor pertains to the sphere of mass communication in Argentina, which during January 2018 felt the impact of the #MeToo movement in the United States and discussed the issue of harassment in the media. This helped create the conditions for introducing the importance of the abortion debate as a debt of democracy in Argentina, as part of a broader gender justice agenda. This circumstance, which came about on a highly rated television program, allowed for greater participation of members of the Campaign in mass media outlets that had never previously included this issue on the public agenda. The second significant event was the organization of a *pañuelazo* (a large public action using the Campaign's emblematic green kerchief/*pañuelo*) on February 19, 2018 in front of the National Congress. This event exceeded all expectations and forced the representatives to listen to society's voices. Finally, in the opening of the Ordinary Sessions of Congress, on March 1, President Mauricio Macri gave a green light to the debate.

This set of factors led the Campaign to present its bill on March 6, 2018 in the Chamber of Deputies with the signatures of 71 legislators. At the head of this list were four legislators with different political backgrounds: Silvia Lospenato (PRO), Mónica Macha (FPV), Brenda Austin (UCR), and Romina del Pla (FIT).[13] The bill was initially reviewed by four commissions: General Legislation, Criminal Legislation, Health, and Minority and Family. During a single plenary session of the commissions, preceding the legislators' debate, more than 700 members of civil society were invited to speak in favor of and against abortion legalization, in equal proportions. In this process of negotiation, modifications were made to the original bill, including personal conscientious objection for healthcare professionals.

Campaign activists participated through a number of strategies: speaking during the plenary of commissions in Congress, organizing actions in public spaces during what became known as "Green Tuesdays," appearing in mass media outlets, and intervening at the level of secondary and tertiary schools, as well as in universities. These activities, which built on the Campaign's actions over the years, and the massive social support in the march on June 13, 2018 were evidence of the "social decriminalization of abortion."

The abortion debate in the Chamber of Deputies (lower house) took place on June 13 and 14. Preliminary approval of the bill was achieved with 129 votes in favor and 125 against. This result prompted joy and hope among the Campaign members and various sectors of society, as well as surprise among anti-abortion groups that were strategically (and aggressively) campaigning in the Senate.

The climate of greater listening and exchange in the Chamber of Deputies transformed into a hostile, aggressive, and violent one in the Senate. The particularities of origin and functions of each of the houses of Congress gave a different sense to the climate of exchange and the strategies implemented. Therefore, the Senate debate during August 8–9 culminated with a vote rejecting the preliminary approval of the bill, without proposal of any alternative. The situation for women and other people with the capacity to gestate was left unchanged: clandestine abortion and denial of the right to decide about their own bodies and life projects with autonomy and freedom.

Lines of Argumentation in the Debate

The arguments issued during the debate show contrasting visions on the rights of women and gestating persons. Topics included the freedom and autonomy to decide about one's own body and life projects; understandings from the sphere of public health; the constitutionality or unconstitutionality of a right; the origin of life; the veracity or untruth of scientific information; and others.

The presentations of experts in support of the decriminalization and legalization of abortion laid out their arguments through diverse lines of argumentation: scientific, legal, social, and ethical. We can see from the scientific positions, with internationally validated foundations, the importance of recording the serious public health problem created by the illegality of abortion, with a strong impact on the health of pregnant people and the high rate of pregnancy-related mortality due to unsafe abortions. Calculations were presented on the number of abortions (Mario and Pantelides 2009), the costs for the healthcare system due to clandestine abortions, and the social significance of deaths due to pregnancy. These arguments offered evidence of the value of saving and protecting the lives of women and other people with the capacity to gestate.

The legal arguments pivoted on the constitutionality of the right to abortion with regards to the National Constitution and the international agreements included in it—on the notions of autonomy, equality, and dignity. The importance of decriminalization and legalization was presented. Decriminalization does not solve the right to equality; legalization that guarantees the provision of abortion services is necessary in order to achieve equity of access.

Finally, arguments in favor posited that the discussion should not focus on whether one is for or against abortion but rather on *legal* abortion versus *clandestine* abortion. One is in favor of the right of women and gestating persons to decide about their own bodies and life projects, or one promotes clandestine abortions, underground business, and deaths. It was also argued that the law would not coerce or obligate people to undergo abortions but rather aid those who are in need of terminating an unplanned pregnancy. Those in favor presented a crossroads: legislate for the broadening of citizenship or for restriction and the interests of a particular group.

Arguments against the law centered on the restrictive affirmation of the origin of life at the moment of conception. They employed twisted meanings of science—with the use of images and video—placing the emphasis on the existence of DNA. The moral status of the fetus was another of the arguments (Mayans and Vaca 2018). The lack of serious and internationally recognized research to back up these ideas was apparent.

Another axis of discussion was the progressive autonomy of young people in decision-making. Those opposing abortion rights presented the importance of parental intervention from 13 years of age on and thereby blocking the free decision of young people about their life projects. This was made clear in the campaign launched against modifications to the Comprehensive Sex Education Law, whose slogan summed up the conservative viewpoint on young people: "Don't mess with my children" ("Con mis hijos no te metas").

Recognizing that abortions do take place, anti-legalization activists created the slogan "Let's save both lives" ("Salvemos las dos vidas") and promoted the importance of prevention: they proposed effective implementation of comprehensive sex education provisions and access to reproductive healthcare and information. Both of these proposals (which are part of the Campaign's slogan) have been covered for years by national laws, the enforcement of which has been fervently opposed by anti-abortion groups. The fallacy of these groups' proposals and their intent of leaving the situation unresolved became clear.

Finally, anti-abortion groups laid out criticisms of institutions and financing in relation to abortion by denouncing an "imperialist" policy that supposedly proposed the extermination of poor people rather than eradicating poverty. This accusation denies the paradigm shift of population policy since the 1990s, when a notion of rights was adopted.

These strategies are in line with a transnational anti-abortion and fundamentalist politics that has developed a variety of proposals over the course of many years to act against what they refer to as "gender ideology" (see Vaggione and Morán Faúndes, this volume). It establishes a fight against human rights, feminism, and dissident sexualities. The novelty is that they are not appealing to God or beliefs but rather to science and legal theory as key materials in their argumentation (Vaggione 2011; Esquivel and Vaggione 2015; Correa 2018; Gudiño Bessone 2018).

The "encounter" between the Catholic Church (whose action is deployed among power elites) and Protestant groups (mostly Pentecostal, who mobilize and act among low-income groups) has created significant political events in various countries in the region, organizing parliamentary caucuses and acquiring mass media outlets. This alliance expressed itself in actions taken during the Senate debate, including public protests, religious homilies, use of a pale blue kerchief that mimics the Campaign's green kerchief, a variety of acts of violence and aggression, threats to provincial legislators, and others.

The majority rejection of the bill in the Senate in 2018 was evidence of anti-abortion gains that left unresolved a drama affecting a highly significant number of women and gestating persons across the country and the region.

Post-2018 Strategies

After the 2018 debate, the Campaign reorganized its strategies. It proposed a new modification to the bill[14] centered on an analysis and review of the presentations made by conservative groups in both legislative chambers, and continued to develop its public actions through its networks in different social spheres. In this context, on May 28, 2019, the Campaign presented a new bill with a massive public act in front of the National Congress (Campaña 2019, n.p.). As it was an election year, the possibilities to move forward were limited. However, the presidential candidate (who was later elected) Dr. Alberto Fernández stated in his electoral campaign the importance of and his commitment to the debate on the Voluntary Interruption of Pregnancy Law. When he assumed the presidency, and in the opening of sessions in the legislative chambers on March 1, 2020, he reemphasized his intention to present his own bill.

The different groups that make up the Campaign activated their public initiatives, as well as lobbying with legislators and members of the new Ministries of Health and of Women, Gender, and Diversity sensitive to the debate. While the president stated that he would present his own bill, the Campaign's actions focused on reinforcing the importance of the social support of its own bill to achieve parliamentary debate. The emergence of the global COVID-19 pandemic and the enforcement of Preventative and Mandatory Social Isolation (Aislamiento Social Preventivo y Obligatorio) in Argentina on March 20, 2020 led to a change of priorities among members of government. In May 2020, the Legislative branch began to operate through virtual modes. The Campaign, meanwhile, continued to carry out online advocacy and activist initiatives through social media. By late 2020 a new bill to legalize abortion sent by President Alberto Fernández was debated in Congress and this time approved. It is fair to say that this historic achievement is largely the result of the tenacious activism by the abortion rights movement in Argentina.

The 28th of September Campaign for the Decriminalization and Legalization of Abortion in Latin America and the Caribbean

At the Fifth Feminist Encuentro of Latin America and the Caribbean (V Encuentro Feminista Latinoamericano y del Caribe) held in San Bernardo, Argentina, in 1990, participants decided to launch coordinated regional activities for abortion rights, which led to the creation of the 28th of September Campaign for the Decriminalization and Legalization of Abortion in Latin America and the Caribbean (Campaña 28 de Septiembre por la Despenalización y Legalización del Aborto en América Latina y el Caribe).[15] For many years, this campaign (now also known as 28S) conducted actions across the region. In 2017, it organized the Global Cry for Legal Abortion with interventions across Latin America and the Caribbean, leading to connections between activists from different places. The Argentine abortion rights Campaign was called upon to handle the regional coordination. After several meetings, organization was handed over at the 14th Feminist Encuentro of Latin America and the Caribbean (EFLAC) held in Montevideo, Uruguay, in 2017. The proposal was to coordinate actions, and for each country to move forward according to its conditions and level of organization, with support from 28S. One major act for abortion legalization was region-wide, and there was also global support with *pañuelazos* during the 2018 debate in Argentina.

After the abortion legalization bill was rejected in the Senate in 2018, and at the request of the Network for Women's Health in Latin America and the Caribbean (Red de Salud de las Mujeres de América Latina y el Caribe), 28S organized a regional meeting in Buenos Aires where participants strategized courses of action and adopted the green kerchief as their emblem, with different slogans for each location. Declarations of support were issued for actions in different countries as a result of the debate and/or attacks on abortion rights.

The Green Tide

The Green Tide (Marea Verde)—as the growing mobilization for abortion rights is known—can be traced to more than 15 years of activist construction by the National Campaign for the Right to Legal, Safe, and Free Abortion. Its presence was evident on multiple occasions during the Voluntary Interruption of Pregnancy debate. The green kerchief, a symbol of the fight since the Campaign's beginnings, has spread and expressed feminist demands in unison.

The growth of global feminisms (through Ni Una Menos, the Global Cry, the International Women's Strike, and abortion rights mobilization), as well as the participation of innumerable young people, were not spontaneous or wholly surprising. In Argentina, since the National Encuentros of Women, the participation of feminist and sexual diversity groups has been a testament to an important capacity for organization and demands, and has given rise to a counterhegemonic strategy that, at this stage, confronts the implementation of neoliberal and neoconservative models.

Young people are central actors in the new political configuration. While the Campaign is made up of individuals from various generations, the mass visibility of this new political subject shows the marks of the past and projection into the future (Elizalde and Mateo 2018). It also expresses a variety of oppressions and reflects the strength of a movement that has established itself at the center of the political agenda, providing overwhelming energy and amplifying forms of participation. It is, indeed, the faithful reflection of the "social decriminalization of abortion" and the range of demands by feminists.

Conclusions

Debates surrounding abortion have addressed the weight of cultural principles and biases that made the proposal of legalizing abortion a prolonged utopia. They have focused the question in ways that reveal the impacts of clandestine abortion on central issues such as maternal mortality (i.e., public health) to demonstrate who died or was severely injured, shedding light on the social injustice and the issue of class inequality. The focus on health and social dimensions had no small impact given that the statistics were and are alarmingly convincing (see, e.g., REDAAS, ELA and CEDES 2018). Perhaps this captured the attention of many healthcare professionals and creators of public policy.

At other times, pro-legalization activists brought up and exerted pressure regarding the silence on the part of mass media, and over the years, a critical mass has been achieved that helped place this issue on the media agenda. Activists engaged with various sectors, not without difficulty, to build alliances in support of the demand. Sometimes this was possible, and in other cases, enormous hurdles became apparent for women's movements and the sectors called upon.

This chapter has reviewed the role of different players involved in the abortion debate: doctors, politicians, communicators, the Catholic Church, and particularly abortion rights activists. All of this led to the creation of an idea, or rather a practice, which materialized in the National Campaign for the Right to Legal, Safe, and Free Abortion. The creation of the Campaign marked a turning point in 2005, enabling territorial inclusion beyond the borders of the City of Buenos Aires (often the center of political activity) and incorporating an array of women's and feminist voices and experiences. It also amplified the sound of the demand and articulated other actions in parallel, which allowed for the presentation of a bill supported by legislators from diverse political/ideological leanings. A significant expression of these efforts was the legislative debate in 2018. The Campaign proposed the notions of justice, human rights, and democracy as the axes on which the demand is based. In addition, it created engagement with diverse organizations in society that came together in the Green Tide.

The negation of the right to abortion is an act of violence against the bodies of women and gestating persons. The inability to make decisions about reproduction suggests a narrowing of available life projects and the full exercise of freedom. There is no exercise of human rights without the possibility of deciding freely about one's own body in the same way that there is no bodily freedom if the social, economic, political, and cultural rights that make it possible are not solidified. It is therefore valid to ask about the true potentialities of democracies to accommodate the demands and necessities of women and gestating persons in a heterosexist, patriarchal, speciesist, ableist, racist context rife with other oppressive intersectionalities. The fight for legal abortion, part of an array of emancipatory struggles, entails a sense of inclusion and of reversal of oppressive matrices.

The year 2020 began full of expectations, desires, and a need for efforts and strategies to decriminalize and legalize abortion. Despite COVID-19 and the economic and social crisis, a hope endured that was not naïve. Political leadership expressed the decision to debate the Voluntary Interruption of Pregnancy bill. The Campaign continued to act even in the context of the pandemic; broad sectors of society showed their support. The arguments were expressed in countless situations and spaces. The Green Tide's demand—#LegalAbortionNow (#AbortoLegalYa)—finally became a reality when the year ended and Congress approved a bill legalizing abortion.

Notes

1 In Spanish, Campaña Nacional por el Derecho al Aborto Legal, Seguro y Gratuito. Note that *gratuito*/free means free of charge.
2 In Argentina, the 1921 Penal Code penalized abortion except in cases of risk to the mother's health or life, or in cases of rape or indecent assault (*atentado al pudor*) committed against a woman with mental disabilities. This final clause was clarified by a Supreme Court ruling in 2012 (F., A.L. case), which reaffirmed the right to abortion for any woman who was raped, requiring only the woman's affidavit without the need to file a legal complaint. It also called upon the federal and provincial governments to issue protocols for its effective enforcement. This recommendation, for cases referred to as "non-punishable abortions" were partially enforced, with barriers to its acceptance in some provinces.
3 For the past several years, attention has been called to the need to change the name from National Women's Encuentro to National and Plurinational Encuentro of Women, Lesbians, Travesti, and Trans Women, which reflects the growth in demands and the incorporation of new social actors.
4 See https://comisionporelderechoalaborto.wordpress.com
5 Among other initiatives, in 1997, Dora Coledesky—a legendary abortion legalization activist—organized a campaign that was published in *Revista Tres Puntos*, a magazine with mass distribution. The article entitled "For the First Time, Twenty Women Dare to Say 'I Had an Abortion'" collected the accounts of well-known women from different spheres: academics, psychoanalysts, writers, artists, and others.
6 See the Campaign's website: www.abortolegal.org
7 For further information on the digital activism of the abortion rights movement see Laudano (this volume).
8 See the website of Socorristas en Red—Feministas que Abortamos: socorristasenred.org
9 See the social media presence of the network of Teachers for the Right to Legal, Safe, and Free Abortion in Facebook: www.facebook.com/docentesaborto/
10 See the website of the Network of Health Professionals for the Right to Choose: www.redsaluddecidir.org/
11 See RUDA's social media presence in Facebook: www.facebook.com/rudacatedrasaborto/
12 See the Facebook site of the Colectiva de Actrices por el Aborto: www.facebook.com/actricesarg/. Regarding the Collective of Poets for Abortion Rights (Colectiva de #poetas por el derecho al aborto) see Campaña (2018).
13 The meanings of the political party acronyms are the following: PRO (Propuesta Republicana / Republican Proposal), FVP (Frente para la Victoria / Front for Victory), UCR (Unión Cívica Radical / Radical Civic Union), FIT (Frente de Izquierda y de los Trabajadores / Leftist and Workers Front) (see Fernández Anderson, this volume).
14 After the 2018 debate, a revision and new consultations were carried out in order to formulate a new bill, which was presented in 2019. Among the most relevant points, the reason "fetal malformations incompatible with life outside the womb" was removed

because of the perspectives of groups of people with disabilities and because of attacks during the debate about eugenic abortion. The final version included a reason due to "health," explaining the concept of integral health.

15 Abortion is illegal in Latin America, except in Cuba, Puerto Rico, Uruguay, Mexico City, and the Mexican state of Oaxaca. Argentina joined this group after abortion legalization on December 30, 2020. Other countries have decriminalized abortion for reasons that in many cases have been set forth in criminal codes for nearly a century.

References

Alma, Amanda, and Paula Lorenzo. 2009. *Mujeres que se encuentran. Una recuperación histórica de los Encuentros Nacionales de Mujeres en Argentina (1986–2005).* Buenos Aires: Feminaria.

Anzorena, Claudia, and Ruth Zurbriggen. 2013. "Trazos de una experiencia de articulación federal y plural por la autonomía de las mujeres: La Campaña Nacional por el Derecho al Aborto Legal, Seguro y Gratuito en Argentina." In *El aborto como derecho de las mujeres. Otra historia es posible*, eds. Ruth Zurbriggen and Claudia Anzorena, 17–38. Buenos Aires: Herramienta.

Ávila, Maria Bethania. 1999. "Feminismo y ciudadanía: La producción de los nuevos derechos." In *Género y salud reproductiva en América Latina*, ed. Lucila Scavone, 57–83. Cartago: Libro Universitario Regional.

Bellucci, Mabel. 2014. *Historia de una desobediencia. Aborto y Feminismo.* Buenos Aires: Capital Intelectual.

Campaña Nacional por el Derecho al Aborto Legal, Seguro y Gratuito. 2005. *Declaración Campaña Nacional por el Derecho al Aborto Legal, Seguro y Gratuito.* Mimeo, November 25.

Campaña Nacional por el Derecho al Aborto Legal, Seguro y Gratuito. 2010a. "¿Qué es la Campaña/Quiénes somos?" March 1. https://abortolegalseguroygratuito.blogspot.com/search/label/%C2%BFQu%C3%A9%20es%20la%20campa%C3%B1a%3F.

Campaña Nacional por el Derecho al Aborto Legal, Seguro y Gratuito. 2010b. "Proyecto de Ley de legalización/despenalización del aborto en Argentina," March 26. www.abortolegal.com.ar/proyecto-de-ley-de-legalizaciondespenalizacion-del-aborto-en-argentina/.

Campaña Nacional por el Derecho al Aborto Legal, Seguro y Gratuito. 2018. "CABA: La Marea Verde en poesía," November 22. www.abortolegal.com.ar/caba-la-marea-verde-en-poesia/.

Campaña Nacional por el Derecho al Aborto Legal, Seguro y Gratuito. 2019. "Proyecto de Ley de Interrupción Voluntaria del Embarazo," March 20. www.abortolegal.com.ar/proyecto-de-ley-presentado-por-la-campana/.

Colectiva de Disidencias Sexogeneropolíticas en la Campaña Nacional por el Derecho al Aborto, Legal, Seguro y Gratuito. 2019. "Colectiva de disidencias sexogeneropolíticas en la Campaña," March 31. www.abortolegal.com.ar/colectiva-de-disidencias-sexogeneropoliticas-en-la-campana/.

Correa, Sonia. 2018. "Ideología de género: Rastreando sus orígenes y significados en la política de género actual." *Sexuality Policy Watch*, February 16. http://sxpolitics.org/es/ideologia-de-genero-rastreando-sus-origenes-y-significados-en-la-politica-de-genero-actual/3858.

de Sousa Santos, Boaventura. 2006. *Renovar la teoría crítica y reinventar la emancipación social.* Buenos Aires: Consejo Latinoamericano de Ciencias Sociales.

Elizalde, Silvia, and Natacha Mateo. 2018. "Las jóvenes: Entre la 'marea verde' y la decisión de abortar." *Salud Colectiva* 14(3): 433–446.

Esquivel, Juan, and Juan Marco Vaggione. 2015. *Permeabilidades activas. Religión, política y sexualidad en la Argentina democrática.* Buenos Aires: Biblos.

Gudiño Bessone, Pablo. 2018. "Aborto, sexualidad y bioética en documentos y encíclicas vaticanas." *Acta Bioethica* 24(1): 85–94.

Gutiérrez, María Alicia. 2000. "Mujeres Autoconvocadas para Decidir en Libertad (MADEL): La experiencia reciente del movimiento de mujeres." In *La sociedad civil frente a las nuevas formas de institucionalidad democrática*, eds. Martín Abregú and Silvina Ramos, 83–106. Buenos Aires: Centro de Estudios de Estado y Sociedad and Centro de Estudios Legales y Sociales.

Gutiérrez, María Alicia. 2016. "Eternas indisciplinadas: Repensando la autonomía para el derecho al aborto legal, seguro y gratuito." In *Entre-dichos-cuerpos. Coreografías de los géneros y las sexualidades*, ed. María Alicia Gutiérrez, 17–41. Buenos Aires: Godot.

Honorable Cámara de Diputados. 2018. "Proyecto de Ley. Expediente 0230-D-2018. Sumario: Interrupción voluntaria del embarazo. Régimen," March 5. www.hcdn.gob.ar/proyectos/proyecto.jsp?exp=0230-D-2018.

Maffia, Diana, Luciana Peker, Aluminé Moreno, and Laura Morroni (eds.). 2013. *Mujeres pariendo historia. Cómo se gestó el primer Encuentro Nacional de Mujeres. Reseña íntima y política de las integrantes de la Comisión Promotora*. Buenos Aires: Legislatura Porteña Ciudad Autónoma de Buenos Aires.

Mario, Silvia, and Edith Alejandra Pantelides. 2009. "Estimaciones de la magnitud del aborto inducido en la Argentina." *Notas de Población* 35(87): 95–120.

Mayans, Itzel, and Moisés Vaca. 2018. "Nuevos argumentos en contra del aborto." In *Aborto. Aspectos normativos, jurídicos y discursivos*, ed. Daniel Busdygan, 95–118. Buenos Aires: Biblos.

Morley, Morris. 2000. "Los ciclos políticos neoliberales." In *La izquierda contrataca*, ed. James Petras, 162–188. Madrid: Akal.

Revista Tres Puntos. 1997. "Por primera vez veinte mujeres se atreven a decir: Yo aborté," 1(23).

Red de Acceso al Aborto Seguro - Argentina (REDAAS), Equipo Latinoamericano de Justicia y Género (ELA), and Centro de Estudios de Estado y Sociedad (CEDES). 2018. "Las cifras del aborto en Argentina." March 1. www.redaas.org.ar/nuestro-trabajo-documento.php?a=64.

Rosenberg, Martha, and Elsa Schvartzman. 2014 "La Campaña Nacional por el Derecho al Aborto Legal, Seguro y Gratuito. La lucha por el derecho al aborto: Una deuda de la democracia." *Voces en el Fénix* 5(32): 142–149.

Tarducci, Mónica, Catalina Trebisacce, and Karin Grammático. 2019. *Cuando el feminismo era mala palabra. Algunas experiencias del feminismo porteño*. Buenos Aires: Espacio Editorial.

Theumer, Emmanuel. 2018. "1994 en la memoria feminista. Disputas por la liberación del aborto." *Latfem*, May 30. http://latfem.org/1994-en-la-memoria-feminista-disputas-por-la-liberacion-del-aborto/.

Vaggione, Juan Marco. 2011. "Sexualidad, religión y política en América Latina." In *Sexualidade e Politica na América Latina: Histórias, intersecoes e paradoxos*, eds. Sonia Correa and Richard Parker, 286–336. Rio de Janeiro: Associação Brasileira Interdisciplinar de AIDS.

Williamson, John. 1999. "Lo que Washington quiere decir cuando se refiere a reformas de las políticas económicas." In *La cultura de la estabilidad y el consenso de Washington*, eds. Manuel Guitián and Joaquín Muns Albuixech, 118–138. Madrid: La Caixa.

9

SOCIAL MEDIA DEBATE ON #ABORTOLEGAL IN ARGENTINA

Claudia Laudano

Social Media and Feminist Cyberactivism in the Public Sphere

In the context of the first parliamentary debate on the legalization of abortion in Argentina in 2018, social media platforms—specifically Twitter—became a meaningful site of political debate in the country.[1] Among other strategies, the National Campaign for the Right to Legal, Safe, and Free Abortion[2] (hereafter the Campaign) extensively utilized social media to promote and sustain its point of view. The tweetathons, organized twice a week with different hashtags, including the successful #AbortoLegal (#LegalAbortion), were frequent trending topics and therefore gained widespread public visibility. Yet, feminists were not the only ones using social media to disseminate their ideas on the status of abortion: conservatives did too. Networking became a major site of dispute, with intense and vibrant moments in which feminist cyberactivism led the challenge.

Since the mid-1990s, cyberfeminism has become a noticeable trend within the feminist movement, concerning the relations between women and digital technologies in the era of Internet. The most optimistic viewpoints considered cyberspace as a special political arena where sexism could be subverted and patriarchy dismantled. In a context characterized by the global expansion of information and communication technologies (ICT), feminist and women's groups throughout the world have become progressively more active, using ICT for their own goals (Nuñez Puente 2011; Natansohn 2013; Fotopoulou 2014; Mendes, Ringrose, and Keller 2019).

From that moment on, as Internet connection became more accessible, cheaper, and faster, countless individual and collective feminist actions appeared in different parts of the world, enriching the public sphere and contemporary democracies, as more voices, images, discourses, and testimonies of women and girls could be spread. As for other social movements (Castells 2012; Gerbaudo 2012; Reguillo 2017), social media improved the opportunities to organize and coordinate collective actions on-

DOI: 10.4324/9781003079903-12

and offline with repercussions in the media and the political sphere, as well as to connect globally.

In contrast to the two major theoretical perspectives on technologies, which could be characterized as strong technological determinism and naïve celebration of the power of citizens, the framework of this chapter is based on attention to the social appropriation of technologies. This perspective considers that the appropriation of ICT by women and girls occur as material and symbolic processes, according to their needs and skills, with reproductive or somewhat creative uses (Lago Martínez, Méndez, and Gendler 2017), as "skilled accomplishments" (Thompson 1995, 40).

Although Twitter as a platform has less followers in Argentina in comparison to others like Instagram and Facebook, the twittersphere has become a meaningful site for political debate. The majority of politicians participate in Twitter and use it to make frequent public announcements (Calvo 2015; Galup 2019) and most journalists and media programs also have accounts and follow trending topics as part of their daily routine.

Trending topics may be the result of spontaneous or planned actions. The tweetathon, as an organized e-tactic of intervention in Twitter, is a call to concentrate participation at a certain moment in time around a hashtag: a keyword or phrase introduced by the symbol #, as a label to mark contents about certain topics of conversation. Hashtags are considered successful when they become part of the list of the top local trending topics and therefore visible within the social media and probably offline as well. Besides technical characteristics, hashtags are also a dispositive to articulate political subjectivities (Reguillo 2017), hopes (Clark 2016), and affects (Castells 2012; Papacharissi 2015).

Local trending topics have only been available in Twitter since 2010, and the international appropriation of hashtagging for feminist goals has been increasingly used since that time. #EndSH, #aufschrei, #MachismoMata, #YesAllWomen, #direnkahkaha, #AcosoEsViolencia, #PrecisamosFalarSobreAborto were some of the earliest feminist hashtags in different languages and with variable levels of dissemination (Akyel 2014; Maireder and Schlögl 2014; Rodino-Colocino 2014; Kearl 2015). The effectiveness of these feminist cyberactions, some of them reported by mainstream news, were taken into account as part of the structure of opportunities (Tarrow 1994) in 2015, during the #NiUnaMenos (#NotOneWomanLess) demonstration against violence against women and femicides in Argentina.

#NiUnaMenos went viral in the local and global trending topics and was a milestone for a hashtag in Spanish. Later, during the preparation for the First International Women's Strike in 2017, the hashtags #MujeresEnHuelga (#WomensStrike) and #YoParo8M (#IStrike8M) were used to explain the reasons for the global strike and, moreover, to attract public attention, becoming local and global trending topics (Laudano 2019). Since 2015, there has been a marked increase in feminist hashtags in Spanish and in Latin America in general referring to different forms of violence against women and girls, such as: #Primeiroassédio (#MyFirstAbuse) in Brazil and then #MiPrimerAcoso (#MyFirstAbuse) in Mexico, #NoNosCallamosMas (#WeWillNotBeSilenced), #Cuentalo (#TellUs), #YoSíTeCreo (#IBelieveYou), besides the #MeToo global movement. Sometimes, the hashtags were exclusively e-tactics, as innovation (Earl and Kimport 2011), but others formed part of the hybrid action repertoires of the movements or groups (Chadwick 2007; Van Laer and Van Aelst 2010).

In light of the political significance of cyberactivism, the goal of this chapter is to analyze the main characteristics of the appropriation of digital technologies, especially Twitter, by the Campaign during the debate for the legalization of abortion in Argentina in 2018, and the response of conservative groups opposed to legalization on the same platform. The main argument is that social media are not only part of an extended public sphere which contribute to enrich contemporary democracies in various ways, but that cyberactions as skilled accomplishment in the twittersphere may have repercussions both in the media and in the broader political sphere, with unexpected results. In the weeks leading up to the debate in the Chamber of Deputies in 2018, feminist activism achieved an unprecedented mass mobilization both in public demonstrations and on social networks in favor of abortion legalization, with a notable ripple effect in the national and international arenas.

The methodological tool of virtual ethnography (Hine 2000) informs this study. Data were collected by daily monitoring of the debates related to the legalization of abortion in the trending topics lists of Twitter from January to August 2018, with special attention to the tweetathons. Hashtags were collected by scrapping techniques, to observe the main characteristics of the actions, the number of accounts involved, and tweets generated, the duration of the conversation, the main arguments, and the top tweeters, among other issues. A sample of trending topics which appeared in different mainstream media was also registered.

A Brief Summary of Cyberactivism for #AbortoLegal in Argentina

Since its creation in 2005, the National Campaign for the Right to Legal, Safe, and Free Abortion has used many different digital sites and platforms for internal organization and debates as well as to publicize its aims and influence the public opinion, as part of its dual strategy as a counterpublic (Fraser 1991). The Internet has created enormous potential to disseminate information about abortion, which for decades had been a difficult issue to include in the media agenda (Laudano 2001). Lists of emails, webpages, blogs, and the commercial platform Facebook were the initial main sites in a gradual process of appropriation of digital technologies by feminist groups in general in Argentina (Laudano 2019).

However, a significant moment in digital activism occurred in 2016, when the hashtag #AbortoLegal (#LegalAbortion) was a trending topic for the first time on Twitter for 14 hours and reached the top of the list. The Campaign called for support through social media in preparation for the sixth presentation of its bill for legal abortion in Congress. The tweetathon gained massive support from feminists and the general public as well as obtaining repercussions in global trends.

From that moment on, digital technologies were frequently used, especially the tweetathon as an e-tactic to install the issue in Twitter's agenda. In 2017, during the

#GritoGlobal (#GlobalCry) Campaign for September 28, the day for the legalization of abortion in Latin America since 1990, the hashtag #AbortoLegal spread virally and obtained a new record on the platform, topping the trends for many hours and sparking a discussion that continued for three days. These successful actions formed the backdrop to the digital activism of 2018, when the Campaign's abortion legalization bill was presented to Congress for the seventh time, as described below.

How the Social Media Debate Started in 2018

In January 2018, two spontaneous cyberactions concerning feminist issues took place on Twitter with outstanding results. The first of them was on January 2 when an actress responded by tweet to the televised comments of an actor who said that becoming a mother makes a woman whole. After the massive mobilizations against gender violence in #NiUnaMenos in 2015 and the first Women's Strike in #8M in 2017, that comment on motherhood as women's main form of fulfillment generated anger across social networks. One of the persons who responded on Twitter, the actress Muriel Santana, posted that she had interrupted a pregnancy as a life choice. That testimony, in first person in cyberspace, stimulated a series of other testimonies from women from different social backgrounds, ages, and moments in life stories. The actress was also subjected to a series of denigrating insults on Twitter. This controversy stimulated a vigorous return to the discussion about #AbortoLegal across the social networks, which continued for two consecutive days.

The second action originated in the verbal exchange between two Argentine celebrities. The first week of January 2018 had seen the Golden Globe Awards with widespread media coverage of the speeches of Hollywood actresses as the finishing touch to the relentless "Time's Up" campaign against harassment and sexual abuse which had begun with the hashtag #MeToo. At the same time, in Argentina several actors and presenters were publicly exposed for the same reasons, and one well-known singer over 70 years old casually said, "if you suffer rape, relax and enjoy," without realizing that the expression was no longer admissible.

Another actress criticized the comment, but emphasized that she was not a feminist, that she had a beautiful son and husband and respected men. This generated widespread anger, and cyberfeminism immediately responded with the hashtag #SoyFeminista (#IAmFeminist), which was quickly popular throughout the social network. In fact, statements of pride and self-identification as feminists became the leading topic on Twitter for three days with repercussions in the global ranking of the platform and brought together the enthusiasm of both Latin American and Spanish participants just at the time that the Second International Women's Strike was being organized for the #8M, International Women's Day.

The media astutely reported the unprecedented success of both cyberfeminist actions which, in just 20 days, sent shock waves across different media channels, with debates on the freedom to choose motherhood, practices to terminate pregnancy, the legalization of abortion, media sexism, sexual harassment, the history of feminism as a movement, and personal experiences of being a feminist.

As a consequence of the viral spreading of the hashtag #SoyFeminista like a choral "we," several feminists were invited to participate on different television programs in the context of reports of sexual abuse against certain actors and television presenters. A highly-rated show decided to continue the debate for a whole week, interviewing different feminists on topics such as the feminist movement, sexual abuse, and the different forms of discrimination in the media. The successful television ratings (You-Tube videos of the program also had more than 500,000 visits) and daily trends on Twitter favorable to the shows guaranteed the continuity of feminist interviews, even where the discussions fell outside the normal scope of the program.

What happened next was an unexpected surge in the demand for the legislative debate on the legalization of abortion, which was immediately converted by feminists into the hashtag #AbortoLegalYa (#LegalAbortionNow), and it once again led the trends on Twitter, with news coverage. For two consecutive days, the trending topic of abortion legalization not only crowned a week of feminist appearances on television but showed that social networks were reverberating with the demand which had long been heard in the streets and intermittently in the media: "The time for legal abortion is now."

At this point in time, a fluid dynamic could be seen between digital activism and media coverage, clearly revealing the skills of cyberfeminists to make their voices heard and enable the debate for abortion legalization to transcend exclusively feminist spaces into different areas of society. In fact, these two spontaneous and powerful cyberactions in Twitter were a major trigger for the abortion law debate in Congress.

Time for Tweetathons by @CampAbortoLegal

Organizing the Day of Green Action for the Right to Abortion on February 19, 2018, the Campaign proposed a combined action of mobilization on social networks and in the streets (on- and offline). Online, the communication commission of the Campaign decided to use the tweetathon strategy of #AbortoLegalYa (#LegalAbortionNow) for two hours at midday to show a demonstration of strength which would position the urgency of the demand online and stimulate the successive street demonstrations.

Within minutes, the hashtag #AbortoLegalYa suddenly climbed to reach among the top network trends. It reached the top place in local trends, and within an hour also appeared in global trends. These outstanding results were immediately reported by news agencies and featured on different digital media.

The data collected shows that in just two hours of planned action, 40,500 accounts (twice the number of previous actions) generated 107,000 tweets. Most of these were related to arguments to legalize abortion from the perspective of public health, human rights, and information on the legislative proposal, including the Campaign's slogan, jingles, videos, drawings, graphics, and green emojis: a combination of current multimedia language in which the networks were "painted green," the color that came to be identified with the Campaign and support for abortion rights more broadly.

The cyberaction had achieved unprecedented enthusiasm, which was spread not only by feminist activists and sympathizers but also a wide range of politicians, celebrities, intellectuals, journalists, and academics. Then, during the afternoon, photos and videos of the huge *pañuelazos* (green kerchief demonstrations) appeared both outside the National Congress and in city centers across the country.

The tweets continued throughout the day and finished with a record frequency of hashtags, for the fourth time in less than 50 days, but this time as an organized strategy of the Campaign. News on the effective cyberaction of #AbortoLegal continued for several days and increased the visibility of the Campaign. This success strengthened the combined strategy of on- and offline mobilization. Therefore, the digital strategy became an inextricable dimension of the Campaign's strategy of visibility and influence on the public opinion, rather than a mere tactic to organize demonstrations.

Later on, at the beginning of March 2018, the bill for abortion legalization was presented for the seventh time in the National Congress (see Gutiérrez, this volume). On all previous occasions the proposal had been stymied by successive governments, but this time, with a continued high trending of hashtags in social networks and a green tide of activists and sympathizers in the irrefutable massive mobilization for #8M, the second International Women's Strike, the government was under pressure. In fact, the mass multimedia coverage meant that the right-wing government of Mauricio Macri could not ignore the proposal this time, especially since his advisers were particularly concerned about social network tendencies.

After years of waiting for the debate in Congress, #AbortoLegalYa became the irrefutable flagship of the struggle, demanding an urgent solution. While the lower house of Congress, the Chamber of Deputies, convened on April 10, 2018, the hashtag #AbortoLegalYa was again the top local trend in conversations, which continued for 13 hours and achieved global repercussions for ten hours. This historic achievement of gaining visibility in the networks was highlighted in the reports of the Campaign from the outset and would later be a specific topic of discourse in the informative sessions of the Chamber of Deputies.[3]

From this point on, the twice weekly parliamentary report sessions were accompanied by successful online actions with different hashtags: #QueAbortoSeaLey (#Abortion-ShouldBeLaw), #AbortoNosotrasDecidimos (#AbortionWeDecide), #AbortoLegalJusticiaSocial (#LegalAbortionSocialJustice), #AbortoLegalEsSalud (#LegalAbortion IsHealth), #AbortoDeudadelaDemocracia (#AbortionDebtofDemocracy), #YoVotoAbortoLegal (#IVoteLegalAbortion). The change was necessary to avoid the rules of the companies which stop ranking those hashtags that have already trended to provide space for new topics of conversation.

As Marco Bräuer (2008) says, the choice of strategies and the use of a particular repertoire of action in a specific social movement could be conceptualized as the result of a collective decision-making process shaped by the goals of the group, the available resources (time, money, skills, experiences), the collective action frames, and the evaluation of the given political opportunity structures. Feminist cyberactivists euphorically posted "the networks are ours" with every trending success, acknowledging the skills they had acquired and their ability to communicate with a "green community" through the networks, a community which never failed to respond and make the challenge their own. Synchronized participation effectively generates adrenalin and complicity around a common objective, and at the same time contributes to the construction of a community, which is connected on a daily basis and leads to euphoria when the actions result in the achievement of common objectives.

At the same time, the communication commission of the Campaign shared what was happening in the legislature. Although the debates in the Chamber of Deputies and, later, in the Senate were transmitted in YouTube on the National Congress channel, the essential work of editing and citing key discourses concentrated the focus on the arguments for the Campaign's bill, many of which went viral via retweets. Nevertheless, all the discourses were collected on the YouTube channel of the Campaign, together with the 15 parliamentary reports including the most important extracts of every session.

The accounts which were most active from March to May 2018 were the major institutional accounts, such as the @CampAbortoLegal of the Campaign with hundreds of thousands of followers, constituting a type of "authority" with wide powers of dissemination. Another more recent institutional account with less experience in cyberactivism was the @RedSaludDecidir of the Network of Healthcare Professionals for the Right to Choose (Red de Profesionales de la Salud por el Derecho a Decidir), who work in the public health system and create the conditions for access to legal abortions. These accounts posted the highest number of tweets per day and were the most reproduced, a fact showing that they are robust nodes with mass followings favoring the dissemination of the tweets (Entman and Usher 2018).

However, about halfway through the cyberactivism process, a new phenomenon was observed: that of personal accounts—some of which at the time had no more than 300 followers, such as @luciatre86, @c73lima1, @macia753—that made an important contribution to the successfully high ranking of #AbortoLegalYa (#LegalAbortionNow) and #AbortoLegalEsVida (LegalAbortionIsLife). What marks a difference between these Twitter actions and those previously analyzed in Argentina (Calvo and Aruguete 2020) is that the Campaign showed the gradual incorporation and articulation between communities, networks, and subjects who connected and identified in the same process to construct the cyberaction.

To be clear, cyberaction is not just about posting tweets, but also involves a process of collective construction of identity and the socialization of contents: the inclusion of names and profile pictures of symbols and colors of the Campaign; the posting of selfies with the emblematic green kerchief, and the creative production of memes. The conversation continued to grow through an increasing number of accounts taking part, but also of "fans" following the Campaign by retweets, making their voices heard to become protagonists in the conversation. Therefore, as part of the continuum on- and offline, the platform served not only as a conduit for connective actions (Papacharissi 2015), but also for collective ones, in their capacity to negotiate collective identity.

Tweetathons in social networks and feminist demonstrations throughout the country together with the "Green Tuesdays" outside the Congress with speakers, live music, poetry, and dance were the main strategies of action to publicize the Campaign, connect broader publics, and increase intergenerational awareness of the issues involved (Sutton 2020). The simultaneous on- and offline mobilization brought about the historic vote when the bill for legalized abortion was passed in the lower house on June 14, 2018. Huge crowds outside Congress erupted in euphoria and tears of emotion, and once again social networks were painted green for hours.

The twice-weekly cyberactions continued until August 2018 when the bill would be debated in the Senate, although the second stage of activism would be different due to the actions of groups opposed to the bill, as described below. The sustained work of the Campaign in social networks from March to August and the widening feminist coalition made abortion legalization a frequent trending topic with continued local media coverage, and sometimes international attention.[4] On August 8 and 9, the bill was debated in the Senate and 141,000 tweets were created with the hashtag #8ASeraLey (#8AWillBeLaw) with more than 19,000 accounts participating. This was an outstanding number, considering that the average participation in the tweeta-thons of March and April of the same year were between 3,000 and 4,000. As the movement grew, the expression #AbortoLegalYa became the emblem of the Cam-paign, ostensibly publicizing the language of the social networks as part of the cultural framework of the movement.

Cyberactions of Groups Opposed to Legal Abortion

After the bill was passed in the Chamber of Deputies on June 14, 2018, a definite change could be seen in the tactics of the opposition as they began an organized strategy using digital technology and social networks, particularly Twitter. There-fore, the following analysis involves two different stages of the appropriation of digital technologies by this sector.

Initially participation was unsystematic, with sporadic incursions without evidence of planned strategies. In Twitter the posts appeared more as a reaction to the activism of #AbortoLegalYa, rather than a strategic aim. After the success of the bill in the lower house, the opposition began disruptive actions to try to block the extensive publicity of the Campaign. First, the Campaign hashtags were infiltrated by adding simple negative words, for example, No #AbortoLegal (No #LegalAbortion) or #AbortoLegalNunca (#LegalAbortionNever). These actions could be characterized as emotional, angry reactions mostly generated by individuals rather than by institutio-nalized accounts. While these incursions disrupted the messages, they actually con-tributed to increase the number of participants in the hashtag, facilitating a higher position in the ranking of trending topics, so paradoxically they achieved a positive rather than negative effect in the metrics.

The second tactic of participation, in contrast, was directly aimed at blocking the high visibility of the Campaign on the platform through the use of counter-hashtags. These were hashtags created specifically by the opposition to disrupt the Campaign rankings at specific moments in time. An example can be observed on February 19,

2018 when #AbortoLegalYa spread quickly across the networks and became the top-ranking discussion for many hours. The anti #AbortoLegal sectors circulated their classic slogan, this time transforming it into the hashtag #SiALaVida (#YesToLife). It remained for four hours in Twitter conversation, sometimes with the hashtag #NadieMenos (#NobodyLess).[5]

In Argentina, March 25 was established in 1998 to commemorate the day of "the Unborn Child." In 2018, the opposition used the hashtag #SiALaVida online to accompany the street demonstrations mobilized by the Catholic Church. However, on this day the highest ranking image was of a giant *papier-mâché* effigy of a fetus, the "pro-life" emblem. After three decades of using highly emotional icons and figures of exaggerated size and development in Argentina (Laudano 2001, 2012), this time the public reaction was different. The "giant public fetus" became the object of an outpour of ironic memes (a recent addition to digital language), making it an object of ridicule and humor for several days. This response in social media showed a significant turn in the contemporary imaginary of the interruption of pregnancy. Laughter and humor were now freely available resources in the cultural battle for meaning.

The hashtag #SiALaVida (#YesToLife) sustained eight hours of discussion as a trending topic on Twitter, a good result for a debut strategy online. However, it was noticeable that a considerable number of accounts had been set up just before the day of action or on the same day (Galup 2019). This fact alerted suspicions about the authenticity of the accounts and pointed to the use of bots (automated accounts), an artificial strategy which might be employed when faced with a low level of activism across the networks.

In the first stage from April to June 2018 in the run up to the debate in Congress, there were a limited number of opposition posts reacting to the tweetathons of the Campaign, called just a few hours later, as a mirror tactic. Centered on their particular notion of life, the slogans, which had previously been used both nationally (Laudano 2001, 2012; Vacarezza 2012) and as part of a transnational rhetoric, were the following: #SalvemosLasDosVidas (#Let'sSaveBothLives), #CuidemosLas2Vidas (#Take-Careof2Lives), #ArgentinaQuiereVida (#ArgentinaWantsLife), #LaVidaNoSeNegocia (#NoDealOnLife), #MarchaPorLaVida (#MarchForLife), #VotemosVida (#VoteForLife), #AbortoNoEsNiUnaMenos (#AbortionIsNotOneWomanLess), and #ArgentinaEsProVida (#ArgentinaIsProLife). On only one occasion, in the run up to the #MarchForLife held in May of the same year, was there an organized call to a tweetathon as part of the on- and offline demonstration.

To summarize, during the first stage the conservative groups did not prioritize cyberspace as a forum to publicize their standpoint, since actions were sporadic, limited to reacting to the Campaign posts, and tweetathons were used only once to mobilize demonstrations in the traditional public sphere. It is interesting to note that analyses of participant accounts in every action show that most of the top tweeters were men.

Nevertheless, as a communication strategy the Campaign refused to confront the question of the beginning of life, so beloved by the Catholic Church and conservative groups. Instead they chose the hashtag #AbortoNosotrasDecidimos (#AbortionWe-Choose), digitally bringing up to date the classic debate defined as "pro-life" or "pro-choice." The Campaign slogan, "Sex education for choice, contraception to prevent abortion, legal abortion to prevent death"[6] gives another take on the preservation of life. As does the hashtag #AbortoLegalEsVida (#LegalAbortionIsLife) used on May 28, the day on which the Campaign celebrated its 13th anniversary of struggle, referring to the women and girls whose daily lives are put at risk by unsafe and clandestine abortions.

Then, two days before the vote in the Chamber of Deputies, came a moment of decisive confrontation in the public sphere. With conservative groups striving to center the debate on the protection of the fetus, the Campaign managed to turn the debate towards the need to end clandestine abortions that may cause death and severe consequences for future health. The hashtag #AbortoLegalOClandestino (#LegalOrClandestineAbortions) was therefore a skilled accomplishment in a double sense, as it summarized the terms of the public debate in a proper way and showed abortion rights activists' ability to manage the language of social media with symbolic efficacy.

As mentioned above, the turning point in the cyberactivism of conservative groups came after the bill was passed in the Chamber of Deputies in June 2018. From this point on, they began an offensive initiative on Twitter in preparation for the vote in the upper house.

From Amateur Opposition to Cyberactivists

In the second stage, analysis of the main contents of the online debates shows how the groups opposed to abortion legalization intensified the dispute, this time not just responding negatively to the feminist cyberactions but generating their own content. This change shows that social media were now recognized as meaningful sites for political confrontation. Therefore, the groups began to compete for the skillful command of the platform.

While the direct confrontation with the Campaign hashtags continued—counterhashtags such as #RechazoFederal (#FederalRejection) responding as an inverted-mirror tactic to the Campaign hashtag #PañuelazoFederal (#FederalPañuelazo)—at the end of June 2018, conservative groups' own initiatives were more frequent to obtain visibility and reverberations in the public sphere. Previously, they imitated other action repertoires of the Campaign; for example, promoting the use of light blue kerchiefs (as opposed to the massively used green kerchiefs of feminists), promoting demonstrations #PorLaVida (#ForLife), and now imitating the metaphor of the massive "Green Tide" by using the term "Light Blue Wave."

The choice of colors of the opposition was also strategic to outline an identity in social media: they appropriated patriotic symbols and colors, as the light blue and white, the colors of the national flag of Argentina, suggested a national cause. The light blue color began to be used as profile and background photos and emojis, as hearts and waves of the same color flooded social media.

The light blue flyers used to organize the tweetathons with a definite date, time, and hashtag (indications of a planned strategy) contained neither personal nor institutional names. This lack of explicit reference seems a tactic to pretend a spontaneous production of actions online, as expressions of a self-organized (*auto-convocada*) citizenry.

Then, the type of hashtags widened their political content to reject the legalization bill, such as #RuidazoParaElRechazo (#NoiseForRejection) and #DictamenRechazoTotal (#VerdictTotalRejection) as well as those to pressure President Mauricio Macri: #MacriConAbortoNoTeVoto (#MacriWithAbortionIWon'tVoteForYou). The opposition also resorted to false accusations against Planned Parenthood as well as some local organizations with the hashtag #AbortoEsNegocio (#AbortionIsBusiness), as part of a campaign of fake news. The self-identification as "pro-life" was frequent in hashtags such as #SoyProvida (#ImProLife) and #RevoluciónProVida (#ProLifeRevolution) together with the use of the light blue color in the hashtags #LaOlaCeleste (#LightBlueWave) and #ArgentinaCeleste (#LightBlueArgentina).

In this second stage of intense political confrontation, the posts do not mention the Campaign, as the main collective actor leading the process. However, there are references to "the feminists," "the green kerchiefs" (or its diminutive "little green kerchiefs" as pejorative) and to Actrices Argentinas (the collective of actresses that supported the Campaign), usually with the term "feminazis" to discredit the movement. Most likely, there was a strategic decision not to recognize the Campaign as the most important adversary in the contention.

As a result of strategic planning, the opposition obtained a sustained number of tweets during each action, twice and sometimes three times more than in the first stage, with increased accounts in conversation, including bots, and some international support during the tweetathons. They also achieved the position of trending topic for many hours, celebrating their triumph on the same platforms.

As the date approached for the vote in the Senate, the polarized debates on the platform became increasingly more intense. On July 31, 2018, one week before the vote, there were five topics with the following hashtags: #MartesVerde (#GreenTuesday) and #LegalOClandestino (#LegalOrClandestine) (this time simplified, without "abortion") and the critical #EsMuyDeLosProvida (#ItIsVeryProLife), for the Campaign. While the trending topics for the opposition were #MacriConAbortoNoTeVoto (#MacriWithAbortionIWon'tVoteForYou) and #RechazoTotal (#Total Rejection). This intense level of dispute for hegemony in the days leading up to the vote meant that the networks became an incessant battlefield for meaning.

Opposition cyberactions at this time were complemented by the simultaneous planning of demonstrations such as that in the center of Buenos Aires by Evangelical groups, #MarchaFederal on August 4, 2018 with the tweetathon #SalvemosLas2Vidas (#Let'sSaveThe2Lives). This joint mobilization on- and offline made visible the opposition in both spaces and also gave them mainstream media time, just a few days before the vote in the Senate. The abortion legalization bill was finally defeated by a meager margin.

One unfortunate development in the second stage of the dispute was the virulence of the attacks against individual, group, and institutional accounts in favor of abortion legalization by means of insults and derogatory remarks, unsolicited photos and drawings (for example, the hanging of feminists or gory bloody fetuses). There were also massive intimidating attacks organized against certain accounts which were forced to change their status from public to private as a protective tactic (Amnistía Internacional 2019). And that is exactly the aim of these campaigns: to expel and silence certain voices (Calvo and Aruguete 2020). However, attacks were not only online, as activists with green kerchiefs were attacked in public places, and women's murals were defaced.

Conclusions

The year 2018, without doubt, marked a milestone in the long struggle for the legalization of abortion in Argentina and as such encouraged feminist activism throughout Latin America and other regions of the world. In the run up to the debate in the legislature, the appropriation of digital technologies formed a fundamental dimension in the overall mobilization strategies of the Campaign, as part of the structure of political opportunities.

While the activism of the Campaign should not be reduced to one exclusive digital platform, the political reverberations of Twitter in the country showed that it merited a specific strategy. The most important result of this strategy was the visibility of the arguments for the legalization of abortion in the wider public sphere.

There had been spontaneous calls for mobilization before and during this period, going viral with varying degrees of success and with repercussions in the media, but this time it was different. The specific tactic of tweetathons with certain hashtags at specific times and dates in the context of a general mobilization of public opinion was far removed from occasional tweeting and hashtagging. On the contrary, it constituted the skilled feminist appropriation of hashtag tactics in a specific political scenario: that of the long-awaited bill for legal abortion.

Once the groups opposing legal abortion realized the mutual implications for media coverage, operating between social networks and the general media, they decided to battle in Twitter. As a countermovement, at first they imitated to the letter the accomplishments of cyberfeminism and achieved certain favorable results, but in general without significant media coverage. However, in the time lapse before the bill was debated in the upper house, feminist hegemony in the network underwent a change as cyberspace became the forum of intensely polarized political contention.

Rather than a logical, rational, and democratic public debate, in which the best arguments would win, the opposition's interventions included arguments with varying doses of fake news, denigrating remarks, and organized violence. They resorted to their classic hyper-emotional tactics. A hashtag-based synthesis for 2018 could be: #AbortoLegalOClandestino (#LegalOrClandestineAbortion) versus #SalvemosLas2Vidas (#Let'sSaveThe2Lives).

From the time that the abortion legalization bill was rejected in the Senate in 2018 until the end of 2020, the countermovement continued its activities in cyberspace. These included frequent social media campaigns that became trending topics and even called into question the 1921 Penal Code, specifically in cases of rape (one of the exceptions to penalization). Then, during the COVID-19 pandemic in 2020, which led to social distancing measures, the countermovement's presence in digital platforms increased. Abortion rights opponents engaged in online mobilizations to extend their audience, with a multicentered strategy that included tweetathons in Twitter, dissemination of their message through websites, Facebook, Instagram, and TikTok, and marches that gained followers via YouTube live gatherings. These events included the Evangelical #MarchaPorLaVida (#MarchForLife) in May and the online mobilization for #8A, the international day for "the two lives," celebrating the Senate's rejection of the abortion bill in August 2018. The latter was an initiative by Unidad Provida (Pro-Life Unity), the Catholic and Evangelical coalition against legal abortion.

At the same time, the Campaign for the legalization of abortion in Argentina continued with #AbortoLegal2020 (#LegalAbortion2020) and presented a new bill for debate in Congress. As part of the challenges of the new context, during the preventative isolation required by the pandemic, the Campaign focused on a digital repertoire that included dissemination through different platforms, public presentations, and the emblematic *pañuelazos* (protests in which activists hold up the green kerchiefs/*pañuelos* that are symbolic of the movement). This time the *pañuelazo* was in the form of a collective photo of thousands of screens, with supporters holding the green kerchiefs simultaneously, during a Zoom meeting on September 28, the day for the legalization of abortion in Latin America. With December 2020 coming to a close, after intense legislative debate, abortion rights activists were able to celebrate a major victory as abortion became legal in Argentina and #EsLey (#ItisLaw) was the final hashtag that put a stamp on the movement's success.

Notes

1 This chapter is part of the ongoing research project, H817 "Contemporary feminisms and ICT: Modalities of appropriation of ICT by feminist groups in Argentina." Instituto de Investigaciones en Humanidades y Ciencias Sociales. Facultad de Humanidades y Ciencias de la Educación. Universidad Nacional de La Plata (Research Institute of Humanities and Social Sciences, School of Humanities and Science of Education, National University of La Plata, Argentina).
2 In Spanish, Campaña Nacional por el Derecho al Aborto Legal, Seguro y Gratuito. See Gutiérrez (this volume) for a discussion of the history and multipronged strategies of the Campaign.
3 See, for example, in the report of the first informative session in the Chamber of Deputies: www.youtube.com/watch?v=HjCX91BJHpU&t=6s. Then, during the informative session on May 22, 2018, the importance of social media could be seen in this discourse: www.youtube.com/watch?v=FUqtKW3pWTc
4 See, for example, Montoya (2018).
5 #NobodyLess is a counter-hashtag used by some individual men and conservative groups since 2015 in Argentina instead of the hashtag #NotOneWomanLess, as a reaction to the feminist demonstration in streets and social media about violence against women and girls.
6 In Spanish, Educación sexual para decidir, anticonceptivos para no abortar, aborto legal para no morir.

References

Akyel, Esma. 2014. "#Direnkahkaha (Resist Laughter): 'Laughter is a Revolutionary Action.'" *Feminist Media Studies* 14(6): 1093–1094.

Amnistía Internacional. 2019. "Corazones verdes. Violencia contra las mujeres online durante el debate por la legalización del aborto en Argentina." https://amnistia.org.ar/corazonesverdes/informe-corazones-verdes.

Bräuer, Marco. 2008. "Citizen Action Groups and Online Communication. How Resource Mobilisation Theory Can Help to Understand the Appropriation of Enhanced Repertoires of Action." In *Democracy, Journalism, and Technology: New Developments in an Enlarged Europe*, eds. Nico Carpentier, Pille Pruulman-Vengerfeldt, Kaarle Nordenstreng, Maren Hartmann, Peeter Vihalemm, Bart Cammaerts, Hannu Nieminen, and Tobias Olsson, 229–240. Tartu: Tartu University Press.

Calvo, Ernesto. 2015. *Anatomía política de Twitter en Argentina*. Buenos Aires: Capital Intelectual.

Calvo, Ernesto, and Natalia Aruguete. 2020. *Fake news, trolls y otros encantos*. Buenos Aires: Siglo Veintiuno.

Castells, Manuel. 2012. *Redes de indignación y esperanza*. Madrid: Alianza.

Chadwick, Andrew. 2007. "Digital Network Repertoires and Organization Hybridity." *Political Communication* 24(3): 283–301.

Clark, Rosemary. 2016. "'Hope in a Hashtag': The Discursive Activism of #WhyIStayed." *Feminist Media Studies* 16(5): 788–804.

Earl, Jennifer, and Katrina Kimport. 2011. *Digitally Enabled Social Change. Activism in the Internet Age*. Cambridge, MA: MIT Press.

Entman, Robert M., and Nikki Usher. 2018. "Framing in a Fractured Democracy: Impacts of Digital Technology on Ideology, Power and Cascading Network Activation." *Journal of Communication* 68(2): 298–308.

Fotopoulou, Aristea. 2014. "Digital and Networked by Default? Women's Organizations and the Social Imaginary of Networked Feminism." *New Media and Society* 18(6): 989–1005.

Fraser, Nancy. 1991. "Rethinking the Public Sphere: A Contribution to the Critique of Actually Existing Democracy." In *Habermas and the Public Sphere*, ed. Craig Calhoun, 109–142. Cambridge, MA: MIT Press.

Galup, Luciano. 2019. *Big data y política*. Buenos Aires: Penguin Random House.

Gerbaudo, Paolo. 2012. *Tweets and the Streets: Social Media and Contemporary Activism*. London: Pluto Press.

Hine, Christine. 2000. *Etnografía virtual*. Barcelona: Editorial de la Universitat Oberta de Catalunya.

Kearl, Holly. 2015. *Stop Global Street Harassment: Growing Activism around the World*. California: Praeger.

Lago Martínez, Silvia, Anahí Méndez, and Martín Gendler. 2017. "Teoría, debates y nuevas perspectivas sobre la apropiación de tecnologías digitales." In *Contribuciones al estudio de procesos de apropiación de tecnologías*, eds. Roxana Cabello and Adrián López, 75–86. Rada Tilly: Del Gato Gris.

Laudano, Claudia. 2001. "Direitos reprodutivos e aborto na mídia argentina dos anos 90." In *Saúde Reprodutiva na Esfera Pública e política na América Latina*, eds. María Coleta Albino de Oliveira and María Isabel Baltar da Rocha, 209–236. Campinas: Editora da Unicamp.

Laudano, Claudia. 2012. "Reflexiones en torno a las imágenes fetales en la esfera pública y la noción de 'vida' en los discursos contrarios a la legalización del aborto." *Temas de Mujeres* 8(8): 57–69.

Laudano, Claudia. 2019. "Acerca del uso estratégico de TIC en movilizaciones feministas." In *Tecnologías digitales. Miradas críticas de la apropiación en América Latina*, eds. Ana Laura Rivoir and María Julia Morales, 357–369. Buenos Aires: Consejo Latinoamericano de Ciencias Sociales; Montevideo: Red de Investigadores sobre Apropiación de Tecnologías Digitales.

Maireder, Axel, and Stephan Schlögl. 2014. "24 Hours of an #Outcry: The Networked Publics of a Socio-political Debate." *European Journal of Communication* 29(6): 687–702.

Mendes, Kaitlynn, Jessica Ringrose, and Jessalynn Keller. 2019. *Digital Feminist Activism. Girls and Women Fight Back Against Rape Culture.* New York: Oxford University Press.

Montoya, Angeline. 2018. "Le débat sur la légalisation de l'avortement s'ouvre enfin en Argentine." *Le Monde*, March 8. www.lemonde.fr/ameriques/article/2018/03/08/le-debat-sur-la-legalisation-de-l-avortement-s-ouvre-enfin-en-argentine_5267539_3222.html.

Natansohn, Graciela (ed.). 2013. *Internet en código femenino.* Buenos Aires: La Crujía.

Nuñez Puente, Sonia. 2011. "Feminist Cyberactivism: Violence Against Women, Internet Politics, and Spanish Feminist Praxis Online." *Continuum: Journal of Media & Cultural Studies* 25(3): 333–346.

Papacharissi, Zizi. 2015. "Affective Publics and Structures of Storytelling: Sentiment, Events and Mediality." *Information, Communication & Society* 19(3): 307–324.

Reguillo, Rossana. 2017. *Paisajes insurrectos: Jóvenes, redes y revueltas en el otoño civilizatorio.* Madrid: Ned Ediciones.

Rodino-Colocino, Michelle. 2014. "#YesAllWomen: Intersectional Mobilization Against Sexual Assault Is Radical (Again)." *Feminist Media Studies* 14(6): 1113–1115.

Sutton, Barbara. 2020. "Intergenerational Encounters in the Struggle for Abortion Rights in Argentina." *Women's Studies International Forum* 82: 102392.

Tarrow, Sidney. 1994. *Power in Movement. Social Movements and Contentious Politics.* New York: Cambridge University Press.

Thompson, John B. 1995. *The Media and Modernity. A Social Theory of the Media.* Cambridge: Polity Press.

Vacarezza, Nayla. 2012. "Política de los afectos y tecnologías de visualización en el discurso de los grupos contrarios a la legalización del aborto." *Papeles de Trabajo* 6(10): 46–61.

Van Laer, Jeroen, and Peter Van Aelst. 2010. "Internet and Social Movement Action Repertoires." *Information, Communication & Society* 13(8): 1146–1171.

10

TRANSFORMING ABORTION ACCESS THROUGH FEMINIST COMMUNITY-BASED HEALTHCARE AND ACTIVISM

A Case Study of Socorristas en Red in Argentina

Brianna Keefe-Oates

Introduction

Feminist activists have long supported people in need of abortions. In the 1970s in the United States a collective known as Jane, comprised of young feminists, learned how to perform abortions themselves and safely provided abortions in the Chicago area (Kaplan 1997). Other movements in France and Italy also created underground networks to facilitate abortion access (Bracke 2014). In Mexico, along the United States–Mexico border, clandestine abortion services have been provided for people on both sides (Murillo 2018). Until relatively recently, however, even safe clandestine services required relying on medical providers at some point in the process, with travel (at sometimes great distances) to a clinic for the procedure.

Over the past 20 years, the increased availability of medications that can be taken in the privacy of one's home to induce abortion has provided more choice in abortion methods and improved access for many people who live in areas where an abortion is illegal and/or clinics are inaccessible (Berer and Hoggart 2018; Kapp et al. 2018; Kapp and Lohr 2020). The use of these medications, which include a regimen of misoprostol alone or a combination of misoprostol and mifepristone, is considered safe by the World Health Organization (WHO), which provides protocols on the correct dosing and regimen (WHO 2018). The medications have increasingly meant that laypeople who are not medical providers can effectively learn and teach others how to take these medications safely.[1] Those who learn these methods are able to note any warning signs of complications and manage them appropriately (Berer and Hoggart 2018; Kapp et al. 2018; Kapp and Lohr 2020). As the use of medications for abortion has increased, various models have been developed to provide information on how to use and access these methods outside of the formal healthcare sector.[2] The medications have been especially transformative in places where abortion is highly restricted, as feminist activists,

DOI: 10.4324/9781003079903-13

health promoters, and community-based providers have created models in which they legally provide information on how to use the medication, and support people seeking abortion in a discreet way.[3]

In this context, feminist activists around the world have worked with researchers and medical providers to develop protocols to safely use the medications in areas where abortion is illegal or inaccessible in clinics. Their protocols incorporate WHO guidelines on safe use of the medication as well as procedures to emotionally support people seeking abortion (Zurbriggen, Keefe-Oates, and Gerdts 2018; Krauss 2019; Moseson et al. 2020). One such model often practiced by feminist activists is that of *accompaniment*, whereby activists offer information and emotional support to people in need of an abortion—the vast majority women—before, during, and after the process. In these cases, the activists often meet or speak on the phone with the people seeking abortion, communicating with them throughout their abortion process to ensure they have a safe, high-quality abortion (Zurbriggen, Keefe-Oates, and Gerdts 2018; Krauss 2019; Moseson et al. 2020).

These feminist groups are distinguishable from many other community-based models that provide information about abortion services in that they are grassroots organizations, often beginning as volunteer-led initiatives, dedicated to ensuring access to high-quality, compassionate abortion services, while also advocating from a feminist perspective to change laws and policies in the country.[4] These groups are often seeking not just increased abortion access but also truly fighting to dismantle patriarchal systems and incorporate feminist values into all levels of society—abortion access is an important, though not the only, topic that they advocate for.

Through their organizing and services, feminist collectives in Latin America have been crucial to improving abortion access. One such group that has had an enormous impact on abortion access and rights in their country is the Socorristas en Red—Feministas que Abortamos (Network of First Responders—Feminist who Abort). This network of feminist collectives in Argentina exists to support people seeking abortions throughout the country, where the practice was illegal—except for cases of rape or when the woman's health or life was at risk (Ruibal 2018)—until the December 2020 congressional approval of a bill to legalize abortion on demand up to the 14th week of pregnancy. Previous to this legislative change, the Supreme Court clarified in 2012 (in the F., A. L. case) the interpretation of the rape exception and recommended that authorities formulate and implement protocols to guarantee access to non-punishable abortions.

In 2019, the Argentine government instituted a federal protocol to determine who was eligible for a legal abortion under the law's exceptions. This protocol characterized health using the WHO definition, which conceptualizes health as a "state of complete physical, mental and social well-being and not merely the absence of disease or infirmity" (WHO 2020, n.p.). The new federal protocol had the potential to expand access with the new, specified regulations. Yet each province also sets policies that determine how broadly the law is interpreted, and many of these provinces chose not to adhere to the protocol, making abortion services in clinics inaccessible in many regions (Ruibal 2018; Franco and Volij 2020). Indeed, even now with legalization of abortion through 14 weeks gestation, access is likely to vary due to provincial differences in its implementation. Although abortion access has been changing in the country, the Socorristas en Red continue to provide information and support to thousands of people seeking abortion every year (Socorristas en Red 2020c).

The Socorristas en Red span the entire country, and its members focus not only on abortion accompaniment, but also actively engage in efforts to make the democratic state responsive to the need for legal, safe, and free abortion. They collaborate with and hold public health services accountable, advocate for a change in policies, and increase awareness of the issue through a feminist and democratic lens. This chapter will discuss the case study of the Socorristas en Red to demonstrate the power of merging both service provision and activism in the context of abortion rights and public health. The Socorristas show how feminist activists who provide abortion accompaniment have changed the landscape of abortion access and care. They also reflect a theoretical health perspective in line with Latin American Social Medicine, where those who provide healthcare are not only service providers but also active participants in advocacy in the context of democracy. They work to ensure equitable and just access to health services.

This chapter will show how the Socorristas have a multidimensional relationship with the Argentine state: they have provided extralegal abortion services that compensate for the state's historic failure to offer such services, while also demanding that the state legalizes abortion, and guarantees access in the cases that qualify for a legal abortion. The Socorristas are part of the National Campaign for the Right to Legal, Safe, and Free Abortion,[5] a coalition formed to demand the decriminalization and legalization of abortion as a "debt of democracy" (see Gutiérrez, this volume). Although the Socorristas' model may change after implementation of the abortion legalization bill, they will likely continue to support women seeking services, and advocate for better services in the new legal context.

Research Approach and Theoretical Framework

I utilize a case study of the Socorristas to demonstrate how feminist activists engage with the public health system and the state to ensure abortion access in a restrictive context. This analysis draws on a review of documents, websites, social media posts, and blogs produced by Socorristas en Red, academic articles about the network, as well as my own experiences and personal correspondence working directly with La Revuelta (The Revolt), one of the founding feminist collectives of Socorristas en Red.

The Socorristas' feminist principles influence all of their actions, and their work is extensive.[6] They fight not only for abortion access but for broader human rights and social justice from a feminist standpoint. This chapter will specifically analyze the Socorristas' practices from a public health perspective, assessing how their work reflects the theoretical health framework of Latin American Social Medicine (LASM), also known as "Collective Health."

LASM/Collective Health is a theoretical health framework developed in the 1950s and 1960s which focused on social theory and a critical analysis of how social structures, especially class, influence health (Tajer 2003; Granda 2008; Krieger 2011). As Débora Tajer, one of the former leaders of the Latin American Association of Social Medicine explains,

> Although LASM is basically considered as a stream of thought and knowledge, it has strong roots in a political practice, carried out by a social actor of heterogeneous characteristics, known as the LASM movement. The link between theory and practice makes LASM an approach with explicit ideological objectives that has undergone important changes throughout its nearly 40 years.
>
> *(Tajer 2003, 2023)*

LASM takes a rights-based approach to health, focusing on how the state has an obligation to ensure the right to health in an equitable fashion. It is rooted in anti-hegemonic principles that reject neoliberal and capitalist forms of healthcare; it addresses the dynamic relationship between health, illness, and care; and it emphasizes the importance of civil society, healthcare providers, and social movements in creating changes in governance to improve healthcare. The theory pays special attention to social determinants as the basis of health inequities and the means by which to improve health equity.[7] LASM aligns with a host of epidemiologic theories focused on social structures and health, termed social epidemiology (Krieger 2011).

LASM is unique in its explicit focus on the importance of social movements, particularly those with a focus on health, to pressure and transform societal structures—both from outside and inside of government—to impact on health (Tajer 2003; Krieger 2011; Vasquez, Perez-Brumer, and Parker 2019). As this case study will illustrate, the Socorristas' work aligns with the LASM framework due to their participation in a movement to ensure access to a fundamental human right—abortion care—which the state has traditionally failed to guarantee. They use the tools available in a democratic system to pressure the state in various forms to ensure equitable access to the right to abortion.

Case Study: Socorristas en Red—Feministas que Abortamos

Socorristas en Red—Feministas que Abortamos is a network of feminist collectives which began in 2012 and is now comprised of more than 50 individual collectives, all of whom provide accompaniment to people seeking abortions, and also engage in local and national advocacy to improve reproductive health services and rights (Burton 2017c; Socorristas en Red 2019; Piccinini 2020). Although each collective is unique in that it works in a certain region and tailors its actions to that specific cultural context, all of the network's collectives have similar values and protocols to provide abortion accompaniment. In addition to this service provision, the Socorristas have a political agenda to ensure that people can access abortion rights as well as other human rights that they believe the government should guarantee (Burton 2017b; Socorristas en Red 2020b). As they describe on their website:

In 2014 the Socorristas en Red became a clear network of accompaniers, focused on protecting the lives and health of those who decide to have an abortion, acknowledging that our experiences and empirical evidence show that when a person decides to have an abortion, they will do it, regardless of restrictive and criminalizing laws. The poorest and most vulnerable will do it and often put their lives at risk. Under this situation in which the state has abandoned [those choosing to have an abortion], networks that provide information and accompaniment are a response to this uncertainty, harm, and contempt that we hope to avoid. The Socorristas en Red have arisen from and are made possible by a complex network of groups advocating during a specific time period; [the Socorristas] are influenced by the strong presence of the groups comprising the National Campaign for the Right to Legal, Safe, and Free Abortion that, together with the broad women's movement, gender and sexual rights movements, researchers, health professionals, and other social sectors, bring and generate new political agendas.

(Socorristas en Red 2020b, n.p.)

As the Socorristas describe here, their mission is supported by a feminist agenda to ensure abortion access, recognizing the importance of collaboration and the need to guarantee social justice more broadly.

Activists from one of the founding collectives of Socorristas en Red, La Revuelta (The Revolt), developed an abortion accompaniment service in 2010 called Socorro Rosa (Pink Relief). In 2012, they coalesced with several other feminist collectives around the country who were also providing accompaniment and began to train other collectives to provide accompaniment, forming the current network. As the network was formed, participants developed a shared set of values and common practices (Maffeo et al. 2015; Burton 2017b). The expansive growth in collectives over the years has allowed the Socorristas to extend their reach and impact. In 2014 the entire network provided support to approximately 1,100 women who were accompanied in their abortion with medication. By 2019, the Socorristas had registered more than 12,500 women who had been accompanied in that year (Socorristas en Red 2020c). Yet the Socorristas en Red is more than a network that accompanies women who have abortions outside of the formal sector; the collectives that constitute the network also engage in advocacy and activism, at both the local and national levels, to change the status quo of Argentine society.

Providing a Crucial Health Service When "the State Abandons Us"

The most tangible, and one of the most visible, actions of the Socorristas is their model of accompaniment. This model has evolved over the years, and although implementation can vary across collectives and regions depending on the context, the model has four main "stages," as described by two of the groups' leaders, Belen Grosso and Ruth Zurbriggen of La Revuelta in Neuquén, Argentina (2016).

The first stage of accompaniment includes a publicized, local telephone number that women can call to speak to the Socorristas collective in their region. As described by

Grosso and Zurbriggen (2016, 3), "This is the first moment to listen, without judgment, calm anxieties, reassure, reduce fears, confirm decisions, listen to reasons without judging them, think through possible strategies if women are in situations of violence, etc." The second stage of the Socorristas' process is a group meeting. During the telephone call in the first stage, the Socorristas find a time when the person seeking an abortion can attend a group meeting. This is a meeting with several Socorristas and those who are seeking information on medication abortion. Grosso and Zurbriggen (2016, 3) describe the meetings as a place to "[s]how that abortions can be shared, they are not individual acts, we look to remove the weight of guilt and stigma that often surround this decision." During these meetings women share their experiences and see that other women may be in similar situations. At this time the Socorristas also provide a brochure on how to use medications for abortion, and review key information on how to take the medication, common side-effects, and any signs of symptoms that might merit a check from a doctor.

Following the group discussion, one Socorrista will meet individually with the person seeking an abortion—a time which Grosso and Zurbriggen refer to as the most intimate—to fill out a document that collects sociodemographic information and a medical and social history, as well as to discuss that person's specific situation at that time (Grosso and Zurbriggen 2016; Burton 2017b). This document helps the collectives gather information on who they serve. It also provides an opportunity for the Socorrista and the individual to speak in private and address any other concerns they may have (Burton 2017a). After this,

> Every woman that is at the meeting leaves with the telephone number that will help her connect to the Socorristas, who will provide follow-up and accompaniment. This will be the person [Socorrista] who they have just met, who has a face, name, body, who they know they can call for any question that is needed.
>
> *(Grosso and Zurbriggen 2016, 3)*

The final step in the accompaniment process is a post-abortion medical consultation, which is when the person who was accompanied can go to a "friendly" healthcare provider who the Socorristas work with and know is trustworthy, and who can provide a check-up to ensure the abortion is complete. The health professional may also provide contraception if it is desired, and answer any questions that arise (Grosso and Zurbriggen 2016; Burton 2017a).

Throughout the accompaniment process, a crucial aspect is the focus on providing people with the kind of support they need at the time, respecting their wishes and decisions, and ensuring their physical and legal safety (Zurbriggen, Keefe-Oates, and Gerdts 2018). In one study using a focus group methodology with Socorristas, accompaniers described how they worked to ensure people received support according to their desires, without imposing the Socorristas' own views. As one participant put it: "We are a service. We give you information and ultimately the decision is yours. As long as we are confident that we passed the information along … for us, their health is the most important" (Zurbriggen, Keefe-Oates, and Gerdts 2018, 111).

This support is especially significant during the third stage, when the woman is in touch with the accompanier during her abortion process. This direct line to someone they know and trust allows them to ask questions, share their fears, and feel reassured about their process. It also ensures that any warning signs of complications, which are very rare, can be identified quickly and addressed (Grosso and Zurbriggen 2016; Zurbriggen, Keefe-Oates, and Gerdts 2018).

When providing this care, the Socorristas are essentially community-based lay health providers with a feminist lens: they assess what people want in their abortion experience, use the knowledge learned from trainings with other Socorristas and medical professionals, help women identify potential side-effects and whether medical attention might be needed, refer women to post-abortion care if necessary, and continue to provide emotional support through the entire process. The Socorristas model of provision of health services and support in the community, outside of healthcare settings, has parallels with the *promotores de salud* (health promoters) models and other types of community health worker programs, which have grown in popularity over the years. In these models, health workers help to carry out health campaigns, such as vaccinations and health education, as well as support individuals in managing their chronic diseases in communities and households. The primary theoretical basis for these programs is that by providing the support for individuals where they are at, with ongoing care, they will be healthier and major health issues will be prevented rather than having to treat acute problems in the hospital. By this definition, the Socorristas are also community health workers, meeting people where they are at to ensure they get the high-quality service they need, and preventing unsafe abortions (WestRasmus et al. 2012; Balcazar et al. 2016; Zurbriggen, Keefe-Oates, and Gerdts 2018). Yet in these circumstances, the dedication of the Socorristas goes above and beyond community-based service provision; they provide a personalized, supportive, empowering model which ensures a quality of care that is rare in any health service.

The Socorristas are often quoted saying "The state has abandoned us," referring to the steady need for abortion services throughout the country and abortion as a human right, while the state refused to actually allow or provide those services (Socorristas en Red 2018, 2019). Although abortion in Argentina was largely illegal until very recently, post-abortion services (including check-ups, treatment of complications, and provision of contraception) have been offered through the public and private health systems, and legal abortions were allowed under certain circumstances depending on the province (Ministerio de Salud de la Nación Argentina 2017; Ruibal 2018; Franco and Volij 2020). The fact that these services existed demonstrates that the state may have recognized that illegal abortion was less safe, and thus provided post-abortion services and some additional allowances for legal abortion to try to decrease morbidity and mortality due to unsafe abortion. However, due to the largely illegal status of abortion, the state itself did not provide services for abortion on demand (this should change as a result of abortion legalization in December 2020). By providing support to people seeking abortions themselves, the Socorristas have provided a necessary service that is given in a compassionate, caring way, in the face of a democratic government system that has been traditionally unresponsive to the specific needs of gestating women, trans, and gender non-conforming individuals.

Holding the Public Health System Accountable

Although the Socorristas step in when the state does not guarantee the right to abortion, they also work to ensure that women are able to exercise the rights accorded by the state to the fullest of their ability. Here I outline several instances in which Socorristas en Red have worked to ensure people can be treated with dignity and respect under Argentine law and public health regulations. These interventions place abortion care as a fundamental human right and involve both collaboration with and pressure on the Argentine health system.

The Socorristas proactively work with many "friendly" healthcare providers who offer comprehensive sexual and reproductive services, post-abortion care, and often are available to consult on any cases of women who reached out to the Socorristas (Burton 2017a, 2017b; Grosso and Zurbriggen 2016). The Socorristas have built these relationships over the years, often through personal and work relationships, and participation in groups such as REDAAS[8] (Safe Abortion Access Network in Argentina) and the Red de Profesionales de la Salud por el Derecho a Decidir (Network of Health Professionals for the Right to Choose) (Grosso and Zurbriggen 2016).

One example of a comprehensive, local collaboration with health professionals began in 2012, when La Revuelta worked with the head of the Obstetrics and Gynecology program at the regional hospital in their city to create a post-abortion care clinic within the hospital, called Te Acompañamos [We Accompany You]. This was a clinic that opened each week for anyone who may want to consult a medical provider after their abortion. Gynecology residents staffed the service, while the Socorristas let women know they would have a safe place for post-abortion care should they want it. Although post-abortion care is not necessary for everyone, this initiative provided a safe space and an extra layer of attention and support for people having abortions (Grosso and Zurbriggen 2016). This work also served to grow the network of friendly medical providers who would collaborate with the Socorristas.

While the Socorristas on the one hand collaborate with allied health professionals, they also demand that the health systems carry out their mandates. This is how Socorrista Débora Machuca explained the relationship between her organization and the public health system during a public hearing in the Argentine Congress:

> Our responsibility as feminists is to demand that medical practices in the health system are provided from a rights perspective, taking into account the international treaties, and current international legal, economic, social, and cultural laws that ensure access to scientific advances and a benefit from its progress and application. We know this is possible because the Socorristas have been working with the health system in different regions of the country.
>
> *(Socorristas en Red 2018, 12)*

The Socorristas work to ensure that people can have a respectful, compassionate abortion, not only through their accompaniment outside the health system, but also within the health system in cases of legally permitted abortions. In order to ensure this right, the Socorristas pressure the public health and legal systems through formal complaints and lawsuits if such systems do not uphold existing laws and policies. For example, in 2015 in the city of Rosario a young woman was denied an abortion in the health system, even though she should have qualified under the law given her specific circumstances. In this case, the Socorristas lodged formal complaints against several medical providers and a lawyer involved in the case, decrying the denial of this right (*La Capital* 2015). In 2020 in the province of Río Negro, a woman who was the victim of domestic violence sought and received a legal abortion but was accused by some government authorities of having an illegal abortion. The woman's personal health information was released as legal authorities investigated the case, and some conservative media outlets acquired the information as well. The Socorristas lodged formal complaints against those authorities, and launched a public campaign to highlight this injustice. Although the case was still ongoing at the time of writing, most assumed that those in the government who had been involved in charging the woman would resign due to the malpractice and abuse they put the woman through (Gonzalez 2020).

Advocating for Legal and Social Change

The Socorristas not only work to ensure that women can access abortion services outside the formal health system, or through current Argentinean laws and public health regulations; they also actively participate in their democratic right to advocate to change the system (Socorristas en Red 2018). The Socorristas have long been part of the National Campaign for Legal, Safe, and Free Abortion (hereafter, the Campaign), which was launched in 2005 (Socorristas en Red 2019; Burton 2017b, 2017c; see also Gutiérrez, this volume). As a Campaign member, the Socorristas sign on to the coalition's agenda and participate in the advocacy activities that the Campaign promotes. In 2018, during the abortion legalization debates in the Argentinean lower house of Congress (Chamber of Deputies), multiple Socorristas from throughout the country testified about the importance of abortion law reform and in support of the Campaign. Many of their arguments included stories of the women they had accompanied. They spoke about how the existing laws violated women's rights while not preventing abortion, and how this denial of rights led to deaths due to unsafe abortion procedures. They also addressed how many of those who were denied these rights had less education, wealth, and privilege. In contrast, women who were able to pay for a costly extralegal abortion did not have to undergo dangerous procedures. The Socorristas underscored that individuals who end up in unsafe abortion situations are the same people who the state does not support with other rights such as education and labor (Socorristas en Red 2018). These arguments reflect a comprehensive feminist analysis of how the denial of abortion is part of a larger patriarchal system that violates people's fundamental rights.

In addition to their advocacy work at the national level with the Campaign, the Socorristas are constantly conducting local demonstrations, protests, and artistic activism to raise awareness of feminist agendas and abortion rights, and demanding action from the state. For example, in 2017 La Revuelta held a demonstration in their city center to denounce patriarchal values, hosting a march downtown, with many Socorristas wearing their signature pink wigs. They also offered a collective "learning opportunity," encouraging people to sit with leader Ruth Zurbriggen to discuss feminist values. The group then burned wooden pallets that created the words MACHO, accompanied by speeches and songs in support of feminist values and reproductive rights (La Revuelta 2017).

In another example in the city of Córdoba, a Socorristas group, currently called Socorristas Córdoba Hilando, incorporated several activist groups that were formally separate including the group Las Hilando, a collective that conducted "artivism," combining public artistic interventions with activism. This Socorristas group often conducts public art events to bring attention to feminist values and the unjust patriarchal system (*Medionegro* 2017). All of these events and local activism serve to raise awareness regarding abortion rights, pressure local governments to change their practices, and also publicize the accompaniment model and phone number of Socorristas so that more people will know how to find quality abortion care if needed.

Throughout the years, as their work has become more visible, the Socorristas have seen their ranks increase, as evidenced by the growth in the number of collectives that are part of the network (Socorristas en Red 2019). Women who were accompanied by the Socorristas sometimes join the collectives, and others who participated in public activities also decide to join and become more active participants. Socorristas en Red provides multiple opportunities for training in feminist values and the network's abortion accompaniment model specifically. They host teach-ins, workshops, and local and regional conferences, where new activists are trained and all of the participants continue to refine their strategies, discourses, and ideas (La Revuelta 2019; Socorristas en Red 2020a). In providing these various opportunities for learning and participation, the Socorristas are passing on knowledge to not only provide a crucial abortion service but also participate in the Argentine democracy to both hold it accountable and improve it.

Concluding Remarks

The Socorristas are first and foremost a feminist organization. Feminist values and perspectives drive their work—from abortion accompaniment, to activism to improve abortion laws, to other initiatives to achieve feminist social justice in society as a whole. At the same time, the Socorristas' model also serves an important public health purpose, ensuring safe abortion access, and improving sexual and reproductive health and rights in the country. As such, it also reflects the values and theoretical underpinnings of Latin American Social Medicine, one of whose pillars is a focus on the role of government in health equity (Granda 2008; Eslava-Castañeda 2017). LASM suggests that economic structures such as capitalism and who is in power create differential access to resources which influence a person's ability to lead a healthy life. As seen in their organizational declarations and their speeches to Congress, the Socorristas' feminist values and practices reflect similar principles, whereby they argue that those who have fewer resources and are more marginalized face more challenges to access and an increased risk of having an unsafe abortion, leading to increased risk of morbidity and mortality linked to those practices.

The Socorristas' accompaniment practices provide a person-centered model of care that is anti-hegemonic and rejects the notion of the medical provider being the sole expert. The Socorristas want to ensure that the people who seek their services are able to make their own decisions and choose the kind of care and experience that works best for their situation. They also provide equitable care; they aim to serve everyone and ensure that they can receive services regardless of class, age, disability status, gender identity, ethno-racial background, and other forms of marginalization in Argentina. They are constantly thinking about how to ensure that everyone can access their services; for example, during the coronavirus pandemic and quarantine in Argentina in 2020, they switched to holding online meetings, and worked to publicize their services as much as possible during the global health crisis.[9] Incorporating these principles so that people can have access to important health services in an equitable fashion reflects the practice of LASM.

The feminist views of anti-capitalism and equality are also reflected in LASM, which posits that many different social structures, especially political and economic, influence health. For the Socorristas, intersecting systems of inequality and oppressive relations in society (i.e., capitalism, patriarchy) influence abortion rights and access. They recognize that those who are most impacted by restrictive abortion laws and public health systems are those who have been marginalized in multiple ways. They carry these beliefs with them as they work with and pressure the public health and legal systems for change. All in all, the Socorristas are a powerful social movement organization and reflect important principles of Latin American Social Medicine.

The Socorristas are not the only feminist group that employs a multidimensional strategy to improve abortion access. Throughout the world, different feminist collectives have been working to provide quality services and actively engage the state to change laws. These activists are unique in their positioning in society and in their ability to participate in democratic movements to improve reproductive health, rights, and justice in their countries and regions. They straddle the worlds of medicine, public health, democratic governance, feminism, and often other social movements. They offer a comprehensive view of the need for abortion services through a feminist, health, and human rights lens. These collectives, which work directly with individuals seeking abortion, are also successful in engaging civil society. They are a crucial part of democratic movements for health and human rights, with a special focus on how abortion access itself is a human right.

Notes

1 Access to these medications varies by country and region; while they are readily available in pharmacies as abortifacients in some countries, in other countries misoprostol can be

purchased for its original use (treating ulcers) and used off-label. Other countries require a doctor to prescribe or even administer the medications (usually mifepristone), while in still other countries mifepristone is not available through legal means. In many contexts, people access the medications through online means, either through online pharmacies in other countries or teleinternet abortion services that send the medications through the mail. For information on access to these medications see Consorcio Latinoamericano Contra el Aborto Inseguro (2017), Footman et al. (2018), Endler, Cleeve, and Gemzell-Danielsson (2020).

2 See Drovetta (2015), Gerdts and Hudaya (2016), Labandera, Gorgoroso, and Briozzo (2016), Aiken et al. (2017), Grossman et al. (2018).
3 See Erdman (2012), Labandera, Gorgoroso, and Briozzo (2016), Foster, Arnott, and Hobstetter (2017), Erdman, Jelinska, and Yanow (2018), Zurbriggen, Keefe-Oates, and Gerdts (2018).
4 See McReynolds-Pérez (2017), Zurbriggen, Keefe-Oates, and Gerdts (2018), Krauss (2019), Singer (2019), Walsh (2020).
5 In Spanish, Campaña Nacional por el Derecho al Aborto Legal, Seguro y Gratuito.
6 See Reynoso and Zurbriggen (2011), Grosso and Zurbriggen (2016), Burton (2017a, 2017b, 2017c).
7 See Tajer (2003), Granda (2008), Eslava-Castañeda (2017), Vasquez, Perez-Brumer, and Parker (2019).
8 In Spanish, Red de Acceso al Aborto Seguro de Argentina.
9 Information about the Socorristas' response to the coronavirus pandemic was gathered through personal correspondence and reviews of their social media pages in 2020.

References

Aiken, Abigail R. A., Irena Digol, James Trussell, and Rebecca Gomperts. 2017. "Self Reported Outcomes and Adverse Events after Medical Abortion through Online Telemedicine: Population Based Study in the Republic of Ireland and Northern Ireland." *BMJ. Clinical Research* 357: 1–8.

Balcazar, Hector, Ana Bertha Perez-Lizaur, Ericka Escalante Izeta, and Maria Angeles Villanueva. 2016. "Community Health Workers-Promotores de Salud in Mexico: History and Potential for Building Effective Community Actions." *The Journal of Ambulatory Care Management* 39(1): 12–22.

Berer, Marge, and Lesley Hoggart. 2018. "Medical Abortion Pills Have the Potential to Change Everything about Abortion." *Contraception* 97(2): 79–81.

Bracke, Maud Anne. 2014. *Women and the Reinvention of the Political: Feminism in Italy, 1968–1983*. New York: Routledge.

Burton, Julia. 2017a. "Registrar y acompañar: Acciones colectivas por el derecho al aborto en la ciudad de Neuquén." *Zona Franca. Revista de Estudios de Género* 25: 89–125.

Burton, Julia. 2017b. "Prácticas feministas en torno al derecho al aborto en Argentina: Aproximaciones a las acciones colectivas de Socorristas en Red." *Revista Punto Género* 7: 91–111.

Burton, Julia. 2017c. "De la Comisión al Socorro: Trazos de militancia feminista por el derecho al aborto en Argentina." *Descentrada* 1(2): 1–17.

Consorcio Latinoamericano Contra el Aborto Inseguro. 2017. "Resumen ejecutivo. Mifepristona y misoprostol en seis países de América Latina: Procesos de registro y disponibilidad," January. http://clacaidigital.info:8080/xmlui/handle/123456789/999.

Drovetta, Raquel Irene. 2015. "Safe Abortion Information Hotlines: An Effective Strategy for Increasing Women's Access to Safe Abortions in Latin America." *Reproductive Health Matters. An International Journal on Sexual and Reproductive Health and Rights* 23(45): 47–57.

Endler, Margit, Amanda Cleeve, and Kristina Gemzell-Danielsson. 2020. "Online Access to Abortion Medications: A Review of Utilization and Clinical Outcomes." *Best Practice & Research Clinical Obstetrics & Gynaecology* 63: 74–86.

Erdman, Joanna N. 2012. "Harm Reduction, Human Rights, and Access to Information on Safer Abortion." *International Journal of Gynecology & Obstetrics* 118(1): 83–86.

Erdman, Joanna N., Kinga Jelinska, and Susan Yanow. 2018. "Understandings of Self-Managed Abortion as Health Inequity, Harm Reduction and Social Change." *Reproductive Health Matters* 26(54): 13–19.

Eslava-Castañeda, Juan C. 2017. "Pensando la determinación social del proceso salud-enfermedad." *Revista de Salud Pública* 19(3): 396–403.

Franco, Juan Victor Ariel, and Camila Volij. 2020. "Nuevo protocolo para la interrupción legal del embarazo en Argentina." *Evidencia. Actualizacion en la práctica ambulatoria* 23(1): e002029.

Footman, Katharine, Katherine Keenan, Kate Reiss, Barbara Reichwein, Pritha Biswas, and Kathryn Church. 2018. "Medical Abortion Provision by Pharmacies and Drug Sellers in Low- and Middle-Income Countries: A Systematic Review." *Studies in Family Planning* 49(1): 57–70.

Foster, Angel M., Grady Arnott, and Margaret Hobstetter. 2017. "Community-Based Distribution of Misoprostol for Early Abortion: Evaluation of a Program along the Thailand–Burma Border." *Contraception* 96(4): 242–247.

Gerdts, Caitlin, and Inna Hudaya. 2016. "Quality of Care in a Safe-Abortion Hotline in Indonesia: Beyond Harm Reduction." *American Journal of Public Health* 106(11): 2071–2075.

Gonzalez, Carolina. 2020. "Tarde." *En Estos Días. El Contexto es la Noticia*, June 13. www.enestosdias.com.ar/4584-tarde.

Granda, Edmundo. 2008. "Algunas reflexiones a los veinticuatro años de la ALAMES." *Medicina Social* 3(2): 217–225.

Grossman, Daniel, Sarah E. Baum, Denitza Andjelic, Carrie Tatum, Guadalupe Torres, Liza Fuentes, and Jennifer Friedman. 2018. "A Harm-Reduction Model of Abortion Counseling about Misoprostol Use in Peru with Telephone and in-Person Follow-up: A Cohort Study." *PloS One* 13(1): e0189195.

Grosso, Belén, and Ruth Zurbriggen. 2016. "Coaliciones y alianzas entre activistas feministas y el sistema de salud: Relato de una experiencia situada en pos del derecho a abortar." *Serie Documentos REDAAS* 8. www.redaas.org.ar/archivos-actividades/38-Doc8_pdfweb_GrossoZurbri_ok.pdf.

Kaplan, Laura. 1997. *The Story of Jane: The Legendary Underground Feminist Abortion Service*. Chicago: University of Chicago Press.

Kapp, Nathalie, and Patricia A. Lohr. 2020. "Modern Methods to Induce Abortion: Safety, Efficacy and Choice." *Best Practice & Research Clinical Obstetrics & Gynaecology* 63: 37–44.

Kapp, Nathalie, Kelly Blanchard, Ernestina Coast, Bela Ganatra, Jane Harries, Katharine Footman, Ann Moore, Onikepe Owolabi, Clementine Rossier, Kristen Shellenberg, Britt Wahlin, and Cynthia Woodsong. 2018. "Developing a Forward-Looking Agenda and Methodologies for Research of Self-Use of Medical Abortion." *Contraception* 97(2): 184–188.

Krauss, Amy. 2019. "The Ephemeral Politics of Feminist Accompaniment Networks in Mexico City." *Feminist Theory* 20(1): 37–54.

Krieger, Nancy. 2011. *Epidemiology and the People's Health: Theory and Context*. New York: Oxford University Press.

La Capital. 2015. "En todos los hospitales de la provincia se garantiza el acceso al aborto," August 19. www.lacapital.com.ar/la-ciudad/en-todos-los-hospitales-la-provincia-se-garantiza-el-acceso-al-aborto-n495140.html.

La Revuelta. 2017. "Declaración colectiva de las feministas organizadoras del 'Domingo contra los machos.'" *Colectiva La Revuelta: Prácticas Callejeras*, August 28. http://larevuelta.com.ar/2017/08/28/declaracion-colectiva-de-las-feministas-organizadoras-del-domingo-contra-los-machos/.

La Revuelta. 2019. "Encuentro Plurinacional en La Plata: 'Fuimos miles con la sangre revuelta de las ganas que las cosas cambien.'" *Colectiva La Revuelta: Prácticas Académicas*, October 26. http://

larevuelta.com.ar/2019/10/26/encuentro-plurinacional-en-la-plata-fuimos-miles-con-la-sa
ngre-revuelta-de-las-ganas-que-las-cosas-cambien/.

Labandera, Ana, Monica Gorgoroso, and Leonel Briozzo. 2016. "Implementation of the Risk and Harm Reduction Strategy Against Unsafe Abortion in Uruguay: From a University Hospital to the Entire Country." *International Journal of Gynecology & Obstetrics* 134 (S1): S7–11.

Maffeo, Florencia, Natalia Santarelli, Paula Satta, and Ruth Zurbriggen. 2015. "Parteras de nuevos feminismos. Socorristas en Red - Feministas que Abortamos: Una forma de activismo corporizado y sororo." *Revista Venezolana de Estudios de la Mujer* 20(44): 217–227.

Medionegro. 2017. "Las Socorristas Hilando bajo el viento soleado de septiembre," October 9. www.medionegro.org/las-socorristas-hilando-bajo-el-viento-soleado-de-septiembre/.

McReynolds-Pérez, Julia. 2017. "No Doctors Required: Lay Activist Expertise and Pharmaceutical Abortion in Argentina." *Signs: Journal of Women in Culture and Society* 42(2): 349–375.

Ministerio de Salud de la Nación Argentina. 2017. "Atención integral de personas en situación de aborto." *Diccionario Enciclopédico de la Legislación Sanitaria Argentina (DELS)*, March. www.salud.gob.ar/dels/entradas/atencion-integral-de-personas-en-situacion-de-aborto.

Moseson, Heidi, Kimberley A. Bullard, Carolina Cisternas, Belén Grosso, Verónica Vera, and Caitlin Gerdts. 2020. "Effectiveness of Self-Managed Medication Abortion between 13 and 24 Weeks Gestation: A Retrospective Review of Case Records from Accompaniment Groups in Argentina, Chile, and Ecuador." *Contraception* 102(2): 91–98.

Murillo, Lina-Maria. 2018. "Reproductive Freedom along the U.S.-Mexico Borderlands." *Scholars Strategy Network*, November 20. https://scholars.org/contribution/reproductive-freedom-along-us-mexico-borderlands.

Piccinini, Emiliano. 2020. "Socorristas en Red no entra en cuarentena." *La Tapa*, May 29. https://latapa.com.ar/socorristas-en-red-no-entra-en-cuarentena/.

Reynoso, Mónica, and Ruth Zurbriggen. 2011. *Colectiva feminista La Revuelta: Una bio-genealogía.* Buenos Aires: Herramienta.

Ruibal, Alba. 2018. "Federalism, Two-Level Games and the Politics of Abortion Rights Implementation in Subnational Argentina." *Reproductive Health Matters* 26(54): 137–144.

Singer, Elyse Ona. 2019. "Realizing Abortion Rights at the Margins of Legality in Mexico." *Medical Anthropology. Cross-Cultural Studies in Health and Illness* 38(2): 167–181.

Socorristas en Red. 2018. "Compilación de intervenciones de feministas socorristas en el debate por el derecho al aborto legal, seguro y gratuito en el Congreso Nacional," November. https://socorristasenred.org/wp-content/uploads/2018/11/Socorristas-en-Red.pdf.

Socorristas en Red. 2019. "Declaración de la 8va. Plenaria Nacional de Socorristas en Red–Feministas que abortamos– en Argentina," April 30. https://socorristasenred.org/declaracion-de-la-8va-plenaria-nacional-de-socorristas-en-red-feministas-que-abortamos-en-argentina/.

Socorristas en Red. 2020a. "Encuentro de formación política sub-25—Socorristas en Red," February 2. https://socorristasenred.org/encuentro-de-formacion-politica-sub-25/.

Socorristas en Red. 2020b. "Quiénes somos – Socorristas en Red." https://socorristasenred.org/quienes-somos/.

Socorristas en Red. 2020c. "Sistematización de acompañamientos a abortar realizados en el año 2019 por Socorristas en Red (feministas que abortamos)." https://socorristasenred.org/sistematizacion-2019/.

Tajer, Débora. 2003. "Latin American Social Medicine: Roots, Development During the 1990s, and Current Challenges." *American Journal of Public Health* 93(12): 2023–2027.

Vasquez, Emily E., Amaya Perez-Brumer, and Richard G. Parker. 2019. "Social Inequities and Contemporary Struggles for Collective Health in Latin America." *Global Public Health. An International Journal for Research, Policy and Practice* 14(6–7): 777–790.

Walsh, Aisling. 2020. "Feminist Networks Facilitating Access to Misoprostol in Mesoamerica." *Feminist Review* 124(1): 175–182.

WestRasmus, Emma K., Fernando Pineda-Reyes, Montelle Tamez, and John M. Westfall. 2012. "Promotores de Salud and Community Health Workers: An Annotated Bibliography." *Family & Community Health* 35(2): 172–182.

World Health Organization (WHO). 2018. "Medical Management of Abortion." www.ncbi.nlm.nih.gov/books/NBK536779/.

World Health Organization (WHO). 2020. "About WHO: Frequently Asked Questions." www.who.int/about/who-we-are/frequently-asked-questions.

Zurbriggen, Ruth, Brianna Keefe-Oates, and Caitlin Gerdts. 2018. "Accompaniment of Second-Trimester Abortions: The Model of the Feminist Socorrista Network of Argentina." *Contraception* 97(2): 108–115.

PART IV
Chile

11

BETWEEN THE SECULAR AND THE RELIGIOUS

The Role of Academia in the Abortion Debate in Chile

Lidia Casas Becerra

Introduction

Among the various players that came to be involved in the abortion debate in Chile are academic institutions. Far from a unified field, the tensions and divisions within academia permeate divergent stances on the status of abortion, often along religious and secular lines, among other cleavages. Educational institutions' involvement in public affairs, particularly their law schools, shows varying degrees of influence in Chilean politics. Since the end of the dictatorship and the transition to democracy in 1990, legal scholars have been important social and political players, shaping public policy in various areas, including family law and the administration of justice. After the total ban on abortion was enacted by the regime of General Augusto Pinochet toward the end of the dictatorship, different sectors of society endeavored to decriminalize abortion or to defend its prohibition.[1] In this chapter, I examine the role of secular and confessional scholars in the abortion debate in Chile, considering the university as an important site of contestation and potential influence. Additionally, from my position as a lawyer and scholar, and in accordance with the feminist adage that "the personal is political," I present a personal account regarding my relationship with abortion as a both personal and academic concern.

Jaime Caiceo Escudero (2013) describes the construction of two university models in Chile that initially competed in the consolidation of the republic: one of liberal inspiration, with great influence of the masons and centered on the idea of a secular state; the other organized under the edicts of the Catholic Church. The creation of the Pontifical Catholic University of Chile (Pontificia Universidad Católica, PUC) was a response to the secularization of the state, to ensure the provision of a space of belonging in education, culture, and politics, especially after the enactment of the 1884 secular laws. It aimed at "crafting an intellectual Catholic Chilean elite to conduct the destiny of the country. This institution has trained many political and

DOI: 10.4324/9781003079903-15

intellectual leaders in its century of tradition; however, only two have become President of Chile"[2] (Caiceo Escudero 2013, 93). The Chilean Catholic Church and the conservatives of the 19th century considered the prerogatives of the state in organizing public secular schools a threat, especially since the government created the University of Chile (Universidad de Chile) and had the monopoly over education (Serrano 2016). The University of Chile educated the liberal elite of political and intellectual leaders of Latin America and it even had a Theology School, but few were interested in pursuing theology (Serrano 2016). Today no one debates the creation of confessional universities; however, contemporary heated discussions—as a result of the decriminalization of abortion on three grounds—center on what obligations private universities have when they receive public funds and have voluntarily accepted to provide healthcare services (Serrano 2016). In addition, the tension arises between two rights: the right to education and the right to organize educational institutions.

Currently the conflict between the secular and the confessional tradition is represented by the tension between the two main Chilean universities mentioned, which eventually extended to other institutions. Since 1982, the creation of new private universities followed the same rationale of secular or confessional institutions of higher education. Some higher education institutions emerged under the financial control of powerful economic groups, some of them related to fundamentalist Catholic religious groups such as the Opus Dei or the Legionnaires of Christ. As expected, these institutions have been instrumental in promoting conservative and religious ideologies (Ramm et al. 2020). The secular academia, which roughly speaking I consider liberal,[3] was committed to a public agenda supporting the rebuilding of a democratic society, including the recognition of rights and equal protection for children born out of wedlock. In contrast, the Catholic University Law School professors had an important role in shaping Pinochet's constitution and new legal order, making future changes difficult. Chile has had a divorce law only since 2005, and abortion was decriminalized on three grounds even more recently, in 2017.

Silence about Abortion and the Debate on Emergency Contraception

The process of legal reform in family law was a long journey of continuous confrontations; other issues simply remained unattended in the public agenda but also in the scope or interest of academia. Ignacio Walker, a former Senator, eloquently pointed this out at the end of the 1990s:

> There is a situation that remains pending, and which is still taboo in our society, the situation of abortion.... Until now we have simply chosen to avoid facing this situation. And we are quiet because abortion is a criminal offence. Personally I am not for legalizing abortion, because I believe in the right to life, anyway, we could argue this another day, but I do believe that we have to face the situation.... I believe that we have to decriminalize some forms of abortion, for example, in the case of rape.
>
> *(Walker 1998, 235)*

The politicians on the left did not take seriously the demands or the importance of the feminist movement, which was weakened during the 1990s. Merike Blofield (2001) described the state of feminism by quoting former Senator José Antonio Viera Gallo who commented: "Look out the window, I don't see any feminist movement here, nothing compared to what I saw in Italy in the seventies" (34). The hope for change took a wrong turn in the 1999 presidential election. President Ricardo Lagos reaffirmed an explicit anti-abortion stance in September 2000. Feminists at that point had little influence in Congress, even to promote lukewarm changes in the law (Blofield 2001). The politicization of the consequences of clandestine abortions and the support of public opinion were required to achieve partial decriminalization—without these, there would be no changes in the future (Blofield 2001).

However, a relevant development preceded the abortion debate: the inclusion of emergency contraception in the public health services from the late 1990s onwards. For the first time, those who opposed and those in favor in the governing center-left coalition confronted each other with unusual vehemence. The main argument was that emergency contraception acted as an abortifacient, so some considered it unconstitutional. The confrontation was long and in slow motion from the end of the 1990s until 2008, going through different judicial channels from regular courts, passing through the Supreme Court before arriving at the Constitutional Court.[4] Legislators, ministers, and deputy ministers had opposing views. For example, the relationship between the ex-minister of the National Women's Service (SERNAM),[5] Cecilia Pérez, and the ex-minister of health, Pedro García, was not particularly good at one point because he had delayed to issue a clinical guide that would allow the use of emergency contraception in situations of rape in 2004.

The participants in the debate that took place in academic circles, and later on in court, remained a reduced group of scientists and doctors from social organizations, led by the Chilean Institute of Reproductive Medicine (ICMER).[6] The Institute's work was backed up publicly and decidedly by the professors of the School of Medicine at the University of Chile and the director of the School of Public Health of the same university.[7] On the other side, there was also a group of people from the University of the Andes and the Pontifical Catholic University.[8] Faculty from secular and confessional medical schools revealed, once again, opposing views while there were few legal scholars who weighed in, posing their favorable legal opinions.[9]

Only with the emerging litigation in the Constitutional Court in 2008, challenging the Ministry of Health Fertility Clinical Regulations, did a few professors (in particular constitutionalists) see the significance of the debate. Indeed, it pertained to the scope of article 19 No. 1 of the Constitution, the right to life provision, and its relation to a potential liberalization of abortion. In a literature review on legal doctrine, Antonio Bascuñán Rodríguez (2001) concluded that there had been little concern for abortion. Constitutionalists—all men except for Medina Quiroga (2005)—started to write (Gómez Bernales 2012; Figueroa García-Huidobro 2008; Bascuñán Rodríguez 2016). Some others decided to actively participate in the litigation at different levels: Jorge Contesse Singh and Rodrigo Barcia Lehmann prepared Law Reports (Barcia Lehmann 2007; Contesse Singh 2007),[10] and I became a litigator on the case, as I had been working with the ICMER on the legal aspects since 1997. Samuel Buzeta participated in public hearings, representing the Chilean Association for the Protection of the Family (APROFA)[11] affiliated with the International Planned Parenthood Federation (he had been a clinical professor of Public Interest and Human Rights at the University Diego Portales). Jesús Vicent, counsel for ICMER, and I represented—in the hearings before 52 legislators (including right-wing congresswoman Karla Rubilar)[12]—the position in favor of the constitutionality of the Ministry of Health Fertility Clinical Regulations (Sarmiento Ramírez and Walker Echenique 2018).[13] Once again, the members of academia on either side of the debate, including the scholars and their institutional affiliation, were recognizable. Among the religious universities, there were well-known lecturers and professors: Angela Vivanco (Pontifical Catholic University and currently a member of the Supreme Court), Professor Alejandro Romero (University of the Andes),[14] and José Joaquín Ugarte from the Catholic University, among others. A group of conservative constitutionalists mostly from confessional universities signed an *amicus* brief in the public annulment trial, and two years later two of them would be part of the Constitutional Court during the constitutional challenge against the inclusion of emergency contraception in the Fertility Regulations. The justices Raúl Bertelsen[15] and Enrique Navarro Beltrán[16] behaved differently: the former refused to recuse himself, while the other did, declaring unconstitutional by one vote the prescription and use of the emergency contraception in the public healthcare services.

The Archbishop of Santiago made a call to invoke conscientious objection in case the use of the morning-after pill was approved, which in turn generated various criticisms. The Pontifical Catholic University reacted in defense of the Catholic Church:

> The dean of the School of Law at the Catholic University, Arturo Yrarrázaval C., academic secretary Carlos Frontaura and the Vice dean Roberto Guerrero, manifested their energetic rejection of the accusations made to the Archbishop of Santiago and his categorical support to the Cardinal on the insinuations that the Archbishop of Santiago could have incurred in a call to "civil disobedience" or even sedition. The accusations against the Cardinal appear to reflect a secularism that we believed had disappeared from the national debate. Secularism that has always attempted to negate Christians their right to express their opinion on public matters and act according to their conscience.
>
> (Dides 2006, 97)

Similar expressions were manifested later in the discussion on abortion on the question of freedom of conscience. The conservatives won an important battle but lacked legitimacy due to the composition of the Court and the militant role played by Raúl Bertelsen, the president of the Court. For the first time close to 30,000 women rallied in protests.

Abortion, a Concern for a Few Academics

There was a handful of people who researched, wrote, or spoke on abortion and the reproductive rights of women. I would say that many scholars were not aware that in 1998 the Senate voted a bill aimed to increase penalties for women who had undergone an abortion. The bill was defeated only by two votes.[17] Women's rights seemed to be out of the scope of academic interest. Among that handful, a few women, myself included, did write about the issue from an academic perspective: Yanira Zúñiga of the University Austral, Verónica Undurraga of the Adolfo Ibáñez University, and Alejandra Zúñiga Fajuri from the University of Valparaíso (Zúñiga Fajuri 2011). I met Verónica Undurraga when she was presenting a seminar in the University of Chile and she invited me to her class in 2002. Each one of us continued developing complementary academic work—some sponsored by the National Fund for Scientific and Technological Development (Fondecyt)[18]—in the process of writing their doctoral dissertations,[19] and in my case, conducting sociolegal studies. The relationship between us grew both in terms of being academics with a shared concern over abortion and sharing the wider agenda of equal gender rights.[20] As for me, I have also contributed to the Annual Report on Human Rights in Chile, produced since 2002 by the Center of Human Rights, a platform to report on human rights violations. We would report on the limited public discussion and the recommendations by human rights treaty bodies on different issues including abortion.

The silence of academia seemed to show total indifference. A possible explanation could be that abortion was not a concern for the media, although a couple of cases became prominent when two women made a public request to have an abortion. Gladys Pavez in 2002 and later Griselle Rojas, who lived the experience of a partial molar pregnancy of a malformed fetus (Centro de Derechos Humanos 2004). The Minister of Health, a Christian Democrat, Osvaldo Artaza, made the following statement:

> With respect to the request for a therapeutic abortion, the Ministry of Health states that at the present time there is no legal rule allowing such procedure, and as a result, no person or authority has the power to authorize or carry out such actions which have the aim of causing an abortion.
>
> *(Centro de Derechos Humanos 2004, 227)*

The minister later added that in the case of Griselle, she underwent a cesarean operation at 22 weeks, so in his opinion, it was possible to provide care under the legislation preserving the values and defending the lives of both, the unborn and the woman. The statement was made right after visiting Cardinal Errázuriz (Dides, Benavente, and Sáenz, 2011). The hypocrisy lies in waiting until 20–22 weeks of gestation to call the procedure a premature birth (Casas and Vivaldi 2017).

The changes in the composition of Congress timidly opened up these apparently closed issues. At the end of the first government of the President Michelle Bachelet (2006–10), there were a series of bills proposing partial decriminalization of abortion. The bills did not reach a majority for its approval; however, this scenario changed during the first term of right-wing President Sebastián Piñera (2010–14), whose early days in office saw massive rallies demanding environmental and education rights. Feminist demands would soon follow.

Politicians and Academics in the Abortion Debate

The force of the stubborn facts of abortion and growing support for decriminalization showed that it was not possible to postpone some public debates permanently. The crisis of the center-left coalition by the end of the first government of Bachelet and the unusual rejection to include abortion in the public agenda, added to the social discontent regarding politics. The self-imposed political censorship extended beyond politicians. The scientific Society of Gynecologists and Obstetricians was reluctant to debate up to that point and the Committee of Ethics at the Medical College of Chile in 2003 insisted that it was not necessary to legislate over the possibility to intervene when there is a serious risk to the woman by virtue of the double effect theory (Comité de Ética del Colegio Médico de Chile 2003; Shepard and Casas Becerra 2007).[21]

Bachelet's government during her first administration had to confront the issue at the Council of Human Rights. The government presented two reports for the Universal Periodic Review of the United Nations, a political body of the Council of Human Rights where governments participate and observe each other. The reports and the official responses were communicated under different governments: that of President Michelle Bachelet (2006–10) and that of Sebastián Piñera (2010–14). The delegation in 2009 (Bachelet administration), headed by the ex-minister of the Secretary General of the Government, José Antonio Viera Gallo, plainly rejected Sweden and Finland's recommendations regarding the decriminalization of abortion, indicating that these did not have Chile's support, compared to other recommendations that would indeed be studied by the government. He stated:

> The objective and subjective conditions [do not exist] to make this change. Without prejudice to the aforementioned, our country will not consider contraceptives or any methods which could cause an abortion, to this end, they will not be part of any public policy relating to fertility. Therefore, with regard to the recommendations 19 and 20, it should be noted that our legal order protects the life of the unborn which means an absolute ban of abortion in any form.
>
> *(Casas Becerra 2014, 585–6)*

The "objective and subjective" political conditions—using the minister's language—continued to change and Congress started to gradually become more open to dealing with abortion.

At that point, it was evident the government was immune to the international criticisms regarding the criminalization of abortion. The government was prepared to take on the cost in order to maintain the cohesion of the governing center-left coalition. In 2014, the rejection to the recommendations came from the Piñera government, so that the reaction to the VI Report of the Universal Periodic Review of the United Nations confirmed its commitment to respect the Constitution and right to life—therefore, there would be no changes.

International pressure from human rights treaty bodies is important but not sufficient; the persuasion had to come from within the country. By 2013, I had decided that the Annual Report on Human Rights in Chile would include empirical research on the effects of the criminalization of abortion and its effect on women's human rights (Casas and Vivaldi 2013). Sociolegal work soon started, but it required much labor. As is customary for the elaboration of the human rights report, law students became involved as volunteers, and another colleague, Lieta Vivaldi from the University of Chile, who had finished her Master's in England, also volunteered.[22] These were months of intensive work, preparing interviews, obtaining ethical approval, and starting the difficult fieldwork, which included interviews with women who had undergone abortion, men and women who had helped with these decisions, and health professionals who had collaborated directly in abortions. It was an investigation that showed the true impact of the legal ban on abortion. It was bringing abortion out in the open and avoiding the easy slogan "the body is mine," which did not carry much meaning with the public opinion. The work was presented in a small discussion group with activists and scholars. Activists had not shared a common space for a long time to discuss different political views and strategies available on abortion. The work also attracted criticism from some scholars. Someone told me that the research was journalism and sociology, but not law.

The entire work was also published by an important digital media source and prompted openness to dialogue. The most salient event occurred months later, in August 2014 after the announcement of President Bachelet (in her second term) that her government was preparing a bill to amend the abortion law. I received an invitation to a public forum of around 70 attendees, which included laypeople and Jesuits. A prominent journalist acted as a moderator, and two other people participated: a well-known theologian, Tony Mifsud, and an anti-abortion epidemiologist, Elard Koch (Arzobispado de Santiago 2014). Later on, some Jesuits, without agreeing on the issue, wanted to meet with me to know more about the situation of abortion in the country and Bachelet's proposal. It was interesting to have reserved conversations with priests on the need for a reform.

There were two political-technical opportunities for reform. The first was when criminal law scholars were summoned by President Piñera in 2013 to draft the blueprint of the penal code. The following professors participated: Bofill (University of Chile), Acosta (University of Development), Bascuñán (University Adolfo Ibáñez), Hernández (University Diego Portales), Maldonado (University of Talca), Cox (University Adolfo Ibáñez), and van Weezel (Catholic University). A majority of the experts presented a blueprint legalizing abortion up to 12 weeks. The recommendation on abortion reform was rejected by the government. Later, during the second term in office, Bachelet also convened a commission in 2015. The participants included Hernández (University Diego Portales), Couso (University Diego Portales), Mañalich (University of Chile), Ortíz (University of Chile), Wilenmann (University Adolfo Ibáñez), and Acosta (University of Development). Again, a majority maintained the proposal to decriminalize abortion.[23] However, the blueprint was not sent to Congress.

The Presidential Message of Bachelet in 2014

Independent women supporting Bachelet and feminist members of the coalition's political parties were key in incorporating abortion into the new government's program (see also Fernández Anderson, this volume). The women compelled the coalition parties to find an agreement; the consensus was a partial decriminalization. For some, this was the least of the needed changes, while for others it was the maximum they would tolerate. The program became a window of opportunity, born over many years, for the partial decriminalization in case the woman's life is at risk, when the fetus has severe fetal malformation incompatible with life, and in the case of rape.

Feminists awaited anxiously the Bachelet's Statement to the Nation of May 21, 2014. There was no certainty whether Bachelet would announce the bill to decriminalize abortion. The reaction to the announcement was both applauded and attacked. In any case, Bachelet showed political will to continue. The Ministry of Women's Affairs and the Ministry of Health recruited feminists for different key tasks: a department of legal reform and a team of health professionals leading the debate (Sarmiento Ramírez and Walker Echenique 2018). Scholars participated as advisors, and feminist Verónica Undurraga's (University Adolfo Ibáñez) work as a consultant to the Ministry of Health was key. Additionally, Gastón Gómez Bernales (University Diego Portales), who comes from a liberal right and secular tradition, prepared a report on constitutional law.

There was some discussion among feminist scholars on how to organize, coordinate, and prepare for a debate. Some years before, Verónica Undurraga and I had created a conversation between scholars from various secular universities and litigant lawyers to discuss strategic litigation (see also Borland, this volume).[24] Legal reform seemed unlikely to occur. The outlook even for litigation was not encouraging; a lawyer privately confessed he had an agreement in his law firm that he would not take on cases of abortion and the partner would not take sexual offence cases.

Legal reform in any jurisdiction is always a difficult task. It was evident that in order to open a public debate there was a need to build alliances beyond feminist organizations with little political influence, and to position abortion as an academic interest. The expert group that prepared the first blueprint of the Penal Code in 2013 was a start.

The confessional scholars had begun working on arguments against any potential reform to reinstate therapeutic abortion more than a decade before. In 2002, the Center of Bioethics of the Pontifical Catholic University prepared a document titled "'Therapeutic' Abortion. Medical, Ethical, Legal Considerations and from the Magisterium of the Catholic Church" (Besio et al. 2002). This work was a preamble of a book published in 2015 by the University of the Andes, right after Bachelet made her announcement. This book was a collection of papers from philosophy, medicine, and law presenting the arguments against abortion law reform (Aguirrezabal Grünstein and Bertelsen Simonetti 2015). The authors were well-known; some of them had been involved in the legal debate on emergency contraception. In the opinion of a secular constitutionalist, the book was the best that the confessional academics had produced.

In the process of preparing the bill, during 2014, the government acted in strict privacy. Little was known how the bill would look like, causing many doubts among feminist organizations.[25] Some insiders explained that, if conversations filtered through, it could risk the success of the bill; there were far too many people interested in seeing the failure of the project.

Given the circumstances, I took the stand to support the government bill knowing the limited scope of the reform. Its approval would be not only an important legal, but also a symbolic and cultural victory. It was important to look for other organizations that would support the bill, or at least be open to dialogue while recognizing the political differences. This was a unique opportunity to debate abortion openly. The polls showed consistent opinions in favor of a law permitting abortion under the three circumstances specified. In fact, the approval among the public did not diminish, but increased during the legislative debate (Instituto de Investigación en Ciencias Sociales UDP 2015; Radio Cooperativa, Imaginacción, and Universidad Central 2015; CADEM—Plaza Pública 2018).

In 2015, when the bill was tabled (two years before the law's approval), I convened constitutional law professors, Yanira Zúñiga and Rodolfo Figueroa García-Huidobro, and criminal law professor Javier Wilenmann with support from Jaime Couso, to work on reports that would serve as *amicus curiae* in the Constitutional Court. There was a shared opinion that if the law were to be approved in Congress, the right-wing opposition would take the case to the Constitutional Court. By 2017, the report prepared by Wilenmann was later openly backed by other criminal law scholars.

The legislative process in Congress started in March 2015 in the Commission of Health in the Chamber of Deputies, in my opinion, in a disorganized manner. Universities, secular and confessional, played an important role with participation from specialists from the social sciences, medicine, and law. Among the active participants were Fernando Zegers (University Diego Portales), Adela Montero and Irma Palma (University of Chile), and Alejandra Zúñiga Fajuri (University of Valparaíso) from secular universities; meanwhile on behalf of the confessional institutions were Ignacio Sánchez (the chancellor of the Catholic University) and members of the Pontifical Catholic University (PUC). Legal experts would be the main actors in the Constitution, Legislation, and Justice legislative committee; the same would happen later in the Senate.

In the Senate, the full spectrum of scholars from all the universities participated: Austral, Concepción, Santísima of Concepción, Talca, Valparaíso, Chile, Diego Portales, Adolfo Ibáñez, the Andes, PUC and the Catholic University of Valparaíso, Development, and Finis Terrae.[26] They represented regional and national universities, confessional and secular, showing all legal traditions and ideological viewpoints.

University authorities played a significant role presenting their opinions in Congress: Ennio Vivaldi (chancellor of the University of Chile and medical doctor), Carlos Peña (chancellor of the University Diego Portales and lawyer), and the ex-chancellor of the University of Valparaiso, Agustín Squella (lawyer), gave their favorable opinions, while Ignacio Sánchez (medical doctor) of the Pontifical

Catholic University was fully opposed. It is possible that no other bill in Chilean history had shown such involvement from academia and, with some exceptions, most scholars and professors from the secular universities gave their support. Meanwhile, among scholars from religious universities, there was an unambiguous vote against the decriminalization of abortion. They stated from the outset that the bill was unconstitutional.

The experts from the Jesuit University Alberto Hurtado remained silent during the legislative debate. A few other well-known constitutional law specialists from the governing coalition did not express publicly an opinion either. It is possible that they would support two of the grounds for decriminalization (risk of life and fetal malformation incompatible with life outside of the womb), but not in the case of rape. For many people, the rape ground represented abortion on demand because the decision rested solely on the woman's choice. It would require neither a criminal report nor the participation of doctors; and most importantly, the fetus was healthy. The final text considered the participation of a psychosocial team that would examine the woman's rape account and establish whether she could be eligible for a legal abortion.

For and Against

The discussion remained alive in the media and other public venues. Editorials, letters to the editor, and articles appeared on a regular basis. Universities held seminars and debates which had never been seen before.[27] With an academic spirit, the Center of Human Rights of the University Diego Portales decided to foster a true debate inviting specialists for and against the bill to present their arguments in two publications ensuring gender equality and representation from every type of university, secular and confessional, public and private (Casas and Lawson 2016). Within the School of Law at the University of Diego Portales not all shared the idea of decriminalizing abortion, but the mutual academic respect for diverse opinions, the leitmotif of a university, allowed us to engage in healthy dialogues.

Scholars from completely opposing views presented their arguments on conscientious objections, but the publication revealed the nuances even among those who were against on the issue of institutional objection. The Constitutional Court in its later ruling did not even distinguish between institutions with or without ideologies that could justify an exemption to comply with the law (Tribunal Constitucional 2017). Criminal justice experts also confronted views, including Professor Héctor Hernández and Professor Magdalena Ossandón. To be in favor or against abortion law reform in academia was only a starting point; the question was how to make this reform a moment of academic and civic dialogue (Casas and Lawson 2016; Casas Becerra and Vargas 2018). We thought that this would be our contribution.

From my end, I considered it important to include empirical data and not only strict legal opinions because law needs to be anchored in people's daily lives. This prompted me to conduct research on rape resulting in pregnancy. The rape ground was sensitive in the public opinion—laden with prejudice and stereotypes. It was also most resisted among politicians making offensive statements about women and their condition as victims of sexual violence. It was noteworthy that a new argument emerged from the opposition: allowing decriminalization on the basis of rape could promote greater impunity for the perpetrators. Little was known about rape and pregnancy and how the administration of justice, or the victim support networks of sexual violence, confronted the issue. The study's fieldwork took place between 2015 and 2016 in three regions of the country, considering as criteria prevalence of sexual violence, migrant population, and ethnicity/rurality. We interviewed prosecutors, judges, technical advisors (social workers or psychologists) to family courts, midwives, lawyers, psychologists, and social workers. All of them showed a bleak scenario. There were no clear estimates on pregnancy and rape; generally the victims were minors; the crimes revealed high levels of impunity for the perpetrators; and there was high prevalence of secondary victimization. Furthermore, there was poor support from health networks and, worse still, a discourse among many promoting maternity at any cost (even amongst professionals working in organizations that provide psychosocial support for victims of sexual violence) (Casas et al. 2018). This research would be the basis for a later intervention in Congress and in the Constitutional Court.

Constitutional Court: Professors and Prominent Lawyers on the Stage at the Public Hearings

In the legal community, we were cognizant that the last battle on the passing of the law would be in the Constitutional Court. It was a step-by-step process: summoning enough votes in Congress, gathering sufficient support from the law branches of academia, and later performing during the last act at the Constitutional Court. Sarmiento Ramírez and Walker Echenique (2018), feminist lawyers in the Ministry of Women's Affairs, recounted how it was necessary to present in Court a range of voices from different disciplines, expressing legal opinions that went beyond politics. The preparation for the Constitutional Court became another step in a coordinated and collective effort.

From April 2015, mostly feminist organizations and women from different academic disciplines joined a loose coordination to monitor the legislative process.[28] Until March 2015, the feminist organizations were very disjointed.[29] My personal trajectory with some feminist organizations enabled me to facilitate a relationship between activism and academia, whereby there would be sharing of information and perspectives as well as a process of learning from each other. Feminist organizations maintained a healthy skepticism towards the negotiations taking place in Congress, toward the government, and also extending somewhat to academia. It was crucial to be coordinated for the final stage at the Constitutional Court, to have a core consensus, for me and many others to defend the rape ground.

My experience litigating emergency contraception since 2001, and especially in the Constitutional Court in 2007, suggested the need to have a clear plan for civil society to intervene in the public hearings that the Court would likely convene. A young lawyer, Belén Saavedra, who was a teaching assistant in constitutional law at the University Diego Portales and a new hire of the legal reform department with the Ministry of Women's Affairs, shared the same opinion regarding a stronger role for civil society in the coming litigation. Her knowledge and relationship with civil society helped the government to engage with organizations on a different spirit. As the legislative process was ending, there was a certain division of labor: Verónica Undurraga managed the relationships with colleagues in some universities and organizations, while I managed others. This was very intense and collaborative work with constant dialogue and mutual respect.

As we organized, the same was happening with the opposition. For them, their political stand was unequivocal—the total rejection of the bill—but not so among feminist and human rights organizations. There was no common discourse, there were misgivings about a restrictive bill; some of them had to be persuaded. Yet as evidenced, organizations showed political maturity to not conflict with the government supporting the bill at the Constitutional Court hearings. In this context a collaboration was born between social organizations and the government.

Academics, all from secular universities, as well as prominent lawyers would present their arguments in favor of the constitutionality of the bill on behalf of social organizations.[30] The opposition to the bill also organized, but the differences between the types of organizations (for or against abortion reform) jumped out. First, differences emerged in relation to the number of presentations (those opposing the bill exceeded those in favor). With respect to those in support, we find workers' unions, women's organizations, association of female lawyers, collectives of sexual diversity, organizations of women and children with disabilities, and social organizations defending children's rights. On the opposite, we find organizations linked especially to the Catholic Church, Evangelical churches, and anti-abortion organizations. It was noteworthy that four confessional universities, as higher education institutions, made a plea against the law. This could be explained since the bill approved in Congress would not permit institutional objection, and therefore they would be affected in relation to the health services they might have to provide and with respect to changes to curricula. The Catholic University chancellor, Ignacio Sánchez, was the main actor to lead the battle on conscientious objection (Montero et al. 2017).[31]

The University of Chile also participated at the hearings represented by the Dean of Law, Davor Harasic, who in the past had litigated representing the government in the case of the morning-after pill. There was concealed criticism among some academics claiming that positioning the University of Chile on one side of the debate disregarded the fact there is not a single perspective among the faculty.

A second difference is that the professors presenting before the Constitutional Court against the bill were mostly from the Catholic University and the University of the Andes. There were a few exceptions from secular universities, from the University of Chile and the University of Development. Conversely, those who were in favor of the project all came from the secular universities: the University of Chile, University Diego Portales, University Adolfo Ibañez, and University of Valparaiso.

In two days of televised hearings, two types of religiosity became distinctively displayed, giving a glimpse of one of the main features of Chilean society. On one hand, the Catholic elite spoke from a privileged political and economic standpoint, including owners of great fortunes in the country and people who have protected prominent priests accused of sexual abuse. On the other hand, the growing Evangelical churches from working-class communities (Emol 2017).[32] I argue that the Catholic elite was required to have a strategic and political alliance with the growing Evangelical sectors.

The secular and confessional academia may move in different social networks and enjoy distinct levels of political influence among business people and politicians; however, due to the small community of academic and prestigious legal professionals, they share other spaces. This account reveals a sum of political, cultural, and social continuities where secularism and religious traditions have been in opposition, particularly with respect to abortion.

Abortion carries stigma. It took quite a while before legal scholars were to engage in the public debate. For instance, for prestigious liberal lawyers to be associated with abortion had significant costs when their clients (say, some executive officers of large corporations) belong to powerful Catholic elites. The secular universities could at the end of the day show their capacity to accommodate diverse views and facilitate dialogue among peers. Yet the same cannot be said for the confessional universities, which remain firm in their ideology and where dissent could mean academic reprisal.[33]

A Final Reflection

I cannot finish this chapter without reflecting upon the reasons that led me to focus on abortion as an academic interest. Preparing my presentation for the Constitutional Court hearings, my grandmother's story came to my mind, which I incorporated in my plea by saying that "the rape ground has the face of a child, the face of an adolescent, it is a woman's story." This was my grandmother's story as a little girl, her account hidden for many years in the same way as the daughter born as a result from a rape—the rapist being the landowner of where she lived. She never saw her daughter as an adult because she left her behind in the countryside when the baby was only six months old.

After my intervention, people's reactions to the story were unimaginable. A doctor approached me to tell me that he now understood my commitment to the legalization of abortion. Another woman—a lawyer—told me this was also her grandmother's story. Other women wrote to me telling me the stories of their friends, or of themselves. Even the gentleman who parked cars in the streets of the university neighborhood stopped me to give me his own account. This was not a "legal argument," there was no legal doctrine. Instead it was a narrative revealing that legalizing abortion in the case of rape was a small amount of justice for many women who have confronted sexual violence.

My concern about abortion can be traced to my grandmother, but not just due to her forced pregnancy, but rather her courage to fight with doctors in a hospital emergency ward at the end of the 1950s, demanding care for her daughter-in-law who was hemorrhaging because of a clandestine abortion. This story was also another family secret, which I discovered when my family and I left Chile in the 1980s. I was able to speak a few times with my mother about abortion, far away from Chile and its taboos. It was possible to have conversations when the women in Canada protested in the streets to defend Dr. Henry Morgentaler's demanding women's right to choose. My mother did not know that when I was an adolescent I had a friend who had also undergone a clandestine abortion.

When I returned to Chile in 1990, and realized that the absurd and unjust prohibition on abortion continued, I was lucky to have the opportunity to do work that has meaning. I wrote a paper for an elective course with Carlos Peña, the current chancellor of the Diego Portales University. This work was later published, which connected me to feminist organizations and later led to a series of sociolegal research projects regarding abortion. I took up the task to study the criminalization of abortion, which meant reviewing old files in the public defender's office in the city of Santiago's women's prison in 1994.[34] This was the first time that I conducted interviews. Being a novice, I completed two emotionally difficult interviews in the prison: the first with a young woman 20 years old, who had come to Santiago to work as a domestic worker and to study at night. I do not remember her name but I remember her fortitude. She had become pregnant by her boyfriend, who did not want anything to do with her once he found out about the pregnancy. At the end of the interview, she told me that she did not know her own father; for he had not recognized her as his daughter. Later she was never treated the same as her other brothers and sisters, so she did not want the same life for her child. The other woman I interviewed had been in prison for a year; she performed abortions with a probe. Her last client died from septic shock even though she had taken the woman to emergency services at the hospital. She cried through the interview, repeating that if the woman had told her the truth about the gestational time of the pregnancy, she would not have performed an abortion at six months because it was too dangerous.

Each time that I read files about women behind bars, I asked myself what ultimately happened to these women, until I managed to arrive at the home of one of them. She was serving a three-year sentence under probation. The abortion resulted in a serious case of septicemia causing her to have an arm amputated and a complete hysterectomy—she almost died. She could not work as a domestic worker any longer; instead she sold second-hand clothes at the local market, clothes which she washed with one hand. I was strongly affected by the sight of the poor conditions in which she lived.

This first study was published, and my professor of international human rights law, Cecilia Medina (who later was the president of the United Nations Human Rights Committee and the Inter-American Human Rights Court) presented her comments at the book's launch (Casas Becerra 1996). Afterwards, I conducted further research with a more strategic aim, analyzing criminal files in four cities over four different years, during the dictatorship and in the first two years of democracy.

In conducting my studies, I also thought of the people who reported those women to the police and the conditions in which the women carried out the abortions. The files had the names of doctors and midwives who reported the women, sometimes their names would repeat, just like the names of hospitals would repeat. Chilean bureaucracy at work, sometimes the report would contain a long list of names of women who sought medical attention due to the consequences of clandestine abortions. In this way, I came to the name of a well-known doctor and professor of a confessional university. He acted as a court clerk, taking the statements of the women he reported. I could never look at him without thinking of these women. The findings were predictable: poor working women were prosecuted, many of them domestic workers; their medical records sometimes indicated they wanted to have no more children and had requested a sterilization prior to the abortion. One of them, by the time she was questioned was pregnant again.

Years later, in 2003, and in the context of another research project on the criminal justice system, I found myself waiting in the maternity ward for my interviewee who was late because he was in a clinical meeting deciding whether a woman who had been hospitalized as a result of an illegal and unsafe abortion should be reported or not. A little while later, in another investigation, I interviewed women prosecuted on abortion charges. All of them were ordinary women, with a sense of moral justice, conscious of their lives, their difficulties, and their decisions. In this way, I got to know first-hand the consequences of criminalized abortion that marked my work and reputation as a researcher. However, I also received comments from colleagues who discredited my research as activism and not scholarly work. To debate, conduct research, and write about abortion has costs because of stigma and prejudice. It also means writing about marginalized issues, beyond the interest of traditional legal doctrine. In any case, a secular university made it possible for me to complete this critical commentary and to continue with determination my investigation and writing about abortion. If this is activism, so be it.

Notes

1 See for example, Fernández Anderson (this volume) on the role of political parties.
2 The two presidents that Caiceo Escudero refers to are Eduardo Frei Montalva and Sebastián Piñera Echeñique (the latter was in office from 2010 to 2014, and was elected as Chile's president again in 2018).
3 I refer to "liberal" academia in the sense of being an institution that understands processes of social and cultural modernization, that supports individual civil liberties, and defends democracy, human rights, and government measures to increase opportunities for those in subordinate positions.
4 The Supreme Court is the highest adjudicating court and carries judicial review. The Constitutional Court is an independent body in charge of a preemptive constitutional control of bills and legislation and *ex post facto* abstract control of legislation.
5 In Spanish, Servicio Nacional de la Mujer.
6 In Spanish, Instituto Chileno de Medicina Reproductiva. The experts alluded to were doctor Soledad Díaz Fernández, biologist María Elena Ortíz Scarlazetta, and doctors Horacio Croxatto Avoni and Fernando Zegers Hochschild, both medical doctors specializing in human reproduction.
7 The doctor and Dean of Medicine Cecilia Sepúlveda and the doctor Giorgio Solimano coincided along with Professor Ramiro Molina at the Constitutional Court. Before the Constitutional Court, Molina provided expert opinions in a case in regular courts that attempted to invalidate the permit for the sale of the contraceptive.

8 This group included Sebastián Illanes, Mercedes Bisquertt, and Professor Ventura Juncá, all from the University of the Andes.
9 Among them were Jorge Contesse Singh, Rodolfo Figueroa García-Huidobro, Gastón Gómez Bernales, and Antonio Bascuñán Rodríguez.
10 A law report was requested regarding the inability that weighed over the justices of the Constitutional Court, Raúl Bertelsen Repetto and Enrique Navarro Beltrán. They had participated in the elaboration of a report on constitutional law in support of the annulment of the drug registry of one brand of emergency contraception.
11 In Spanish, Asociación Chilena de Protección de la Familia.
12 Rubilar later supported the abortion bill. Currently she is a cabinet minister and held up to July 2020 the post of spokesperson for President Sebastián Piñera's government.
13 Opposed to what is suggested by Sarmiento Ramírez and Walker Echenique, legislators of the political alliance were organized by Congresswoman María Antonieta Saa. There was some concern in the government that the staging of the 52 legislators would reveal the political divide that existed with the Christian Democrats.
14 He started the public annulment trial against the sanitary registration of the emergency contraception brand Postinor 2—a case he finally lost in the Supreme Court 5–0 in 2006 (Corte Suprema 2006, No.1039). He was later the Dean of Law of the Andes University.
15 He was Chancellor of the Andes University and was part of the group that drafted the constitution under the dictatorship.
16 Professor at University of Chile and the religious Finis Terrae.
17 A feminist non-governmental organization, the Instituto de la Mujer (Women's Institute), prepared a brief for the senators outlining who the prosecuted women in Chile were and the consequences of criminalization.
18 In Spanish, Fondo Nacional de Desarrollo Científico y Tecnológico. Yanira Zúñiga undertook a research project in 2015 on reproductive rights: "Sexual and Reproductive Rights: From the Control to Autonomy."
19 Undurraga undertook her doctoral research on abortion. This work was key for the argument about the futility of the criminal law's abortion prohibition.
20 In the case of Alejandra Zúñiga Fajuri, I met her in the School of Law in the University Diego Portales due to our work in human rights.
21 According to canon law, a pregnancy can be terminated before viability to save the woman's life, even if it causes the death of the fetus. This is viewed ethically by the Church as "indirect abortion" because the main intent is to save the woman's life; the loss of the fetus is an unfortunate and secondary consequence.
22 See Vivaldi and Stutzin's contribution in this volume.
23 The last commission was summoned in 2018. A majority (Hernández, Couso, Wilenmann, Mañalich, and Acosta) maintained the original proposal to decriminalize abortion.
24 This was organized under the auspice of the Alas Network (Red Alas: Red Latinoamericana de Académicos/as del Derecho) of academics of gender, sexuality and law. See, www.redalas.net
25 One group agreed to advance as much as possible while others considered this too little. At the end of the day, there was no boycott to the legislative process, and many of the skeptics came out to celebrate in the streets the day the law partially won in the Constitutional Court.
26 This institution belongs to the Movimiento Regnum Christi related to the Legionaries of Christ.
27 The Observatory of Bioethics and Human Reproduction at the University Diego Portales organized a seminar together with the University of Edinburgh at the end of 2015: "Abortion and Reproductive Rights, Implications from Ethics, Law and Medicine." In this seminar, people from different disciplines from the government to academia participated. The presentations were later published in a book edited by Salas, Zegers and Figueroa García-Huidobro (2016).
28 Previously, there was a coordination effort that later became the Working Action Group for Legal Abortion in Chile in which individuals, social organizations, and political parties representatives are involved.

29 Despite what appeared in the press, social organizations hardly managed to survive financially due to lack of funding.

30 Some academics wanted to represent some organizations more than others. Paradoxically, another showed a strong interest in participating in the hearings even though he never participated in the public debate, not even writing letters to newspapers in support, and he requested that we would find an organization to represent.

31 Montero et al. (2017) in their research project, "Discursive Representations on Professional Rights and Duties, Institutions and the Role of the State, Related to Health Conscientious Objection and the Decriminalization of the Voluntary Interruption of Pregnancy, for Three Causes in Chile," established that institutionally the Pontifical Catholic University appears with 15.1 percent of mentions in informative pieces in comparison to 3.7 percent for the University of Chile. However, in terms of individual actors during this period, the Catholic University chancellor Ignacio Sánchez appears with 12.7 percent of mentions, and in second place the Minister of Health Carmen Castillo with 4.8 percent.

32 The national census showed that the atheist and evangelical population is growing while Catholicism is decreasing.

33 Many outstanding professors have been fired for dissenting. Ciro Colombara who was a lecturer in the law school was dismissed after he took the case of censorship of the film *The Last Temptation of Christ* to the Inter-American Human Rights Court. The same occurred with the scientists Horacio Croxatto, María Elena Ortíz, and Soledad Díaz, who were conducting research on contraceptives, and more recently with theologian Jorge Costadoat. Horacio Croxatto, an outstanding international scientist and expert on contraceptives was fired in 2006 for his research on emergency contraception and a public letter condemning the criminalization of abortion.

34 I owe the idea of this work to two people: former feminist Professor Mirtha Ulloa and the director of Legal Aid, Benito Mauriz, who authorized access to the files.

References

Aguirrezabal Grünstein, Maite, and Soledad Bertelsen Simonetti (eds). 2015. *El aborto. Perspectivas filosófica, jurídica y médica*. Santiago: Ediciones Universidad de Los Andes.

Arzobispado de Santiago. 2014. "CVX Invita A Foro Acerca De La Despenalización Del Aborto," August 6. www.iglesia.cl/detalle_noticia.php?id=25140.

Barcia Lehmann, Rodrigo. 2007. "Fallos y comentario a los fallos de la Corte de Apelaciones de Santiago y Corte Suprema sobre recurso de protección, interpuesto por la distribución de laboratorios de la denominada píldora del día después a adolescentes (menores mayores de catorce años)." *Revista Ius et Praxis* 13(2): 409–422.

Bascuñán Rodríguez, Antonio. 2001. "Límites a la prohibición y autorización legal del aborto consentido en el derecho constitucional comparado." *Revista de Derecho Público (Universidad de Chile)* 63: 209–233.

Bascuñán Rodríguez, Antonio. 2016. "Límites a la prohibición y autorización legal del aborto consentido en la jurisprudencia constitución chilena." In *Aborto y derechos reproductivos. Implicancias desde la ética, el derecho y la medicina*, eds. Sofía Salas, Fernando Zegers, and Rodolfo Figueroa García-Huidobro, 171–206. Santiago: Universidad Diego Portales.

Besio, Mauricio, Fernando Chomalí, Jorge Neira, Ángela Vivanco, Paola Rivas, Eliana Zúñiga, Carla Robledo, and Pilar Rogat. 2002. *Aborto "terapéutico." Consideraciones médicas, éticas, jurídicas y del Magisterio de la Iglesia Católica*. Santiago: Centro de Bioética de la Pontificia Universidad Católica de Chile.

Blofield, Merike. 2001. *The Politics of Moral Sin: A Study of Abortion and Divorce in Catholic Chile since 1990*. Santiago: Facultad Latinoamericana de Ciencias Sociales-Chile.

CADEM—Plaza Pública. 2018. "Encuesta Plaza Pública. Primera Semana de Julio—Estudio 234." www.cadem.cl/wp-content/uploads/2018/07/Track-PP-Jul-S1-N234.pdf.

Caiceo Escudero, Jaime. 2013. "La enseñanza universitaria laica y gratuita versus la enseñanza particular y católica: Un debate de ayer y de hoy en Chile." *Acta Scientiarum. Education* 35(1): 89–95.

Casas Becerra, Lidia. 1996. *Mujeres procesadas por aborto.* Santiago: Foro Abierto de Salud y Derechos Sexuales y Reproductivos.

Casas Becerra, Lidia. 2014. "El examen periódico universal: ¿Un instrumento de rendición de cuentas y diálogo?" In *Anuario de Derecho Público 2014,* ed. Javier Couso, 572–588. Santiago: Universidad Diego Portales.

Casas Becerra, Lidia, and Gloria Maira Vargas (eds.). 2018. *Visiones contrapuestas sobre el artículo 19 n° 1 de la Constitución: Reflexiones sobre la constitucionalidad de la ley de despenalización del aborto en tres causales.* Santiago: Facultad de Derecho, Universidad Diego Portales.

Casas, Lidia, Juan José Álvarez, Paulina Larrondo, and Gloria Maira Vargas. 2018. "Respuesta del Estado de Chile a casos de embarazo producto de la violencia sexual." In *Los efectos de la violencia sexual contra niñas y mujeres. Los casos de la violación con resultado de embarazo y de la violencia sexual contra las mujeres migrantes en la ruta hacia Chile,* 23–107. Santiago: Centro de Derechos Humanos, Facultad de Derecho, Universidad Diego Portales.

Casas, Lidia, and Delfina Lawson (eds.). 2016. *Debates y reflexiones en torno a la despenalización del aborto en Chile.* Santiago: Centro de Derechos Humanos, Facultad de Derecho, Universidad Diego Portales.

Casas, Lidia, and Lieta Vivaldi. 2013. "La criminalización del aborto como una violación de los derechos humanos de las mujeres." In *Informe anual sobre derechos humanos en Chile 2013,* ed. Tomás Vial Solar, 69–120. Santiago: Facultad de Derecho, Universidad Diego Portales.

Casas, Lidia, and Lieta Vivaldi. 2017. "Pregnancies and Fetal Anomalies Incompatible with Life in Chile: Arguments and Experiences in Advocating for Legal Reform", *Health and Human Rights Journal* 19(1): 95–108.

Centro de Derechos Humanos. 2004. *Informe Anual Sobre Los Derechos Humanos en Chile. Hechos 2004,* ed. Felipe González, 219–239. Santiago: Universidad Diego Portales.

Comité de Ética del Colegio Médico de Chile. 2003. "Aborto: Interrupción del embarazo como medida terapéutica en casos de gestantes con riesgo de muerte al continuar la gravidez." www.colegiomedico.cl/wp-content/uploads/2018/12/Aborto.pdf.

Contesse Singh, Jorge. 2007. "Implicancias y recusaciones: El caso del Tribunal Constitucional. Informe en derecho sobre la inhabilidad constitucional para conocer de un caso en el que se ha vertido opinión pública con anterioridad." *Revista Ius et Praxis* 13(2): 391–405.

Corte Suprema. 2006. *Corte Suprema No. 1039–2005.* Santiago: Corte Suprema.

Dides, Claudia. 2006. *Voces en emergencia: El discurso conservador y la píldora del día después.* Santiago: United Nations Population Fund and Facultad Latinoamericana de Ciencias Sociales-Chile.

Dides, Claudia, Cristina Benavente, and Isabel Sáenz (2011). *Sistematización hitos noticiosos sobre aborto en la prensa. 1998–2010. Brasil, Chile, México y Nicaragua.* Santiago: Facultad Latinoamericana de Ciencias Sociales-Chile.

Emol. 2017. "Encuesta Bicentenario: 59% de los chilenos se declara católico y 17% evangélico," October 25. www.emol.com/noticias/Nacional/2017/10/25/880610/Encuesta-Bicentenario-59-de-los-chilenos-se-declara-catolico-y-7-evangelicos.html.

Figueroa García-Huidobro, Rodolfo. 2008. "Concepto de derecho a la vida." *Ius et Praxis* 14(1): 261–300.

Gómez Bernales, Gastón. 2012. *Derechos fundamentales y recurso de protección.* Santiago: Ediciones Universidad Diego Portales.

Instituto de Investigación en Ciencias Sociales UDP. 2015. "Encuesta Nacional UDP 2015." http://encuesta.udp.cl/2015/11/09/acuerdo-con-que-se-despenalice-el-aborto.

Medina Quiroga, Cecilia. 2005. *La convención americana: Teoría y jurisprudencia. Vida, integridad personal, libertad personal, debido proceso y recurso judicial.* Santiago: Centro de Derechos Humanos, Universidad de Chile.

Montero, Adela, Jorge Vergara, Mauricio Ríos, and Raúl Villarroel. 2017. "La objeción de conciencia en el debate sobre la despenalización del aborto por tres causales en Chile." *Revista chilena de obstetricia y ginecología* 82(4): 350–355.

Radio Cooperativa, Imaginacción, and Universidad Central. 2015. "Encuesta," September 8. http://encuesta.cooperativa.cl/temas/site/artic/20150908/asocfile/20150908101314/presentaci__n_encuesta_8_de_septiembre.pdf.

Ramm, Alejandra, Lidia Casas, Sara Correa, C. Finley Baba, and M. Antonia Biggs. 2020. "'Obviously There is a Conflict Between Confidentiality and What You are Required to Do by Law': Chilean University Faculty and Student Perspectives on Reporting Unlawful Abortions." *Social Science & Medicine* 261: 113220.

Salas, Sofía, Fernando Zegers, and Rodolfo Figueroa García-Huidobro (eds.). 2016. *Aborto y derechos reproductivos. Implicancias desde la ética, el derecho y la medicina.* Santiago: Universidad Diego Portales.

Sarmiento Ramírez, Claudia, and Elisa Walker Echenique. 2018. "Tramitación del proyecto de ley que despenaliza la interrupción del embarazo en tres causales específicas." In *Visiones contrapuestas sobre el artículo 19 No 1 de la Constitución: Reflexiones sobre la constitucionalidad de la ley de despenalización del aborto en tres causales,* eds. Lidia Casas Becerra and Gloria Maira Vargas, 139–160. Santiago: Facultad de Derecho, Universidad Diego Portales.

Serrano, Sol. 2016. *Universidad y Nación. Chile en el siglo XIX. 2nd ed.* Santiago: Centro de Investigaciones Barros Arana, Editorial Universitaria, and Dirección de Bibliotecas y Archivos.

Shepard, Bonnie L., and Lidia Casas Becerra. 2007. "Abortion Policies and Practices in Chile: Ambiguities and Dilemmas." *Reproductive Health Matters: An International Journal on Sexual and Reproductive Health and Rights* 15(30): 202–210.

Tribunal Constitucional. 2017. *Tribunal Constitucional No 3729–17.* Santiago: Tribunal Constitucional.

Walker, Ignacio. 1998. "La familia real y la familia ideal." In *A partir de Beijing. La familia chilena del 2000,* ed. Sergio Marras, 229–237. Santiago: Universidad Diego Portales, Ediciones de Chile 21, and RIL Editores.

Zúñiga Fajuri, Alejandra. 2011. "Aborto y derechos humanos." *Revista de Derecho (Valdivia)* 24(2): 163–177.

12

EXPLORING ALTERNATIVE MEANINGS OF A FEMINIST AND SAFE ABORTION IN CHILE

Lieta Vivaldi and Valentina Stutzin

Introduction

The prohibition of abortion in Chile can be traced back to the dictatorship led by General Augusto Pinochet (1973–90), which, alongside its exponential increment of political violence, imposed a social and economic model of deep social reach. The dictatorship's ideological apparatus underpinned legislation that represented and supported the interests of conservative and religious groups. In this sense, it is no surprise that the implemented policies were largely detrimental for women's bodily integrity. More surprising, however, is the fact that this tendency was not alleviated after the fall of Pinochet's regime. Consider, for instance, the privatization of the healthcare and education systems in the 1990s. Additionally, the protection of the patriarchal Catholic family and the division of gender roles were key during the dictatorship, placing motherhood at the center of "rebuilding the nation," and their roots continued to run deep.

The transition to democracy was based on agreements and moderation (Richard 2001; Blofield and Haas 2005; Shepard and Casas Becerra 2007). During this period, we can observe different strategies regarding sexual and reproductive rights, and abortion in particular. In general terms, framing strategies focused on public health, social justice, and fair access. However, it is useful to distinguish between two types of strategies. First, the strategy of legal reform, deployed by "institutional feminists," sought to effect changes through new governmental regulations and public policies. Paradigmatically, reform efforts aimed to legalize abortion at least on certain grounds, and in relation to the Ley Marco sobre Derechos Sexuales y Reproductivos (Framework Law on Sexual and Reproductive rights) of 2000. Second, feminist groups also implemented strategies based on the creation of their own spaces for discussion and consciousness-raising about the common experience of abortion.

After the 1990s, several events have challenged and reshaped the political landscape of the transition to democracy: the student movement in 2011, the *mayo*

DOI: 10.4324/9781003079903-16

feminista (Feminist May, also known as "Feminist Tsunami") in 2018, and finally the general uprising of October 2019. Largely, these political events relate to the fact that democratic governments not only failed to reverse the dictatorship's neoliberal policies, but rather strengthened and further developed them. Feminists have had a crucial role in bringing people to the streets and protesting around issues such as gender violence, sexist education, heteronormativity, and the political and economic system. Abortion has been another important arena of political struggle.

In the context of abortion illegality in Chile, the pharmaceutical misoprostol has been very important for the safety of clandestine abortions since the late 1990s (Casas and Vivaldi 2013; Vivaldi and Varas 2015). Its commercialization, however, was restricted for the first time in 2001, and nowadays it is not possible to buy it in pharmacies. However, the pills are clandestinely sold on the Internet, and can be bought in other countries. While there are some international non-governmental organizations (NGOs) that send misoprostol to Chile via mail, the abortion prohibition generates an underground market, and most women are left on their own to find out how and where to acquire misoprostol (Etcheberry 2016; Palma Manríquez et al. 2018).

As in many parts of the world, the use of misoprostol in Chile has decreased the risks associated with clandestine abortion. Additionally, it has the potential to give greater autonomy to women. For instance, when access to healthcare services is difficult or even threatening, it is certainly liberating not to require a doctor or a hospital to perform an abortion. Moreover, by the use of misoprostol women can generate solidarity networks that resonate with new forms of imagining the political and the ethical (for example, notions of relational autonomy, vulnerability and care as a condition of possibility of the political, forms of sorority and accompaniment, and reimagining the body as a territory of decolonization). However, the hopeful face of these new discovered possibilities runs the risk of leaving the unjust face of current health policies and official channels untouched and unimproved. As the state fails on its responsibilities towards women, many see themselves forced back to forms of clandestine agency and various marginalized spaces.

As in the 1990s, recent years have seen the development of different strategies and discourses on abortion: some of them focusing on the legal reform, and others on the social decriminalization of abortion and accompaniment practices. With respect to legal reforms, in general, feminists have invoked the concept of human rights to demand the legalization of abortion and the construction of reproductive rights as individual rights highlighting the claim for self-determination and autonomy (see, for instance, Matamala Vivaldi 2014), not always problematizing the underlying liberal paradigm of choice. Some of these discourses are based on rhetorics that construct women as passive victims in need of protection, under humanitarian logics (Vivaldi and Stutzin 2017), not without critique from other feminist perspectives. Nevertheless, the boundaries between legal, social, state, and autonomous strategies and activisms have often blurred since the approval of the 2017 law permitting abortions for three reasons (rape, risk to life, and fetal unviability). Considering that the bill guarantees access to abortion to a minimum percentage of women, certain feminist groups have formed coalitions to help women use the law, and to monitor its implementation, while at the same time continuing the fight for "free" abortion, meaning without restrictions.

Focusing on collective action for abortion rights in Chile, this chapter examines feminist activist discourses and practices for free abortion from the 2000s onwards. We particularly analyze the strategies of activists who provide information on pregnancy termination with pills as well as give physical and emotional accompaniment to women undergoing abortions. These activisms operate in partial (il)legality, clandestinity, and opacity to the state's legibility—in that porous and contentious field of what Veena Das and Deborah Poole (2004) call "the margins of the state." As we will argue, these direct-action practices have created, in a context of prohibition and urgency, collective solutions operating in "the radical in-between of prefigurative politics and the politics of survival" (Lin et al. 2016, 302). In doing so, they have broadened the horizons of the desired democracy, bringing into practice new imaginaries of agency and autonomy, in ways that defy neoliberal conceptions of subjectivity, humanitarianism, and rights. Thus, beyond the traditional venues of struggle and debate (e.g., changes in the legislation based on discourses of human rights, choice, and autonomy), we will focus on the ways different women have been "doing the work of the state," in their own independent networks of solidarity and accompaniment, exploring and including new perspectives, actors, and voices in the abortion debate, particularly those of sexual dissidence and decolonialism.

Activisms, and more generally, feminisms, are *"fluid, dynamic and heterogeneous fields of contestation* in which participants adopt varied forms and degrees of engagement with one another, with hegemonic discourses, and with dominant institutions, including the state" (Thayer and Rubin 2017, 333, emphasis in original). Currently in Chile, feminists find themselves involved in a large and diversified plurality of discourses and actions; feminism is multi-located and internally heterogeneous (Alvarez 2019). Considering that activism occurs in a wide range of modalities and venues, as Sonia Alvarez et al. (2017) point out, is it useful to distinguish between "the permissible, authorized, tolerated forms of activism and participation and their 'others', the prohibited unauthorized, intolerable" (3). Following these authors, rather than determined by venues and political forms, a given practice or discourse is authorized or unauthorized (as poles in a continuum with shades of gray) depending on the effects of activism and its relationship to dominant discursive formations and constellations of power. From this perspective, transgression and counterhegemonic effects are not embedded in particular locations or strategies, and activist effects may be contradictory and heterogeneous.

In developing these arguments, we draw on interviews with 12 activists, conducted by both authors between 2017 and 2020; public documents produced by the organizations; activist websites and social media; and interviews published in media sources. We elaborate on reflections that come from a broader analysis of abortion politics in Chile, regarding biopolitics and governmentality (Vivaldi 2020), issues of neoliberalism, vulnerability, and agency (Vivaldi and Varas 2015), and affects and visualities (Vivaldi and Stutzin 2017).

Abortion, Feminism, and Sexual Dissidence

> I know that now there is more visibility of women in the "front line," as we were not there before… We have always been there, doing the same things […]. In the political history of clandestine political organizations, history professors or super radical activism, very patriarchal, do not consider abortion as part of this history. They don't think of us as doing radical clandestine political organizing in post-dictatorship. For instance, women in prison for abortion are not part of the history of political prisoners. It's because they don't care about these issues […] and because they don't care, they don't know […]. In our feminist circles, we all know how hard it is. The secrecy, for instance: I don't mean the moral secrecy of abortion, which exists, but rather the secret organizing that takes place when you have a law that forbids the pills, and the risks we then have to face. […] However, we are also not that kind of "traditional front line," or "traditional revolutionaries." We are constructing other models. We have our own criticism against this heroic, masculinist kind of martyr, this left-wing ideal of clandestine revolutionary […]. If we are afraid or oversaturated, we are not afraid to say so. We have a feminist commitment and that includes taking care of ourselves and trying to support each other. Women do not have to give their lives away for an abortion or to be heroines.
>
> *(Lesbofeminist and abortion accompaniment activist, personal communication, 2020)*

As the state takes a step back, feminist women and groups fill the gap creatively and courageously regarding abortion. From within neoliberal constraints and dilemmas, and facing clandestinity, difficult access to medication, and precarity, they have proposed other ways of experiencing and representing abortion. They have demanded rights from the state along with producing new participatory processes and struggles over representation, unsettling meanings and the power relations upon which hegemonic meanings are produced (Alvarez et al. 2017). Particularly, activisms rooted in sexual dissidence perspectives have gone beyond the languages of legality and rights to embrace broader debates on health, collective care, and relational agency. They engage in what we argue are embodied prefigurative politics of care.

Moreover, recovering lesbian and *cuir* (queer) voices in abortion activism is crucial to dismantle the gay homonormative trends of the expansion of sexual democracy in Chile and Latin America. As noted by various scholars (Hernández 2014; Tabbush et al. 2016), in recent decades, processes of social and legislative openings to sexual diversity have coexisted with the prohibition of abortion. In the words of Iris Hernández, a lesbofeminist decolonial activist in Chile:

> Sexual democracy has omitted the lesbian voice, in that it doesn't question the narratives that populate our conception of sexuality […] Sexual democracy has meant an openness for masculine sexual diversity, but it hasn't been enough to open the debate about the liberty of women to decide about their own bodies.
>
> *(Hernández 2014, n.p.)*

Within sexual dissidence activism, there are two main groups that have been actively fighting for unrestricted abortion: Lesbofeminists (organized in different groups) and Colectivo Utópico de Disidencia Sexual (Utopian Collective for

Sexual Dissidence, CUDS). Lesbofeminist organizations include Línea Aborto Libre (Free Abortion Hotline, LAL)[1] and Con las Amigas y en la Casa (With Friends and at Home, CLAYELC)[2]. By calling to "abort heterosexuality," the perspectives of sexual dissidence emphasize that abortion is a relevant issue not just for cisgender heterosexual women. Abortion matters to gestating persons who are neither women nor heterosexual (such as trans identities, lesbians, queer), and because its prohibition is part of the heterosexual regime (Wittig 1992). By drawing on feminist and queer theorizations, lesbofeminists see the prohibition of abortion as "the tip of the iceberg" in a society based on heteronormativity, mandatory motherhood, patriarchy, and capitalism. As activists from LAL state:

> If asked why lesbians are working on the issue of abortion, we answer that it is a strategy of solidarity, of love, and care between women. A strategy against patriarchy and, consequently, against capitalism and the "system." […] Love between women is the first step to put an end to the reproductive commandment and that cell of capitalism and patriarchy that is the family.
>
> *(Loaíza Cárdenas 2016, 100–1)*

Indeed, lesbofeminist groups have played a crucial role in what they call the "social decriminalization of abortion," organizing the distribution of abortion information, support, and accompaniments as well as forming solidarity networks. They have also been very active in political demonstrations and cultural production. Members of CUDS, who define themselves as *cuir*/queer and post-feminist, have produced several artistic performances aimed at dislocating the hegemonic visual and affective representational politics of abortion; particularly the status of the fetus as a human being (Henríquez Murgas 2015). These strategies, not merely focused on legal reform, have been an alternative to the narrow law-based language of human rights that dominates the public debate. In the words of Amy Krauss, it is a narrowing that happens "not only through the assumption of a liberal discourse of individual rights, but also the way 'the legal' comes to take precedence over the moral, social and ethical terms of care" (2018, 689). For instance, CUDS have put abortion in the center of a more general debate regarding access to healthcare in neoliberal Chile. *Por una vida mejor: Dona por un aborto ilegal* ("For a better life: Donate for an illegal abortion") was a 2012 performance by CUDS. It was a parody of NGO-like campaigns for solidarity and donations, and the performance included recruiting volunteers and having them ask for money in public spaces. The idea was to provoke a conversation about abortion and put it in the scenario of everyday life in the city, in order to make people think that if the state failed to support abortions, people should collaborate and donate, as abortions should be part of our public concerns (Henríquez Murgas 2015). Moreover, it was a statement against the precarious healthcare system in neoliberal Chile, where most people who cannot afford treatments have to rely on the solidarity of their families and neighbors or resort to self-organized activities to raise money (such as parties and raffles). Only a few extreme cases become high profile, receiving public attention and donations from NGOs or private companies.

A priority for these groups is the social decriminalization of abortion, led by feminists and lesbofeminists in particular. Strategically, they aim to remove negative affects associated with abortion such as shame, guilt, secrecy, and condemnation (Vacarezza 2017; Vivaldi and Stutzin 2017). That was, for instance, the idea behind the public campaign *Yo amo aborto, yo amo misoprostol* ("I love abortion, I love misoprostol") led by the Colectiva Feminista Las Sueltas[3] in 2012 or the LAL slogan *¡Sin doctor ni policía nuestro aborto es alegría!* ("Without a doctor or the police, abortion is joy!"). Nevertheless, activisms still give space to the possible mourning or grief, or to the pain, dangers, and possible criminalization associated with unsafe abortion, because as Nayla Luz Vacarezza notices "leaving aside these forms of injustice, violence and suffering would imply denying past and present injustices still suffered by women" (2017, 1). Additionally, they aim for abortion to be publicly recognized as a reality, and something to be taken care of collectively. In this sense, CLAYELC activists have repeatedly noted that just like women get baby showers, gifts, solidarity, and some kinds of state help and recognition when they are pregnant, women should also receive "abortion shower" solidarity. As this kind of support has yet to exist, activists have taken upon themselves to do abortion accompaniments.

Here, we will focus on accompaniment activism as forms of experimental, prefigurative politics of care. In a context of prohibition and urgency, activists have collectively created solutions in "a radical in-between of prefigurative politics and the politics of survival" (Lin et al. 2016, 302). "Politics of survival" because they are born from the necessity to perform abortions, under an unwanted clandestinity regime imposed by the state. But even though they act upon a necessity in the present, without knowing beforehand the pregnant people that they will get to accompany, the particular way of solving this necessity involves a kind of political imagination that is transformative. It is not only about giving access to abortion, but to make the abortion experience an imaginative political opening (Siskindovich 2018).

We follow Luke Yates' understanding of prefiguration as the "attempted construction of alternative or utopian social relations in the present, either in parallel with, or in the course of, adversarial social movement protest" (Yates 2015, 1). The term is originally embedded in a genealogy of scholar and political praxis in social movements, radical left politics, and collective action. We apply it as a part of our analytical toolbox, since it resonates with feminist attention to the politics and politization of everyday life and lived experiences, the importance of reflexivity and intersubjective relations, as well as with structural transformations. Therefore, a feminist approach to prefiguration politics (see for example Lin et al. 2016; Carmo 2019; Ishkanian and Peña Saavedra 2019) "expands the theory, practice, and aspirations of prefigurative politics" (Lin et al. 2016, 303), shedding light on the engendered, affective, and embodied dimensions in these kinds of political actions.

Furthermore, as Íris Nery do Carmo (2019) points out, Judith Butler's (2015) reflections on vulnerability and assemblies can be a complementary theoretical input to prefigurative politics. Indeed, Butler (2015) focuses on the embodied and performative forms of collective action. Public gatherings of bodies in alliance exercise the performative right to appear, by defying the norms that have constrained the field of the intelligible and "calling into question the inchoate and powerful dimensions of reigning notions of the political" (Butler 2015, 8). In the action of alliance, a new "between" of bodies is created that enacts "the social order it seeks to bring about by establishing its own modes of sociality" (Butler 2015, 84). The "we" that is enacted by the assembly of bodies produces a new sense of the collective: plural, persistent, acting, interdependent; the assembly "enacts a provisional and plural form of coexistence that constitutes a distinct ethical and social alternative to 'responsibilization'" (Butler 2015, 16) and the privatization of care. In this way, as we will consider in the next section, abortion accompaniments rely on collective strategies and gatherings of bodies, which constitute these kinds of alliances.

Reimagining Feminist Friendships and Notions of Safety

Under prohibition and without legal access to misoprostol, the value of personal networks and economic resources becomes a decisive factor for the safety/risk involved in the practice of abortion, or even if the abortion will take place at all. Tackling this unequal distribution of opportunities is one of the motivations behind feminist support networks such as LAL and CLAYELC.

Feminist abortions imply the (re)distribution and sharing of collective resources and risks—a collective responsibility for care. Indeed, CLAYELC's name (With Friends and at Home) comes from the perceived need for reaching women who did not have a feminist activist friend or someone else "inside the circuit" who would know where to get information, the pills, and access to a feminist doctor in case of need. Consequently, the idea was to expand the "circle of friends," transforming friendship into a political decision, and making friendship and care a model of political organizing.

> If you don't have a feminist friend, you still can be treated as a friend, with the care and love and intimacy that friendship means, by a lesbofeminist activist that is willing to be there in the process with you.
>
> *(CLAYELC activist, personal communication, 2020)*

Friendship is an interpersonal relation that involves mutual trust, shared learning experiences, and also conflict. That is the type of abortion accompaniment that CLAYLEC has in mind. Women seeking an abortion have to trust the *acompañantes* (person who accompanies), but also *acompañantes* have to trust unknown women in an activity that has legal risks. It is through risk-sharing that other forms of safety arise, beyond "not dying" or the World Health Organization's (2012) definition of safe abortion. As an activist put it:

> A safe abortion is not only about not dying. It is so much more. It depends on emotional and psychological issues too. That's why we call our network "friends" [*amigas*]. With friends you have a relation of *apañarse* [be there for each other] and trust. It is a space of peers. Hospitals and doctors are not peers.

Friends you trust; you can feel scared or embarrassed, or disagree, but still you trust, still you know that you can count on each other. There may be laughter, love, crying, and fear. Just like in abortions.

(CLAYELC activist, personal communication, 2018)

Thus, safety also involves unprejudiced listening and a space for diverse, even contradictory affects. It is about sharing the risks and responsibilities, not feeling so alone, and exchanging knowledge in peer-to-peer non-hierarchical relationships. This project, however, poses many challenges. Even though horizontality is a desired goal, there are differential power positions that need to be acknowledged. Women are in urgent need of abortions and asking for help. Yet, activists prefer the word "accompaniment" rather than "help," because it puts them in a position of learning and reciprocity:

I think every feminist should accompany an abortion, have the experience of accompanying an abortion as part of her feminist formation. Because you learn a lot of things. Many times, you are accompanying women that aren't feminists, that don't think like you do, or, as it might be the case, you don't like them. Or they are in really unimaginable situations. And all the time you're listening to another woman, trying to make a plan with this other woman you don't know, but you've decided to trust her, and she has decided to trust you. […] It is a great feminist learning. It locates you in reality, it brings you out of the feminist ghetto, and it helps you to work on your own prejudices.

(CLAYELC activist Viviana Díaz, in Espinoza 2019, n.p.)

The concept of safety that we are considering is not about total control over uncertainty. It is not a homogenizing script with no space for transformative encounters or mistakes. In this sense, both LAL and CLAYELC have actively participated in a broader debate within contemporary feminisms and *cuir*/queer politics regarding the responsible, liberal sexual subject behind the hegemonic imaginary of the sexual rights-bearing subject (Sabsay 2016a). Consider, for instance, the problematization of a typical abortion-rights slogan: "Educación sexual para decidir, anticonceptivos para no abortar, aborto legal para no morir" ("Sex education for choice, contraception to prevent abortion, legal abortion to prevent death"). Abortion, in this case, is something that should be exceptional, a last resort that could and should be prevented.

The boundaries of what is considered right and wrong regarding sexuality have shifted dramatically in recent decades and, as Sérgio Carrara (2015) points out, currently the dominant discourse around sexuality seems to revolve around the notion of responsibility (responsible/irresponsible sex) more than around reproductive/non-reproductive sex. Accordingly, Josefina Brown (2016) indicates that sexuality is not an isolated phenomenon in a world where the pervasive neoliberal rationality permeates everything: risk (Giddens 1991; Beck 1992), the logic of self-sufficiency, anticipation, resilience, and responsibility as individual imputation redefines our experience and understanding of sexuality. Therefore, with the possible exception of cases resulting from unforeseen sufferings (such as rape or serious fetal illness), abortion is conceived, even in feminist discourses, as a failure of the neoliberal subject (Brown 2016). That is, a failure of a subject that must embody the ideal of autonomy as independence, self-control, rationality, and calculation. In this way, blame comes swiftly denouncing irresponsibility and lack of control (for instance, for failing to adopt adequate contraceptive methods). This leaves no space for mistakes or chance, or for changing minds about a pregnancy, with the consequent toll on women's minds, bodies, and social environments. In this sense, CLAYELC *acompañantes* have explicitly worked to move beyond internalized commonsense views about abortion:

> Women have compelled us to think a lot about our boundaries, what is possible to do, or what we thought was impossible, ethical limits, every kind of limit […]. What happens when a woman comes for an abortion one, two, three times? What happens to you with that? Do you accompany her again or not? And if you feel something about that, how much is related to your own misogynist prejudice? […] You are never still, you are always thinking, you are forced to reflect on many issues.
>
> *(CLAYELC activist Viviana Díaz, in Espinoza 2019, n.p.)*

Finally, feminist abortion activism has publicly underscored the issue of care within social movements and as part of transformative politics. This positioning of care is not just about organizing around care-related issues, but also about questioning and reflecting on how organizations and movements implement care practices. CLAYELC, for example, has organized "schools of *acompañantes*" not only to guarantee the quality of accompaniments, but also to connect "unorganized *acompañantes*" (*acompañantes sueltas*) and promote the construction of groups, networks, and collective instances for accompanying the *acompañantes*.

Home, Belongings, and Coalitions: Alternatives to State Legibility

As an alternative to problematic abortion experiences in hospitals, accompaniment groups actively call for home-based abortions. As the lyrics of a reggaeton song by CLAYELC put it: "If the senate approves of you / or wants you in prison / you don't give a fuck about that / you will abort with your friends / if you are a threat to the state / be happy and abort at home with friends."[4] This claim has not been without controversy in feminist circles, as it remains anchored in the tension between "doing the work of the state" or "being an apologist for clandestinity."

Indeed, critically reflecting on the contradictions involved in "doing the work of the state" is important (Etcheberry and Vivaldi 2016, 40). In the extreme case, "doing the work of the state" goes hand in hand with a situation of vulnerability and dispossession that can be interpreted in terms of Giorgio Agamben's *nuda vita*, bare life (1998). That is the argument of Barbara Sutton when she reflects on the clandestinity of abortion as a form of state violence "implicated in the production of hidden bodies (in particular those of women), bodies that are nonetheless exposed to danger with total impunity" (2017, 890). It is a paradoxical position for them: women who abort clandestinely are constructed as *nuda vita* and dispossessed of basic rights, but also exert (constrained) agency: "They are affirming and reclaiming their whole humanity through the active rejection of the commandment to be merely reproductive wombs" (Sutton 2017, 899).

From another perspective, accompaniment activism develops in what Das and Poole (2004) call "the margins of the state." This notion refers to "the many different spaces, forms, and practices through which the state is continually both experienced and undone through the illegibility of its own practices, documents, and words" (9). It also considers the margin as a space between bodies, law, and discipline:

> The point is not whether the desires, fears, and hopes nourished in the margins and then projected onto the state are somehow more ethical, just, or pure. Rather, the complexity of lived experience inflicts notions of justice and law with different kinds of imaginaries from those available in the official sites and representations of justice and law.
>
> *(Das and Poole 2004, 23)*

In this sense, "aborting at home with friends" can pose an opportunity to defy hegemonic representations and producing new meanings around the experience of abortion and care.

What is the scope of reclaiming "home" as the political space for abortion? The call for home-based abortions involves a dismantling of the private/public dichotomy and an expansion of the conception of home itself. Reclaiming "home" as a political space is not new in feminist politics. In one sense, for feminist theorizing on the troublesome private/public distinction and domesticity, "home" is fraught with sexual and gendered exploitation, oppression, conflict, and power relations. But also, for some women of color, migrant, lesbofeminists and queer, reclaiming "home" is political in the sense of constructing an alternative place of belonging and care. The "home" imagined and fostered by CLAYELC resembles bell hooks' (1990) notion of *homeplace*. For hooks, the nurturing and care work done by Black women at home, as a humanizing place, creates an intimate enclave for resisting and opposing racist oppression and violence, by materially and subjectively enabling the reproduction of the community. In this way, care becomes radically subversive by fostering their personal and their community's self-determination.

In conditions of abortion illegality, the space generated by feminist networks of trust can become a homeplace where a new public space for assemblies of bodies is rendered recognizable, resisting and bypassing the state's gaze. Thinking about public assemblies, Judith Butler argues that bodies in their relational materiality, vulnerability, and spatial appearance, seize upon "an already established space permeated by existing power seeking to sever the relations between the public space, the public square and the existing regime" (Butler 2015, 85) wrestling their legitimacy and recognizability from the state.

Therefore, producing new collective feminist homes as a space of belonging appears against the background of the "exposed" space of the public, understood as a field of recognition controlled by state legibility (Trouillot 2001; Das and Poole 2004). According to this legibility—dominated by the language of humanitarianism in Chile—victimhood and exceptionality are the only legitimate ways of accessing an abortion. In this sense, going through abortions collectively produces (re) assemblages and resignifications of political social spaces: social media, the streets in which massive feminist gatherings and popular uprisings unfold, venues where abortion groups meet and feminist talks take place, and the space where a pregnant person takes the pills and goes through an abortion, among others. These gatherings defy crystalized figurations of public space as well as which subjects and types of abortion can be rendered recognizable. It is in this sense that accompaniments are intended to be "radical homeplaces to foster relationality and identifications out of longing" (Lin et al. 2016, 307), where there is no need to ask the state for permission to abort.

This kind of homeplace may be concrete, such as the meetings and the experience of reclaiming the house as a place to interrupt the daily routine and produce a time-space for self-care:

> Generally, we don't have spaces for us women even inside our homes, where we are full of responsibilities towards others, always caring and reproducing life for others in an overload of sexual division of labor, with no intimacy and space for our own desire. It is about arranging a time-space for an abortion, whether it takes place in your own physical house, or in a friend's house or with our [CLAYELC] help for the logistics of finding a concrete space. Because you know it is impossible for some women to abort at their homes because of the kids, the parents, or the presence of a violent male partner.
>
> *(CLAYELC activist, personal communication, 2018)*

Thus, feminist activism tries to open a space to imagine, remember, and desire a different home. A home that reflects an experience of longing to be with others (Carrillo Rowe 2005), and a realization of what home should be and feel like, what relationships make us feel that we belong. Feminist networks are a homeplace where one can go back to in order to engage in feminist activism or accompany other women. Moreover, these networks enable different kinds of work and labor. As Sara Ahmed (2017, 7) points out, "[f]eminism is homework" because we have to work out from not being at home in worlds that are violent and that limit us, not giving us space to fit: "Feminist housework does not simply clean and maintain a house. Feminist housework aims to transform the house, to rebuild the master's residence" (7). Thus, home-building is a world-building practice; it is an ongoing, unfinished project, between survival and prefiguration, because it is a question of how to build a feminist world while we still inhabit the world we oppose.

Understanding accompaniments through the lens of prefiguration raises questions about temporality, durability, and transcendence involved in this kind of political action. How can they be prefigurative, if they are what Amy Krauss—who considers accompaniments of abortions in Mexico—calls "ephemeral politics," characterized by fleeting intimacies? Abortion accompaniments "require a quality of attention in spite of the fact that connections dissolve, and in this sense, they are a form of political action that inhabits a space in-between world-making and repair" (Krauss 2019, 3). Indeed, there is no real opposition between repairing and world-making, between making this world more livable and constructing new worlds. Our attempts to repair and make some situations more livable are usually the way in which we imagine and construct new worlds.

The notion of "feminist abortions as accompanied abortions" is crucial, because it emphasizes both the possibility of agency beyond the control of the state and taking advantage of the available pharmacological resources, as well as including the "other women" invisibilized behind the abstract and isolated women of "choice" (Pampín 2014). Behind the scenes are all the people who enable the abortion and exercise of freedom—a notion that acquires meaning only in relation to others, in the context of others' practices, and in an engagement of power relations. It is in that sense, an important example of Butler's idea that beyond determinism and radical voluntarism, the space of freedom is a struggle and practice without beginning or end (Butler 2008).

In this regard, recent feminist attempts to reconceptualize autonomy in terms of "relationality" or "relational autonomy" help incorporate the values of inter-dependency and care, producing new imaginaries of freedom and agency. They are premised on the shared conviction "that persons are socially embedded, and that agents' identities are formed within the context of social relationships and shaped by a complex of intersecting social determinants, such as race, class, gender, and ethnicity" (Mackenzie and Stoljar 2000, 4). Furthermore, Leticia Sabsay argues that

> freedom as autonomy can reveal itself as a mechanism of control, for instance, by undermining the ideal of freedom and the freedoms we might imagine for ourselves, or detaching questions of freedom 'as a subjective capacity' from the social and economic conditions in which subjects could be actually free.
>
> *(Sabsay 2016a, 167–8)*

Another problem with neoliberal conceptions of autonomy is the obviation or denial of the relational and sociopolitical background of choice. Relations between people are dismissed, because "neoliberalism operates as a technique of 'govern-mentality' that aims to shape citizens' attitudes and behaviors by reinforcing the autonomy of individuals as against the agency of politicized collectives" (Undurraga 2015, 14). Furthermore, the practice of abortion has often been considered an "individual choice" for some part of the feminist movement and leftist thought. In this sense, collectively organizing and enabling abortions shed new ways of understanding political agency for social movements.

As a popular feminist slogan says: *Abortamos hermanadas, abortamos en manada* ("We abort together, we abort as a pack"). In this bodily experience of togetherness individual boundaries are blurred. In the words of Viviana Diaz from CLAYELC:

> The woman that we are accompanying has also accompanied another woman before, or knows about someone else [who has aborted]; somehow, we all

have aborted, because we've done it in our life or because we have accompanied someone else, which is also a way of aborting.

(Etcheberry and Vivaldi 2016, 40)

Therefore, when the inter-bodily dimension is at the center of agency, alternative ways of thinking and experiencing action are enabled, ways that are unthinkable when agency is conceived merely in terms of an individual narrative (Macón 2013). These are forms of agency embedded in and made possible by vulnerability. As Leticia Sabsay notes, vulnerability "emerges from a subject's relationality and it is constitutive of our capacity for action" (2016b, 285).

But, even though shifting away from the liberal rhetoric of choice or the ownership-based notion that "my body is mine," and producing practices that through the action of "aborting together" problematize agency as individual freedom, abortion activism still somehow encourages "a melodramatic view of agency in the temporality of the event of the decision" (Berlant 2011, 97). Particularly by framing abortion as a feminist decision. For example, as stated in a declaration: "We recognize the decision to abort as a contempt against the heterocapitalist and patriarchal system, understanding that to accompany is a lesbofeminist strategy of resistance" (Con las Amigas y en la Casa 2019, n.p.).There is a risk in seeing this moment of "affirmation as a subject" in terms of neoliberal and individualist understandings of freedom and agency. There is also the risk of reinforcing new norms on how a feminist abortion should be and what it should mean, as well as reifying it as an ontological meaningful and radical experience.

From the activists' perspective, abortions are embodied and subjective performative experiences that can produce us as feminist subjects. Feminist abortions are not just the pregnancy termination procedure, but the web of embodied relations in and through vulnerability and resistance, the circulation of affects, and the explicit attempt to make abortions a locus of conscious confrontation against gender mandates. In this way, abortion activism produces a counter-ritualization of abortion. Ritualization is the social practice of distinguishing, highlighting, and giving more relevance and significance to certain practices and actions over others, regarding how they contribute to the emergence of subjects (Bell 2009). This contextualized operation of distinction is performative, it produces meanings and subjects. If not necessarily traumatic anymore, should then abortions become a meaningful and subjectively transcendent experience? How, for instance, would our perspective on reproductive rights politics shift "if we understood the situation of abortion as more, or at least as much akin to ordinary illness experience as to sovereign decision-making" (Krauss 2019, 13)? As a LAL activist commented,

Sure, abortion means a lot because of the prohibition, the fear, the pressure, the moral pressure, and we can turn that meaning into a liberatory meaning through feminist accompaniment. But, yes, an ideal non heteropatriarcal world, maybe abortions shouldn't be such an issue. It is this system that imposes so much meaning on this act.

(LAL activist, personal communication, 2017)

From our perspective, another limitation of these lesbofeminist and *cuir*/queer abortion activisms has been not fiercely including a broader notion of reproductive justice or feminist reproductive resistance beyond abortion as a liberatory act, even though this is starting to change. According to activist Viviana Diaz, the prohibition of abortion is "the tip of the iceberg of many forms of gender violence" (Etcheberry and Vivaldi 2016, 44)—a common idea across feminist activism in Chile. The problem is that it has not been analyzed from an intersectional perspective beyond an arithmetic understanding of the oppressions that different kinds of pregnant bodies face when pursuing an abortion.

For instance, Graciela Di Marco (2017) examines how, after the 2001 economic and political crisis in Argentina, the demand to legalize abortion has become an "empty signifier" in the sense of Laclau (2005), articulating demands for democratic laicism and pluralism through a chain of equivalences enabling the emergence of what Di Marco refers to as *pueblo feminista* ("feminist people"). In this *pueblo feminista*, diverse political forces have formed coalitions that exceed the category "women," while also acknowledging that feminist and women's movements were a nodal point for its constitution (Di Marco 2017). We wonder how much of this capacity of being an "empty signifier" may have been grounded in the neoliberal common sense of the sexual rights–bearing-subject (Sabsay 2016a).

Decolonizing the Abortion Frame

Another important approach for understanding abortion politics and activism in Chile is the recent and increasing influence of the decolonial, indigenous, and communitarian feminisms of Abya Yala (e.g., Lugones 2008; Suárez Nava and Hernández Castillo 2008; Gargallo 2012; Espinosa Miñoso, Gómez Correal, and Ochoa Muñoz 2014; Mujeres Creando 2014) and lesbofeminist decolonial antirracist reflections (e.g., Espinosa Miñoso 2016, 2019; Hernández 2017).

In the last few years, groups like LAL, CLAYELC, and Coordinadora Feministas en Lucha (Coordination of Feminists in Struggle, CFL)[5] have engaged in self-reflection from the perspective of their indigenous heritage and knowledge, for instance, going back to Mapuche cultural heritage and including forms of care related to indigenous medicine (Valderrama Cayuman 2017). Additionally, feminist practices have incorporated considerations regarding the immigration to Chile from other countries of South and Central America. Recently, the handbook with the information on how to perform safe abortions using the pill was translated into Creole, thinking especially of those women who have migrated from Haiti, in order to guarantee their access to the information (Línea Aborto Libre, 2017). However, the organizers emphasized the importance of knowing how the process of abortion was understood in the country of origin of these women, in order to improve accompaniments and understand the fears, expectations, and intercultural diversities and similarities involved.

On 2019, the seventh demonstration organized by CFL for "*aborto libre, seguro y gratuito*" ("abortion that is free, safe, and without monetary charge") was coordinated for the first time with the anti-racist organization Microsesiones Negras (Black Microsessions).

They advanced an intersectional approach aiming to engage reproductive rights with antiracism, which organizers felt it is still needed in Chile's feminisms (Magnet 2019). The demonstration's date, July 25, coincided with the Afrolatin, Afrocaribbean, and Diaspora Women's Day. Juliete Micolta, from Microsesiones Negras, promoted an integral reproductive justice frame, not only focused on abortion. As she denounced: "There are many black immigrant women in Chile that have been to the hospital for x or y pain, but they end up without their uterus, and this hasn't happened once or twice, but many times" (Magnet 2019, n.p.). As a gesture of commitment with the antiracist struggle, from this year on, the eighth demonstration for "aborto libre, seguro y gratuito" was held on July 30.

Along with the shifting from "my body is mine" and "my body, my choice" paradigm to a more complex one, there has also been an inclusion of the notion of *territorio-cuerpo-tierra* and *cuerpo-territorio* ("territory-body-earth" and "body-territory") (Cabnal 2010) as a political site for resisting colonization and the extractivist capitalist model. Slogans like the one popularized by the Bolivian communitarian feminist group Mujeres Creando (Women Creating) have brought together feminist, socioenvironmental, and indigenous struggles: "Neither our women's bodies nor the Earth are territories to be conquered."

For indigenous women, is not just the body that has been expropriated by capitalism, the state, and men, forced to function as a means for reproduction and labor-force accumulation (Federici 2004), but their land as well. Therefore, indigenous, communitarian, and ecofeminist perspectives are part of Latin American territorial feminisms that defend life against capitalist colonial expropriation and contemporary extractivist neoliberal politics (Ulloa 2016) based on accumulation by dispossession (Harvey 2003). The concept of body-territory articulates and unifies the struggle for the recuperation of land and bodies (Cabnal 2010). Land is understood as a communal good and as the basis for collective—not just human—reproduction of life. Thus, territory from indigenous standpoints is not related to the juridical-geographical property-based comprehension of modernity (Tzul Tzul 2018). And body is seen as the first territory to be recuperated, a body that is memory, site of enunciation, and needs to be healed and emancipated. As Francesca Gargallo notes about Abya Yala's feminisms:

> To think of women is to do it from bodies that have been subjected to repeated attempts at definition, submission, and control to be expelled from rationality and turned into a reproduction machine. It is to think from the place that bodies are, from the body-territory that resists the modern idea that women embody the kind of animality that we should defeat, the lack of self-control and the non-historicity, and that with their indiscipline they have built the possibility of an alternative to the universal individual subject.
>
> *(Gargallo 2012, 47)*

In relation to abortion politics, the notion of body-territory has been sometimes interpreted in the sense of a body-uterus as the fundamental locus of patriarchal, capitalist, and colonial control, where women's sovereignty has to be reclaimed.

Accordingly, some of the uses of the category body-territory or body-uterus are problematic because they rely on a modern property-based notion of sovereignty and a reductive, universalistic, deterministic synecdoche-like use of the uterus as a symbol for women (Vivaldi and Stutzin 2017). In addition, sometimes it is invoked in calls for self-determination that depend on individual notions of autonomy, choice, and resistance or even so, consumer-based calls to self-care. Therefore, they differ from the indigenous feminist reflections that gave birth to the notion.

When articulated as resistance to the precarization of lives, capitalist dispossession, and extractivism, abortion as one dimension of the body-territory frame gains new meanings. Abortion then can be understood in relation to health and environmental issues, reproductive injustices such as forced sterilization, infertility caused by contamination, racially motivated custody removal of children, and criminalization and incarceration, among others. A research path that follows the practical political implications of a decolonized abortion frame may shed light on whether or not this expression reflects a reorganization of the current feminist fields of discursive action in Chile (Alvarez 2019).

Conclusion

Abortion politics serve as an interesting point to engage in critical questions about democracy, sexual democracy, and embodied dimensions of collective action in neoliberal times, precisely because of the inherent tensions between the critique of neoliberalism and the neoliberal rationality that still lurks in feminist discourse. We have shown some ways in which embracing these paradoxes, ambivalences, and tensions can transform them in rich and dense sites for creative political imagination. Thus, the gap left by a retreating state though unjust has been resignified through feminist creativity and courage.

Accompaniment practices are a remarkable example of the kind of political resistance embodied by feminism in the midst of neoliberal governmentality. The impetus for such political resistance is born from within the constraints of prohibition and vulnerability. Certainly, activism has never flourished in some abstract "ideal" space. In particular, the contribution of feminist activisms rooted in sexual dissidence and decolonial perspectives shows us a way of going beyond the languages of legality and rights. This expansion of the ground for resisting, debating, and imagining new ways of caring redefines not only what we usually consider in relation to abortion, but also reveals how the dynamics of democracy cannot be fully understood without these dimensions in the margins of the law and the state.

Notes

1 Since 2009, the Chilean abortion hotline Línea Aborto Libre created by the Colectivo de Lesbianas y Feministas por el Derecho a Información (Collective of Lesbians and Feminists for the Right to Information) has provided legal advice and information on misoprostol-based abortion.

2 Some of the activists from LAL moved on to form CLAYELC, launched in September 2016. They went further than LAL accompanying women in an abortion situation (see www.fa cebook.com/conlasamigas/). They were influenced by the Argentinian feminist organizations and movement of *Socorristas* (first responders) (see Keefe-Oates, this volume).
3 Roughly translating as Feminist Collective on the Loose.
4 See Tumblr post, https://conlasamigasyenlacasa.tumblr.com/post/163950828447/si-el-senado-te-aprueba-o-te-quiere-encarcelar
5 Coordinadora Feministas en Lucha is a collective of feminist individuals and organizations formed in 2013.

References

Agamben, Giorgio. 1998. *Homo Sacer: Sovereign Power and Bare Life*. Stanford: Stanford University Press.

Ahmed, Sara. 2017. *Living a Feminist Life*. Durham: Duke University Press.

Alvarez, Sonia E. 2019. "Feminismos en movimiento, feminismos en protesta." *Revista Punto Género* 11: 73–102.

Alvarez, Sonia E., Gianpaolo Baiocchi, Agustín Laó-Montes, Jeffrey W. Rubin, and Millie Thayer. 2017. "Introduction: Interrogating the Civil Society Agenda, Reassessing Uncivic Political Activism." In *Beyond Civil Society: Activism, Participation, and Protest in Latin America*, eds. Sonia E. Alvarez, Gianpaolo Baiocchi, Agustín Laó-Montes, Jeffrey W. Rubin, and Millie Thayer, 1–24. Durham: Duke University Press.

Beck, Ulrich. 1992. *Risk Society: Towards a New Modernity*. London: Sage.

Bell, Catherine. 2009. *Ritual Theory, Ritual Practice*. New York: Oxford University Press.

Berlant, Lauren. 2011. *Cruel Optimism*. Durham: Duke University Press.

Blofield, Merike H., and Liesl Haas. 2005. "Defining a Democracy: Reforming the Laws on Women's Rights in Chile, 1990–2002." *Latin American Politics and Society* 47(3): 35–68.

Brown, Josefina. 2016. "El aborto en cuestión: La individuación y juridificación en tiempos de neoliberalismos." *Sexualidad, Salud y Sociedad* 24: 16–42.

Butler, Judith. 2008. "Gender Is Extramoral: Judith Butler Featuring Fina Birulés." *Genius*, February 1. http://genius.com/Judith-butler-gender-is-extramoral-annotated.

Butler, Judith. 2015. *Notes Toward a Performative Theory of Assembly*. Cambridge, MA: Harvard University Press.

Cabnal, Lorena. 2010. "Acercamiento a la construcción del pensamiento epistémico de las mujeres indígenas feministas comunitarias de Abya Yala." In *Feminismos diversos: El feminismo comunitario*, eds. Lorena Cabnal and Asociación para la Cooperación con el Sur, 10–25. Spain: Asociación para la Cooperación con el Sur—Las Segovias.

Carmo, Íris Nery do. 2019. "O rolê feminista: Autonomia e política prefigurativa no campo feminista contemporâneo." *Cadernos Pagu* 57: e195704.

Carrara, Sérgio. 2015. "Moralidades, racionalidades e políticas sexuais no Brasil contemporâneo." *Mana* 21(2) :323–345.

Carrillo Rowe, Aimee. 2005. "Be Longing: Toward a Feminist Politics of Relation." *NWSA Journal* 17(2): 15–46.

Casas, Lidia, and Lieta Vivaldi. 2013. "La penalización del aborto como una violación a los derechos humanos de las mujeres." In *Informe Anual sobre Derechos Humanos en Chile 2013*, ed. Tomás Vial Solar, 69–122. Santiago: Universidad Diego Portales.

Con las Amigas y en la Casa. 2019. "Declaración Pública. Preparando el Segundo Encuentro Latinoamericano y del Caribe de Acompañantes de Aborto a realizarse en Perú en enero del 2020," December 22. www.facebook.com/conlasamigas/photos/a.666953213481236/1474313196078563/?type=3.

Das, Veena, and Deborah Poole. 2004. "State and Its Margins: Comparative Ethnographies." In *Anthropology in the Margins of the State*, eds. Veena Das and Deborah Poole, 3–33. Santa Fe: School of Advanced Research Press.

Di Marco, Graciela. 2017. "Social Movement Demands in Argentina and the Constitution of a 'Feminist People'." In *Beyond Civil Society: Activism, Participation, and Protest in Latin America*, eds. Sonia E. Alvarez, Gianpaolo Baiocchi, Agustín Laó-Montes, Jeffrey W. Rubin, and Millie Thayer, 122–140. Durham: Duke University Press.

Espinoza, Josefina. 2019. "Viviana Díaz de Con las Amigas y en la Casa: 'Creo que toda feminista debería acompañar un aborto.'" *Observatorio Género y Sociedad*, September 24. https://oge.cl/viviana-diaz-de-con-amigas-y-en-la-casa-creo-que-toda-feminista-deberia-acompanar-un-aborto/.

Espinosa Miñoso, Yuderkis. 2016. "Y la una no se mueve sin la otra. Descolonialidad, antiracismo y feminismo: Una trieja inseparable para los procesos de cambio." *Revista Venezolana de Estudios de la Mujer* 21(46): 47–64.

Espinosa Miñoso, Yuderkis. 2019. "Hacer genealogía de la experiencia: El método hacia una crítica a la colonialidad de la Razón feminista desde la experiencia histórica en América Latina." *Revista Direito e Práxis* 10(3): 2007–2032.

Espinosa Miñoso, Yuderkis, Diana Gómez Correal, and Karina Ochoa Muñoz (eds.). 2014. *Tejiendo de otro modo: Feminismo, epistemología y apuestas descoloniales en Abya Yala*. Popayán: Universidad del Cauca.

Etcheberry, Lorena. 2016. "Internet y acceso a información, medicamentos y abortos seguros. Entrevista a activista de Women Help Women." *Rufián Revista* 6(26): 81–85.

Etcheberry, Lorena, and Lieta Vivaldi. 2016. "Con las Amigas y en la Casa. Entrevista a Viviana Díaz Muñoz." *Rufián Revista* 6(26): 39–45.

Federici, Silvia. 2004. *Caliban and the Witch: Women, the Body, and Primitive Accumulation*. New York: Autonomedia.

Gargallo, Francesca. 2012. *Feminismos desde Abya Yala: Ideas y proposiciones de las mujeres de 607 pueblos en Nuestra América*. Bogotá: Ediciones Desde Abajo.

Giddens, Anthony. 1991. *Modernity and Self-Identity: Self and Society in the Late Modern Age*. Cambridge: Polity Press.

Harvey, David. 2003. *The New Imperialism*. New York: Oxford University Press.

Henríquez Murgas, Tomás. 2015. "Hacerse la víctima: Aborto, performance y teatralidades liminales." *Universitas Humanística* 79: 193–210.

Hernández, Iris. 2014. "Aportes lesbianos al debate sobre aborto." *Miles Chile*, November 21. http://mileschile.cl/?p=1482.

Hernández, Iris. 2017. "Colonialidad feminista, sociosexual y aportes lesbofeministas anti-rracistas descoloniales." *Revista Nomadías* 24: 67–87.

hooks, bell. 1990. "Homeplace: A Site of Resistance." In *Yearning: Race, Gender, and Cultural Politics*, 41–49. Boston: South End Press.

Ishkanian, Armine, and Anita Peña Saavedra. 2019. "The Politics and Practices of Intersectional Prefiguration in Social Movements: The Case of Sisters Uncut." *The Sociological Review* 67(5): 985–1001.

Krauss, Amy. 2018. "Luisa's Ghosts: Haunted Legality and Collective Expressions of Pain." *Medical Anthropology. Cross-Cultural Studies in Health and Illness* 37(8): 688–702.

Krauss, Amy. 2019. "The Ephemeral Politics of Feminist Accompaniment Networks in Mexico City." *Feminist Theory* 20(1): 37–54.

Laclau, Ernesto. 2005. *On Populist Reason*. London: Verso.

Lin, Cynthia S., Alisa A. Pykett, Constance Flanagan, and Karma R. Chávez. 2016. "Engendering the Prefigurative: Feminist Praxes That Bridge a Politics of Prefiguration and Survival." *Journal of Social and Political Psychology* 4(1): 302–317.

Línea Aborto Libre. 2017. "Protocolo en CREOLE: ¡A la calle!" *Info Aborto Chile*, April 14. http://infoabortochile.org/?p=810.

Loaíza Cárdenas, Cecilia. 2016. *Estrategias de amor e información entre mujeres: La Línea Aborto Libre. Una propuesta de investigación feminista.* Undergraduate thesis, Universidad de Chile.

Lugones, María. 2008. "Colonialidad y género: Hacia un feminismo descolonial." In *Género y descolonialidad*, ed. Walter Mignolo, 13–54. Buenos Aires: Ediciones del Signo.

Macón, Cecilia. 2013. "Sentimus ergo sumus. El surgimiento del 'giro afectivo' y su impacto sobre la filosofía política." *Revista Latinoamericana de Filosofía Política* 2(6): 1–32.

Mackenzie, Catriona, and Natalie Stoljar. 2000. *Relational Autonomy: Feminist Perspectives on Autonomy, Agency, and the Social Self.* New York: Oxford University Press.

Magnet, Camila. 2019. "Organizaciones feministas convocan a marcha antirracista por el aborto libre." *Radio Juan Gómez Millas*, July 24. https://radiojgm.uchile.cl/organizacio nes-feministas-convocan-a-marcha-antirracista-por-el-aborto-libre/.

Matamala Vivaldi, María Isabel. 2014. "Aborto en Chile: Cuerpos, derechos y libertades." In *Voces Sobre el Aborto: Ciudadanía de las mujeres, cuerpo y autonomía*, eds. Articulación Feminista por la Libertad de Decidir, 7–20. Santiago: Articulación Feminista por la Libertad de Decidir and Universidad de Chile.

Mujeres Creando. 2014. *El tejido de la rebeldía. ¿Qué es el feminismo comunitario?* La Paz: Moreno Artes Gráficas.

Palma Manríquez, Irma, Claudia Moreno Standen, Andrea Álvarez Carimoney, and Alondra Richards. 2018. "Experience of Clandestine Use of Medical Abortion among University Students in Chile: A Qualitative Study." *Contraception. An International Reproductive Health Journal* 97(2): 100–107.

Pampín, Ayelén Marina. 2014. *Misoprostol para todxs: Objetivos y alcances del activismo lésbico en la lucha.* Paper presented at I Jornadas de Género y Diversidad Sexual. La Plata, October 24–25.

Richard, Nelly. 2001. "La problemática del feminismo en los años de la transición en Chile." In *Estudios latinoamericanos sobre cultura y transformaciones sociales en tiempos de globalización*, ed. Daniel Matos, 227–239. Buenos Aires: Consejo Latinoamericano de Ciencias Sociales.

Sabsay, Leticia. 2016a. *The Political Imaginary of Sexual Freedom: Subjectivity and Power in the New Sexual Democratic Turn.* London: Palgrave Macmillan.

Sabsay, Leticia. 2016b. "Permeable Bodies: Vulnerability, Affective Powers, Hegemony." In *Vulnerability in Resistance*, eds. Judith Butler, Zeynep Gambetti, and Leticia Sabsay, 278–302. Durham: Duke University Press.

Shepard, Bonnie L., and Lidia Casas Becerra. 2007. "Abortion Policies and Practices in Chile: Ambiguities and Dilemmas." *Reproductive Health Matters. An International Journal on Sexual and Reproductive Health and Rights* 15(30): 202–210.

Siskindovich, Julieta. 2018. "La experiencia de aborto como apertura política imaginativa. Lugares del deseo y la esperanza." *Crítica y Resistencias. Revista de Conflictos Sociales Latinoamericanos* 7: 122–136.

Suárez Nava, Liliana, and Rosalva A. Hernández Castillo (eds.). 2008. *Descolonizando el feminismo: Teorías y prácticas desde los márgenes.* Madrid: Cátedra.

Sutton, Barbara. 2017. "Zonas de clandestinidad y 'nuda vida': Mujeres, cuerpo y aborto." *Estudos Feministas* 25(2): 889–902.

Tabbush, Constanza, María Constanza Díaz, Catalina Trebisacce, and Victoria Keller. 2016. "Matrimonio igualitario, identidad de género y disputas por el derecho al aborto en Argentina. La política sexual durante el kirchnerismo (2003–2015)." *Sexualidad, Salud y Sociedad* 22: 22–55.

Thayer, Millie, and Jeffrey W. Rubin. 2017. "Conclusion: Uncontained Activism." In *Beyond Civil Society: Activism, Participation, and Protest in Latin America*, eds. Sonia E.

Alvarez, Gianpaolo Baiocchi, Agustín Laó-Montes, Jeffrey W. Rubin, and Millie Thayer, 331–337. Durham: Duke University Press.

Trouillot, Michel-Rolph. 2001. "The Anthropology of the State in the Age of Globalization: Close Encounters of the Deceptive Kind." *Current Anthropology* 42(1): 125–138.

Tzul Tzul, Gladys. 2018. "Sistemas de gobierno comunal indígena: La organización de la reproducción de la vida." In *Epistemologías Del Sur: Epistemologias Do Sul*, eds. Maria Paula Meneses and Karina Bidaseca, 385–395. Buenos Aires: Consejo Latinoamericano de Ciencias Sociales.

Ulloa, Astrid. 2016. "Feminismos territoriales en América Latina: Defensas de la vida frente a los extractivismos." *Nómadas. Revista de Ciencias Sociales* 45: 123–139.

Undurraga, Tomás. 2015. "Neoliberalism in Argentina and Chile: Common Antecedents, Divergent Paths." *Revista de Sociología e Política* 23(55): 11–34.

Vacarezza, Nayla Luz. 2017. *Affects, Mourning and Justice in Visual Productions about Women's Incarceration and Deaths for Abortion in Latin America.* Paper presented at the 13th Mundos de Mulheres & Fazendo Gênero, Florianopolis, July 30–August 4.

Valderrama Cayuman, Ange. 2017. "Aborto libre: Una reflexión desde la mirada interseccional." *Fondo Alquimia*, June 21. www.fondoalquimia.org/derecho-a-decidir/aborto-libre-una-reflexion-desde-la-mirada-interseccional/.

Vivaldi, Lieta. 2020. "Critical Possibilities on Social Research: The Abortion Dispositif from a Feminist Perspective." *Pléyade. Revista de Humanidades y Ciencias Sociales* 25: 105–124.

Vivaldi, Lieta, and Valentina Stutzin. 2017. "Mujeres víctimas, fetos públicos, úteros aislados: Tecnologías de género, tensiones y desplazamientos en las representaciones visuales sobre aborto en Chile." *Zona Franca. Revista de Estudios de Género* 25: 126–160.

Vivaldi, Lieta, and Benjamín Varas. 2015. "Agencia y resistencia feminista en la prohibición del aborto en Chile." *Derecho y Crítica Social* 1(1): 139–179.

Wittig, Monique. 1992. *The Straight Mind and Other Essays.* Boston: Beacon Press.

World Health Organization (WHO). 2012. *Safe Abortion: Technical and Policy Guidance for Health Systems. Second Edition.* Geneva: World Health Organization.

Yates, Luke. 2015. "Rethinking Prefiguration: Alternatives, Micropolitics and Goals in Social Movements." *Social Movement Studies: Journal of Social, Cultural and Political Protest* 14(1): 1–21.

AFTERWORD

Embodying Democracy: Abortion Protest and Politics in the Southern Cone

Sonia E. Alvarez

As I finalize this Afterword, Buenos Aires is drenched in green. The so-called Green Tide—the broad-based, heterogeneous constellation of social and political forces that since 2018 has filled the streets, festooned in the green kerchiefs that have come to symbolize the struggle for abortion rights—is again sweeping across Argentina, now in ebullient celebration. On November 10, 2020, a date selected to coincide with International Human Rights Day and the one-year anniversary of Alberto Fernández's presidency, the lower house of Congress approved a bill—introduced by the president and endorsed, with some reservations, by the National Campaign for the Right to Legal, Safe, and Free Abortion—that promised to finally settle what the Campaign has long dubbed democracy's "debt" to women and other "persons who gestate." The bill passed at the end of December 2020, with the approval of a Senate controlled by Fernández and Cristina Kirchner's electoral coalition, the Frente de Todos (Front for All).

This momentous achievement is the product of the manifold successes documented in this unprecedented collection. Although Argentina's bill, like Uruguay's 2012 abortion law, allows for conscientious objection by providers, the bill's passage means that the two countries are the only places in the South of the Americas where abortion is available up to the 14th or 12th week of pregnancy, joining Cuba, Guyana, and the Mexican Federal District and state of Oaxaca. The Green Tide, which as several chapters in the book show, has extended transnationally into Chile, everywhere in Latin America, and indeed, into many parts of the world, has been the leading edge of a broader, radical upsurge of mass-based feminist politics over the past two decades.

Local translations of the global "Slut Walk" phenomenon have mobilized young women against violence throughout the region ever since the early 2010s. And since the mid-2010s, feminists across the Americas have joined women around the globe in International Feminist Strike actions that involve the mobilization of hundreds of thousands who stop or withhold both productive and reproductive labor on March 8,

DOI: 10.4324/9781003079903-17

International Women's Day, now known as 8M. In Brazil, we had the so-called Feminist Spring of 2015 in defense of even restricted abortion rights under threat and the mass mobilizations against Bolsonaro's candidacy in 2018, known as #EleNão or #NeverHim, along with the Black Women's 50,000-strong March on Brasília in 2015 and the hundreds of thousands of rural, popular feminists who have marched on the capital with the Marcha das Margaridas on four occasions since the early 2000s.[1] In Chile, during the so-called Mayo Feminista or Feminist May in 2018, we witnessed *tomas* or occupations of dozens of universities and secondary schools, demanding an end to sexual harassment and the establishment of gender-sensitive curricula, along with street protests of a size rivaled only by the mass mobilizations of the current *estallido social* or social uprising. More than two million protested in Santiago alone for 8M in 2020 and activists bedecked in green have been prominent among participants of the Chilean uprising as well as other "social explosions" that shook Colombia, Ecuador, Haiti, Peru, Guatemala, and other parts of Latin America in 2019–20.

Indeed, as feminist theorist Silvia Federici eloquently put it, Latin American feminisms are the "punta del diamante de una insurgencia internacional," the diamond tip of an international insurgency (Furtado and Menéndez 2020, n.p.). The fact that Latin American feminists made the "tierra temblar," the "earth tremble" in the 2010s, in the words of Argentine NiUnaMenos intellectual-activist Verónica Gago (2018), provides the larger regional backdrop to the manifold successes in the Southern Cone—continued restrictions and obstacles to full autonomy notwithstanding—to which I now turn.

Successes, I want to suggest, are cultural as well as political, the products of artful and recombinant articulations of cultural politics, protest politics, direct action, coalition politics, cause lawyering, and policy advocacy pursued by activist constellations like Argentina's National Campaign for the Right to Legal, Safe, and Free Abortion; Uruguay's National Coordination of Social Organizations in Defense of Reproductive Health, and Chile's Action Committee for Abortion. As amply illustrated in the preceding chapters, those constellations unsettled dominant discourses that stigmatize and criminalize those who choose to interrupt their pregnancies and changed the national conversation about abortion and bodies that abort.

A feminist cultural politics was enacted through protests and direct action that mobilized affects as well as, ultimately, in the case of Uruguay and Argentina, electoral will and congressional votes. Green kerchiefs—worn on the neck, the head, the wrist, as a blouse or other vestment, tied to backpacks and purses—extend feminist protest to the realms of the corporeal and the quotidian; more than a "style of protest," Barbara Sutton insists, the ludic, embodied politics of Green Tide protests "transforms the stigma associated with abortion" and enables protesters to "exuberantly celebrate their right to freedom" (2020, 8). Symbols like the green kerchief and the orange voting hand of Uruguayan origin, writes Vacarezza (this volume), "convey ideas, arguments, interpretative frames, and also politically significant emotions." And coordinated symbolic acts such as the *pañuelazos* typically unfurled at the end of abortion protests large and small, she further suggests, generate "a collective emotional climax and powerful images for spectators."

Affect is also central to abortion rights activists engaged in one of the most subversive if least visible forms of protest/direct action, one that enacts an embodied, prefigurative feminist politics of autonomy and care: the feminist organizations that engage in abortion "accompaniment," providing information and accompanying people seeking to end their pregnancies with abortifacient medications, discussed in Vivaldi and Stutzin's chapter in this volume. Often led by lesbian-feminist and sexual dissidence organizations, accompaniment networks also seek to "abort heterosexuality," emphasizing that abortion is not just relevant to cisgender heterosexual women and working to "dismantle patriarchal systems and incorporate feminist values into all levels of society" (Keefe-Oates, this volume).

These radical actors also engage in policy advocacy, working in broad-based coalitions of other feminist and human rights organizations, trade unions, student groups, LGBTQ organizations, neighborhood groups, professional associations, and more—a key dimension of what I am calling success. In doing so, advocates construct the right to abortion as "a matter of democracy, equity, and social justice, a public health issue, and a central axis of human rights," as we learn from López-Gómez, Couto, and Berro Pizzarossa in their chapter. Diverse pieces of complex activist tapestries, such as those woven across the more than 500 organizations that compose Argentina's Campaign, work in specialized action areas, such as lobbying and communications, as well as in concert around moments of intensive and extensive protest mobilization (Gutiérrez, this volume).

Activist tapestries also include advocates working in academia (Casas Becerra, this volume), engaged in cause lawyering and legal mobilization (Borland, this volume), and organizing inside political parties (Fernández Anderson, this volume). To be sure, while mass protest in recent years has captured the imagination of activists and observers alike, "institutional activists"—people at work in feminist party caucuses, in elected office, and in government bureaucracies "with the purpose of advancing the political agendas or projects proposed by [feminist] social movements" (Abers and Tatagiba 2015, 78)—are a crucial part of the story of abortion rights politics in the Southern Cone, striving to promote sexual and (non)reproductive rights since the onset of transitions from authoritarian rule. Democratic institutionality in all three cases, although biased in favor of elites and significantly constricted by neoliberalism and race and class inequalities, has been deployed creatively and insistently in ways that at once extend democracy's parameters and *embody* it.

In the Argentine case, the sustained conjoining of institutional activism, direct action, and protest politics has resulted in one of the abortion rights movements' greatest achievements: what the Campaign calls the "social decriminalization" of abortion, which crucially preceded and created the cultural and political conditions that made possible the bill passed in Congress in December 2020. Social decriminalization, in turn, was a product of what feminist sociologist Graciela Di Marco has referred to as the emergence of a Laclauian *Pueblo Feminista*, or "feminist people," which congealed through the "chains of equivalence" established in broad-based coalitions that transformed issues such as abortion rights into "empty signifiers" that articulated diverse forces such as unions and leftist parties (Di Marco 2017). Social media has, of course, also played a key role in enabling those chains and in shaping the abortion debate in all three cases (see Laudano, this volume). And deliberately and painstakingly assembling wide-ranging constellations in support of abortion rights as part of broad-based democratic and social justice agendas was a strategy pursued by activists across the Southern Cone and is one of the key political and strategic take-aways from this volume for abortion rights advocates everywhere, including in contexts where there are mounting obstacles to access and guardianship and limits on bodily autonomy—as has been the case in Uruguay since 2012 and in a number of countries around the world where abortion is legal but increasingly restricted, including many parts of the United States.

A further key takeaway then concerns the centrality of building and sustaining a new feminist transnationalism, one that travels through shared, constantly shifting global imaginaries as well as through formal networks and intra-organizational linkages and that journeys from South-to-North and South-to-South, and not just North-to-South, as was too often the case with the United Nations-centered policy advocacy of the 1990s and early 2000s (Phillips and Cole 2009). In the Southern Cone, for instance, a feminist imaginary has traveled both on- and offline via potent symbols that reveal the regional construction of "shared interpretative frames and common affective repertoires" (Vacarezza, this volume). And the South-to-North travels of feminist discourses and practices is facilitated by processes of cultural translation (Alvarez et al. 2014), as well as by the kind of rigorous and engaged feminist scholarship represented in this volume.

Today's green soaked streets of Buenos Aires notwithstanding, abortion rights, and women's, gender, sexual and (non)reproductive rights more generally, will no doubt confront a number of challenges in the years to come. Access is likely to continue to be difficult, especially for the poor, the racialized and the *disidencias sexuales*, even when abortion is legal, as has been increasingly the case in Uruguay, where conscientious objector clauses to the Voluntary Interruption of Pregnancy Law did not end the state's tradition of guardianship, but rather as Rostagnol and Caccia contend in their chapter, shifted it from "repressive guardianship to healthcare guardianship" that is protected by scientific, medical, and religious arguments. In Chile, of course, repressive guardianship remains firmly in place via the *tres causales* or three grounds for abortion. In both Argentina and Uruguay, an anti-abortion, anti-rights right is increasingly encroaching into the party system, blurring the boundaries between the religious and the secular. Right-wing groups are constructing empty signifiers of their own by linking feminist and LGBTQ agendas to a "supposed cultural Marxism with a global character" that propagates "gender ideology," thereby bringing together disparate conservative actors "around the lowest common denominator: their rejection of progressive and left-wing parties" (Vaggione and Morán Faúndes, this volume). This is a phenomenon that today is rampant throughout the Americas, including in neighboring Brazil under Bolsonaro, and in many parts of the world, of course. The Green Tide protestors in Buenos Aires in December 2020 had to share the plaza with (a far smaller number of) opponents donning celestial blue kerchiefs, the chosen color of anti-abortion rights coalitions that have usurped many of rights advocates' symbols and strategies—as is also the case with the so-called "pro-life" movement in the United States.

As the right maneuvers to gain greater command of the abortion debate in the Southern Cone and other world regions, feminist activists can learn from the effective strategies and discourses summarized in the chapters assembled here. The continuation of the *estallido social* and upcoming Constituent Assembly process it enabled in Chile represent exceptional opportunities to expand and consolidate broad-gauged abortion rights constellations and work toward social decriminalization. Uruguayans can seek to contest guardianship through continued accompaniment and legal mobilization strategies. And the multifaceted Campaign in Argentina will no doubt continue to creatively articulate advocacy, cultural politics, and protest in pursuit of effective implementation and access.

We can think of social decriminalization as a genre of feminist strategy that seeks to secure rights in practice, contesting dominant discourses and transforming meanings alongside, or even in advance of, efforts to transform policy. Such strategies would seem to be essential when dealing with what the activists discussed in this book refer to as "cuerpos-territorio," "body-territory-earth," realms that have proven particularly more resistant to policy regulation or intervention. As Rostangol and Caccia suggest in their chapter, the body "is disputed territory; as women take ownership of it, democracy is deepened." Assembling heterogeneous coalitions and enacting a cultural politics of embodied democracy no doubt will be crucial to securing and expanding abortion access and sexual and (non)reproductive rights, and thereby deepening democracy.

Note

1 The name "Margaridas" is in remembrance of murdered union leader, Margarida Maria Alves.

References

Abers, Rebecca Neaera, and Luciana Tatagiba. 2015. "Institutional Activism: Mobilizing for Women's Health from Inside the Brazilian Bureaucracy." In *Social Movement Dynamics: New Perspectives on Theory and Research from Latin America*, ed. Federico M. Rossi and Marisa von Bülow, 73–101. Burlington: Ashgate.

Alvarez, Sonia E., Claudia de Lima Costa, Verónica Feliu, Rebecca Hester, Norma Klahn, and Millie Thayer (eds.). 2014. *Translocalities/Translocalidades: Feminist Politics of Translation in the Latin/a Américas*. Durham: Duke University Press.

Di Marco, Graciela. 2017. "Social Movement Demands in Argentina and the Constitution of a 'Feminist People.'" In *Beyond Civil Society: Activism, Participation, and Protest in Latin America*, ed. Sonia E. Alvarez, Jeffrey Rubin, Millie Thayer, Gianpaolo Baiocchi, and Agustín Laó-Montes, 122–140. Durham: Duke University Press.

Furtado, Victoria, and Mariana Menéndez. 2020. "El feminismo es la punta de diamante de una insurgencia internacional." *Zur: Pueblo de Voces*, February 20. https://zur.uy/el-feminismo-es-la-punta-de-diamante-de-una-insurgencia-internacional-entrevista-a-silvia-federici/.

Gago, Verónica. 2018. "Critical Times/The Earth Trembles." *Critical Times* 1(1): 158–164.

Phillips, Lynne, and Sally Cole. 2009. "Feminist Flows, Feminist Fault Lines: Women's Machineries and Women's Movements in Latin America." *Signs: Journal of Women in Culture and Society* 35(1): 185–211.

Sutton, Barbara. 2020. "Intergenerational Encounters in the Struggle for Abortion Rights in Argentina." *Women's Studies International Forum* 82: 102392.

INDEX

Number entries in **bold** denote tables; number entries in *italics* denote figures.

CPSIA information can be obtained
at www.ICGtesting.com
Printed in the USA
LVHW082142240921
698679LV00014B/920

9 780367 529413